Forms of Dictatorship

OXFORD STUDIES IN AMERICAN LITERARY HISTORY

Gordon Hutner, Series Editor

Family Money
Jeffory A. Clymer

America's England
Christopher Hanlon

Writing the Rebellion
Philip Gould

Antipodean America
Paul Giles

Living Oil
Stephanie LeMenager

Making Noise, Making News
Mary Chapman

Territories of Empire
Andy Doolen

Propaganda 1776
Russ Castronovo

Playing in the White
Stephanie Li

Literature in the Making
Nancy Glazener

Surveyors of Customs
Joel Pfister

*The Moral Economies of
American Authorship*
Susan M. Ryan

After Critique
Mitchum Huehls

Forms of Dictatorship
Jennifer Harford Vargas

Unscripted America
Sarah Rivett

Forms of Dictatorship

POWER, NARRATIVE, AND AUTHORITARIANISM
IN THE LATINA/O NOVEL

Jennifer Harford Vargas

Oxford University Press is a department of the University of Oxford.
It furthers the University's objective of excellence in research, scholarship,
and education by publishing worldwide. Oxford is a registered trade mark of
Oxford University Press in the UK and certain other countries.

Published in the United States of America by Oxford University Press
198 Madison Avenue, New York, NY 10016, United States of America.

© Oxford University Press 2018

First issued as an Oxford University Press paperback, 2020

All rights reserved. No part of this publication may be reproduced,
stored in a retrieval system, or transmitted, in any form or by any means,
without the prior permission in writing of Oxford University Press,
or as expressly permitted by law, by license, or under terms agreed with
the appropriate reproduction rights organization. Inquiries concerning
reproduction outside the scope of the above should be sent to the
Rights Department, Oxford University Press, at the address above.

You must not circulate this work in any other form
and you must impose this same condition on any acquirer.

Library of Congress Cataloging-in-Publication Data
Names: Harford Vargas, Jennifer, 1980– author.
Title: Forms of dictatorship : power, narrative, and authoritarianism in the
Latina/o novel / Jennifer Harford Vargas.
Description: New York, NY : Oxford University Press, 2017. |
Series: Oxford studies in American literary history
Identifiers: LCCN 2017008679| ISBN 9780190642853 (hardback) |
ISBN 9780190079673 (paperback) | ISBN 9780190642877 (epub)
Subjects: LCSH: American fiction—Hispanic American authors—History and
criticism. | Dictators in literature. | Authoritarianism in literature. |
Social control in literature. | Point of view (Literature) | American
fiction—20th century—History and criticism. | American fiction—21st century—History
and criticism. | BISAC: LITERARY COLLECTIONS / Caribbean & Latin American.
Classification: LCC PS153.H56 H37 2017 | DDC 813.009/868—dc23
LC record available at https://lccn.loc.gov/2017008679

A previous version of chapter 1, "Dictating a Zafa: The Power of Narrative Form in Junot Díaz's *The Brief Wondrous Life of Oscar Wao*," was published in *MELUS: Multi-ethnic Literature of the United States* 39.3 (Fall 2014): 8–30, and was reprinted in *Junot Díaz and the Decolonial Imagination*, ed. Monica Hanna, Jennifer Harford Vargas, and José David Saldívar (Durham, NC: Duke University Press, 2016).

For Mom and Dad, because you taught me to love books

For Manuel, because you reminded me to imagine

{ ACKNOWLEDGMENTS }

Do not be deceived by the title page; I am not the dictator of—oops, I mean sole author of—this book. Just as it takes an elaborate network to uphold a dictator, it takes an elaborate network of colleagues, mentors, friends, and family to write a book. While academic convention prevents me from listing you as coauthors, I could not have written this without the innumerable conversations, motivating encouragement, productive criticism, and much needed distractions you provided. With deep gratitude, I want to acknowledge the people who have been instrumental in helping me write, rethink, delete, rewrite, revise, and produce this book.

I feel incredibly privileged to have worked with such generous and engaged mentors who have modeled for me how to be a scholar. Paula Moya, you always understood what I was really writing about and helped guide me there; thank you for your invaluable intellectual, professional, and personal mentorship. José David Saldívar, I am grateful that I have had the immense benefit of your decolonial imagination on my work. Ramón Saldívar, this book owes much of its conceptualization to the formal and transnational questions you have posed over the years. Michele Elam, the enthusiasm and knowledge you bring to our conversations always reminds me anew why I want to be in this profession. I am also appreciative of Laura Lomas, Ralph Rodriguez, Josie Saldaña-Portillo, and David Vázquez for aiding me at key stages in this book's development and in my career. Josie, your comments helped me refine my intervention, and Laura and Ralph, your feedback helped me nuance my arguments. David, I am indebted to you for agreeing to read the first full draft of this book; your feedback helped me articulate the contours of the project and my scholarly investments more clearly. Rodrigo Lazo, I work on Latina/o literature because of your appearance at Pizza and Profs so many years ago; thank you is not enough for how formative you were in helping me envision myself as a Latina and an academic, but I hope it is something.

Bryn Mawr College and the Tri-College Consortium have been a generative space where my scholarship and teaching mutually nourish each other. It has been exciting to work alongside colleagues who are intellectually and pedagogically exacting and adventurous. Thank you to my colleagues, including Inés Arribas, Farid Azfar, Osman Balkan, Linda-Susan Beard, Peter Briggs, Karisa Butler-Wall, Jen Callaghan, Kim Cassidy, Lara Cohen, Anne Dalke, Andrew Friedman, Ignacio Gallup-Díaz, Martín Gaspar, Aurelia Gómez Unamuno, Colby Gordon, Jane Hedley, Gail Hemmeter, Sylvie Honig, Homay King, Anita Kurimay, Evelyne Laurent-Perrault, Baki Mani, Erica Márquez, Edwin Mayorga, Verónica Montes, Hoang Nguyen, Mary Osirim, Gina Patnaik, María Cristina Quintero, Roya Rastegar, Lyndsay Reckson, Katherine Rowe, Bethany Schneider, Monique Scott, Asali Solomon, Eric Song, Rosi Song, Gus Stadler, Ellen Stroud, Jamie Taylor, Kate Thomas, J. C. Todd, Dan Torday, Michael Tratner, Elly Truitt, Sharon Ullman, and Alicia Walker. Andrew, I value all our conversations on my nascent ideas; they helped solidify this project. Bethany and Rosi, thank you for helping me image how to turn this into a book, and Kate, a special thanks to you for pushing me (Titch!) to submit my work even when I did not feel ready. Thank you to Bryn Thompson for all her heartfelt labor. My students have been ideal sounding boards for my interpretations of the texts I write about, and being in dialogue with them has improved this book. I am grateful to them for expanding my scholarship and pedagogy and to Sofi Chávez for teaching me a great deal about mentoring research projects.

Conferences, institutes, and working groups may very well be my favorite part of academia. They have been sources of rich intellectual exchanges and helped shaped my overall project as well as my individual readings of the novels I analyze herein. First, I want to express my gratitude to Latina/o studies colleagues who have inspired me to contribute to the field and who have made being in conversation with them so much fun. Thank you to Frederick Aldama, Jesse Alemán, Mary Pat Brady, María Elena Cepeda, Raúl Coronado, Arlene Dávila, Jazmín Delgado, Lyn Di Iorio, Daynalí Flores-Rodríguez, Armando García, Maia Gil'Adi, John Morán González, Alma Granado, Kirsten Silva Gruesz, Laura Halperin, Michael Hames-García, Natalie Havlin, Renee Hudson, Ylce Irizarry, Christina Lam, Carmen Lamas, Enrique Lima, Johana Londoño, Marissa López, Elena Machado Sáez,

Enmanuel Martínez, Ernesto Martínez, John Mckiernan-González, Claudia Milian, Michelle Nasser, Gabriela Nuñez, Marcia Ochoa, Ariana Ochoa Camacho, Randy Ontiveros, Bill Orchard, Yolanda Padilla, Daniel Enrique Pérez, Richard Perez, Juan Poblete, Jennifer Ponce de León, Sarah Quesada, Jennifer Reimer, Belinda Rincón, Ana Patricia Rodríguez, Cristina Rodriguez, Ricky Rodríguez, Eliza Rodriguez y Gibson, Marion Rohrleitner, Alicia Schmidt Camacho, Silvio Torres-Saillant, Eric Vázquez, and Ariana Vigil. John Alba Cutler, I am especially grateful for all your support of my work and am excited to be Oxford University Press book buddies. Juana Alicia, thank you for the powerful beauty of your artwork and for providing me with your vision on the murals.

Second, I want to express how appreciative I am of the folks in the Faculty Working Group in American Studies at Haverford College, the Colloquium for the Study of Latina/o Literature and Theory, the Penn Humanities Forum, the Trans-American Studies Working Group at the Stanford Humanities Center, the American Literature reading group at the University of Pennsylvania, the Working Group on the Novel at the Stanford Humanities Center, the Tepotzlán Institute for Transnational History of the Americas, the Future of Minority Studies Research Project and Summer Institute, the Futures of American Studies Institute at Dartmouth College, and the UCD Clinton Institute Summer School, as well faculty at Stanford University and colleagues at various conferences, because they have all been important in helping me develop my work. Thank you to Linda Martín Alcoff, Magalí Armillas-Tisyera, Munia Bhaumik, Ximena Briceño, Anna Brickhouse, Al Camarillo, Darrais Carter, Jason Chang, Mary Jean Corbett, Kavita Daiya, Claire Decouteau, Harry Elam, James English, Shelley Fisher Fishkin, Jay Fliegelman, Susan Gillman, Tanya Golash-Boza, Roland Greene, Richard Grijalva, Héctor Hoyos, Miyako Inoue, Gavin Jones, Marcela Junguito, John Pat Leary, David Luis-Brown, Andrea Lunsford, Nelson Maldonado-Torres, Saikat Majumbar, Eduardo Mendieta, Sophia McClennen, Walter Mignolo, Carol Moeller, Satya Mohanty, Donald Pease, Gaile Pohlhaus, H. Q. Quan, Virginia Ramos, April Shemak, Tyrone Simpson, Stephen Sohn, Chandra Talpade Mohanty, Bronwen Tate, Michelle Tellez, Tyler Williams, Carla Wojczuk, Alex Woloch, Chi-ming Yang, and Yvonne Yarbro-Bejarano. I am grateful to the following for funding my research: the Woodrow Wilson National Fellowship Foundation; the Research Institute for the Comparative Studies in Race and

Ethnicity at Stanford University; the Diversifying Academia, Recruiting Excellence Fellowship Program at Stanford University; El Centro Chicano at Stanford University; and the Andrew W. Mellon Foundation. Thank you to the various administrators, librarians, and research assistants for the many ways they have helped along the way, including Judy Candell, Oliva Cardona, Anika Green, Chris Golde, Frances Morales, Elvira Prieto, Chris Queen, Kelsey Rall, Margaret Sena, and Arleen Zimerlee. I also want to express my appreciation for Kerry Anne Rockquemore and the National Center for Faculty Development and Diversity for helping me write every day and develop a sense of balance.

I am deeply grateful for the people at Oxford University Press who have made this book's publication possible. It has been a privilege to work with Gordon Hutner, whose guidance has been invaluable throughout this process. This book has benefited from the professional skills and the careful attention of Sarah Pirovitz, Gwen Colvin, Abigail Johnson, Martha Ramsey, Hannah Doyle, Dan Earley, and Enid Zafran. Though he is no longer at OUP, I thank Brendan O'Neil, who first believed in this project. I will be forever grateful for my external reviewers, whose feedback helped clarify and extend the through lines of this book.

Elda María Román, you have read every word, and the afterlives of our countless conversations permeate this book. Thank you for making me a better scholar with your astute insight and curiosity and for giving me confidence when all I had was doubts; I won the lotería having you as my writing partner. Jillian Hess, thank you for our (radical practical!) writing sessions and our many meditations on life and work as well as for sharing the world of book making with me. Guadalupe Carrillo, thank you for teaching me to be vulnerable; I am thrilled that we have been able to create working groups and go on international adventures together. EM, Jill, and Lupe, I will forever be grateful that grad school let me create familia from scratch, as you are the sisters I never had. Monica Hanna, you make all our intellectual exchanges fun and your outlook always helps center me; I hope we find many more scholarly and life projects to collaborate on. Julie Minich, your advice and textual interpretations are always illuminating; I am so grateful for your mentorship and for the wittiness you bring to my life. Rio Riofrio, I have appreciated learning from your comments, whether they are based on the connections you observe or on conference bets. Ulka Anjaria, thank you for the numerous discussions we have had about global dictator novels

Acknowledgments xi

because they were crucial to this project. Jayson Gonzalez Sae-Saue, you have been a perceptive interlocutor for my work through its various iterations, and I feel fortunate to have had your friendship since our first year in grad school. I am very grateful for the friends I have made during my time in academia who have provided much needed community, writing dates, idea exchanges, workouts, and festivities over the years, including Yveline Alexis, Sarah Allison, Amada Armenta, Mike Benveniste, Magdalena Barrera, Rashida Braggs, Felipe Cala, Niambi Carter, Micaela Díaz-Sánchez, Justin Eichenlaub, James Estrella, Harris Feinsod, Maura Finkelstein, Vida Mia Garcia, Lee Gayle, Marissa Gemma, Nigel Hatton, Heather Houser, Michael Hoyer, Cristina Jimenez, Teresa Jimenez, Nina Johnson, Doug Jones, Jenny Kelly, Ju Yon Kim, Marisol LeBron, Long Le-Khac, Kenny Ligda, Shantal Marshall, Tim McCall, Natalie Phillips, Adam Rosenblatt, Robert Samet, Peter Samuels, Joe Shapiro, Jessica Weare, Mary Zaborskis, and Austin Zeiderman.

I am also very grateful for all of my friends outside of academia who have helped me more fully enjoy life amidst all the work. Thank you to two healers: to Rohan Radhakrishna for always reminding me who I am, and to Radhka Jurkech for always putting things in perspective. Jenn Jacquet, I can't believe it has been over twenty years since we started Baboom Comics; thank you for making me laugh and teaching me something new every time we talk. Thank you also to Jim, Kristiania, Sage, and Reed Anderson-Knipler; Julie Charay; Califia Hess; Leah Kahler; Amanda Levinson; Whitney Martinko; Mir Masud-Elias and Jamal Elias, Manuel Rivera and Natalia Rodríguez; Lara Thoreson; Fabian Toro; and Diana Velásquez for their friendship. Josh, Nancy, Zoe, and Theo Gnass, being part of your family has enriched my life; I will forever miss being your neighbor and always look forward to our next vacation adventure.

Finally, I would not have written this book, let alone these acknowledgments, if it weren't for the love and patience of my family. Agradezco toda mi familia Colombiana. Che Che, he disfrutado tanto viajar por el Caribe contigo, escribiendo las aventuras de la cándida nietecita y su abuela desalmada. Tus cuentos y tus chistes quedarán siempre en mi memoria y mi corazón. Tere, mi mamá Barranquillera, admiro tu espiritú de berraquera y aprecio todo lo que has hecho por mí. Para todos mis tíos, tías, primas, y primos, incluyendo Jorge, Salma, Milena, Rafa, Jhonny, Lucho, Raisa, Beto, Soraya, Mayra, Martha, Laura, Daniela, Claudia, Daniel, Melissa,

Karol, Eric, Olga, Valentina, Isabella, Antonella, Vanessa, Elias, Yuris, Alquileo, Samuel, Sandra, Rosita, Miria, y Lucy, les quiero mucho y siempre me hacen muchísima falta. To Gloria López; Greg Seegers and Luis López; Sergio Herrera, Silver Rodríguez, Damian Rodríguez, Aria Herrera; Miguel, Eva, Dylan, and Blake Herrera; Alejandro Herrera and Roxana Arvanaghi; and Gabriela Canziani and Cesar Belchez: thank you for embracing me as family and for bringing so much joy and entertainment to my life. I am also appreciative of Jim and Char Floyd, Mary Harford, Tim Harford, and Anne Poole. Michael Harford and Lydia Floyd, I admire your creative talent and your intense work ethic, and Ian, I adore hearing your laughter over the phone but wish I didn't have to be a long-distance aunt. Tom and Rosa Harford, you have been more than parents; you have been unwaveringly supportive friends. Thank you for keeping me nourished in more ways than one with encouragement, cards, and prayers. Dad, your generosity humbles me, and Mom, your affection moves me.

Manuel, Melquiades, and Machete Vargas López, yours were the faces that kept me grounded as I finished this book. Melquiades and Machete, I am grateful for your furry head bumps, your purring cuddles, and for all the "writing" you did lying on my laptop. Manuel, thank you for bringing all my pieces together and for allowing me to see the world through your eyes. The breadth of your knowledge and your daily dedication to putting social justice into practice inspires me. I can't imagine composing this book without you beside me; your love bookends these pages, mi vida.

{ CONTENTS }

Acknowledgments — vii

Introduction: Literary Form and Authoritarian Power in the Latina/o Dictatorship Novel — 3
The Latina/o Counter-dictatorial Imaginary 5
An Américan Tradition 9
The Power of Form and the Form of Power 14
Postdictatorship and Postmemory Hauntings 18
Pan-Latina/o and Trans-Latina/o Fictions 24
Chapters in the Latina/o Dictatorship Novel 29

1. Dictating Narrative Power — 34
The Dictator as Minor Character 38
A Marginalized Hero 46
Underground Storytelling 51

2. The Borderlands of Authoritarianism — 60
The Author as Dictator 64
Narrative Territory 71
Plotting Resistance and the Typography of Dissent 74
Narrative Rights and Narrative Disclosure 79

3. The Floating Dictatorship — 86
Captain of a Dictator-ship 89
Ships of Death 96
Navigating the Discourse of a Shipwreck 103
Scraps, Holes, Ruins 108

4. Plotting Justice — 118
Ordering Disorder 121
Individual Retribution against Collective Impunity 129
Narrative Scales of Justice 135

5. The Fall of the Patriarchs — 148
Foiling Hypermasculine Hero Myths 151
A Resolver Aesthetic 160
Defiant Daughters 168

Coda — 177
On Placas and Palimpsests of Paint   179
Creating Political Memory   192

Notes — 195
Works Cited — 235
Index — 249

Forms of Dictatorship

{ Introduction }

LITERARY FORM AND AUTHORITARIAN POWER IN THE LATINA/O DICTATORSHIP NOVEL

> *Beware the plague of amnesia, America.*
> *Or have you forgotten Chile? Not just a name. Chile?*
> *Democratic Chile? Demonized, destabilized by your government in 1973?*
> *Chile? That country misruled for 17 years by a dictator you helped to install?*
> *And other countries, other names.*
> *Iran, Nicaragua, the Congo, Indonesia, South Africa, Laos, Guatemala.*
> *Just names? Just footnotes in history books, your creatures?*
> —ARIEL DORFMAN, *Other Septembers, Many Americas*

> *To the immigrant mexicano and the recent arrivals we must teach our history.*
> *The 80 million mexicanos and the Latinos from Central and South America*
> *must know our struggles. Each of us must know basic facts about*
> *Nicaragua, Chile, and the rest of Latin America....*
> *We need to meet on broader communal ground.*
> —GLORIA ANZALDÚA, *Borderlands/La Frontera*

Carolina de Robertis's novel *The Invisible Mountain* (2010) begins and ends with a mother, Salomé, in Uruguay writing a letter to her daughter, Victoria, in the United States, who grew up in San Francisco and knows nothing of the violent circumstances of her birth under the Uruguayan dictatorship, let alone the fact that the parents who raised her are actually her uncle and aunt. Salomé was a Tupamaro revolutionary in Uruguay who was imprisoned, tortured, and raped, thereby becoming pregnant with Victoria. The novel opens relating that "when Salomé finally wrote to her daughter—by now a young woman, a stranger, thousands of miles away—she said *everything that disappears is somewhere*" (3). The use of "disappears" evokes the hundreds of thousands of "los desaparecidos" (the disappeared) under the dictatorships in the Southern Cone and Central America in the 1970s and 1980s, at the same time that it creates a link between the

Latin American mother and her Latina daughter. Salomé is a political prisoner who is lucky to have survived when so many remain disappeared, their fates unknown and their bodies still missing. Yet, in another sense, Salomé *is* disappeared because her own daughter does not know about her past and has never met her mother. Salomé strives to render their link into narrative and pass down her story to her daughter so that Victoria might know her history—which is simultaneously a national history, of Uruguay, and a transnational history, of the United States' support of the dictatorship through Operation Condor—and how her identity as a Latina is directly shaped by both.

The Invisible Mountain highlights the central role of memory, genealogy, writing, and the violent history of dictatorships that separate families and link Latina/os and Latin Americans. As she composes the letter to her daughter, Salomé strives to "tie women back together" through her writing, which metonymically stands in for the cultural and memory work of the novel (3). This book also ties together Latin American and Latina/o writings about dictatorship and illuminates how the violence of dictatorial regimes reappears somewhere: in the "here" of Latina/o literature. According to Salomé, "energy is neither lost nor created. Nothing truly goes away"; rather, it changes form (3). Her words symbolically capture a dual concern among Latina/o writers with regard to dictatorship. The first is the haunting presence of the past in the present moment. The second is the way in which the signification of dictatorship can take different forms, the way it changes given a particular historical moment and geopolitical context.

As a result of Salomé's traumatic imprisonment and torture for resisting the authoritarian state, she gives birth to the Latina daughter to whom she seeks to pass on her story. Salomé reflects on how her brother has "raised his daughter, her daughter, what a twisted family tree, spliced and splayed all over the world" (5).[1] This image of a family tree, its branches cut in different pieces and spread out in different directions, metaphorically captures how I conceptualize the dictatorship novel tradition in the Americas.[2] This book is centrally concerned with the migration of the dictatorship novel to the United States and the ways Latina/os have developed a new set of dictatorship novels. This book explores what these novels and their formal literary devices can tell us about the haunting afterlives of dictatorship and about the dictatorial power relations that Latina/os grapple with in the United States.

The Latina/o Counter-dictatorial Imaginary

In the past two decades a wide range of English-language Latina/o novels have been published that depict historical dictatorships and use dictatorship as a literary trope. Daniel Alarcón, Julia Alvarez, Junot Díaz, Cristina García, Francisco Goldman, Demetria Martínez, Salvador Plascencia, Carolina de Robertis, Héctor Tobar, and others have all written novels that represent myriad kinds of authoritarian power.[3] While their novels are rooted in differing local and national histories—moving between New Jersey and the Dominican Republic, Los Angeles and Guatemala, Miami and Cuba, New Mexico and El Salvador, San Francisco and Montevideo, among other sites—they are all haunted by the specter of dictatorship. This literature, I argue, constitutes a new subgenre of contemporary Latina/o fiction that I term the Latina/o dictatorship novel. While scholars have studied the Spanish-language dictatorship novel as a canonical Latin American literary form, I reveal how Latina/o writers insert distinct visions of dictatorial power into the genre. The novels depict the aftermath of Latin American authoritarian regimes on Latina/o communities alongside authoritarian structures and discourses of power that minorities and migrants face in the United States. Moreover, they dramatize these linkages at the levels of both content and form.

This book examines what these novels reveal about the transnational afterlives of dictatorship and about the forms of dictatorial power that shape Latina/os' experiences as U.S. ethnic minorities. It analyzes how Latina/o novels imagine various kinds of dictatorial power, paying particular attention to the central role that narrative form plays in capturing local and hemispheric relations of power. By extending the Latina/o literary field-imaginary beyond the nation, it uncovers the trans-American production of dictatorship novels and illuminates Latina/os' central contributions to the literary history of the dictatorship novel.

Using "Latina/o" and "the dictatorship novel" as frameworks, I examine texts written by Latina/os from varying national-origin groups that explore authoritarian power from diverse angles. Reading these texts alongside one another reveals an overarching concern on the part of Latina/o writers to represent resonances and dissonances between hierarchies of power and modes of repression in the Americas. Having grown up in the United States, the authors I examine in this book, as well as many of their novels' characters, are at a geographic and generational remove from Latin American dictatorships. Their experiences as minorities living in the United States—in what José Martí has famously described as living in the entrails of the monster—rather than living in the belly of the beast of a Latin American dictatorship, give rise to a different conceptualization of domination and thereby of dictatorship. I argue that Latina/o novels have a double vision of state violence both abroad and domestically, and they position dictatorship along a spectrum of authoritarian power in the United States and Latin America. By portraying dictatorship along a continuum of domination, they generate what I term the Latina/o counter-dictatorial imaginary, which draws connections between authoritarianism, imperialism, white supremacy, heteropatriarchy, neoliberal capitalism, and border militarization in the Americas.

That Latina/o counter-dictatorial imaginary accounts for multiple manifestations of authoritarian power and hierarchies of privilege and oppression. Because of their intimate knowledge of imperialism and dictatorship, Latina/os see and experience the United States differently and recognize the traces of dictatorial power in foreign *and* domestic sites. The novels insert a trans-American memory of dictatorship and U.S. interventionism into the Latina/o literary imaginary. The fictional productions are a cultural response to the history of the United States' support of repressive dictatorships and counter-insurgency campaigns, drawing attention to what Ariana Vigil calls the "war echoes" that reverberate in contemporary narratives and community relations (*War Echoes*, 3). Latina/o dictatorship novels suggest that, contrary to the United States' projected image of itself as the exemplary model for democracy in the hemisphere, the United States functions like a dictator abroad. This figuration of the United States as dictatorial interrogates "the occult artistry whereby empire parades behind a mask of democracy" (Lomas, xv). The novels further suggest that the drama of U.S. imperialism is not just something that unfolds in foreign countries but that it plays out in our own domestic dictatorial hierarchies of power in the United States.

Though interventionism, racism, machismo, labor exploitation, and the policing of undocumented subjects may not be as visibly and spectacularly violent as dictatorships, they are oppressive systems of control. Depicting authoritarian power along a continuum, Latina/o representations of dictatorial power challenge us to see the United States not only as a site of freedom but as a perpetrator of oppression that masks its inequalities and modes of dominance more covertly than dictatorships do. By representing dictatorship both literally as a political system and abstractly as a discursive system, Latina/o novels highlight more ubiquitous modes of domination and expand the ways we conceptualize dictatorial power.

The Latina/o counter-dictatorial imaginary is embedded in what scholars have theorized more broadly as the "social imaginary," the "trans-American imaginary," and the "Latino imaginary." The "social imaginary" is a "symbolic matrix within which a people imagine and act as world-making collective agents" (Gaonkar, 1). This symbolic field is the means through which people create a sense of themselves in relation to one another and in relation to the material, social, and historical conditions in which they live.[4] The social imaginary is not limited to a national community but can be shared by a group of people across geopolitical boundaries. In the context of the hemisphere, Paula M. L. Moya and Ramón Saldívar term this the "trans-American imaginary," which is "a very real but fundamentally different syntax of codes, images, and icons, as well as the tacit assumptions, convictions, and beliefs that seek to bind together the varieties of American national discourses. The transnational imaginary is thus to be understood as a chronotope, a contact zone, that is both historical and geographical and is populated by transnational persons whose lives form an experiential region within which singularly delineated notions of political, social, and cultural identity do not suffice.... It is an interpretive framework that yokes together North and South America instead of New England and England" (2). The trans-American imaginary is the experiential field in which Latina/o cultural producers imagine and forge transnational symbolic representations that make sense of their world. The novel is one expressive mode through which Latina/os imagine their existence, using fiction and its world-making possibilities to understand, and sometimes even reconfigure, social relations and discourses. As an interpretive framework, the Latina/o counter-dictatorial imaginary yokes together the United States, Mexico, and various countries in Central and South America and the Caribbean that have experienced authoritarian political regimes, and draws links among various Latina/o novels that remember the violent histories of these regimes and other kinds of systematic violence in the United States.

The Latina/o counter-dictatorial imaginary is a symbolic field of representation that arises out of the experiences of Latina/os from various national-origin groups. Juan Flores's concept of the "Latino imaginary" is a politically strategic means of grouping together a disparate group of heterogeneous people, signaling a sense of unity amid the diversity and of diversity amid the unity. It creates "a unity fashioned creatively on the basis of shared memory and desire, congruent histories of misery and struggle, and intertwining utopias" (193). The Latina/o imaginary precisely enables difference and similitude to coexist while stressing, like Gloria Anzaldúa and Ariel Dorfman in the epigraphs to this chapter, that an awareness of a shared history in "Nuestra América" (Our America) is key.[5] Interwoven into these memories of political, structural, and discursive violence in the Latina/o novel is a utopian desire for a future in which authoritarian power is no longer a reality of the present but a relic of the past. The Latina/o counter-dictatorial imaginary expresses this in terms of both an oppositional response and an "alternative ethos" that does not simply resist authoritarianism but is rooted in an anticipatory and decolonial consciousness that longs for a future otherwise (Flores, 200).

This study reveals how Latina/o novels expand the traditional thematic concerns of Latin American and Latina/o literature and develop new narrative strategies for depicting dictatorial power relations. The novels offer a contrapuntal critique of authoritarian power abroad and at home. Examining the complex geopolitical and formal contours of the Latina/o dictatorship novel illuminates how Latina/os conceptualize and creatively resist sociopolitical, socioeconomic, and discursive domination in their various structural manifestations. In reading narrative form and hemispheric geopolitics together, I contend that we cannot fully understand Latina/o literature without considering Latin American literature and how certain genres, literary tropes, and histories migrate to the United States and undergo a process of transformation, transculturation, and reformulation through the pens of Latina/os.[6]

An American Tradition

Gustavo Pérez Firmat's edited collection *Do the Americas Have a Common Literature?* posed a titular question in 1990 that encapsulates the field of trans-American literary studies. Affirmative answers to Pérez Firmat's question abound.[7] This book argues that the Americas have a common literature of dictatorship fiction. The Latin American dictatorship novel, written in Spanish, depicts authoritarian regimes such as caciquismo, caudillismo, dictatorship, and the military junta in Latin America. The tradition is a long and rich one, with scholars consistently beginning their genealogies of the genre with Domingo Faustino Sarmiento's influential 1845 *Facundo: Civilización y barbarie* (*Facundo: Civilization and Barbarism*).[8] The tradition includes such early works as José Mármol's *Amalia* (1851), Ramón de Valle-Inclán's *El tyrano banderas* (*The Tyrant Banderas*) (1926), Miguel Angel Asturias's *El señor presidente* (*The President*) (1946), and Enrique Lafourcade's *La fiesta del rey acab* (King Ahab's Feast) (1959). During the 1970s, the boom generation of writers produced the most famous and heavily studied novels: Augusto Roa Bastos's *Yo el supremo* (*I, the Supreme*) (1974), Alejo Carpentier's *El recurso del método* (*Reasons of State*) (1974), and Gabriel García Márquez's *El otoño del patriarca* (*The Autumn of the Patriarch*) (1975). The tradition has continued to grow in subsequent decades, in particular due to dictatorships in the Southern Cone and in Central America and the creative production of writers such as Roberto Bolaño, Diamela Eltit, Cristina Peri Rossi, Sergio Ramírez, Luisa Valenzuela, and Mario Vargas Llosa.[9] Yet, to fully understand contemporary developments in the genre, we must look beyond the geopolitical boundaries of Latin America and the linguistic boundaries of Spanish and follow the other forking paths of the dictatorship novel in the Americas. Using a more expansive lens that includes the writings of Latina/os in the United States illuminates the dictatorship novel's geographic and formal range and accounts for its canon of texts, its expressive aesthetics, and its archive of experiences.

Numerous scholars have developed typologies of the Latin American dictatorship novel by identifying multiple stages in the development of the tradition. Scholars generally split the various phases of the genre's evolution by literary period—romantic, modern, and contemporary—and by the shift from the early novels that have a distanced view of dictatorship to the novels of the 1970s that focus on the perspective of the dictator.[10] Scholars have also chronicled the common thematic and stylistic features of the Latin American dictatorship novel.[11] The centrality of these features varies depending on whether or not the dictator is the primary focus of the novel. For example, when the novels focus on the dictator's consciousness, they often emphasize his solitude and egocentrism, whereas when the dictatorship is in the background, they generally focus more on the atmosphere of fear, censorship, and violent repression.

Latina/o dictatorship novels vary widely, traversing countries and time periods, ranging from minimal to fully developed dramatizations of life under authoritarian political regimes. Though some of the novels are set during or in the aftermath of Latin American dictatorships, many of them take place in the United States and are peppered with references to life under dictatorship or contain backstory conflicts and flashback sequences that occur under dictatorship. The novels' characters are shaped by Latin American state violence *and* by U.S. structural and discursive violence that they must navigate as racial minorities and migrants in the United States. I argue that we can read the Latina/o dictatorship novel both as a subgenre of Latina/o fiction and as a new stage of the dictatorship novel in the Americas, delineating the ways the writers I examine fuse the sociopolitical and aesthetic concerns of Latina/o and Latin American literatures.

Latina/o dictatorship novels broaden the thematic concerns, the geographic and temporal scope, and the character types and stylistic features of the Latin American dictatorship novel. They enlarge the geographic scope transnationally by bringing their plots into the United States. They extend the temporality of the dictatorship by exploring its afterlife[12] in the United States as experienced by Latina/o citizens and migrants. They expand the language of production into English and code-switch between English and Spanish.[13] Moreover, they widen the political concerns of the Latin American dictatorship novel by intertwining the critical concerns of Latina/o literature— with regard to race, class, gender, sexuality, ability, migration, citizenship, language politics, and cultural mestizaje—with those of Latin American literature. They also insert a new set of protagonists, antagonists, and transnational characters.

Latina/o authors take up the historical condition of dictatorship, the figure of the dictator, and the concept of authoritarianism, adapting them to and transculturating them with the themes and tropes common to Latina/o literature. I use the term "dictatorship novel" to draw attention to regimes of power instead of to a single figure in power. Though there is no critical consensus on the name of the genre and few Latin Americanists use the same terminology, in general, we can parse the difference between dictator novels and dictatorship novels, with the former referring to those that focus on the dictator as a main character and the latter referring to those that focus more broadly on the system of dictatorship.[14] My use of "dictatorship novel" in a more expansive sense allows me to consider novels that fit neatly into the category and those that fit more awkwardly but bring interesting and important considerations of dictatorial power to the discussion.[15] This links a novel like Cristina García's *King of Cuba*, in which the dictator is a central character, Junot Díaz's *The Brief Wondrous Life of Oscar Wao*, in which the dictator is a minor character and a historical reference in a plot that is partly set in the United States decades after the death of the dictator, and Salvador Plascencia's *The People of Paper*, which uses the trope of the author-as-dictator but is not based in a real historical dictatorship. My use of "dictatorship novel" also emphasizes that "dictatorship" and "authoritarianism" do not have to refer only to political governments. Rather, these terms can usefully describe intimate relationships within a family (what in chapter 5 I call domestic dictatorship, to capture heteropatriarchy and domestic abuse), transnational and transhistorical relations of empire (the dictatorship of imperialism and interventionism that I examine in chapters 3 and 4), and the formal and metaphorical use of authority (what in chapters 1 and 2 I call *author*itarianism, to highlight the slippages between authorship, authority, and authoritarianism).[16] In other words, I explore at length how Latina/o writers exploit dictatorship and authoritarianism as literary tropes to critique different modes of repressive power.

Dictatorship novels by Latin Americans and Latina/os share a critical and oppositional stance toward their subject of representation. By identifying the primary attitude of the narrative and reader toward the dictator as inherently an antagonistic or contestatory one, Carlos Pacheco and Juan Carlos García capture how the dictatorship novel is commonly written and interpreted as a political form of literature and as a politically and socially committed genre.[17] Given the genre's roots in the anti-dictatorship writings against Juan Manuel de Rosas in Argentina in the mid-nineteenth century, this oppositional function is built into the genre, with the written word functioning as a weapon in the struggle against tyranny.[18] While subsequent Latin American writing attempts to understand the psychology of dictatorial power and the mechanisms of state control, portraying the complexity of domination and consent and making simple denunciation more difficult, it has done so with the desire to imagine the end of authoritarian regimes. Resistance is also a common stance and trope in Latina/o literature. Latina/os infuse anti-dictatorship writing with interrogations of racism, colorism, heterosexism, class exploitation, the surveillance of undocumented migrants, and pressures to assimilate at the expense of cultural heritage. In short, they fuse the oppositional strands of Latina/o and Latin American narrative traditions.

At the same time, Latina/o novels grapple seriously with complicity and compromise. For example, the dictator at the heart of Salvador Plascencia's *The People of Paper*, which I analyze in chapter 2, is a Chicano novelist, and the characters in his novel stage a revolution against the author, who omnipotently rules over his characters' life stories, omnisciently reads their thoughts, and materially profits off of their consciousnesses. The novel asks us to take seriously the limitations of the novel genre as a mode of contestation, due to the power dynamics inherent in its formal structures and its status as a commodity in the literary marketplace.

A common rhetorical trope in the Latin American creative and scholarly tradition is to position dictatorships and dictatorship novels as indigenous to Latin America, whereas the Latina/o dictatorship novel puts pressure on this formulation. Gabriel García Márquez proclaimed: "El tema [del dictador] ha sido un constante en la literatura latinoamericana desde sus orígenes, y supongo que lo seguirá siendo. Es comprensible, pues el dictador es el único ser mitológico que ha producido América Latina, y su ciclo histórico está lejos de ser concluido." (The dictator as a theme has been a constant since the origins of Latin American literature, and I suppose that it will continue to be. It is understandable since the dictator is the only mythological being that Latin America has produced and his cycle in history is far from finished.) (*El olor*, 137). For his part, Roberto González Echevarría declared: "The most clearly indigenous thematic tradition in Latin American literature [is] the dictator and the dictator-book" (206).[19] This prevailing assumption that the dictator is an archetype and a means to understand Latin American reality allows writers to represent and critics to study a literary, social, and historical phenomenon simultaneously. Yet the danger of justifying the literary or critical tradition with the idea that dictatorship is "un mal endémico de América Latina" (an evil endemic to Latin America) is that it keeps the focus exclusively on Latin America and Latin American writing (Ramos, 7).[20]

Moreover, this justification problematically, even if inadvertently, reinforces popular stereotypes of Latin America and elides a more rigorous accounting of the United States' role in aiding and abetting right-wing authoritarian regimes across the hemisphere. Especially in U.S. popular culture and political discourse, Latin America is stereotypically represented as the land of dictatorships.[21] This "tropicalizes" Latin Americans and, by extension, Latina/os. "To *tropicalize*," as Frances R. Aparicio and Susana Chávez-Silverman define it, "means to trope, to imbue a particular space, geography, group, or nation with a set of traits, images, and values," which in this case is essentialist, condescending, and colonialist (8). Moreover, tropicalism "is intrinsically connected to the history of political, economic, and ideological agendas of governments and of social institutions. Furthermore, these inscriptions facilitate the popular acceptance and justification of imperialist interventions, invasions, and wars" (8). The hemispheric binary that aligns Latin America with dictatorship and the United States with democracy not only demonizes Latin America and romanticizes the United States, it also veils and disavows the United States' constitutive and imperialist role in fomenting and colluding with authoritarian regimes in Latin America. Latina/o novels directly confront and interrogate this tropicalizing binary by indicting both Latin American dictatorships and U.S. imperialism, and they foreground more ubiquitous modes of domination to indict structural discrimination in the United States, as well as repressive power hierarchies in general.

The Latina/o counter-dictatorial imaginary also positions individual authoritarian regimes alongside broader hemispheric configurations of coloniality in Latin America and the United States. This is crucial, because while dictatorship is a primary feature of what Jean Franco has called "cruel modernity," it is one moment in the long history of domination in the Americas, which originates with colonialism but continues in the present, drawing attention to the *longue durée* of coloniality in the Americas. According to theorists such as Aníbal Quijano, Walter Mignolo, María Lugones, and José David

Saldívar, "modernity/coloniality" is a world-system that came into being in the sixteenth century during the colonization of the "New World," that is, during the "contact" with the Americas. Coloniality, they argue, is constitutive of modernity; therefore, one cannot speak of modernity without speaking of coloniality, its dark underside. "Coloniality" enabled the enactment of domination and exploitation through the creation and imposition of hierarchical classifications of race, labor, and gender relations and through new capitalist modes of production. As a result, non-European people in particular were placed at the bottom of racial hierarchies and characterized as intrinsically inferior, primitive, without civilization, and outside history. Europe and later the United States, in contrast, were constructed as the bearers of civilization, reason, and progress. Both Latin Americans and Latina/os have been mutually, though differently, relegated to subordinate and inferior positions in relation to Europe and Anglo-America. Like Latin Americans, Latina/os produce "postdictatorial texts that remind the present that it is the product of past catastrophe," while also reminding us that the present is catastrophic too and that the dictatorship of coloniality is far from over (Avelar, 3).

While Latin America has certainly produced the most novels about dictatorship and has the most robust scholarly tradition for considering this textual production, if we read the dictatorship novel only as a Latin American cultural form, we foreclose fruitful comparative alignments with Latina/o writers.[22] Using a trans-American framework, I reveal how attending to the genre of the novel adds another layer to the variegated set of "transamerican literary relations" that other scholars have untangled (Brickhouse). While much of trans-American literary criticism has been archival, thematic, genealogical, or discourse-oriented, my study demonstrates the critical import of genre-based hemispheric studies. I elucidate how we can read hemispheric relations of domination through the circulation and modification of the dictatorship novel and through the transnational subjectivities, aesthetic forms, and discursive tropes that constitute the imaginative horizon of the Latina/o dictatorship novel.

The Power of Form and the Form of Power

Dictatorial power serves as a trope and an aesthetic problem that enables us to rethink the relationship between different forms of power and the power of form—that is, between various instantiations of repressive power structures and the effect of different narrative structures in representing, reproducing, or contesting repressive power. Latina/o authors manage their critiques of dictatorial power by deploying narrative techniques. Precisely how Latina/os use the novel as a genre—in particular how they manipulate specific literary devices and how they overlay different geographies and histories—to construct a counter-dictatorial imaginary is at the center of the formalist analyses I offer in each chapter.

Through my readings of formal devices and discursive tropes, I unpack dictatorial power and dictatorial relations in the Latina/o novel. I focus on the novels' formal features so as to excavate the mechanisms through which the novels are conceptualizing dictatorial power. I attend to the ways Latina/o writers mobilize the novel genre—how they use formal devices such as footnotes, focalization, analepsis, and metafiction—to interrogate various political, economic, and social hierarchies of power. I build on narrative theories of plot, character, temporality, and perspective to show how the Latina/o dictatorship novel stages power dynamics. Engaging in socioformal analysis, I draw connections between structures of power, narrative control, and social location.

Moreover, writing is a form of power that manifests in the novel as discursive and representational control. I thus track the dual literary and political connotations of puns and analogies in the novels to expose the links between writing and domination and to trouble the correlation between writing and resistance. For instance, "dictate" and "plot" have different meanings: a novelist dictates a story, but a politician or military officer also dictates an order; alternatively, plot is the structure of events in a novel, but plot is also a plan to overthrow an abusive power figure and attain justice. Analyzing the different wordplay and narrative strategies running throughout the novels, I sketch out the contiguities between different kinds of dictatorial power, be they political, social, economic, or discursive. Examining the Latina/o dictatorship novel's complex formal and geopolitical literary imaginary illuminates how Latina/os creatively and critically contend with domination in its various sociopolitical, socioeconomic, and sociocultural structural manifestations.

This book deliberately attends to the underlying political messages about power running through the novels *and* to the surface of the page and the complexity of the literary tactics being employed.

My attention to form and genre is part of a renewed interest in formalist criticism in literary studies more broadly and more specifically among Latina/o literary critics, who are increasingly attending to the issue of form.[23] As John Morán González observes, the "question of form within Latina/o studies has been a vexed one. For the most part, scholars in this field have been fixated on thematic analysis, and specifically on how texts reveal the unequal operations of power at the level of expressed content. While certainly necessary, this approach neglects how the formal parameters of a text negotiate that very terrain of power in ways that both compliment and complicate its manifest content" (430).[24] Latina/o novels do not simply represent real historical dictatorships and relations of power in an unmediated way. Since formal literary devices mediate the novels' representations of reality, we cannot approach "literary works sociologically, reading them as transparent repositories of cultural description" (Cutler, 18). In order to grasp how Latina/os are theorizing dictatorial power in the realm of the aesthetic imagination, I attend to their representational structures as well as the content of their storyworlds. For I am precisely interested both in "how texts mean" and in the meanings that exist below the surface of the text (R. E. Rodriguez, "In Plain," 88). Form matters as much as content and theme, and this is particularly salient in dictatorship novels because these novels wrestle so centrally with questions of authority and how authoritarian regimes manipulate reality through structures that are themselves forms of power.

I focus on the power of narrative form and the form of sociopolitical power in each novel, with form serving as the connective link between literary and sociopolitical structures of power.[25] An attention to narrative form is crucial because form is a constituting feature of literature and of the social world. As Caroline Levine puts it, "social hierarchies and institutions can themselves be understood as *forms*. What emerges is a cultural-political field in which literary forms and social formations can be grasped as comparable and overlapping patternings operating on a common plane" (626). Levine explains that hierarchies of identity such as race, gender, class, and sexuality are "formalized, disciplined into recognizable, repeatable oppositions. And so: if cultural studies has taught us to see power relations as systemic and patterned—as formalized—then it is time to think about culture in terms of its forms" (631).[26] Following this, I read forms of power in the novels in terms of hierarchies of identity such as race, class, gender, and citizenship; furthermore, I demonstrate how in thinking through the category of dictatorship—at least the way Latina/o novels conceptualize dictatorship—we can also see authoritarianism and imperialism as forms. Indeed, Latina/o novels ask us to make these links so we can see dictatorial power functioning through various forms even as it functions differently depending on the pattern or structure it takes.

Over the course of this book, I focus on the power of form and the form of power. I probe the plethora of ways that Latina/o novels represent, trouble, reinforce, and topple dictatorial hierarchies of power. I analyze how a novel inverts hierarchies of power by making the dictator a minor character and the marginalized subject a major character, for example, at the same time that I explore how a novel reproduces the panoptic disciplinary gaze of a dictatorship through omniscient narration. In doing so, I demonstrate how literary forms and sociopolitical forms can be at odds with or can collude with each other.

By analyzing the forms through which Latina/os narrate dictatorial power, I capture the ways their novels are reconceptualizing the forms in which we are subject to dictatorial power. My readings of the Latina/o dictatorship novel are rooted in the premise that literature is "a mode, as well as an object, of inquiry" (3) and thus that it is an "act of interpretation" (Moya, 8). As an interpretive mode of inquiry, Latina/o novels about dictatorship seeks to understand authoritarian power, not simply to represent or to denounce it. The Latina/o writers I examine in this book use literary form as a mode of inquiry into the legacy of dictatorship and into systemic violence and structural marginalization. Literature and especially narrative devices are their means to identify and narrate various forms of dictatorial power. The counter-dictatorial imaginary their writings collectively generate functions as a means of raising our consciousness about how hierarchies of power dictate social identities. This increases our literacy to read such operations of power in terms of intersectionality and multiplicity[27] as well as transnationally and across various forms of domination. By depicting dictatorial power along a spectrum that includes authoritarianism, imperialism, white supremacy, heteropatriarchy, neoliberalism, and border militarization, the Latina/o counter-dictatorial imaginary challenges us to recognize how these are forms of power that dictate our agency and restrict our ability to build more just futures.

Postdictatorship and Postmemory Hauntings

In a 1998 op-ed in *La Insignia,* Nicaraguan writer Sergio Ramírez notes how Latino novelists Daniel Alarcón and Junot Díaz are both plagued by

> los fantasmas de la realidad latinoamericana que nos persiguen a todos, escribamos en español, o en inglés. Y cuando digo realidad estoy hablando de la que tiene que ver con la vida pública, los horrores y alucinaciones de la realidad social y política, la que proviene de la historia reciente, o de la historia lejana. Los pasmosos excesos dictaduras, el crimen, la tortura, los desaparecidos. República Dominicana y la dictadura de Trujillo; Perú y Sendero Luminoso. Los viejos fantasmas salidos de los sótanos de los palacios presidenciales, no dejan de hacer sonar sus cadenas al arrastrarlas.
>
> Y esos fantasmas traspasan las fronteras de Estados Unidos como tantos otros clandestinos, escondidos en los genes, o en el equipaje de los emigrantes que un día serán escritores de primera línea. Fantasmas mojadas, que no se dejan quitar de en medio.

> the ghosts of the Latin American reality that persecute us all, whether we write in Spanish or English. And when I say reality I mean the reality of public life, of the horrors and hallucinations of social and political reality, a reality that comes from recent history or from distant history. The astonishing excesses of dictatorships, crime, torture, the disappeared. The Dominican Republic and the Trujillo dictatorship; Peru and the Shining Path. The old ghosts that have come out of the basements of the presidential palaces do not stop the sounds of the chains they are dragging.
>
> And these ghosts have crossed the United States border like many other clandestine migrants, hidden in the genes or in the luggage of the immigrants who will one day be first class writers. Wetback ghosts who refuse to get out of the way.

While the primary focus of Ramírez's op-ed is to provocatively ask whether the new Latin American novel will be written in English, he vividly captures how Latina/o fiction is haunted by the violent histories of dictatorship. Latina/o novelists nuance Ramírez's formulation that the ghosts originate in Latin America, for Latina/o writers invite us to grapple with the horrors of domination and violence in both Latin America *and* the United States, with how we are haunted by multiple kinds of repressive regimes.

In Ramírez's description, the violence is mobile, which he figures as traveling north by hiding in the bodies and the trappings of migrants. The trauma of dictatorship is part of the baggage of migrants, figured here in terms of the material belongings carried in a suitcase but also present in the emotional and psychological baggage of inherited trauma. While Ramírez imagines the ghosts as migrants who cross the border into the United States, his assertion that the ghosts are hidden in one's genetic make-up gestures toward an intergenerational inheritance of memory.[28]

Ramírez's image of the ghost is also provocative given the "Los padres de las patrias" (The Fathers of the Homelands) project, which a group of prominent boom generation Latin American writers conceived and agreed to collectively undertake in 1967. The project was to be a collection of novellas about Latin American dictators, each one focusing on a different historical dictator, by a dozen writers from a number of different Latin American nations. While the project was never realized, it shaped, in part, the production of the three most famous dictatorship novels: Carpentier's *El recurso del método*, Roa Bastos's *Yo el supremo*, and García Márquez's *El otoño del patriarca*.[29] As Carlos Fuentes relates, he and Mario Vargas Llosa were in London when they got the idea for the collection. Curiously, Fuentes describes this moment using the image of ghosts: "Sentados en un pub de Hampstead, se nos ocurrió que no estaría mal un libro comparable sobre América Latina: una galería imaginaria de retratos. En este instante, varios espectros entraron al pub londinense reclamando el derecho a encarnar. Eran los dictadores latinoamericanos" (Sitting in a pub in Hampstead, it occurred to us that it would be a good idea to do a comparable book about Latin America: an imaginary portrait gallery. In that instant, various ghosts entered the London pub claiming their right to embodiment. They were the Latin American dictators) (91). In Fuentes's story, the ghosts of the dictators cross national borders and appear far from their homelands to materialize in the space of the pub. Sergio Ramírez's image of enchained ghosts emerging from the basements of presidential palaces switches the focus from the spectral dictators who demand narrative space to the ghosts of those persecuted by the dictatorships smuggling themselves into the stories told by Latina/o writers. Rather than focus on the authorial and authoritarian dictators who claim the right to become fictional protagonists of the envisioned group of short stories, Ramírez grants a different kind of authority that comes from underground, literally from the basements and places of imprisonment and torture but also symbolically from the underground or clandestine organizations of people who resisted the dictatorships. This shifts the narrative focus onto the victims rather than the perpetrators and grants them narrative agency. As I argue in the case of Junot Díaz's *The Brief Wondrous Life of Oscar Wao* in chapter 1, this authority is embedded in the novel's footnotes, which structurally embody under-the-radar or coded modes of communication, since footnotes are positioned below the main text and these paratexts narrate a counter-history to Trujillo's dictatorship. Focusing on the tortured Abelard, his abused daughter Beli, and his murdered grandson Oscar, Díaz's novel represents the ghostly transnational and transgenerational impact of dictatorship from the perspective of the Dominican diaspora.

It is also important to note that Ramírez develops his conjectures based on two male Latino writers and that men conceived "Los padres de las patrias" and selected mainly male writers to participate. This is not surprising given that the dictatorship novel is predominately a male-authored genre that focuses on male dictators. While I have translated "Los padres de las patrias" as "The Fathers of the Homelands," highlighting the nation-state implied in the term "patria" (homeland), we can also translate it as "The Fathers of the Fatherlands" to highlight the male gendering of leadership and heroism. The dictatorship novel entails "cosas de hombres," as Gabriela Polit Dueñas puts it, using a colloquial expression that means something is "a man's thing" to do or say (13). Polit Dueñas's repurposed turn of phrase captures how political power and the authority to write have been seen as the domain of men and how women are typically at the margins of dictatorship novels. Cristina García's *King of Cuba*, as I demonstrate in chapter 5, satirizes the hypermasculinity of the dictatorship novel genre as well as the heteropatriarchal histories that construct men as the ideal agents of revolutionary and counter-revolutionary movements. The specters of dictators past that enter the London pub are all male ghosts speaking to male writers, whereas moving away from focusing on the dictators allows women and other kinds of protagonists to enter the novels, as well as write them.

While Ramírez asks that we be attentive to the ghosts of "Latin American reality and public life," Latina/o authors also track the ghosts of U.S. interventionism and U.S. sociopolitical and socioeconomic structures that plague Latina/o subjects. For example, the "phantom owners" and their "ghost ship" at the heart of Francisco

Goldman's *The Ordinary Seaman*, which I analyze in chapter 3, do not emerge from the basements of Latin American presidential palaces but from the basement of U.S. history, where racialized subjects—in this case, African-origin slaves—were the foundational basis for a socioeconomic system in the United States (and Latin America) that profited off of Black bodies and where a foreign site—in this case Central America—was central in U.S. economic imperial designs. The use of the ship as a trope brings together the slave ship, the filibustering ship, and the novel's neoliberal ship that profits off of undocumented laborers. The novel provokes us to think more broadly about dictatorship and authoritarian power in a post–Cold War world where neoliberal capitalism and multinational corporations monopolize power.

The Latina/o novels at the center of this study are postdictatorship textual productions. I employ the prefix "post" in postdictatorship in multiple different ways. I also use it as a geographic category to indicate that the novels are produced outside Latin America. Additionally, I use it as a temporal category to indicate that they are written after the official ends of the Latin American political regimes they reference. I also use it as a generational category to indicate that they are written by authors who have not lived under or directly experienced these Latin American political regimes. Furthermore, I use it as a thematic category to indicate how the topics of concern in Latina/o novels depart from as well as align with those of Latin American novels.[30] Finally, I also use it as a conceptual category to indicate that Latina/os put pressure on a strictly governmental definition of dictatorship.

In marking a geographic, historical, generational, thematic, and conceptual distance and difference, the "post" does not explicitly signal the end of dictatorial power. Anne McClintock warns about the problematic developmental teleology suggested by the "post" in "postcolonialism," which is "organized around a binary axis of time rather than power, and which, in its premature celebration of the pastness of colonialism, runs the risk of obscuring the continuities and discontinuities of colonial and imperial power" (88).[31] McClintock draws attention to "the United States' imperialism-without-colonies" and to "'post-colonial' Latin America," pointing out how the United States has invaded Latin American "over a hundred times this century alone. Each time, the US has acted to install a dictatorship, prop up a puppet regime, or wreck a democracy" (89).

Latina/o novels critique U.S. imperial power in Latin America at the same time that they highlight the continuities and discontinuities between different kinds of authoritarian domination in the United States and Latin America. My use of "postdictatorship" is meant to foreground this dynamic of dictatorial power.

Moreover, I use the "post" to highlight how the novels pose important conceptual questions about what meaning the idea of dictatorship holds for Latina/os in the United States. My use of "postdictatorship" evokes a similar post-ness ascribed to recent "postrace" novels. "The term 'postrace' does not mean that we are beyond race; the prefix 'post' here does not mean a chronological superseding, a triumphant posteriority," Ramón Saldívar explains; "rather, the term entails a conceptual shift to the question of what meaning the idea of 'race' carries in our own times." For Saldívar, the "post" "refers to the logic of something having been 'shaped as a consequence of' imperialism and racism." ("Historical Fantasy," 575). I use the "post" in "postdictatorship" in this broader terminological way to signal the logic of something having been "shaped as a consequence of" three broad structures of power: Latin American authoritarian regimes, U.S. imperialism, and U.S. structural discrimination. Latina/o novels depict these as simultaneously interlocking structures of power. In doing so, their counter-dictatorial imaginary insists that dictatorship, imperialism, white supremacy, heteropatriarchy, neoliberalism, and border militarization are all dictatorial modes of control. The "post" in "postdictatorship" therefore does not signal the triumphant end to a system of domination but a provocation to consider the links between different kinds of dictatorship and histories of violence.

As postdictatorship texts, the novels are also postmemory texts. According to Marianne Hirsch, "'postmemory' describes the relationship that the 'generation after' bears to the personal, collective, and cultural trauma of those who came before—to experiences they 'remember' only by means of the stories, images, and behaviors among which they grew up" (5). At a temporal, geographic, and generational remove, Latina/o authors' relationship to dictatorships in Latin America is indirect, shaped by family stories (or even silences), by research, and by their imaginations, rather than by direct, firsthand experience.[32] They grapple with how to capture in fiction collective atrocities that they have not lived through, as well as how to understand those atrocities in dialogue with the present conditions affecting them as racial minorities in the United States.

This postmemory or mediated relationship positions Latina/o fiction differently in relation to Latin American national memory projects. Macarena Gómez-Barris uses the term "memory symbolic" to denote how the national public sphere transitioning to democracy in Chile after the Pinochet dictatorship was shaped by state-led initiatives and other memorializing strategies that managed and consolidated national narratives about the authoritarian past in the service of official history and state hegemony. Gómez-Barris posits that cultural representations can offer "alternative memory symbolics" that challenge these national narratives with productions of memory that are "complex, fluid, unending, and incomplete" (*Where Memory Dwells*, 6). Latina/o novels contribute to this production of alternative memory symbolics in transnational contexts, in effect creating postmemory symbolics. They reshape how authoritarian pasts are remembered and resituate debates about how to attain justice in more transnational terms. For example, Héctor Tobar's novel *The Tattooed Soldier*, which I analyze in chapter 4, recalls the genocide perpetrated against indigenous communities in Guatemala alongside the racial profiling and police brutality exerted against racial minorities in the United States. The Rodney King uprisings in Los Angeles in 1992 serve as a contrapuntal backdrop for a Guatemalan leftist's killing of the death squad member, trained in counter-insurgency tactics at the United States' School of the Americas, who was responsible for the murder of his wife and child. The novel exposes the transnational roots of authoritarian violence at the same time that it denounces the impunity granted to military and police apparatuses in both Guatemala and the United States, opening up a dialogue about how to attain justice.

Latina/o novels are haunted by various forms of authoritarian power. Latina/o postdictatorship and postmemory textual production highlights the necessity of attending to ethnic, national, and transnational contexts to fully understand how this literature is shaped by the residual afterlife of the state violence perpetrated in Latin America and by the residual and dominant modes of violence in the United States. Their hemispheric counter-dictatorial visions provide one salient case study on the benefits of a comparative and trans-American Latina/o literary studies that is attentive to congruent and contiguous forms of oppressions across the Americas.

Pan-Latina/o and Trans-Latina/o Fictions

This investigation is rooted in panethnic and transnational Latina/o literary studies.[33] A pan-Latina/o lens compares various Latina/o national-origin groups and highlights continuities and discontinuities among Latina/o groups, whereas a trans-Latina/o lens highlights the transnational relations between Latina/o groups and their home countries in Latin America.[34] Though this study is not comprehensive and some national-origin groups receive more attention than others, I deliberately touch on the major Latina/o groups: Chicana/o, Latina/o Caribbean, Latina/o Central American, and Latina/o South American.[35] While scholars have examined the looming presence of the Trujillo dictatorship in U.S. Dominican fiction, war and trauma as key tropes in U.S. Central American literature, and the force that the Cuban Revolution has had on shaping U. S. Cuban literary production, these different themes and literatures are usually not studied in dialogue with one another.[36] Using the framework of the Latina/o dictatorship novel to examine these divergent literary representations enables us to see a shared Latina/o literary tradition, which in turn highlights a set of shared historical experiences that links different Latina/o groups. To put it another way, if the category of Latina/o assumes a fiction of unity, then the category of the Latina/o dictatorship novel demonstrates the utility of fiction for illuminating unity.

I use the rubric of the Latina/o dictatorship novel conscious of the disparate national-origin groups and diversity of subject positions that the pan-ethnic category "Latina/o" links together and of its homogenizing effect.[37] As numerous scholars have pointed out, the term "Latina/o" obfuscates a vast number of differences between the people and experiences collected under the category, including national-origin, generation, type of migration, history of colonialism and imperialism, citizenship status, race, color, gender, sexuality, class, regional location, residential pattern, language, political affiliation, ideology, religion, and so on.[38] Indeed, Latina/o is a "fiction" (Gruesz, "The Once," 117) whose "descriptive legitimacy is premised on a startling lack of specificity" (Beltrán, 6). Rather than privilege commonality at the expense of the differences, it is essential to be attentive to both. A comparative Latina/o lens enables us as scholars "to be *more* nuanced about particular trajectories and dynamics by comparing and contrasting the various Latino groups" (Caminero-Santangelo, *On Latinidad*, 17). My comparative Latina/o approach captures the way writers from various Latina/o groups use fiction to grapple with discrete but resonating and analogous histories of dictatorship and authoritarian power relations.

Moreover, scholars have argued for the political, rather than descriptive, utility of the pan-ethnic term "Latina/o," and it is precisely in this strategic coalitional orientation that I root my theorization of the category of the Latina/o dictatorship novel. Asserting that "Latino is a verb," Cristina Beltrán conceptualizes Latina/o identity as "something we *do* rather than as something we *are*" (157, 19). It is open-ended, ongoing, and contingent on affinities and building alliances. For their part, Rosaura Sánchez and Beatrice Pita argue for the strategic value of Latina/o in terms of "collectivity-in-difference" (28). What they call the "Latino Bloc" is oriented toward the pursuit of "emancipatory politics," forging solidarity at the juncture of differences (27). Sánchez, Pita, and Beltrán all highlight the active process of mobilizing Latina/o as a category rooted in heterogenous connections and strategic coalitions.[39] By bringing together various texts by writers from disparate Latina/o groups, I illuminate how they develop a counter-dictatorial imaginary based on the premise of a strategically shared oppositional orientation that challenges authoritarian power in its various manifestations.

Contemporary Latina/o writers are inheritors of the 1960s and 1970s civil rights movements and the ethnic nationalisms they propagated. Their novels are part of what Raphael Dalleo and Elena Machado Sáez have identified as "post-Sixties literature." According to Dalleo and Machado Sáez, critics too frequently "juxtapose the marginalized but politically committed writers of the 1960s and 1970s with the market success of the literary professionals from the multi-cultural post-Sixties era" who are labeled as "apolitical or even conservative" (2). Disputing this interpretation, Dalleo and Machado Sáez show how "rather than turning away from politics, contemporary Latino/a writers are renewing that political tradition by engaging with the triumphs and defeats of the past, formulating political projects that will mark our future horizons in substantial and creative ways" (7). The authors I examine—including Junot Díaz, Cristina García, and Héctor Tobar—enjoy both market and critical popularity; notwithstanding that, their fiction is deeply invested in the pursuit of a more just future by tracing the haunting effects of state violence and impunity in the present, interrogating contemporary forms of dictatorial power, and probing new ways of imagining social transformation. Like the first person Latina/o narratives that David J. Vázquez has analyzed, Latina/o dictatorship novels "creatively rearticulate 1960s oppositional paradigms" in both their content and their form (*Triangulations*, 5). Moreover, they explicitly engage with the transnational and anti-colonialist dimensions of these oppositional paradigms. Latina/os involved in the civil rights movement and in radical organizations such as the Brown Berets and Young Lords had decidedly internationalist and anti-imperialist politics, variously inspired by the Cuban Revolution, Salvador Allende's socialist movement in Chile, and the Sandinista Revolution.[40] Latina/o literary-political consciousness has historically been rooted in and inspired by both local and hemispheric decolonial struggles for equality and justice, and the Latina/o counter-dictatorial imaginary that interrogates the spectrum of authoritarian domination across the Americas inherits and extends these oppositional legacies.

As a result of the Cuban Revolution, Cuba fits awkwardly in the Latina/o dictatorship novel tradition because Cuba has been criticized as a dictatorship by some Cuban exile and Cuban American writers and celebrated as an anti-imperialist, socialist alternative in the hemisphere by Latina/o writers. As Marta Caminero-Santangelo points out, "in the imaginary of non-Cuban Latino writers, the revolution has often been represented sympathetically," while, in contrast, "the most visible and vocal strain of Cuban exile population...is vehemently anti-Communist and politically conservative, taking a stance of non-negotiation with regard to the evils of Castro's regime that seems increasingly anachronistic in today's post–cold war, post–Soviet Union world" (*On Latinidad*, 166–167). Latina/o dictatorship novels often celebrate the Cuban Revolution and identify with its anti-imperialist and egalitarian aspirations and use its iconic figures as symbols of liberation. For example, in de Robertis's novel *The Invisible Mountain*, which I began this introduction discussing, a young Argentinian medical doctor named Ernesto Guevara helps Eva give birth to her daughter Salomé. Years later, having become a Tupamaro revolutionary against the Uruguayan dictatorship and having been tortured and raped in prison, Salomé gives birth to a daughter and names her Victoria, inspired by the revolutionary slogan most associated with Ernesto "Che" Guevara: "¡Hasta la victoria siempre!"[41] In contradistinction, Cristina García's *King of Cuba* is markedly more critical of the Cuban Revolution and the current state of affairs in Cuba. U.S. Cuban writers are caught in a "double bind" of both needing to be politically progressive to fit in the Latina/o canon and needing to be politically conservative to be approved by the Miami establishment. Equally critical of the exile generation, *King of Cuba* attempts to carve out a "third space" that puts pressure on this double bind (Dalleo and Machado Sáez, 160, 162).[42] By attending to dictatorship novels by writers from varying national-origin groups, I strive to foreground the "generative contradiction" that Latina/os have differing experiences of and definitions of dictatorship while sharing a commitment to challenging authoritarian hierarchies (D. Vázquez, *Triangulations*, 15).

A further conceptual utility of Latina/o as a coalitional grouping is that it reminds us that Latina/os are the "harvest of empire," to invoke Juan Gonzalez's now famous phrase. The United States' cultural, economic, and political imperialism, which is often accompanied by overt and covert military interventions, has generated the current population of migrant and U.S.-born Latina/os.[43] The now common phrases "We didn't cross the border, the border crossed us" and "We are here because you were there" stress how U.S. imperialism is responsible for the Latina/o presence in the United States. This imperial trace is encapsulated in the fact that "no Latin American country is untouched by US intervention, and, as such, there is no Latina/o immigrant population in the United States which does not bare the trace of this imperial legacy" (Saldaña-Portillo, "From the Borderlands," 509). The genre of the Latina/o dictatorship novel is evidence of how directly this Cold War imperial history has shaped Latina/o literature, for the legacy of the United States' overt and covert support of right-wing civilian and military dictatorships and persecution of left-wing and socialist activists and political leaders in Latin America currently haunts Latina/o cultural production.[44]

Including a Latina Cuban text in this examination of Latina/o dictatorship novels speaks to the tenuousness of "Latina/o" as a unifying term for different national-origin groups with divergent political histories at the same that it highlights the ways the U.S. imperial project has shaped the discourse about Latin American dictatorship. As an institutionalized revolution that toppled a U.S.-supported dictatorship, resisted U.S. imperialism, and built a more egalitarian society based on the principles of socialism, the regime in Cuba under and after Fidel Castro is difficult to classify as a dictatorship of the same kind as the long list of right-wing dictatorships that have plagued Latin America.[45] Regardless, the United States insists on demonizing the Cuban government as the vilest and longest dictatorship in the Americas. Louis A. Pérez demonstrates how this arises in part from the ways the United States has historically imagined Cuba as an extension of its own economic and political designs. Thus, Pérez explains, the "Cuban revolution deeply offended North American sensibilities. Fidel Castro's continuance in power served as a constant reminder of the inability of the United States to will the world in accordance with its own interests, made all the more egregious by the fact that this was a country upon which the United States had routinely imposed its will.... The North American response was exorcism in the guise of policy, an effort to purge Fidel Castro as an evil spirit who tormented North American equanimity for five decades" (273). García's *King of Cuba* both reinforces and satirizes this view of Fidel Castro with its fictional dictator, El Comandante.[46] At the same time, the novel suggests that the Cuban revolutionary project, the U.S. imperial project, and the Cuban exile project are all problematically heteropatriarchal in orientation.

My inclusion of Cristina García alongside Junot Díaz, Salvador Plascencia, Francisco Goldman, Héctor Tobar, and the like accomplishes a threefold purpose. It underscores how U.S. imperial designs shape the development of the Latina/o dictatorship novel tradition. It also accounts for the complex and sometimes conflicting attitudes toward different Latin American regimes that run across the Latina/o novels. Finally, it theorizes how these novels represent dictatorial power in broader and more metaphorical terms, elucidating the necessity of interrogating the full spectrum of authoritarian forms of power. This book thus offers one response to María Josefina Saldaña-Portillo's "plea for a transnational and comparative model of Latina/o studies." In Saldaña-Portillo's view, this pan-ethnic comparative and transnational hemispheric approach places "comparison and the critique of US empire at the center of our field" ("From the Borderlands," 511). Examining the Latina/o dictatorship novel allows us to center a critique of U.S. empire abroad as it intervenes in Latin America *and* domestically as it shapes the lives of U.S.-born and migrant Latina/os.

When we use the category of Latina/o to give a sense of coherence to disparate fictional texts about dictatorship, we also gain a new perspective on a comparative literary history. As Kirsten Silva Gruesz reflects on the need to develop Latina/o literary histories, she points out: "it seems to me that if 'Latino' is to have any long-term conceptual staying power, it must grapple with the construction of a usable past that would be, if not *common* to all Latinos (what historical stories are?), intelligible and meaningful to that constituency" ("The Once," 117). Rather than seek a widespread common applicability—which would be similar to claims about a common "Latino" culture or identity that problematically obscures and erases differences—Gruesz imagines a literary history that is rooted in "hidden continuities—or simply contiguities" (132). Though Latina/os have different experiences of authoritarianism, continuities and contiguities resonate meaningfully across and between Latina/o subgroups. By looking at contemporary Latina/o fiction through the category of the dictatorship novel, we see how Latina/os develop nuanced transnational critiques of state terror, repression, displacement, exploitation, and marginalization. This enables us to trace resonant and dissonant representations of dictatorial power across Latina/o literary history.

What emerges from tying together different Latina/o novels is a set of linked memories about disparate kinds of systemic violence in the Americas. Illuminating these forms of oppression, the Latina/o counter-dictatorial imaginary reveals the productive possibilities of pan-ethnic alliances that collectively resist the various manifestations of authoritarian power. Arguing that Latina/o novels critically unveil histories of dictatorial domination in the United States and Latin America, this book reveals the ways Latina/os are beset by multiple types of violence and how they connect and contest these various forms of authoritarian power in the Americas through the power of fiction.

Chapters in the Latina/o Dictatorship Novel

My socioformal readings explicate the literariness of each novel I analyze and provide sustained explorations of dictatorial forms of power. Each individual chapter centers on a single novel as an exemplary case study in the Latina/o counter-dictatorial imaginary and includes shorter readings of other Latina/o fiction when pertinent. The novels I have selected do not represent a singular response to or imagination of dictatorship. Rather, each novel approaches dictatorship from a different angle and mobilizes varying narrative strategies. In chapters 1 and 2, I investigate the vexed relationship between authorship and authoritarianism by examining how Latina/o writers manipulate narrative form—especially, character-space, orality, narrative perspective, and page layout—to contest dictatorial power while cognizant of the contradiction that writing is itself a form of power. In chapters 2 and 3, I examine the ways Latina/os portray the author-as-dictator and the capitalist-as-dictator to interrogate labor exploitation, in particular in the context of the militarization of the U.S.-Mexico border and neoliberal shipping schemes. In chapters 4 and 5, I consider the means by which narrative form is used as a tool for imagining justice, whether by playing out fantasies of retributive justice against racialized state violence and conditions of impunity or by interrogating hypermasculinist hero narratives and heteropatriarchal revolutionary movements in order to imagine social transformation in a more feminist and decolonial manner.

Chapter 1 foregrounds the tensions between the two definitions of "to dictate": to order or command authoritatively and absolutely, and to speak aloud words that are to be written down or transcribed. Using Junot Díaz's novel *The Brief Wondrous Life of Oscar Wao*, I argue that narrative techniques and formal structures can dictate, or tell, a story against dictatorship without reproducing dictatorial power dynamics. I explicate how the "zafa," or counter-curse, against the "fukú" of oppressive domination is performed and enacted through the form in which the story is told, focusing on the distribution of attention between major and minor characters and on the storytelling modes of hearsay, footnotes, and silences that mimic evasive patterns of communication under dictatorship. Fracturing narrative hierarchies and rife with ambiguity, the novel, I ultimately argue, dictates without dictating; that is, it tells a story without fixing that story monologically.

Chapter 2 teases out the fraught links between authoritarianism, authority, and authorship. Using Salvador Plascencia's metafictional *The People of Paper*, I explore the ways the novel as a genre and as a mode of contestation is limited by the power dynamics inherent within its structural scaffolding. The chapter argues that Plascencia's novel symbolically represents power, control, and agency in the U.S.-Mexico borderlands though the novelistic processes of creation, emplotment, and narration. I situate omniscient narration as a form of panoptic narration to demonstrate how the analogy of the author-as-dictator imagines a surveilling and controlling narratorial apparatus. I then analyze how the characters and fictional author vie for narrative control and how this struggle for narrative power plays out typographically on the space of the page. I conclude by considering how the novel grapples with the problem of how to defend the rights of agricultural laborers and people without papers (i.e., undocumented migrants), in the pages of a novel that circulates as a commodity.

Chapter 3 considers the figure of the neoliberal dictator. Using Francisco Goldman's *The Ordinary Seaman*, I examine the presence of authoritarianism under neoliberalism by reading the white captain and first mate as capitalist dictators and the *Urus*, their marooned ship, as their technology of domination. I interpret the *Urus* as a floating dictator-ship that symbolically functions as a microcosm of authoritarian relations and as a floating signifier for hemispheric histories of domination and exploitation. I then shift course and read the shipwreck as a metaphor for the crew's situation as well as a narrative device, using the term "discourse" to argue that the novel is structured through breakage and stranded temporality. I end by tracing the multiple significations of scraps and holes in the novel, demonstrating how the crew resist their exploitation by repurposing scraps and revaluing holes to find sustenance and safe harbor.

Chapter 4 explores how a novel can plot out fantasies of justice. Using Héctor Tobar's *The Tattooed Soldier*, I argue that the novel contests mass impunity in the Americas. I analyze how the individual act of retributive violence against the Guatemalan military apparatus supported by the United States and the mass uprisings in Los Angeles are crossed in the novel, each made to resonate with the other through disruptive flashbacks, iterative events, and rotating points of view. I subsequently use the idea that plot consists of narrative order and desire to unpack the political and formal valences of plot, arguing that the novel's structure is at odds with the two main protagonists' narrative desires for order and justice. Though its revenge plot is resolved, the novel does not resolve the larger plot for justice. *The Tattooed Soldier* does not offer a solution; rather, it opens up a dialogue about how to move forward, on both individual and communal levels.

Chapter 5 examines the figure of the patriarch as dictator. I analyze how Cristina García's *King of Cuba* interrogates the heteropatriarchal investments of the two main characters. I argue that the novel foils both characters' desires to die heroically, demythologizing the masculinist celebratory narratives of the revolution and the freedom fighters that have dominated in Cuba and in Miami, respectively. I also demonstrate that, while the two men monopolize narrative attention, the novel fractures their dominance through what I call its "resolver" aesthetic, which captures the creative forms of survival and the strategic means of dealing with scarcity on the island. I end by suggesting that when we recenter the narrative focus on the defiant Latina daughters of the conservative exile generation who are artist figures, we see an alternative articulation of revolution and art in the service of decolonial critique.

In the coda, I offer some conjectures on how a number of other cultural producers contribute to the Latina/o counter-dictatorial imaginary using non-print-based artistic forms. I focus in most depth on the murals in Balmy Alley in San Francisco's Mission District, analyzing how their depictions of authoritarian repression in Central America are related to representations of gentrification and undocumented migration in the United States. The murals generate linked histories of domination and displacement and stand as material testaments to interracial solidarity and the collective struggle for social justice. Analyzing the palimpsests of paint and the visual polyphony across the walls of Balmy Alley provides another texture and layer to the counter-dictatorial imaginary I trace in the preceding chapters.

Ultimately, Latina/o dictatorship novels do not offer a permanent resolution to the problem of authoritarian power, for violence and impunity continue to haunt Latina/o Americans' lives. Yet it is precisely the power of the counter-dictatorial imagination to express anti-authoritarian longings and to challenge our horizons of sociopolitical possibilities that makes these Latina/o novels urgent and compelling. Latina/o dictatorship novels contribute to the ongoing struggle to decolonize extant hierarchical power structures. In doing so, they exhibit what Monica Hanna, José David Saldívar, and I have called the "decolonial imagination," which we define as the projective power of the imagination to envision a radically different world that is structured through solidarity rather than through dominance (9).

As socially symbolic acts, the Latina/o novels I examine in this book interrogate transnational modes of domination and use the critical and creative faculty of the imagination to envision an ending to dictatorial power in its myriad configurations and manifestations. Latina/o novelists are continuing a long tradition of dictatorship novels in the Americas that fan the spark of hope for an end to authoritarianism, for the appearance of the disappeared in the archives of fiction and history, and for justice for the oppressed. In a Gramscian moment marked by pessimism of the intellect and optimism of the will and of the imagination, the Latina/o counter-dictatorial imaginary opens up a dialogue about how to envision revolutionary transformation anew—on an individual, a communal, and a transnational level—and how to build a truly "post" dictatorship future that will no longer be haunted by the traumas of the past and mired in the persistent inequalities and oppressions of our present.

{ 1 }

Dictating Narrative Power

*Escribir no significa convetir lo real en palabras
sino hacer que la palabra sea real.
To write does not mean to convert the real into words
but to make the power of the word real.*
—AUGUSTO ROA BASTOS, *Yo el supremo (I, the Supreme)*

*Dizzy, peripheral, inverted, infatuated, insomniac, stargazing, fat:
what manner of hero is this?*
—SALMAN RUSHDIE, *Shame*

*There was of course no way of knowing where you were being watched
at any given moment. How often, or on what system, the
Thought Police plugged in on any individual wire was guesswork.
It was even conceivable that they watched everybody all the time.
But at any rate they could plug in your wire whenever they wanted to.
You had to live—did live, from habit that became instinct—in the
assumption that every sound you made was overheard, and,
except in darkness, every moment scrutinized.*
—GEORGE ORWELL, *1984*

Reflecting creatively in 1967 on the production of his dictatorship novel *El señor president* (*The President*; 1946), the Guatemalan writer Miguel Ángel Asturias creates an imaginary scenario in which the dictator declares to the novelist that he, not the writer, is the real author of the novel because "toda dictadura es siempre una novela" (every dictatorship is always a novel) (470). With this self-authorizing claim, the dictator wrestles power from the author by declaring himself the supreme meaning maker. While the dictator—or, more accurately, the dictatorship—trumps the novelist in Asturias's text, the Dominican American narrator of Junot Díaz's novel *The Brief Wondrous Life of Oscar Wao* (2007) expounds in a footnote: "Rushdie claims that tyrants and scribblers are natural antagonists, but I think that's too simple; it lets writers off pretty easy. Dictators, in my opinion, just know competition when they see it. Same with writers. *Like, after all, recognizes like*" (97, emphasis in original). Much as Asturias's dictator sees the novelist as his competitor, Yunior the narrator recognizes the slippery similarities between dictators and writers: they are both narrative makers and narrative controllers. The dictator and the novelist both create metanarratives and produce meaning. They are fabulous inventors and can make the unbelievable believable. They also control subjects and exercise their authority through words to dictate their subjects' or characters' actions and thoughts.[1] As Alejo Carpentier once succinctly and eloquently observed, there is "un contrapunteo delicioso" (a captivating counterpoint) between dictators and writers (qtd. in Polit Dueñas, 42).[2]

In this chapter, I use the trope of dictation to tease out how *The Brief Wondrous Life of Oscar Wao* circumnavigates the problematic similitude between dictators and writers. The novel plays on the tensions between the two definitions of "to dictate": to order or command authoritatively and absolutely, and to speak aloud words that are to be written down or transcribed. There are two types of competing dictators at the center of the novel: the political dictator (Rafael Trujillo), who rules over the subjects of his regime, and the narrative dictator (Yunior), who retrospectively recounts the novel's events. As the primary narrator and storyteller, Yunior loosely functions as a dictator in both senses because he controls and orders representation and because he collects, writes down, and reshapes a plethora of oral stories that have been recounted to him.[3]

Through the novel Yunior chronicles the life of Oscar de León, an obese Dominican American growing up as a social outcast in New Jersey from the mid-1970s to the mid-1990s. Oscar is obsessed with women and with what he calls the "more speculative Genres," meaning science fiction, fantasy, and comic books (43). The book's middle sections center on the lives of Oscar's mother, Hypatía Belicia Cabral ("Beli"), and his grandfather, Abelard Cabral, in the Dominican Republic under the dictatorship of Trujillo. Yunior pieces together Abelard's, Beli's, and Oscar's lives through oral interviews, historical research, snooping in Oscar's journals, and a bit of imaginative recreation. In doing so he recounts the family's sufferings under a transgenerational cycle of violence: Abelard is imprisoned and tortured, purportedly for refusing to hand over his beautiful eldest daughter for Trujillo's sexual pleasure; Beli is beaten nearly to death in a cane field, for having an affair with "the Gangster," the husband of Trujillo's sister; and Oscar is killed in a cane field for having an affair with Ybón, the girlfriend of "the capitán," a policeman in post-Trujillato Dominican Republic.

Yunior opens the book's preface by giving an origin story for the cursed fate of the de León and Cabral family:

> They say it came first from Africa, carried in the screams of the enslaved; that it was the death bane of the Tainos, uttered just as one world perished and another began; that it was a demon drawn into Creation through the nightmare door that was cracked open in the Antilles. *Fukú americanus*, or more colloquially, fukú—generally a curse or a doom of some kind; specifically the Curse and the Doom of the New World.... It is believed that the arrival of the Europeans on Hispaniola unleashed the fukú on the world, and we've all been in the shit ever since. Santo Domingo might be the fukú's Kilometer Zero, its port of entry, but we are all of us its children, whether we know it or not. (1–2)

The fukú serves as a local folk hermeneutic for reading relations of domination in the Americas more generally and in the novel specifically. The result of colonization, slavery, and the eradication of indigenous peoples, the fukú "ain't just ancient history, a ghost story from the past with no power to scare," Yunior explains ominously (2). Under the thirty-year reign of the "dictator-for-life Rafael Leónidas Trujillo Molina," the fukú "was real as shit" and to this day continues to haunt "its children" across the Dominican diaspora (2). Interlocking Spanish colonialism, Trujillo's dictatorship, and Oscar's temporally and geographically distanced story, the fukú operates as a symbolic chronotope for the ruination caused by domination. The Trujillato is a crystallization of one violent epoch in a five-hundred-year New World apocalyptic saga whose modes of oppression are continually regenerating and transforming. The fukú—or the "fukú americanity" as José David Saldívar terms it—thus generates a multilayered analysis of dictatorship that inserts it into the *longue durée* of the coloniality of power in the Americas ("Conjectures," 125). The fukú foundational fiction that Yunior narrates establishes a trans-American community through an act of imagined identification across forms of domination, spaces of imperial violence, and histories of subalternization. The fukú also offers an explanatory paradigm for the novel's events, based on a folk history of coloniality and the hemispheric ("Great American Doom") and personal apocalypses ("Doom of the Cabrals") that it engenders (5, 143).

Yunior imagines a way out of this American curse of violent domination via another folk belief in the ability to ward off a curse, positing resistance to the fukú as the novel's other central governing politic. He explains:

> Anytime a fukú reared its many heads there was only one way to prevent disaster from coiling around you, only one surefire counterspell that would keep you and your family safe. Not surprisingly, it was a word. A simple word (followed usually by a vigorous crossing of index fingers).
>   Zafa.
>   ....Even now as I write these words I wonder if this book ain't a zafa of sorts. My very own counterspell. (6–7)

Based on the Spanish verb "zafar," meaning "soltar algo" (to let go of or to release something) or "liberarse de un una molestia" (to escape or liberate oneself from harm), the novel represents zafa as a form of protection that enacts a liberatory function through the oral word combined with the physical action. Yunior transvaluates the power of the spoken word into the power of storytelling by envisioning the zafa as a speech act that occurs through his hand's narratorial act. That is, Yunior imagines that writing "this book," which is the text of the novel he narrates, is a zafa, a counter-spell, a Latino counter-dictatorial act.

Yunior takes a complex history of power hierarchies with dire structural, material, physical, and psychic effects and metaphorizes it as the fukú; by creating a narrative encapsulation of oppressive power, he creates a way to respond through another metaphor: the zafa. The novel thus stages a conflict between the fukú and the zafa—between dictating as an authoritarian act and dictating as a resistant act. The two organizing symbolic principles embody the dual signification of dictating as dominating (the fukú) and dictating as recounting or writing back (the zafa). Yunior's self-proclaimed narrative zafa places him in competition with the novel's most salient incarnation of the fukú: the dictator Rafael Trujillo. Yunior's capacity to produce a narrative zafa is predicated on his ability to be a Janus-like narrator, since his challenge is to critique dictatorial power without reproducing it in his own text. He has to beware of *author*itarianism—that is, the precarious link between authorship, authority, and authoritarianism. Yet, due to "the decisive influence that the discourses of power have in constituting the discourses of resistance," Yunior is partially overdetermined by what he is critiquing (Moraña, Dussel, and Jáuregui, 19). I contend that the novel mitigates this problematic formally. Examining the novel's narrative structure, I articulate how the text successfully negotiates between being complicit with and resisting authoritarian discourses and structures of power.

The zafa in the novel, then, is not Yunior's "book" per se but the narrative techniques and formal structures in the book that interrogate dictatorial power in its various sociohistorical manifestations. I focus in particular on how the zafa functions through the character-system and through modes of narration. Initially, I explicate how the novel structurally marginalizes and parodies the dictator and centralizes socially marginalized characters to challenge authoritarian power and hegemonic discourses. Subsequently, I illustrate how the novel mobilizes underground storytelling modes—specifically hearsay, footnotes, and silences—to formally represent and contest the dissemination and repression of information under dictatorship. The novel's zafa is performed and enacted through the counter-dictatorial form in which the story is told. Dictating a zafa against domination, I ultimately argue, entails an open-endedness that does not dictatorially prescribe the successful ends of its critique, especially given that we continue to be haunted by the residual effects of past dictatorships and plagued by contemporary modes of dictatorial power that I trace in this chapter and throughout this book.

The Dictator as Minor Character

A fundamental component of the novel's zafa is the text's representation of Rafael Leónidas Trujillo Molina and his thirty-year dictatorship (1930–1961) over the Dominican Republic.[4] The historical subject with the most power—the dictator Trujillo—is a minor, flat character whose representation is mediated by the narrator Yunior and the author Junot Díaz. The novel orders Trujillo as a minor character in the text's temporal and geographic crisscrossing and prevents him from focalizing the narrative. A dictator who is a *minor* character and is *represented by* other characters seems oxymoronic because a subordinate narrative position runs counter to the dominant position a dictator occupies in the political structure. In order to understand the importance of the subordination of Trujillo in the novel's narrative structure, I start with the premise that the narrative structures that allocate space and focalize perspective in a novel are structures of power. In other words, the uneven distribution of characters and perspectives in a novel can be analyzed as a system of power hierarchies.

The paradigm of dictatorship has its structural basis in the one dictator against the many subjects of the regime, making the novelistic tension between one protagonist and many minor characters particularly significant for a Latina/o dictatorship novel. In *The One vs. the Many: Minor Characters and the Space of the Protagonist in the Novel*, Alex Woloch theorizes the dialectics of narrative form and social power through an examination of the system of characterization. Woloch observes that novels are constructed around a "distributional matrix," meaning that "the discrete representation of any specific individual is intertwined with the narrative's continual apportioning of attention to different characters who jostle for limited space within the same fictive universe" (13). He terms "character-space" the relationship between an individual character's personality and that character's position in a narrative structure, while "character-system" refers to the various arrangements of these character-spaces in a narrative's overall structure. The asymmetrical configuration of major round characters and minor flat characters in a novel, Woloch argues, "reflects actual structures of inequitable distribution" (31). A social configuration of hierarchies of power is realized in narrative form, which for Woloch is evident in the unequal distribution of attention to characters and the distorted stylistic representation of them.

As I discuss in the introduction, there are a number of Latin American dictatorship novels, as well as "Trujillato narratives,"[5] that make the dictator a minor figure and background presence, causing some scholars to distinguish between dictator novels and dictatorship novels so as to capture the difference between those that are centered on and through the dictator and those in which the dictatorship is the backdrop. Díaz's novel falls in the latter category, but for the sake of contrast, in order to highlight what Díaz's strategic use of the character-system and Trujillo's subordination within it accomplishes, let us consider *The Brief Wondrous Life of Oscar Wao* in relation to Latin

American novels produced by the boom generation of writers: Alejo Carpentier's *El recurso del método* (*Reasons of State*; 1974), Augusto Roa Bastos's *Yo el supremo* (*I the Supreme*; 1975), Gabriel García Márquez's *El otoño del patriarca* (*The Autumn of the Patriarch*; 1975), and Mario Vargas Llosa's *La fiesta del chivo* (*The Feast of the Goat*; 2000).[6] In these novels, what Conrado Zuluaga calls "novelas de personaje" (character novels), the dictator is the underlying bearer of the novelistic world—that is, narrative action and perspective are principally constructed around and mediated through him (15). To use Woloch's terms, the dictator's character-space dominates these novels' character-systems. These novels' fictional worlds are organized around an anonymous dictator, and the narrative perspective and action are principally mediated through and constructed around the dictator, who is both the primary protagonist and antagonist. This narrative structure, which is centered on and through the dictator, creates an inequitable distribution of power and voice similar to the hierarchy of power that exists under dictatorship as the dictator monopolizes the overall character-space.[7] This argument does not assume that the dictator's position is stable or uncontested in these novels (it certainly is), only that the dictator's positioning within a novel's character-system is important because different formal structures differently limit or enable particular kinds of interrogations of power.

The tension between major and minor characters, then, crystallizes a real world tension around social power at the socioformal level of the novel in its organization and representation of characters. Yet, what happens when sociopolitical and socioeconomic structures of inequitable distribution are *not* reproduced structurally in the text in ways that reflect their actual structuring in the real world? How do we understand power differentials in a novel like *The Brief Wondrous Life of Oscar Wao*, which displaces the dictator from the center of the historical narrative and redistributes attention to the subjects at the *bottom* of the hierarchy, at the *margins* of power, and at a geographic remove *after* the dictatorship has fallen? In comparing the boom generation novels to previous texts about dictatorship, Ángel Rama argues that the boom novels effected "una drástica inversión de la vision" (a drastic inversion of perspective) by focalizing on the consciousness of the dictator (16). By moving away from the presidential palace and outside the dictator's head, *The Brief Wondrous Life of Oscar Wao* drastically inverts and shifts the optics by exchanging a dictator-centric character-system for one that is centered on marginalized subjects living in the Dominican Republic under the Trujillato and in the United States after its end. Díaz's novel thus alters the correlation in the character-system between character-space, socioeconomic status, and sociopolitical power. This modification of sociopolitical positions of power in the socioformal character-system of the novel enables the novel to interrogate relations of domination under and after the dictatorship and dictatorial discourses in general. Rather than exploring the now classic Latin American trope of the solitude of power by focusing on the dictator, this novel explores the haunting afterlife of dictatorial power on Dominican American lives in the United States. In other words, I am interested in how this Latino novel stages the dictator as a minor character in its transgenerational narrative that features Oscar as the framing protagonist.

Yunior's narratorial control over the dictator's representation and his manipulation of Trujillo's signification produce the text's critique of the Trujillato and its transnational, transgenerational specter in the present. Trujillo is an overwhelmingly absent presence, a kind of backstage character who is continually invoked and described but whose appearance onstage is extremely brief in relation to his overall manifestation in the narrative. In terms of the plot's fictional events (what narrative theorists call the "story") Trujillo is a minor character who does not occupy much narrative space. He does not materialize as a character in the plot until page 221 of the 335-page novel; as a minor character, he only appears four brief times and actually speaks in only two of these appearances. In contrast to his marginalization in the story and the character-system, Trujillo has a major and pervasive presence in the text's language, structure, and mode of narration (what narrative theorists call the "discourse").[8] Less a fully realized fictional minor character, Trujillo is more of a symbol of dictatorial power and violence with an ominous, haunting presence.[9] The omnipresent traces of the Trujillato that run through the novel imitate the inescapable dominance of the fukú, while the text zafa-s Trujillo through its discursive representation of the dictator.

Trujillo's construction in the novel's discourse occurs principally through Yunior's multitudinous, vivid, and often iconoclastic characterizations of him. The real historical Trujillo acquired over one hundred honorific titles during his reign so as to forge a discourse of sanctified leadership, patriarchal protection, national unity, self-determination, racial homogeneity, and economic progress to legitimate his regime.[10] Title-granting was part of the regime's institutionalized pomp and its "dramaturgy of power" (Derby, 2). Yunior signifies on these titles, creating an alternative set of titles for Trujillo. Yunior demeans him by calling him the "Failed Cattle Thief" (2, 214, 217), "Fuckface" (2, 155, 216), "Mr. Friday the Thirteenth" (225), "our Sauron," (2), and the "Dictatingest Dictator who ever Dictated" (80). Putting him down and parodying him with praise, Yunior draws on pre-existing epithets such as "Your Excellency" and "Your Enormity" and blasphemously employs Trujillo's nickname "El Jefe" throughout the novel. He satirically praises the Trujillato as "the first modern kleptocracy," gesturing toward the vast amounts of wealth and lives that were stolen from the Dominican people as Trujillo profited off of the economic monopolies he established and murdered an estimated twenty thousand people, including political assassinations and the genocide of Haitians and Haitian Dominicans (3). Díaz also creates new and bilingually witty words to name Trujillo's abuses, deeming his regime "the world's first culocracy" (217), and hilariously mocks him as the "consummate culocrat" (154) and "Number-One Bellaco" (217) for his infamously rogue playboy tactics, thereby scathingly condemning his sexual exploitation and terrorization of women.[11] While Trujillo's portentous and prodigious titles contributed to his mythification, Junot Díaz's titles for him creatively and explicitly call out his corruption, violent repression, and predatory sexuality. Moreover, the epithets construct Trujillo as a type and as a figure who metonymically stands in for both dictatorship and heteropatriarchal power, satirically positioning him as the first and the best in a series of world-historical authoritarian leaders.

Considering that such epithets do not develop an interiority for the character Trujillo, it could be argued that Yunior's representation of him is simply emblematic of the flat minor character as defined by Alex Woloch or, before him, by E. M. Forster. Woloch characterizes the flat character as the product of narrative distortion and caricature, resulting in the effacement of interiority as the flat character comes to represent an abstract idea. Forster, who posits that the flat character is constructed around a single idea or quality and can be summarized in a single sentence, additionally argues that flat characters "are best when comic. A serious or tragic flat character is apt to be a bore" (77). When he enters the plot, Yunior describes Trujillo the minor character minimally for comical effect: Trujillo has a "heavily powdered face" (222), a "shrill voice" (218, 221), and a "porcine" face (222) and eyes (233). The descriptions mock Trujillo's desire to be white, jab at his performed hypermasculinity, and highlight his brutality through dehumanizing descriptors. Alongside Yunior's often humorous nicknames for Trujillo, these descriptive caricatures of Trujillo certainly make him a classic flat, single-dimensional character who can be reduced to a sentence, which would perhaps read as follows: Trujillo is a violent, lustful, and immoral dictator. Yet something else in addition to flatness is also being produced through the narrative descriptions and delimited amount of character-space.

Overall, the accumulation of names and descriptions offers a set of alternative significations for the regime that highlights its abuses instead of effacing them as Trujillo's real-historical epithets did. Yunior's falta de respeto (lack of respect) for Trujillo deliberately breaks cultural and linguistic norms of respect for those in power at the same time that it fashions a resistant discursive repertoire vis-à-vis heteropatriarchal dictatorship. The humorously biting wordplay—alongside the footnoted historical references and the overlaid fantasy and science fiction allusions—fashions a discourse about the leader and his regime that is subversively humorous and linguistically capacious. The bilingual, bicultural, and intertextual descriptions for Trujillo humorously satirize dictatorial power. Indeed, the "fukú" folk belief is not without its bilingual irony, for "fukú" signifies on its English homonym "fuck you." Yunior's provocative designation of his narrative as a small "fukú story" (6) evokes a different designation in a homonymic register; it is a "fuck you" story about how the de León and Cabral family has been fukú-ed or "fucked up" by Trujillo as well as the larger fukú-ing of the Américas that began with coloniality. The many zafadas de lengua (zafa-like slips of the tongue) that Yunior uses freely and riotously throughout the novel destabilize dominant power relations. Yunior's creative ability to signify on and talk back to power with parodic irony *and* with total sincerity shapes the book's style, which uses humor as means of critical meaning making and of relief from the weight of oppressive relations.

Doubly made minor in the narrative hierarchy of power, Trujillo is relegated to the position of a minor character in the novel's plot at the same time that he is minoritized as a footnote in the novel's structure. Comparing his representation in the footnotes and the main text, Trujillo is referenced more frequently and described more elaborately and at greater length in the footnotes. In fact, he is initially introduced to the reader in the novel's first and quite lengthy footnote; and he, his "minions," and the violence of his regime appear in three-fourths of the novel's footnotes (12). The positioning of Trujillo within the footnotes literally lowers him on the page. This structural move formally mirrors the way in which Yunior deflates Trujillo linguistically.

The overall structure of flatness and humorous minor-ness produce the novel's counter-dictatorial mode of narration. As a flat minor character, Trujillo is often the butt of the joke (he is, after all, a "culocrat") and the referent of Yunior's parody and expletives. Abstracting from this reveals that Trujillo is an *object* of reference in the narrative. Trujillo is not an omniscient narrator or a major character who directly produces meaning in the text. Meaning is mainly produced *about* him, not *by* him. This loss of narrative power runs counter to the definition literary critic Juan Carlos García gives of the representation of the dictator in Latin American literature: the dictator is "él que da ordenes y él que crea. Esto lo aproxima a un ser entidad todopoderoso" (he who gives orders and he who creates. This approximates him to an all-powerful entity) (27). In *The Brief Wondrous Life of Oscar Wao*, the dictator Trujillo does not create and order like an omnipotent being; rather, he is created by and ordered through Yunior's descriptions. Because he is neither the originator nor in control of the production of meaning and action in the text, Trujillo does not *function as* a dictator in the novel. Instead, he *functions for* the narrative discourse. The novel formally counters, or zafa-s, Trujillo's power by marginalizing and functionalizing him.

These narrative techniques also reinforce the novel's positioning of the dictatorship within various interlocking modes of domination. The novel suggests that the perpetration of violence is not caused solely by Trujillo's authoritarian political regime but also by the five-hundred-year fukú americanus. This move, first, denies Trujillo the power of having a totalizing impact on the development of the story's events; second, it turns Trujillo into a mediating figure of transhistorical modes of domination rather than the only source of domination.[12] Just as Trujillo is not an agent who directly produces meaning in the text, he is not the origin of oppression but one figure, though admittedly a very prominent and brutal one, whose rule upholds and extends the coloniality of power. In chapter 3, I focus more at length on this narrative technique of contextualizing dictatorship transhistorically in relation to Francisco Goldman's *The Ordinary Seaman* to show how Goldman figures a white neoliberal capitalist as a contemporary version of the dictator whose exploitation of undocumented Central Americans aboard a ship is also connected to slave ships and the ships of imperialism. Here I want to highlight how the dictator as a figure is embedded in an entrenched structure of domination, a crystallization of one violent epoch in a five-hundred-year trans-American saga.

Trujillo's loss of total power on a symbolic level is not equated with a total loss of political power. Indeed, his presence is ever palpable, and his regime permanently fractures the de Léon and Cabral family by disappearing and torturing Abelard for fourteen years in Nigüa prison, reducing him to a traumatized shell of a person, and by the near fatal beating in the cane field that forces Beli to flee the United States. Rather, the novel takes away Trujillo's power as the supreme narrative maker. In a Latino novel published almost half a century after the toppling of the dictator, this is important because of how people remember Trujillo and how they conceptualize authoritarianism. The novel formally disavows the mistaken assumption that dictatorships are exceptional regimes and that subjects will be free once dictatorships are toppled. The novel insists that the Trujillo dictatorship may be over but there is still an ongoing history of dictatorial violence that must be interrogated.

Lola's condemnatory response to her brother's brutal murder over three decades after the assassination of Trujillo is the most telling and insightful analysis of power in the novel. "Ten million Trujillos is all we are," declares Lola (324). Lola's denunciation implies that the responsibility for dictatorial relations of domination and social violence must be distributed more widely, that is, among the "ten million Trujillos" in the Dominican Republic and the United States in the postdictatorship present. This allocation of accountability is reflected structurally in the novel's displacement of Trujillo in the overall character-system; its frequent denunciatory and exposé-like footnotes about high-ranking officials in the regime; its continual drawing of attention to those who actively upheld the regime by secretly informing on their neighbors and those like Abelard and Beli who upheld the regime with their passivity; its utilization of minor dictator characters like the Gangster, the capitán, and Yunior; and its multigenerational, transnational narrative arc. Moreover, Lola's use of Trujillo's name as a communal proper noun highlights the ways subjects are complicit in the systems of power that govern them. Lola's words echo and extend the anonymous male in Julia Alvarez's *In the Time of the Butterflies* (1994) who observes that dictatorships "are pantheistic. The dictator manages to plant a little piece of himself in every one of us" (311). Lola's use of the shared "we" implicates not only those who lived under the dictatorship, as Alvarez's novel does, but also everyone in the contemporary moment, including Lola herself, who is a Dominican Latina living in the United States.[13] Her words theorize the afterlife of dictatorship in terms not of mourning and memorialization but of repetition, continuity, and trasngenerational complicity, as everyone has internalized and perpetuated the ideology of domination. They also assert that collective responsibility must be assumed, since a people—not a single figure of power—bears the blame for acts of dictatorial domination, whether they are perpetrated by political or discursive regimes.

A Marginalized Hero

The Brief Wondrous Life of Oscar Wao frames its meditation on dictatorial power through Oscar de León, a multiply marginalized and atypical U. S. Dominican living almost half a century after the Trujillato has officially collapsed. Tracing the fukú americanus through the de León and Cabral family, the novel's structure suggests that understanding Oscar's life requires a transgenerational family story and a trans-American history, just as understanding Trujillo's regime requires remembering the colonial past and acknowledging contemporary dictatorial relations. Based on the lives of subjects who are traditionally deemed too insignificant as well as too temporally and spatially removed from "major" events of Dominican history, the novel positions Oscar as an Afro-Latino on the social margins and within a cyclical family history of violent subordination, making his marginalization a node through which various relations of domination overlap and are interrogated.

The cane field outside Santo Domingo in which Beli nearly dies and Oscar does die serves as a chronotope for the family's experience of dictatorial repression and as the time-space for the re-enactment of intersecting oppressions. The cane field is a primal site where violence is perpetrated against African-origin subjects: slaves, Haitian laborers, Dominican subjects (Beli), and transnational Latino subjects (Oscar). "Plunged 180 years into rolling fields of cane" (146), Beli is taken into the cane fields and "beat[en]...like she was a slave. Like she was a dog" (147). Beli's beating in 1962 establishes a similitude between physical repressions of African-origin subjects across time and space, for when the cane field existed 180 years earlier it was around 1782, during the period of slavery and right before the beginning stirrings of the Haitian Revolution. Slaves were subject to the condition Orlando Patterson calls "social death," which included violent beatings, illiteracy, lack of control over sexuality, and the denial of parental and filial birth ties, in what he terms "natal alienation" (5). It is not mere coincidence that Beli is a very dark-skinned Dominican woman who is nearly killed in a cane field for her romantic relationship or that she slips unconscious into "a loneliness that obliterated all memory, the loneliness of a childhood where she'd not even had her own name...alone, black, fea, scratching at the dust with a stick, pretending that the scribble was letters, words, names" (148). Moreover, the scar that covers Beli's back, the result of the burning she receives living parentless in Outer Azua, is "as vast and inconsolable as a sea" and, with "her bra slung around her waist like a torn sail," calls forth a slave ship in the Middle Passage (51). The novel does not imply that being subjected to slavery or economic servitude is the same as being subjected to dictatorship or heteropatriarchal domination, but it does establish transgenerational resonances between the violence enacted upon Beli and Oscar and the slaves and laborers in the cane fields. It likewise gestures across generations toward an insurrectionary tradition. Silvio Torres-Saillant reminds us of "the primacy of Santo Domingo as an inaugural site of the African presence in the Americas, as birthplace of the plantation—the economic institution that gave Blackness its modern significance—as locus of the first insurrections of enslaved Africans, and as the cradle of the Maroon tradition during the colonial period" ("Divisible Blackness," 463). Later, in 1995, when Oscar is beaten in the cane fields for resisting the capitán's injunction against dating Ybón, the "world seemed strangely familiar to him; he had an overwhelming feeling that he'd been in this very place, a long time ago" (298). Ambiguous about precisely how long ago a "long time ago" is, the description evokes both his mother's and his enslaved ancestors' experiences of violent repression and valiant endurance.

The temporal ambiguity gestures toward the cyclical structure of events in the plot and the residual temporality of dictatorship. As Raymond Williams advises, "it is necessary at every point to recognize the complex interrelations between movements and tendencies both within and beyond a specific and effective dominance" (122). To understand a present hegemony, Williams maintains, we cannot focus solely on its features in the present but must look at its ever-changing contours through a dynamic process-oriented analysis. Díaz's novel enacts such a contextualized analysis vis-à-vis its characterization of Oscar's postdictatorship death at the orders of the capitán, thereby highlighting the residual effects of slavery, imperialism, and dictatorship, because these elements produced in the past continue to have an active impact in the present.[14] The "circumstances directly found, given, and transmitted from the past," to quote Karl Marx, "weigh like a nightmare" on Oscar's life (595). Oscar intuits this before his death, as is evident when in relation to his own suicide attempt he professes: "It was the curse that made me do it" (194). Disavowing Oscar's interpretation, Yunior exclaims, "I don't believe in that shit, Oscar. That's our parents' shit" (194). Undaunted, Oscar retorts, "It's ours too" (194). Inheriting his family's past and the bane of the fukú, Oscar astutely recognizes that his life is overdetermined by the history of authoritarian regimes and dictatorial relations in the Americas. His body is a site "where memory dwells."[15] Like Lola's formulation about ten million Trujillos, Oscar's words encapsulate how Latina/o lives are still being affected by past dictatorships and how Latina/o writing is steeped in postmemory.

Oscar's claim on the curse and the effects of its inheritance on him is also revealing in relation to his own position in the novel's character-system. Given the title and his status as the "hero," Oscar is surprisingly absent for most of the novel (11).[16] His absence, however, directly enables the presence of other family members: Lola, Beli, and Abelard become main characters. In fact, Lola's narrative initiates both of the chapters that take place under the Trujillato. As La Inca begins to reveal to Lola what happened to her mother and grandfather, Lola relates, "She was about to say something and I was waiting for whatever she was going to tell me. I was waiting to begin" (75). With these words Lola's narrative ends, and the chapter about Beli's life under the Trujillato begins. Lola's choice of words is important. She does not say "I was waiting for *her* to begin" but "*I* was waiting *to* begin" as if she herself will only begin as a subject within the story of her family history and as if her identity as a Latina living in the aftermath of dictatorship in the United States is inextricably linked to her family members' lives in the Dominican Republic under dictatorship. Lola comes into being as a subject transgenerationally through connecting to her family's past, and like Oscar, she is moored to that past. The novel's partition of character-space among various main characters in the family reinforces on the level of the character-system the transgenerational vision undergirding Oscar's claim.

Not only does Oscar's "brief" life become part of a series of lives that together trace transnational relations of domination, his "wondrous" life as a *marginalized* and *atypical* Afro-Latino hero also becomes part and parcel of the novel's critique of dictatorial relations, be they political or social. I suggest that the novel uses Oscar's abnormality and his nonnormative body to challenge dictatorial power *and* normative discourses, to draw a link between both forms of domination, and to do so in the context of the Dominican Republic and the United States. The novel introduces Oscar as a kind of aberrant Dominican male and thereby an aberrant Dominican hero. The first chapter, "GhettoNerd at the End of the World," begins: "Our hero was not one of those Dominican cats everybody's always going on about—he wasn't no home-run hitter or a fly bachatero, not a playboy with a million hots on his jock. And except for one period early in his life, dude never had much luck with the females (how *very* un-Dominican of him)" (11, emphasis in original). According to Yunior, as well as the traditional conventions of Latina/o fiction, Oscar is not a typical male or main protagonist. As Maja Horn observes, "Dominican male scripts interact with dominant American scripts of masculinity and ... processes of racialization shape this interaction in the United States" (131). Oscar is thus deemed abnormal in both national contexts and subject to intense social and ideological pressure through multiple scripts that seek to dictate his identity. His overall characterization as un-Dominican in the novel is tied to five main characteristics: gender, sexuality, body type, race, and culture. As a nerdy, overweight, dark-skinned Afro-Dominican heterosexual male fluent in the fantastic genres but illiterate in the game of sex, Oscar "couldn't have passed for Normal if he wanted to," as he fails to be a "Normal" (i.e., socially acceptable) Dominican American male subject (21). Establishing difference and anomaly over norms and stereotypes, the novel begins with negation, highlighting what

Oscar is *not*, and maintains this technique of exaggerating differences throughout.

Oscar's nonnormativity serves as a vehicle for the novel's interrogation of the norms, discourses, and hierarchies of power that dictate marginalization and oppression in the United States and in the Dominican Republic. To mobilize Rosemarie Garland Thomson's term, Oscar's "extraordinary body" is located at the bottom of what she characterizes as "accepted hierarchies of embodiment" (7). Black, Latino, fat, effeminate, poor, and a nerd, Oscar is multiply marginalized. Relegated to the social and economic margins, he suffers ridicule and rejection throughout his life. Yet, in stark contrast to his social ostracism, he is the novel's titular hero, and his life frames the novel. At the same time, the novel draws a complex portrait of what Michael Hames-García would call Oscar's "multiplicity" with respect to his numerous social identities, which are mutually constituting and overlapping (*Multiplicity*, ix). Oscar's privileged status as a hero whose multiplicity of self is fully represented calls into question Oscar's social subalternization and the discourses that produce it.

The novel centralizes the socially marginalized Afro-Latino Oscar as a complex, round character and marginalizes the Dominican dictator as a flat, minor character. The demotion of the figure of power—Trujillo—and the elevation of the figure of marginality—Oscar—work contrapuntally in structuring a critique of dictatorial power and the dictates of heteropatriarchy and white supremacy. Trujillo is figured as the excessive embodiment of traditional Dominican masculinity, while Oscar is depicted as sorely inadequate according to these heteropatriarchal ideals because he does not conform to the dominant forms of masculinity. Trujillo is obsessed with whitening his skin, while Oscar is ridiculed for being a dark-skinned Afro-Latino who does not corporeally embody the ideal of whiteness in either the United States or the Dominican Republic. Using the latter extreme to interrogate the former extreme, the novel breaks down, or zafa-s, these hierarchies. Calling the dictatorial authority of the norm into question through the elevation and satirical exaggeration of difference, Oscar's framing centrality as a protagonist is a key counter-dictatorial narrative strategy that works through characterization, in the senses of both narrative description and distribution of attention.[17]

Far from rejecting Oscar for being a "sci-fi-reading nerd," the novel places Oscar and his beloved Genres, which are traditionally considered low cultural forms, at the very center of its transculturated narrative stylistics (19).[18] The novel harnesses the speculative and boundary-pushing genres of fantasy, science fiction, comic books, and marvelous realism to communicate the magnitude of dictatorial atrocities. The multigeneric modes of representation are epistemic as well as aesthetic, for they explore the hermeneutics used to comprehend absolute power. Each imaginative mode contributes one interpretive lens or set of critical references that differently decipher dictatorial political systems and authoritarian discourses in the Greater Caribbean. Oscar's nonnormativity and reading list contribute to his lifelong social marginalization but, when privileged in the novel, serve instead as vehicles of critical interrogation.

Underground Storytelling

The Brief Wondrous Life of Oscar Wao also employs folk orality, paratextual footnotes, and blank pages to critique dictatorial relations. Subjects living under authoritarian regimes such as the Trujillato must either risk under-the-radar signifying and coded circumlocution or remain silent. Yunior mobilizes oral sources, footnotes, and silences to mimic the dissemination and repression of information under dictatorship and to dictate a story against dictatorship without being dictatorial.

Yunior recounts his story through a wide variety of named and unnamed oral sources, thereby forging an oral, hearsay hermeneutic that functions as a narrative structuring principle and as a means for reading the effects of dictatorial power on postmemory narratives. Yunior's style of narration frequently reflects this oral transcription, highlighting the ways sources have dictated their stories to him and how he has pieced his narrative together out of the stories he has gathered. The novel's narrative construction is situated in an oral chain of communication through which the anonymous folk of the Dominican diasporic community tell their fukú "tales" (5), beginning on the novel's first page with what "they say" about the origin of their bane of domination (1). A series of such phrases are interspersed throughout the text signaling the narrative's imbrication in orally circulating information. The novel's hearsay structure is subtle and is most heavily signaled through phrases indicating the secondhand acquisition of information: "it was said," "it was believed," "there are those alive who claim," "it was rumored," "legend has it," "it was whispered," and so on.[19] These and other phrases appear alongside occasionally specified sources of information such as Beli, La Inca, Lola, Yunior's mother, Yunior's girlfriend Leonie, and others. The anonymous sources of information predominate the novel's vernacular aesthetics, and, importantly, references to these sources appear most often in the sections that recount life under the Trujillo regime. Despite the fact that Yunior is not present throughout most of Oscar's life and therefore has learned much of Oscar's life story secondhand—the same way he hears about Beli's and Abelard's lives—the Oscar sections are rarely narrated in a manner that foregrounds Yunior's sources. In contrast, the sections set under the Trujillato rely on phrases that highlight the ways Yunior has acquired information second- and thirdhand. Though Yunior's style of narration has a generally first person limited omniscient tone, his more frequent pauses to disclose the name of a source or signal an unnamed oral source in the sections of the novel set under the Trujillato imply that the events narrated about that time period are much more pieced together than those sections that deal with Oscar's short life.

If, as James C. Scott has demonstrated in *Domination and the Arts of Resistance*, "the process of domination generates a hegemonic public conduct and a backstage discourse consisting of what cannot be spoken in the face of power," then it is essential to take seriously the contextual significance of the anonymous storytellers (xii). I posit that this stylistic contrast is directly tied to the novel's representation of the effects of the conditions of dictatorship on the formal level of the text. Not by chance does Yunior keep the opinions, hearsay, and versions of events he gathers at the level of anonymity ("they say," for example) and indirection ("it is said," for instance). Such grammatical constructions, rendered in passive voice without a specific subject of the sentence, protect sources' identities and register the dictatorship's effects on patterns of communication.[20] Dominicans avoid direct speech and sometimes even speaking at all because any dissent or perceived discontent with the Trujillato could very quickly result in incarceration, torture, and even death. Yunior relates, "You could say a bad thing about El Jefe at eight-forty in the morning and before the clock struck ten you'd be in the Cuarenta having a cattle-prod shoved up your ass.... Mad folks went out in that manner, betrayed by those they considered their panas, by members of their own families, *by slips of the tongue*" (225–226, emphasis added).[21]

This description of the network of informants and the resulting danger of expressing discontent—verbal slips of the tongue that either betray another person or (even unintentionally) oneself—reflects how Dominicans had to resort to coded narratives. Below the surface of the phrases marking oral history, the anonymous speakers' experiences of negotiating domination under the Trujillato are present and continue to haunt their and their children's patterns of storytelling postdictatorship. This, in turn, gets encoded into the novel, expanding the traditional concerns with bilingualism, code-switching, and linguistic capital (themes that are also certainly present in *The Brief Wondrous Life of Oscar Wao*) in Latina/o literature to include linguistic practices inflected by political repression and trauma.[22]

The paratextual apparatus of the footnotes also symbolically concretizes in narrative form covert styles of communicating. Thirty-three footnotes of varying length run throughout *The Brief Wondrous Life of Oscar Wao*.[23] The book's main text is double-spaced, while all of the footnotes are single-spaced and written in smaller font. Though the footnotes run the length of the novel, thirty out of the thirty-three footnotes are found in the sections about Trujillo's regime.[24] As I have demonstrated with the novel's references to a larger source community that relies on coded speech, the conglomeration of footnotes in the sections set during the Trujillato takes on particular significance.

The footnotes are also important to an analysis of domination and narrative form because they play out power relations structurally within the text. As critics who examine the paratext of the footnote in fictional novels have argued, footnotes are, in their placement and form, "minor elements" (Jackson, xvii) that "are inherently marginal, not incorporated into the text but appended to it" (Benstock, 204).[25] Footnotes are located literally at the bottom of the page and structurally at the bottom of the textual hierarchy, below the main text and peripheral to the primary or dominant storyline. While footnotes are at the "margin of the discourse," as Shari Benstock characterizes them, their secondary relationship is complicated in Díaz's novel because the subordinate footnotes are central to *The Brief Wondrous Life of Oscar Wao* (204). The footnotes establish another set of commentaries and another sequence of events that are below and subordinated to but also central to and constitutive of the main text.[26]

Functioning as "hidden transcripts" that enact "a critique of power spoken behind the back of the dominant," the footnotes evade the limitations imposed on narrative development much in the same way that a dissenting subject rhetorically evades and subverts power through indirection (Scott, xii). As marginalia, the footnotes appear below the main narrative, visually resembling forms of undercover storytelling. That is, the footnotes structurally mimic the ways subaltern agents navigate repressive power by communicating information indirectly, secretly, and below the radar of the repressive regime's gaze. The spatiality of the notational apparatus in *The Brief Wondrous Life of Oscar Wao* reproduces the asides and interruptions that are constitutive of oral narrative; for oral narratives do not strictly follow one single line of thought and often veer into associative connections and tangential stories that build an interrelated network of details and substories around the primary story. Similarly, Díaz's footnotes contain digressions that provide important information and generate other plot networks. This decenters the main narrative, which does not follow a single, direct line but follows multiple ones instead. To borrow Kevin Jackson's vivid description, the footnotes "explode upwards into the soft black-and-white underbelly of the main text on contact with the reader's gaze" (140). The explosive and clandestine power of footnotes is heightened in a dictatorship novel since dictatorship is intent on repressing subversive agency. The under-the-narrative footnotes in Díaz's novel function like underground oral storytelling modes to formally critique dictatorial relations and dictatorial narratives. Cristina García also incorporates notes into her novel *King of Cuba*, but, as I argue in chapter 5, those notes do not formally embody the repressive and violent effects of dictatorship on speech patterns as much as they formally embody the way Cubans creatively and strategically negotiate for resources and survive amid great economic obstacles—whereas in *The Brief Wondrous Life of Oscar Wao*, the footnotes, in conjunction with the oral sources, formally mimic evasive modes of communicating.

In addition to stylistically resembling covert oral forms of storytelling, the novel's single-spaced footnotes and double-spaced main text also cause the novel's structure to resemble that of an academic book. In traditional academic usage, footnotes establish authority, acting as the supportive and evidentiary structure.[27] Yunior draws on the epistemic weight granted footnotes in scholarly convention to insert multiple kinds of sources into his fictional footnotes. The footnotes reference a report available in the John F. Kennedy Presidential Library and cite historians, novelists, and even Yunior's girlfriend and mother, not to mention many science fiction and fantasy texts. Serving as both a "critical appendage" and a creative mode of chronicling the Trujillato's abuses, many of the footnotes expose the dictatorship's atrocities and interject a scathing critique of Spanish and U.S. imperialism in the Americas (Benstock, 204). The footnotes do not privilege academic sources over personal, let alone fictional, ones; instead, they provide alternative historical perspectives on the Trujillato, which is especially important given the univocal, monological nature of dictatorship.[28] In the first footnote, Yunior gives a long list of the Trujillato's "outstanding accomplishments," designating the regime as "one of the longest, most damaging U.S.-backed dictatorships in the Western Hemisphere (and if we Latin types are skillful at anything it's tolerating U.S.-backed dictators, so you know this was a hard earned victory, the chilenos and argentinos are still appealing)" (2–3). The comical discourse of success belies a serious articulation of the violence of the Trujillato and the United States' collusion in supporting numerous right-wing military dictatorships across the Americas that have been responsible for imprisoning, torturing, murdering, and disappearing hundreds of thousands of people, Abelard Cabral being just one of those victims. The first of many such footnotes, the aside provides a metanarrative that intertwines Dominican, Southern Cone, Latin American, and U.S. histories, one that is especially important given the geopolitics of knowledge production in the United States, which subalternizes, or footnotes, so to speak, Latina/o and Latin American histories. The footnotes also insert a trans-American consciousness about U.S.-backed dictatorships into the Latina/o literary imaginary, calling attention to the afterlives of dictatorship in contemporary narratives and community relations.

While the novel chronicles these histories of dictatorial violence and their haunting echoes that reverberate in the present, it simultaneously accounts for how conditions of domination create erasures that can never be fully recuperated. It thereby foregrounds the insurmountable difficulties of recovering a violently repressed and disappeared past. The many gaps and silences throughout the novel create a multileveled portrayal of the effects of dictatorial power on information networks and oral histories. The novel materializes these absences textually in its narrative form. This is most evident through the trope of the "páginas en blanco": Yunior cannot fill in these so-called blank pages due to a lack of complete information. Absent information is the result of several factors: it has simply not been recorded or spoken about; it has been repressed because people are afraid to speak or have been silenced; it has been distorted because narratives about the past have been changed; it has been destroyed because the Trujillato burned the documents; and it has been lost because texts have disappeared. The novel generates a complex textual representation of silence through these various blank spaces in circulating and noncirculating information.

Working in conjunction with the text's oral and footnote structures, the silences give formal shape and thematic space to the habitus of people living under the pressures of dictatorship and what Yunior calls the "Chivato Nation" (225). By describing the nation as a "chivato" (tattletale), the novel demonstrates how the Dominican people, functioning as a network of informants, enacted and enforced the dictatorship. As Lauren Derby has demonstrated, the Trujillato fashioned a "vernacular politics" that turned popular forms of speech, such as gossip, into a "repertoire of domination of the regime" (7). The field of dictatorship structures a subject's linguistic habitus, and the transforming of popular gossip and rumor into modes of terror conditioned folks into silent deference to Trujillo.[29] When Abelard, for example, talks with his best friend, Marcus, about his fear of following Trujillo's order for Abelard to bring his daughter to Trujillo's party, he "waxed indignant to Marcus for nearly an hour about the injustice, about the hopelessness of it all (an amazing amount of circumlocution because he never once directly named who it was he was complaining about)" (229). Unable to openly and explicitly criticize Trujillo, Abelard runs a grave risk with his under-the-radar signifying and coded circumlocution.[30] This restrictive conditioning has long-term effects, evident in the "Source Wall" that prevents Yunior from acquiring accurate or complete information decades later (149). As Yunior explains, "due partially to Beli's silence on the matter and to other folks' lingering unease when it comes to talking about the regime, info on the Gangster is fragmented" (119). Yunior's reliance on oral sources in the present is affected by the residual influence of the dictatorship on the production of contemporary oral stories. Impediment and fragmentation highlight the ways information has been distorted and erased and how the specter of dictatorship continues to shape the way survivors pass on oral histories, as well as how the postmemory generation—that includes Yunior, Oscar, Lola, and Díaz himself—inherits these gaps and silences, which, in turn, condition how they understand and speak about the past.

In relation to what really causes Abelard's imprisonment and the subsequent vanishing of all of his books and papers, Yunior declares:

> So which was it? you ask. An accident, a conspiracy, or a fukú? The only answer I can give you is the least satisfying: you'll have to decide for yourself. What's certain is that *nothing's certain*. We are *trawling in silences* here. Trujillo and Company didn't leave a paper trail—they didn't share their German contemporaries' lust for documentation. And it's not like the fukú itself would leave a memoir or anything. The remaining Cabrals ain't much help, either; on all matters related to Abelard's imprisonment and to the subsequent destruction of the clan there is within the family *a silence that stands monument* to the generations, that *sphinxes all attempts at narrative reconstruction*. A whisper here and there but nothing more to say. Which is to say *if you're looking for a full story, I don't have it*. (243, emphasis added)

In "trawling" the past for information, Yunior catches more silence than information. "Full" access to and knowledge of what truly occurred in the past is impossible because people have been silenced and information has been disappeared. Yunior explains that he relates "what I've managed to unearth and the rest you will have to wait for the day the páginas en blanco finally speak," keeping the integrity of the silences in his narrative (119). Ironically, though, the blank pages *do* speak; for they "stand monument" to the abusive horrors of the dictatorship, functioning as testifying silences. The novel simultaneously foregrounds these absent presences and provides a narrative space in which repressed stories can be dictated and chronicled in the archive of Latina/o fiction.

Moving beyond silence into speech and text is, for the oppressed, a liberatory act, but that act must also acknowledge the silence within its own production. Neither author nor narrator can produce a story that lays claim to full and complete meaning because doing so would produce a dictatorial story. Having a story but not "a full story," as Yunior implies, is the most accurate, ethical, and effective story you can have under dictatorship, about dictatorship, and against dictatorship. Creating a counter-dictatorial narrative or a so-called zafa against domination, the novel suggests, necessitates a plurality of possibilities that are precisely impossible under dictatorship given its "authoritarian univocality" (Tierney-Tello, 15). A dictatorship is univocal and does not allow multiple referents or traces of meaning to exist. It seeks to stabilize and control all meaning and action. In fact, Abelard is imprisoned when his darkly comical signifying "trunk-joke" about there being no bodies in the trunk of his car as he tries to put a bureau in his trunk is taken literally and distorted into a directly stated critique of Trujillo, as opposed to the indirectly implied reference it was (234). The Trujillato cuts down the double-layered ambiguity of Abelard's statement, restricting what it signifies. In literary terms, dictatorships require an *authori*tarian narrative—that is, an authoritative narrative that is closed, controlled, and unitary, composed by an author whose word is sacrosanct and infallible. In contrast, the narrative form of the novel negates this structuring of authority and power by highlighting the process of constructing its postmemory account of the Trujillato and the effect of the dictatorship's afterlife on its Latino textual production.

Far from being an objective observer in the positivist sense, far from being omniscient in the narratorial sense, and far from being panoptic in the disciplinarian and authoritarian sense, Yunior foregrounds the knowledge that is both available and unavailable from his social location as a Dominican raised in the U.S. postdictatorship when he constructs his narrative zafa. By keeping meaning multivalent and by continually interrogating narrative authority, Yunior dictates a narrative that is orally based but not authoritative. He draws attention to the absent, partial, and sometimes inaccurate information on which his story is built, hence his comments about the silence that "sphinxes" his "attempts at narrative reconstruction" and his stated disregard for historical accuracy (243). He consistently foregrounds what he does not know, exclaiming "Who can say?" (22) and "shit, who can keep track of what's true and what's false in a country as baká as ours" (139), declaring to the reader: "you'll have to decide for yourself" (243). Offering uncertainty, silence, self-referential critiques, and a bit of humor as antidotes to dictatorial fixity, the text pointedly disavows certainty and definitive closure. The novel's refusal to offer definitive explanations and its general destabilization of textual authority allow for multiple conclusions and generate multifarious readings, as it deliberately does not fix interpretation or present an infallible account of events. Exhibiting the "paradoxical impulse toward revolutionary deconstruction and toward the production of meaning" that Ramón Saldívar has deemed a characteristic of Chicana/o narrative, this Latina/o novel deconstructs dictatorial discourses while producing its own counter-dictatorial narrative (*Chicano Narrative*, 7). Rife with ambiguity, the novel dictates without dictating; that is, it tells a story without fixing that story monologically.

The open-endedness of meaning, which subverts the dictatorial desire for total control and fixity, exists throughout, all the way through the last page of the novel. Deceptively, the novel's conclusion is not in its last line—Oscar's affirmation "The beauty!" (335)—but in the panel he repeatedly circles in the graphic novel *The Watchmen*, which cautions: "Nothing ends, Adrian. Nothing ever ends" (331). Though the novel literally ends with the next and last chapter titled "The Final Letter," nothing is truly resolved, for the counter-dictatorial zafa against the familial and hemispheric fukú americanus remains unfinished.

Ultimately, Yunior's zafa fantasy of narrative justice does not offer a permanent resolution to the problem of dictatorial power or to the curse of coloniality. It is a fantasy. Yet it is precisely the power of the imagination to express decolonial longings and fantasize new futures that makes the dictatorship novel an enduring and compelling form and an apt generic tradition for Junot Díaz and the other Latina/o authors I examine in subsequent chapters.[31] In thematizing and formalizing the process of critiquing and decolonizing relations of domination through the fukú-zafa dialectic, this novel opens up a dialogue about how to build a new future when the present is haunted by past trauma and mired in varying forms of dictatorial power. The novel thereby engages in what Idelber Avelar articulates as "an untimely reading of the present" that "rescue[s] past defeats out of the oblivion and remain[s] open to an as yet unimaginable future" (20–21). *The Brief Wondrous Life of Oscar Wao* dictates a story against dictatorship without dictating the successful ends of its critique. In this sense, the story must remain unfinished; for interrogation is a continual and necessary process as long as the coloniality of power, and the dictatorial structures and norms it perpetuates, remain. *The Brief Wondrous Life of Oscar Wao*, then, is not just a zafa. It is a zafa-ing.

{ 2 }

The Borderlands of Authoritarianism

Power is the ability not just to tell the story of another person, but to make it the definitive story of that person.
—CHIMAMANDA NGOZI ADICHIE, "*The Danger of a Single Story*"

But you have to understand that this isn't a philosophy or a literary theory or a story to me. It's my life.
—HAROLD CRICK, *in Stranger Than Fiction*

O Jamesy let me up out of this
—MOLLY BLOOM, *in James Joyce, Ulysses*

The plots of a number of Latin American dictatorship novels revolve around the demise of the dictator. Luisa Valenzuela's experimental and allegorical *Cola de lagartija* (*The Lizard's Tail*; 1983) portrays the machinations of El Brujo (the Sorcerer) in a fictional country that mirrors Argentina's military dictatorship with its tortures and disappearances. Luisa, the fictional character of the author, is a member of an underground revolutionary movement that charges her with the task of writing the Sorcerer's biography. She decides that her resistant act will be her silence: "En esta sencilla ceremonia hago abandono de la pluma con la que en otras sencillas ceremonias te anotaba. Ya ves. Somo parecidos: yo también creo tener mi gravitación en los otros. Callanda ahora creo poder acallarte. Borrándome del mapa pretendo borrarte a vos. Sin mi biografía es como si no tuvieras vida. Chau, brujo, *felice morte*." (In this simple ceremony I abandon the pen with which, in other simple ceremonies, I took note of you. So you see. We're alike: I, too, think I have influence over others. By being silent now, I think I can make you silent. By erasing myself from the map, I intend to erase you. Without my biography, it will be as if you had never had a life. So long, Sorcerer, *felice morte*.) (211; Rabassa, 227). The fictional author attempts to kill the novel's fictional authoritarian figure, trusting in the power of narrative production to realize the deed. By terminating his biographical existence in her narrative, Luisa hopes to end the Sorcerer's control and foreclose his domination. Other novels, in contrast, opt for nonmetafictional, plot-based assassinations. Enrique Lafourcade's *La fiesta del Rey Acab* (*King Ahab's Feast*; 1959), for example, revolves around a group of revolutionary characters who conspire to kill the dictator with a bouquet of lilies that contains a hidden bomb, which in the book's denouement kills the fictional political dictator.[1] In *The People of Paper* (2005), the Chicano author Salvador Plascencia imagines a metafictional revolutionary scenario in which the characters wage a revolution against a dictator, but in this case the dictator is the author of the novel in which they appear.[2] Though they try a variety of tactics, from silence to direct confrontation, they ultimately fail in their attempts to overthrow the creator and dictator of their diegetic world.

The People of Paper plays out and modifies two common tropes in the Latin American dictatorship novel tradition: the fall of the dictator and the dictator as writer. Though Latin American novels have explored the relationship between narrative creation and dictatorial control, they have done so by figuring the dictator as a writer.[3] *The People of Paper* turns this trope on its head by figuring the writer as dictator in a compelling critique of *author*itarianism that highlights the relationship between authorship, authority, and authoritarianism.[4] The novel's dictatorial writer omnipotently rules over his characters' life stories, omnisciently reads their thoughts, and materially profits from his novelistic representations of their consciousnesses. In rebellion, his fictional creations wage a "war on omniscient narration," attempting to overthrow the author of their lives and gain their liberation (218). The novel displaces political and economic conflicts onto symbolic terrain. I unpack the trope of the writer-as-dictator to analyze the structure of the novel and how it provokes us to be attune to the writer's *and* the novel's imbrication in systems of power and domination, as well as the attendant problem of *author*itarianism.

The novel embeds the trope of the writer-as-dictator alongside traditional themes in Chicana/o cultural production, such as economic exploitation, cultural imperialism, undocumented migration, folk epistemologies, and vernacular aesthetics. The book's main storyline follows the life of Federico de la Fe and his daughter, Little Merced, after his wife, Merced, abandons them. The pair venture north from Mexico, entering undocumented into the United States and settling in El Monte, California, an agricultural town full of flower fields. Blaming his wife's leaving on Saturn—the mysterious presence in the sky that he senses peering down at him and controlling his fate—Federico de la Fe recruits the local gang, El Monte Flores, or EMF as they are commonly known, to serve as soldiers in a war he orchestrates to topple Saturn. Saturn, as the reader learns halfway through the novel, is Salvador "Saturn/Sal" Plascencia,[5] who appears as a fictional character writing the novel while struggling with his own heartbreak since his lover, Liz, has left him for a white man. The novel's characters declare "one of the greatest wars against tyranny... a war against the future of this story," seeking to topple the author of their world (46). In their "war for volition" they use a variety of resistance tactics, ranging from hiding in silence beneath lead and thinking only mundane thoughts to openly fighting for narrative territory by asserting their voices and claiming control over the narrative space (101). The novel is peppered with a wide range of characters and visual elements that enrich this war storyline. Cameroon is a woman addicted to the venom of bee stings; the masked luchador Santos, whose real name is Juan Meza, is hiding his sainthood from the Vatican; the Baby Nostradamus, a presumably mentally handicapped baby whose narrative appears as a long, black column, has the ability to see the past and the future; and a group of Franciscan monks must perpetually march across the Americas from Alaska to the Patagonia and back again until they accomplish the impossible task of forgetting the location of the factory where they once made people. The novel also contains drawings of lotería cards, gang tags, and a food pyramid with sadness at the base, in addition to black boxes and circles, a mechanical tortoise that narrates in numbers or binary code, holes in the pages where Liz's white lover's name has been cut out,[6] and disclosures of responsibility on the part of the fictional Foundation funding the writing of the novel. *The People of Paper* is a visually engaging metafictional and marvelous real novel.[7] The novel's stylistic fusion provides a richly textured backdrop to the mundane and epic struggles of Mexican migrants and Mexican Americans in the borderlands of Greater Mexico.[8]

This novel depicts what I term the borderlands of *autho*ritarianism. I use the term to designate the peripheries of the definitions of dictatorship and authoritarianism in the transnational site known as the U.S.-Mexico borderlands. After all, the novel is not set under a real historical or even fictional political dictatorship. Instead, it conceptualizes dictatorship and *autho*ritarianism in formal, social, and economic terms. In doing so, Plascencia's representation of the borderlands of dictatorship usefully illuminates the relations of domination that exist in the production of fictional worlds, in the surveillance of undocumented subjects, in the exploitation of migrant laborers, and in the capitalist circulation of the novel as a commodity in global literary markets.

The novel presents a humorous and incisive examination of power, control, and agency in the borderlands though the novelistic processes of creation, narration, emplotment, and page layout. I begin by focusing on the analogy of the author-as-dictator and how it imagines omniscient narration as a form of what I call *autho*ritarian narration, which controls and surveils the novel's characters. I then analyze how the characters and fictional author vie for narrative control and how this struggle for narrative power and narrative territory plays out typographically in the text. I conclude by considering how the novel grapples with the problem of defending the rights of agricultural laborers and people without papers in the pages of a novel, and I read the character of the Baby Nostradamus as symbolizing the possibility of an alternative model of power that can be mobilized in the service of social and narrative justice.

Overall, I use *The People of Paper* as an occasion to explore the epistemic value of nongovernmental definitions of dictatorship and to take seriously the limitations of the novel as a mode of contestation due to the power dynamics inherent within its structural scaffolding and to its status as a commodity in the literary marketplace. The characters' war against the Chicano novelist who authors them puts the traditional representation of the resistant Chicana/o writer under pressure. Ralph E. Rodriguez points out that Chicana/o studies scholars, as well as Chicana/o literary production, have tended to focus on "warrior heroes," given that Chicana/o literature is often about disenfranchisement and developing a resistant ethnic and working-class consciousness. Rodriguez urges us to move away from continually analyzing "the oppositional quality of Mexican-American cultural production" ("Chicano Studies," 180), In contrast to the depiction of a heroic Chicana/o writer with pencil in hand, Plascencia's depiction of a Chicano novelist as a dictator asks us to take into account the relations of domination in the politics of novel production and circulation. David J. Vázquez has argued that contemporary Latina/o literature "is often motivated by political perspectives that creatively rearticulate 1960s oppositional paradigms," but these authors have to "constitute opposition in the contradictory space of contemporary U.S. culture—and in particular in the highly contested realm of global capital" (*Triangulations*, 5–6). Thematically, *The People of Paper* certainly keeps us within the paradigm of oppositional resistance, with its characters who stage a revolution against a dictatorial author and its depiction of the vulnerability of migrants to regimes of surveillance and capitalist exploitation. Formally, though, it pushes us to interrogate the very technology used for discursive resistance: the novel genre.

The Author as Dictator

The People of Paper dramatizes the power dynamics of authorial creation and narration by riffing on the author-as-god analogy with an author-as-dictator analogy. The novel opens with a creation myth that figures the artist as creator: "She was made after the time of ribs and mud. By papal decree there were to be no more people born of the ground or from the marrow of bones. All would be created from the propulsions and mounts performed underneath bed sheets" (11). In defiance of Church authority, Antonio the origami surgeon creates a woman named Merced de Papel "from paper scraps" by forming "cardboard legs, cellophane appendix, and paper breasts" out of leaves of paper he tears from the Bible, works of Miguel de Cervantes and Jane Austen, and the fictional *Book of Incandescent Light* (15). Antonio authors Merced de Papel into being in a palimpsestic, intertextual act through which the text is made flesh. The novel's opening pages throw us into a world of marvelous logic, where a surgeon gets paper cuts while making living organs out of paper, and of anti-authoritarian acts, where the surgeon defies papal authority and becomes the creator. Yet Antonio is "no all-powerful god who could part the rivers of Pison and Gihon, but instead a twice-retired man with cuts across his fingers" who is deserted by his female origami creation while he sleeps exhausted from his labor (2). The opening passages prefigure the novel's other abandoned god, Saturn, who authors and rules over the pages of the novel but is really just "Sal," a love-stricken Chicano living in a disorderly room far from El Monte, California, as he attends an MFA writing program in Syracuse, New York.[9] Sal, we learn, is battling heartbreak through novel writing in the hopes of regaining his lost love, only to be confronted by a cast of rebellious characters who seek to write their own fates. The novel thus stages a metafictional, existential dilemma about the "demiurgic creativity" of the Chicano author (González Echevarría, 207).

As a representation of the difficulty of writing a novel—of creating and then ruling a world—the novel signifies on the often-employed analogy of the author-as-god.[10] Critical debates about omniscient narration have partly focused on this equation of the author with God. This theological analogy is frequently applied to the creative process and the realm of epistemology. That is, "the author creates the world of the novel as God created our world, and just as the world holds no secrets for God, so the novelist knows everything that is to be known about the world of the novel" (Culler, 23). Barbara Olson argues that while the term "omniscience" may not accurately name the narrative techniques it describes, the analogy nonetheless captures authors' experiences of writing.[11] Authors experience writing as "world making," and many novelists describe feeling their characters' resistance to their authorial intentions (344). Plascencia scripts his characters' resistance to him into the very plot of his novel, offering a creative representation of the difficulty of writing a novel and of ruling a world.[12] The novel is a metafictional exploration of control and of the authoritarian tendencies that arise when authors feel they do not have total control over a world they feel entitled to dominate because they have created it.

If the trope of the author-as-god is useful precisely for what it suggests "analogically, theologically," the trope of the author-as-dictator is also analogically illuminating (Olson, 342). Paul Dawson points to the "narrative freedom (in terms of panoramic scope and narratorial judgment) which the trope of a 'god-like' narrator suggests" (145). In contrast, the political analogy of a dictator-like author redirects attention from issues of narrative freedom to those of narrative surveillance and domination. In other words, while the divine equation imagines an all-knowing and all-seeing narrator, the political equation imagines a surveilling and oppressing narratorial apparatus that knows all, sees all, *and* will punish all perceived dissent.

In rising up against Saturn, the characters battle for their liberation against the tyranny of dictatorship, imperialism, and slavery, all symbolically embodied in Saturn. The novel's characters variously call the entity they believe to be controlling their lives a "dictator," a "tyrant," a "master," a "despot," and an "emperor."[13] They employ this vocabulary to express how narrative apparatuses, especially plot development and omniscient narration, feel oppressive, and they attempt to break free of the textual apparatuses they see overdetermining their lives and limiting their agency. They resist the plot of their lives written and controlled by another being. Federico de la Fe declares: "We are here right now. We are being pushed in this direction. Saturn wants to move us into the peaks and then into the denouement. And we must stop before our lives are destroyed" (43).[14] As he speaks, he points to a battle diagram that looks exactly like a traditional plot diagram, Freytag's pyramid, with the ascending line that peaks and then falls into the novel's resolution and denouement. A humorous and defamiliarizing moment occurs when we see the graph, which appears as a hand-drawn image in the book, read the literary term "denouement," and realize that Federico de la Fe has declared war on the plot and the plotter of the novel. At this point in the plot we do not yet know what or who Saturn is. (All we know is that there is a being in the sky observing them from above whom they call Saturn.) This metacritical moment causes us to consider how the developing plot is imposed on the characters. In trying to evade the novel's denouement—the term derives from the French term "dénouement," which means "untying" and is based on the Latin word for "knot"—Federico de la Fe seeks to escape from the knot of the plot and to be free of the unraveling that, he predicts, will end in tragedy. Federico de la Fe's explicit resistance to the novel's denouement recalls Yunior's zafa, which comes from a Spanish word meaning to escape or be freed from something, in Junot Díaz's *The Brief Wondrous Life of Oscar Wao*, as both characters seek to author their own fates and to access decolonized futures.

The People of Paper thus stages a conflict between authorial volition and character volition, between the author-dictator and the characters whose lives he dictates in the space of the novel's pages.[15] Federico de la Fe, for example, asserts that "Saturn drove [Merced] away, just so that there would be this story" (95). What is at stake here is the cause of narrative action. Federico de la Fe charges that character action is produced by the author and functions in service of the plot. Similarly, Sandra laments she cannot reconcile with her ex-lover Froggy because he has killed her abusive father. "I felt as if I could walk into the house and lay on the bed, and everything would be as before. And Froggy would be happy and I would be happy too. But there are forces that don't let you turn back and undo things because to do so would be to deny what is already in motion, to unwrite and erase passages, to shorten the arc of a story you don't own" (85). Sandra expresses an accepted limitation of life itself: you cannot change what has already happened. What, or *who*, impelled Froggy to kill her father, however, is up for debate when Sandra draws her conclusions about her lack of volition in novelistic terms. She cannot "unwrite and erase passages" that have already been written, nor can she change "the arc of a story" she does not "own." Sandra speaks with a sense of urgency about the power of space within the pages of a novel, about its inclement capacity to direct and contort her opportunities, hopes, and life.[16] Sandra's comments imply that someone else is writing the plot and that the plot of the novel—which is simultaneously the plot of her life—is ultimately dictated from outside rather than by her and the other characters' intentions. This also symbolically encapsulates how the dictatorial past conditions people's future horizons of possibilities in the present, which is a common concern among Latina/o dictatorship novels.

The characters imagine that Saturn is omnipotent and can dictate their lives through plot development, "commanding the story where *he* wants it to go"; therefore, they imagine that Saturn's omnipresent omniscience is a violation of their interiority (228, emphasis added). They dissent "against Saturn, against the invasion that infiltrated their thoughts and overheard even their softest whispers, murmurs meant to touch only one ear, and to be retrieved only by memory" (46). Like Federico de la Fe's presentation of the plot diagram, the charges leveled against omniscient narration are defamiliarizing, because omniscient narration is so naturalized that its underlying premise—knowing what characters are doing and thinking—is not traditionally considered spying; it is simply considered more "realistic" and in-depth character narration. Yet the author-as-dictator model problematizes this naturalization of omniscient narration by foregrounding the power dynamics undergirding readers' privileged access to and control over characters' mental and emotional privacy.

The characters' declared resistance against "omniscient narration" could thus more aptly be characterized as resistance to *autho*ritarian narration because their very existence in a novelistic world permits their lives to be observed and controlled.[17] The novel employs a much more varied style of narration than one would expect, given the charges the characters level against omniscient narration and their presumption that this is the force they must battle to gain their freedom. Some portions of the novel are narrated in first person by the characters themselves, whereas other portions are narrated in third person about the characters. Despite the various focalizing characters and the shifting narrative perspectives, the text is oversaturated with Saturn's presence. Though the novel's many characters appear to be narrating, Saturn's gaze filters the first person as well as third person narration, framing the reader's encounters with all the characters in the novel. This *autho*ritarian narration, obscured by the mixture of intimate first person and detached third person perspectives that gives the illusion of other perspectives, serves as a means for the author to assert complete control while disavowing his hegemonic power. *Autho*ritarian narration highlights how plot scripts characters' actions, how multiple unfiltered perspectives are an illusion, and how narration is a form of surveillance.

The novel presents what it sensorially feels like to be omnisciently narrated and hence, according to the logic of the novel, to be narratively oppressed. Federico de la Fe is attuned to an ominous planetary presence whose Big Brother–like gaze he can only escape by hiding in the metal shell of a mechanical tortoise. The novel relates how Federico de la Fe "felt the weight of a distant force looking down on him" (18), how he "sensed that he was being constantly watched from above" (26), and how "the force upon him felt heavier than ever before" (28). The text's language evokes both the heavy weight of a gravitational force and the observational constancy of panoptic power. *The People of Paper* presents the constant gaze as a model of authoritarian narrative power such that the characters are "totally seen, without ever seeing" who is looking at them (Foucault, *Discipline and Punish*, 202).[18] As Subcomandante Sandra puts it in response to Liz's inquiry about what Saturn looks like: "I don't know—he only sees us. We never see him" (211). D. A. Miller employs the term "panoptical narration" to describe the "faceless gaze" of omniscient narration (24), whereas Mark Seltzer asserts that the "most powerful tactic of supervision achieved by the traditional realist novel inheres in its dominant technique of narration—the style of 'omniscient narration' that grants the narrative voice an unlimited authority over the novel's 'world,' a world thoroughly known and thoroughly mastered by the panoptic 'eye' of the narration" (54). Unlike more conventional dictatorship novels in which the dictator relies on secret police and informants, Plascencia's novel presents us with an authorial dictator who does not need an elaborate policing apparatus or informant network since his omniscient knowledge comes from surveilling the inner thoughts of his own creations. These and the many descriptions throughout the novel about how the characters feel omniscient narration bearing down upon them reflect the "structures of feeling" of border surveillance for undocumented migrants and racial minorities (Raymond Williams, 128).

Not only does Saturn generally surveil all the characters because he is the author, he surveils undocumented migrant Mexican and working-class Chicana/o characters in particular. It is significant that this narrative technology of surveillance is situated in the borderlands and on the U.S.-Mexico border in particular. When Federico de la Fe and Little Merced cross undocumented over the nation-state border, Federico de la Fe explicitly makes sure the border patrol is not watching them. As they "stepped over the chalk line and walked toward a world built on cement," Federico de la Fe "looked around to see if anybody was following us or watching through telescopes" (31). Given Federico de la Fe's obsession with "being constantly watched from above" (26) and with Saturn "following him wherever he went" (30), the border-crossing scene analogously aligns the border patrol with the authorial narrator. The ever-watchful border patrol state[19] is depicted again when Julieta crosses undocumented into the United States years later, but this time the chalk line has been replaced by a steel fence:

> When Julieta reached Tijuana, what was once a border marked only with a line of chalk had been replaced with watchtowers and steel fences; cement barricades had been buried directly underneath the fences and no one could burrow to the other side. Stadium lights shone on the border all through the night until the early hours of the morning.... It was not clear whether Julieta had dragged the disease of El Derramadero with her, or if it was just coincidence that she found a gap in the three-hundred-mile-long fence where the steel had corroded, allowing her to pass into the other side. (49)

The novel mixes a metafictional metaphor with material reality in rendering the two different crossings. The replacement of chalk—a technology of writing that can also be erased—with steel captures the difference between a porous border space and a heavily militarized border space. The shift from chalk border to fenced border thereby dramatizes the "enormous growth in the enforcement apparatus in the Southwest border region since the mid-1990s" (Nevins, 6). The two scenes capture the shift from personnel-driven surveillance, in which the border patrol is stationed near the border to guard popular crossing points, to dramatically increased technology-driven surveillance. With the implementation of Operation Gatekeeper in 1994, the border between Tijuana and San Diego saw "the installation of high-intensity floodlights to illuminate the border day and night, as well as an eight-foot steel fence along fourteen miles of border from the Pacific Ocean to the foothills of the Coast Ranges" (Massey et al., 94).[20] The modern security border Julieta encounters, complete with technologies of impediment and constant surveillance, recalls the ever-watchful eye of the dictator and of the authorial narrator. Without collapsing the important differences between border patrol state, dictator, and authorial narrator, it is important to note the ocular image used to represent the optic of power and its emotional effects on undocumented migrant characters who feel its disciplinary *and* its *descriptive* gaze.

As fictional characters, Federico de la Fe, Little Merced, and Julieta are people of paper whose existence is limited to the materiality of the novel's pages. But they are also people without papers who confront the fortification of the border fence and the militarization of the border.[21] The novel's underlying organizing symbolic principle—the trope of the "people of paper"—therefore, points to the existence of fictional characters on paper pages while simultaneously invoking the importance of "papers"—legal documents—for Mexican migrants in the United States. In chapter 3, I examine how Francisco Goldman's *The Ordinary Seaman* tackles the exploitation of undocumented Central American migrants through the technology of the ship; here, *The People of Paper* asks us to consider how the technology of the book and the literary device of omniscient narration can both surveil and exploit people without papers in the U.S.-Mexico borderlands.

Narrative Territory

Though set within and certainly concerned with the borderlands as a "contact zone" where "disparate cultures meet, clash, and grapple with each other, often in highly asymmetrical relations of domination and subordination," *The People of Paper* more prominently foregrounds power relations within the novel as a genre (Pratt, 7). The relations of highly asymmetrical domination and subordination are figured through the relationship between the author and his characters and through the configuration of space on the page rather than through interracial, intercultural encounters between white and Chicana/o characters or through the Anglo-American colonial appropriation of land. In other words, if the Chicana/o novel frequently depicts oppressive *social* and *economic* hierarchies and the dictatorship novel oppressive *political* hierarchies, Plascencia's novel expands these traditional concerns by depicting oppressive *narrative* hierarchies of power.

The structure of this novel is a terrain of power, and we visually see the amount of space characters occupy on the page as an instantiation of their relative power and social importance within the overall character-system. The novel is structured through columnar paragraphs and traditional paragraphs. Half of the chapters have three columns running side by side, with one column on the left-hand page dedicated to "Saturn" and two columns dedicated to varying characters on the right-hand page. Saturn is granted the most amount of space on the page, with an entire page for his character-space. The other chapters are presented in traditional book paragraph format, alternating the focus on individual characters within each chapter. Each individual character's particular amount of allotted narrative space, regardless of whether it takes the form of a paragraph or a column, is labeled with her or his name. As Mary Pat Brady notes, "Literature attends to affect and environment; it uses space and spatial processes metaphorically to suggest emotions, insights, concepts, and characters" (8). Plascencia's metafictional novel explicitly calls attention to its use of space and spatial processes, for example when the characters describe how it feels to have their interiority omnisciently narrated and later when the characters attempt to take over the space of the page. Pointing to the "naturalization of spatial production," Brady observes that realism is rooted in "a representational strategy that too easily solidifies oppressive spatial relations by hiding the processual quality of space" (7). Usually, the existence of paragraphs and the format of chapters are taken for granted as features of a novel, as is the realist novel's reliance on access to character interiority. These are defamiliarized in Plascencia's metafictional novel as the novel foregrounds the production of its own spaces, allows characters to voice how they feel about the spaces they occupy in the novel, and depicts narrative space as territory[22] that characters occupy. The page is a topographic terrain of power where character-space is highly structured and narrative space is territory over which the fictional author and the characters battle.[23]

The spatial organization of narrative power is embodied in Saturn, who, like a dictator, sits atop the representational hierarchy. This dominant position is symbolically instantiated in his being above the fictional social world of El Monte, as a planet in the sky, and physically on the page, since his column always appears first on the page at the far left. Allegorically figured as Saturn, the authorial narrator is the god of time who lords over the space of the novel. Saturn is the Roman god of agriculture who devoured his children so they would not overthrow him, and while the Chicano Saturn in *The People of Paper* does not devour his children—the people he has created on paper—they try to overthrow him, and he goes to war to assert his dominance over them. Prose paragraphs, the most basic structural component of the novel, are a structural feature of Saturn's dictatorship. The characters declare it is unjust "to limit us, to relegate us to strict columns and force us to act in one story and submit to the commands of a dictator" (232). The characters imagine that the physical space they are allotted on the page is a technology of oppressive control. They are repressively constrained by columns of narration, and all of the narrative territory must submit to Saturn's authoritarian dictates. Moreover, the columns, which present most of the war storyline, visually resemble lines of soldiers restricted to orderly formation and standing at attention, as well as the furrows of the fields where the characters, who are agricultural laborers, toil.

Saturn imagines himself a Mexican American Napoleon Bonaparte, seeking to imitate the preeminent European dictator and military strategist of the early nineteenth century so he can dominate the territory of the novel.[24] He reads the autobiography of Napoleon to learn how to more effectively wage war against EMF, studying

Napoleon's military philosophies and reading about "every naval, land, air, and epistolary battle in the history of the Americas" (190). Saturn attributes his identification with Napoleon and his imperial disposition to interracial heartbreak, for his girlfriend, Liz, has left him for a lover who is both taller and white. In response, Saturn acts like a Napoleonic figure waging war against EMF "to prove that I too am a colonizer, I too am powerful in those ways. I can stand on my tippy toes, I can curl my tongue and talk that perfect untainted English, I can wipe out whole cultures, whole towns of imaginary flower people. I can do that too" (238). He compensates for his racialized sense of inferiority—indicated by his sense of bodily and linguistic inferiority vis-à-vis a white man—by seeking power, waging war, and re-enacting conquests. The writer becomes a dictator of fictional worlds, creating a cast of Malinche-like[25] female characters who betray their brown men for white men and provoke Saturn's narratorial wrath. Empire, dictatorship, and racial hierarchies of power come together as Saturn seeks to dominate the fictional world of El Monte.[26]

A very different representation of Saturn emerges, though, at the beginning of part 2, when Smiley infiltrates Saturn's private territory. Peeling back a piece of the California sky and climbing up into Saturn's apartment, Smiley discovers Saturn's identity. Smiley's entrance into the authorial narrator's territory ruptures the constructed divide between the "fictional" El Monte and the "real" El Monte, as fictional character encounters fictionalized author. In this metafictional plot twist, the character meets his creator, only to be supremely disappointed.

> It should have been the moment when the creator acknowledges both the necessity of my existence and the reader's role as witness. But it was not the dignified meeting one might expect: the author sitting in his chair, wearing a starched dress shirt with a double-stitched collar, smoking hand-rolled tobacco, awaiting the visit because, after all, he is omniscient, foreseeing all surprises.
>
> But when I came to Saturn he was no longer in control. He did not foresee that I was coming, nor did he care. He had surrendered the story and his power as narrator. I found him asleep, sprawled and naked, laying on his stomach, pillowcases beneath him but the pillows tossed against the wall. And despite the order he had provided in the form of columns and chapters, he applied none of that logic to his sleeping quarters. (103)

A metafictional explosion of omnipotent omniscience indeed.[27] The scene contrasts the importance of the ordering logic of paragraphs, columns, and chapters in the novel with the heartbroken writer's disorderly abode and his abject body.[28] With his life and creative work falling apart, Saturn is no all-powerful planet or mighty dictator but a depressed Chicano writer.

At the same time, the episode self-consciously highlights Smiley's role as a minor character in the novel. Smiley, who visits Saturn partly because he is curious about his "own place in this novel," is faced with a heart-wrenching truth: not only is Saturn simply a heartbroken Chicano writer named Sal whose life is in shambles, his creator does not even remember him (101).[29] Sal tries to explain "that there are many characters, plots, and devices, and in the jumble of things sometimes minor characters are forgotten, even by the author" (105). Smiley, who is the major protagonist in his own life, is forced to confront the small amount of space his life story occupies in the overall character-system. Distraught, Smiley abandons the characters' revolution against Saturn in favor of the more modest goal of getting Sal to notice him, becoming an exhibitionist for the rest of the novel in the hope of being seen.

*Authori*tarian narration is disturbing to both Federico de la Fe and Smiley but for very different reasons: one feels no sense of privacy and too much visibility, while the other feels no sense of recognition and a total lack of visibility. Federico de la Fe contests *authori*tarian power, while Smiley actively seeks to be its subject. While Federico de la Fe and EMF are reminiscent of leftist revolutionaries, with their use of "comandante" titles, Smiley is reminiscent of minor functionaries who participate in authoritarian regimes for recognition and self-promotion. In this manner, the novel plays out two different modes of responding to dictatorship—resistance and complicity—through the narrative territory and narrative attention the characters seek to occupy.

Plotting Resistance and the Typography of Dissent

In *The People of Paper*, characters exist in a narrative topography that is visually apparent to the reader typographically. As they attempt to depose the creator and dictator of their diegetic world, their revolution against deterministic plot and voyeuristic observation affects the structure of the novel. The characters live in a narrative topography that restricts their actions, so when EMF rises up against Saturn, their battles over narrative territory register typographically. The novel formally registers resistance tactics through split narrative columns, absent text, black boxes, mundane thoughts, and chaotic narrative jumbling—all of which function as typographic technologies of dissent against Saturn's *authori*tarian narration.

The characters plot their resistance in order to alter the development of the plot as Saturn is scripting it.[30] Plot structures and gives an order to the narrative. In chapter 4, I explicate how *The Tattooed Soldier* uses a revenge plot to expose impunity and, while the revenge plot gets resolved, the novel leaves the deeper plot to attain justice unresolved. Here in *The People of Paper*, the characters attempt to foil the plot's resolution and alter the structure of the narrative to reclaim their agency. Engaging in guerilla warfare, Federico de la Fe first calls for an evasive war on Saturn. The members of EMF try to go underground, covering their houses with sheets of lead and mentally concealing their thoughts. Saturn's gaze cannot penetrate lead, so hiding under sheets of lead allows them to think and talk freely. The use of lead as a guerilla resistance tactic is interesting because Saturn is associated with lead in alchemy, and pencils are associated with lead. The characters use a metal linked with writing to defend themselves against the writer who created them. When they first split into two battalions, one group going to Tijuana to collect the lead and the other group shrouding El Monte in smoke from the fires they set around the flower fields to obscure their battle actions, Saturn's single narrative column splits into two, with one column describing what happens in Tijuana and the other following what happens in El Monte. The text typographically imitates Saturn's split gaze, and it registers at the level of the sentence—via missing words and ellipses—how his vision is obscured by the smoke and his auditory powers weakened by their whispers, which are nearly drowned out by the sound of the fire.

Since Saturn is able to read their thoughts, a power invoked by dictatorships but never actually possessed, they must develop their own autochthonous means of blocking Saturn's penetrating eye and foiling his omniscient access. When they are outside and not under the protective covering of lead with which they line their houses, Federico de la Fe instructs them to mentally conceal their thoughts: "If you must think about something, think about picking roses and carnations, about potatoes, about things that Saturn has no interest in" (89). Like an underground resistance movement, they must cloak their plans, "obscur[ing] their thoughts in a loop of irrelevance" (90). By thinking of agricultural matters and not matters of the heart, they hope to bore Saturn into leaving them alone.[31]

The narrative typographically records the characters' mental war. An entire column, for instance, chronicles Pelon's attempts to distract himself from thoughts of the war with an acute attention to every detail of his rural surroundings:

> Think about the brown dirt, the black ashes that float in the sky and land in the pit and then stick to the rake, the red crest of the roosters, the red blood on the razor blade that cuts the fighting cock's crest, the sharp beaks of the hens that pick at the severed tufts, the brown eggs they lay, the ropy mucus that covers the blind hatchlings, the yellow puffy chicks that choke on the shelled corn, the furrows where they are buried, the corn stalks that grow from their mouths, the stalks of carnations that suck the minerals from the soil and into the petals, the chapped hands of the flower pickers that gather the flowers on tarps and drag them to the scales and from the scales to two-ton trucks and then to flower shops, from the flower shop to a wedding.... (91)

The sentence continues, running off the bottom of the page with Pelon's endless stream-of-consciousness associations. His thoughts follow the interconnectedness of life and the often-ignored role of flower pickers in the market of flower consumption, and in a different narrative column, Little Merced's thoughts recall the effects of pesticides on the health of farm laborers. The novel becomes a fragmented series of materially focused stream-of-consciousness narrations and of observations about their everyday environment. Little Merced notes "two crop dusters in the sky. One held level, surveying all of El Monte. The second plane cruised behind at a lower altitude, diving into the fields and spraying insecticide on the budding flowers" (93). The crop dusters that survey and then spray the land with poisonous pesticides are figured in a similar position to Saturn. Though they are different kinds of violent technology, the border patrol and the agricultural industry bear down on the migrant laborers, making them vulnerable to deportation, poor working conditions, and health risks.[32] The characters' mind-blocking tactic stops the plot's forward movement; yet it shifts the narrative focus to the materiality of the characters' agricultural existence, to the chapped hands of the flower pickers, reminding the reader that underneath all the metafiction and marvelous realism this is a Chicano novel about migrant farmworkers embedded in transnational flows of labor and commodities. That is, for all its apparent formal differences, Plascencia's novel fits into the corpus of Chicana/o novels about migrant farm labor, alongside texts such as Tomás Rivera's ... *y no se lo tragó la tierra* (*And the Earth Did Not Devour Him*) and Helena María Viramontes's *Under the Feet of Jesus*.

In another attempt at evading the author-dictator's narrative gaze, Little Merced, under the tutelage of the Baby Nostradamus, learns to hide her thoughts under a Shandyesque black box. The black box, functioning as a typographic technology of dissent, "concealed what was a perfectly legible and discernible thought," making it "impenetrable" to Saturn (160, 164). Entire chunks of text and, later, two entire narrative columns are completely blacked out with large square boxes as Little Merced hides EMF from Saturn's gaze (as well as the reader's) with "her protective shield" (188). Her powers are defeated, however, when she (temporarily) dies from citric poisoning. Federico de la Fe and the rest of EMF likewise fall ill, this time from lead poisoning, and Saturn can once again freely read everyone's minds.[33]

Realizing that they cannot hide forever from Saturn and that their only hope of living autonomously is to risk all-out war, they channel the power of their own voices to defeat Saturn. Froggy rallies them:

> "We are fighting a war against a story, against the history that is being written by Saturn. We believed that silence was our best weapon against the intrusion of Saturn, that our silence would in turn silence Saturn.
>
> "But we have discovered an allergy to the lead, and learned that history cannot be fought with sealed lips, that the only way to stop Saturn is through our own voice."
>
> .... After years covered by lead and the imposed quiet under open air, we were ready to speak. We all went outside and said all the things we had always wanted to say, letting the words float. (209)

Saturn has occupied their narrative; to decolonize it they must switch from a defensive to an offensive war, engaging in an open and collective struggle for liberation. Instead of battling over territories of land, the character-revolutionaries fight for control over narrative territory.

In this parable of subaltern agency, the characters wrest control of the master narrative away from the authoritarian narrator by speaking. They seek to decenter the center of power by "crowding into the page, pushing and trying to press Saturn further and further to the margin," gaining more and more narrative space in the process (208). The novel visually and typographically chronicles this mass takeover, tracing the marginalization of the author-dictator through the multiplication of narrative columns and character-spaces. Narrative voice is linked to narrative space on the page, and with Saturn's character-space reduced, other voices flood the novel. At first more characters appear on the opposite page, and then characters' stories appear on the same page as Saturn's column, until Saturn has only a small paragraph at the top left-hand margin of the page. The fall of the author-dictator, then, is represented as an autumnal decline in his power as well as a fall from main-ness into minor-ness. We can read Plascencia's depiction of the fall of the author-dictator in dialogue with how *The Brief Wondrous Life of Oscar Wao* symbolically lowers the dictator in the hierarchy of the character-system by making Rafael Trujillo a minor character (as I discuss in chapter 1) and with how Cristina García's *King of Cuba* depicts the decline of El Comandante's aged body and his political power before he literally falls dead at the end of the novel (as I discuss in chapter 5). The reduced character-space allotted to Saturn in the character-system visually depicts and symbolically enacts the upsetting of his dominance. The coup staged by the characters in *The People of Paper* is visually rendered in the modified page layout, typographically documenting how the characters push Saturn aside with a mass taking to the page. The dialogized heteroglossia that results alters the previous structuring of the narrative columns, and readers must physically turn the book as some of the characters' stories appear horizontally across the page instead of vertically. The centrifugal power of polyphony is brought to bear against the centripetal power of Saturn's *authori*tarian univocality.[34]

Using laboring metaphors to describe their freedom, Froggy declares: "Our voices bloomed everywhere, like wild unfurrowed flowers. El Monte Flores were finally free to step wherever we wished, to think what we wanted, our story unobstructed, unexploited by Saturn" (212). The metaphor of exploitation is appropriate because the characters are indeed workers in the novel, not just in the literal sense, since they are migrant farmworkers, but also in the narratological sense, since their actions, emotions, and experiences produce the novel. As characters in a novel, they are not compensated for their labor in generating the plot; rather, they are subject to what Michael Denning has called a "wageless life," since they earn no income or other form of recompense for their labor (Denning, 81). In chapter 3 I focus on how Francisco Goldman's *The Ordinary Seaman* depicts another kind of wageless life, with undocumented Central American migrants who are exploited for their physical labor repairing a ship and never getting paid and for their narrative labor as the shipowners use stories about them to impress friends and woo lovers. In this chapter, I want to highlight how the author profits off the commodity the characters produce: the novel. By waging a war against their commodification, the characters resist their discursive exploitation, highlighting the importance of having control over the representational means of producing meaning in the realm of discourse. As they vie for control over the means of production—in this case, the page—they also demand control over their bodies' labor and their emotions. The characters, after all, wage "a war for volition *and* against the commodification of sadness" (53, emphasis added). In analogical terms, then, the characters battle not only the writer-as-dictator but also the writer-as-commodifier.

Narrative Rights and Narrative Disclosure

Exploring the politics and ethics of omniscient narration, and the ways it grants readers' access to characters' interior lives, in *The People of Paper* highlights what is at stake for a resistance novel when we take into consideration that the novel itself is a publically circulating commodity. The women in the novel most fiercely resent Saturn's narrative disclosures, claiming that he has violated the terms of love and presented a distorted portrayal of their relationships with men. As one character asserts early in the novel, "There is a certain etiquette to love, discretions that must be observed: You do not tell others about it, nor do you write about it" (44). The novel violates these so-called discretions of romantic etiquette as it reveals intimate and not-so-flattering details of Sal's relationships with Liz and with Cami. Furthermore, it involves other people—the novel's readers—who, according to Liz, have no right to be involved. "I was going to stay quiet, let you write your own story, let your history as you see it stand.... But this is a novel—it is no longer between you and me," Liz asserts; she contends that while Sal is entitled to hate her, he "cannot pass that right onto others" (137). Sal as Saturn has made the novel too autobiographical, and he should not share their intimacy publically. As with Federico de la Fe's claims to "volition" and its implications for how we think about plot and agency, Liz's claims also pose a challenge to the novel genre, this time regarding how we think about interiority, intimacy, and access. For most novels do not just give readers access to characters' inner lives and relationships, indeed they rely on these for their plot developments and world-building. As Saturn, the author-narrator dictates the terms of representation, disclosing characters' personal shame and wounded feelings, their migrant melancholia[35] and heartbreak, and the details of their love lives. These revelations are seen as personal violations, taking the characters' private lives into the public sphere.

Given that the economy of a novel's plot traffics in character interiority, this novel prompts us to see a relationship between textual exploitation and economic exploitation. Reversing his Malinche accusations against her, Liz claims that Sal is the real sellout: "In a neat pile of paper you have offered up not only your hometown, EMF, and Federico de la Fe, but also me, your grandparents and generations beyond them, your patria, your friends, even Cami. You have sold everything, save yourself. You have delivered all this into their hands, and for what? For fourteen dollars and the vanity of your name on the book cover" (138). Linda Hutcheon has termed metafiction a "narcissistic narrative," using the term in a descriptive rather than pejorative way (1). Yet Liz's remarks about the "narcissistic narrative" of *The People of Paper* precisely invoke the pejorative signification as she charges Sal not just with vanity but with commodifying El Monte and his own life relations and experiences, profiting off of them to the detriment of the people. She condemns him for being a sellout within his own local Mexican American community and the entire "patria" of Greater Mexico.[36] He has done so, she contends, for money and fame, and thereby, she implies, he has forsaken his ethical responsibility as a Chicano writer in an act of "cultural betrayal" (Román, *Race and Upward Mobility*, 108).[37] He has turned El Monte and Mexican American and Mexican experiences into a commodity for consumption as a form of entertainment—that is, into a novel. Moreover, her accusation that he has "sold everything, save yourself," subtly jabs at the fact that Sal has fictionalized himself in the form of Saturn and written about himself in the third person, obscuring his own culpability and his heteropatriachal investments by mystifying himself as the "romantic hero" and portraying the female characters as promiscuous race traitors (137). Liz critiques the entertainment value of literature that makes a profit off of personal crisis and ethnic misery ("the commodification of sadness"), especially when that profit comes at the expense of vilifying women of color.

From Federico de la Fe and EMF to Liz, the characters assert their demands on the basis of what we could call their "narrative rights." They demand agency over the plot of their lives using the discourses of free will and self-determination. At the same time, they claim the right to keep their thoughts and feelings to themselves through the discourses of individuality and privacy. They want the right to "dignity through privacy" and the "right to be unseen" (47). They collectively claim their independence politically and ontologically vis-à-vis the world of the novel. These narrative rights contest conventions of the novel genre, in particular omniscient narration, plot development, the allocation of space on the page, and intimate access to character interiority. The novel denaturalizes reading for us, challenging us as readers (and as literary critics) to be more attune to the hierarchical power dynamics built into the novel's structural scaffolding and to the exploitation that occurs when characters are circulated as commodities through the capitalist book publishing market. *The People of Paper*, therefore, extends the long engagements with liberationist discourses in both the Latin American dictatorship novel and the Chicana/o novel, while cautioning us to be critical of the medium of the novel as a genre and of the privileged position of the author.

Meanwhile, the Baby Nostradamus offers a compelling alternative narratorial and economic model to Saturn's *author*itarian narrative domination and his exploitation of borderlands life. Contrary to surface appearances and medical diagnoses, the Baby Nostradamus is not a mentally handicapped baby. He is a sage prophet of sorts who sees the past and the future of the fictional world of the novel and our real world. He knows things recorded and unrecorded, and he has access to the intimate thoughts and details of the interior lives of people across time and space. He is even more powerful than the *author*itarian Saturn: "The Baby Nostradamus had the power to undercut Saturn by prematurely disclosing information and sabotaging the whole of the novel. Ending everything here by simply listing the character fates" with "a terrorism of summation, prematurely bringing everything forward" (111). The Baby Nostradamus, however, chooses to wield his power very differently from Saturn, abiding by an ethics of omniscience based not on narrative disclosure but on narrative restraint.

This alternative mode of omniscient power is rooted in withholding rather than disclosing information. The "laws for the seers of the future," which the Baby Nostradamus obeys, are strict: you cannot use your power for the state, you cannot exchange services for money, and you cannot declare deaths (167). Importantly, the Baby Nostradamus's omniscience is not aligned with the nation-state or with neoliberal capitalism. Unlike Saturn, he seeks neither dominance nor recompense. Asking nothing in return, he helps Little Merced in the characters' war against Saturn by training her how to conceal her thoughts from the author-dictator whose omniscient gaze surveils and exploits her and her community. The black boxes that cover over Little Merced's thoughts and that appear in place of words in the Baby Nostradamus's character-space are illegible—they are completely filled with black ink and deny Saturn, as well as the reader, access. The Baby Nostradamus sets his own borders, which block the gaze of the dictator-author, and refuses to participate in the capitalist system. His omniscience may be unintelligible, but it not based on policing or disciplining, and it does not produce commodities. The border militarization and surveillance that bears down on undocumented migrants and the capitalist modes of exploiting migrant labor are forms of authoritarianism, and the Baby Nostradamus's omniscient gaze refutes them.

Though he ultimately cannot stop Saturn from taking over the page and regaining control of the novel, the Baby Nostradamus does serve as a useful counter-model to the models of power of the author-dictator, the border patrol state, and capitalism. The Baby Nostradamus embodies a different kind of knowledge production and circulation. Moreover, he is simultaneously represented as disabled and as having exceptional abilities that he freely uses to help others who are struggling under the gaze of authoritarian power. If we read him through Julie Avril Minich's work, which elucidates "the role played by representations of disability in making the rights and benefits of citizenship (both cultural and political) more accessible," the Baby

Nostradamus gestures toward the need for narrating a different kind of belonging and for authoring another form of solidarity (*Accessible Citizenships*, 27). The Baby Nostradamus's anti-authoritarian form of power symbolizes the possibility of an alternative model that could be mobilized in the service of social and narrative justice.

The novel's representation of the novelistic processes of creation, narration, and emplotment symbolically functions as an interrogation of power, control, and agency in Greater Mexico. The characters are undocumented migrant Mexican and Chicana/o farm laborers who resist their representational exploitation in the pages of the book instead of in furrows of the fields. Plascencia's marvelous real metafiction is a formal response to inequitable socioeconomic structures in the borderlands that are exacerbated by the militarization of the border and by the exploitive actions of NAFTA-supported multinational corporations and agrobusinesses. This novel therefore reminds us that novel production is inextricably linked to global literary markets and the NAFTA-dictated borderlands modernity of the U.S.-Mexico border. The novel interrogates capitalist literary markets, racialized transnational labor exploitation, and nationalist policies of exclusion through a fictional allegory about people made of paper, people trapped in paper, and people without papers.

As a metacritical Chicano novel about the borderlands of authoritarianism and authoritarianism in the borderlands, *The People of Paper* ultimately grapples with the contradiction of creating a decolonial resistance narrative. Interpreted from a more idealistic perspective, the metaphor of "the people of paper" is an example of the kind of "insurgent metaphors" Otto Santa Anna calls for to challenge the dominant stigmatizing and xenophobic discourses that are currently used to characterize undocumented migrants in particular but also Latina/os more broadly (295).[38] A number of artists, activists, and cultural producers have joined the migrant rights movement and produced a plethora of images and narratives that seek to reframe the discourse around undocumented migration and national belonging. We can read Plascencia's novel in this vein, as a metaphorical response to and metafictional meditation on the surveillance and exploitation that undocumented migrants and racial minorities face and the rights-based struggles they wage in response.

Yet the novel also cautions against this idealistic celebration of the power of the imaginary, metaphor, and writing. Writing and violence have been linked in the Americas since colonization; as a result,

Aníbal González argues, there is a general conflict-ridden "graphophobia" in twentieth-century Latin American literature that speaks to the way "writing's entanglements with duplicity and oppression generates a far-reaching web of complicity from which no one, neither writer nor reader, emerges untainted" (20). His observations obtain as well for the late twentieth- and early twenty-first-century Latina/o dictatorship novels that I examine, including *The People of Paper*, which dramatize how writing and storytelling can be dictatorial at the same time that they try to harness its oppositional, counter-dictatorial potential. *The People of Paper* exhibits a dual impulse to account for writing as both a mode of domination and a mode of opposition. By simultaneously mobilizing tropes of revolutionary resistance and calling attention to the contradiction of using the novel as a form of oppositional power, Plascencia's novel asks us to seriously consider: How can we use a mode of authority, power, and violence—writing and the novel genre—to represent the repression, exploitation, and discrimination that undocumented subjects and minorities face? How can we critique the socioeconomic exploitation of migrant and minority labor using a market commodity that readers purchase and whose characters' lives they then consume as they read? Furthermore, if the border patrol state regulates migrant bodies through the regime of documentation and visa papers, how can we document on paper the lives of the undocumented or people without papers? The novel poses these questions but posits no facile answers; instead, it presents us with a compromise.

In the novel's final pages, Saturn regains control of the narrative apparatus and EMF: he "press[es] against the columns...buckling the structure and crumbling it to rubble...giving Saturn full control over the story" (242). Saturn's narration takes over the rest of the book's pages as the novel moves into a traditional full-page paragraph structure to visually instantiate this triumph. Yet the victory is bittersweet. Despite having triumphed over his fictional creations, the authorial narrator is forced to acknowledge his inability to dictate his own desired future with Liz, which will never come to pass. As Saturn, he has won the war and retaken control of the narrative terrain, but as Sal, he cannot triumph in the "perilous terrain of love" (219). To fulfill the liberatory logic of the Latin American dictatorship novel and the Chicana/o novel, *The People of Paper* demands that power compromise: the author does not fall, but neither does he retain his authoritarian omnipotence and omniscience. He remains in solitude, dreaming of Liz and the sequel to their love that will never materialize. Meanwhile, presumably hiding under the parasol represented as a large black dot on the novel's final page, Federico de la Fe and Little Merced "walk south and off the page," disappearing forever from Saturn's gaze and escaping Sal's pen, refugees from the novel's dictatorship (245).

{3}

The Floating Dictatorship

If we think, after all, that the boat is a floating piece of space, a place without a place, that exists by itself, that is closed in on itself and at the same time is given over to the infinity of the sea and that... it goes as far as the colonies in search of the most precious treasures they conceal in their gardens, you will understand why the boat has not only been for our civilization, from the sixteenth century until the present, the great instrument of economic development... but has been simultaneously the greatest reserve of the imagination.
—MICHEL FOUCAULT, "Of Other Spaces"

El desarollo es un viaje con más naúfragos que navegantes.
Development is a voyage with more shipwrecks than navigators.
—EDUARDO GALEANO, Las venas abiertas de América Latina (Open Veins of Latin America)

The slaver is a ghost ship sailing at the edges of modern consciousness.
—MARCUS REDIKER, The Slave Ship

Different kinds of ships float in the background of Gabriel García Márquez's dictatorship novel *El otoño del patriarca* (*The Autumn of the Patriarch*; 1975). Most memorably, three Spanish sailing ships replay the arrival of Christopher Columbus to the Americas, and the United States threatens to occupy the country once again with its battleships if the unnamed dictator and titular Patriarch does not sell the Caribbean Sea to the United States as payment for the country's debt. In anachronistic and palimpsestic visions of imperialism, the Patriarch looks out and sees "el acorazado de siempre que los infantes de marina habían abandonado en el muelle, y más allá del acorazado, fondeadas en el mar tenebroso, vio los tres carabelas" (the battleship that the marines had left behind at the dock, and beyond that battleship, anchored in the shadowy sea, he saw the three caravels)

(69; Rabassa, 40). Later, as the United States sucks up the entirety of the Caribbean Sea with massive dredges, he sees "la nao capitana del almirante mayor de la mar océana" (the flagship of the first admiral of the ocean), now a "naufragio" (wreck) on the sea floor (365; Rabassa, 234). The appearance of ships from two different historical moments in one field of vision draws a link between imperialism, capitalism, and dictatorship. Columbus's ruined vessel in turn connects with other iterations of shipwreck imagery. The presidential palace and the dictator's body, both of which symbolize the ship of state, are subtly figured in terms of ruins.[1] In contrast, Guatemalan American Francisco Goldman's novel *The Ordinary Seaman* (1997) brings the ship and the trope of shipwreck from the narrative background to the foreground. I consider in this chapter how this novel captures the destruction wrought by slavery, imperialism, dictatorship, and neoliberal capitalism in the Americas.

The Ordinary Seaman tells the story of fifteen Central American men—one Guatemalan, five Nicaraguans, and nine Hondurans, to be more precise—who are hired by two white neoliberal capitalists named Elias and Mark to repair a broken-down ship. Elias and Mark are the ship's captain and first mate as well as its "phantom owners," who never reveal that they are the owners, either to the crew or on any of the ship's paperwork to avoid detection because they plan to fix the vessel cheaply and use it to run shipping scams. Registered under a Panamanian flag of convenience, the *Urus* is docked at a "barnacle-coated pier" in an abandoned port in Brooklyn (103). The crew come up from Central America to work on the damaged ship, and they are told they must not leave the ship or they will be caught and deported, so they remain on board, endlessly repairing the broken vessel. They labor without pay and without electricity or running water for six months in scorching heat and bitter cold on the rat-infested ship, surviving on what little food Elias and Mark infrequently bring them and the cans of sardines and the cockroach-infested rice they find on the ship. Esteban, the main protagonist of the novel and a former Sandinista revolutionary in Nicaragua, eventually ventures into Brooklyn, using the skills he acquired in guerilla warfare to do reconnaissance and go on night raids to steal food and clothing. Bernardo, an elderly Nicaraguan ship waiter and one of the novel's other main characters, is gravely burned and must be taken to the hospital. Elias and Mark, realizing that they may be discovered if Bernardo notifies the authorities and that it is impossible to find a replacement circuit breaker to make the engine run, literally abandon ship; Mark flees to the Yucatan and Elias into domestic life. Esteban meanwhile acquires a job and a Mexican girlfriend named Joaquina and builds a network of aid among a pan-Latina/o American working-class migrant community to help the crew escape the *Urus*.

The novel is set in 1989, at the height of the civil wars and brutal military dictatorships in Central America, but it continually evokes past and present forms of violence in the Americas, such as slavery, filibustering, occupation, military interventionism, and the exploitation of undocumented migrants. The novel recreates Central America through the Guatemalan, Nicaraguan, and Honduran laborers on a ship with a Panamanian registry (2). With characters from multiple Central American countries, the space of the *Urus* functions as a "transisthmus" that strategically draws attention to Central America as a key site for U.S. imperial economic and military ventures (A. P. Rodríguez, *Dividing the Isthmus*, 2).[2] The novel dramatizes how, in the words of Juan González, "intervention comes home to roost" and to haunt the contemporary moment in the form of the ghost ship of the *Urus* (129). The novel figures the capitalist owners of the *Urus* as modern-day versions of slave owners, explorers, filibusterers, and dictators whose money-making venture keeps the crew trapped on the ship as undocumented laborers.

A Guatemalan American journalist and novelist who grew up in Boston, Francisco Goldman has been an important force in developing U.S. Central American literature as an emergent subfield of Latina/o literature, infusing Latina/o literature with the signs of dictatorship.[3] Ana Patricia Rodríguez observes, "as the political unconscious, or phantom figure, of transnational migration narratives, Central American refugees emplot a U.S. Latino imaginary with signs of war, revolution, and displacement—all part of the history of many Central Americas" ("Refugees," 390). Francisco Goldman's literary and journalistic work is centrally concerned with the wars and revolutions in Central America, which he covered as a journalist for *Harper's* in the 1980s. His concern with the human rights violations caused by death squads and paramilitary operations shape the plot of his first novel, *The Long Night of White Chickens*, about the mysterious murder of an indigenous Guatemalan woman who is running an orphanage, and his nonfiction investigatory account of the murder of the Guatemalan human rights activist Bishop Juan Gerardi in *The Art of Political Murder*.[4] Goldman's interest in the afterlife of dictatorship, impunity, and U.S. interventionism is more transnational and much more encoded in *The Ordinary Seaman*. In my interpretation, the novel metaphorizes dictatorship through the *Urus* to unveil multiple kinds of authoritarianism in the hemisphere.

This novel captures the shift away from Cold War political dictatorships and toward the dominance of neoliberalism and the free market.[5] The neoliberal moment allows for the emergence of a phantom dictator, and I read Elias and Mark as neoliberal dictators and the ship as their technology of domination. To explicate their neoliberal dictator-ship, I focus on the holes and scraps of their shipwreck, which exposes how their regime similarly disappears subjects and creates unlivable lives. In the first half of this chapter, I unpack the trope of the ship as a floating authoritarian space, focusing initially on the hierarchical space of the ship, and in particular on the dictatorial figure of the captain, and then on how the ship as a technology produces social death and undocumented refugees. In the second half of the chapter, I turn from the trope of the ship to that of the shipwreck. I read the shipwreck as a metaphor for the crew's situation as well as a narrative device, using the term "discourse"—which in nautical and literary terms, respectively, refers to the planned route of a voyage and of a narrative—to argue that the novel is structured through breakage and stranded temporality. I end by analyzing the multiple significations of scraps and holes in the novel, demonstrating how the discarded scraps and ruinous holes of the shipwreck are repurposed and repaired in the novel through the narrative form. This novel ultimately offers the opportunity to critically interpret the ruins caused by coloniality—specifically through imperialism, slavery, dictatorship, neoliberal capitalism, and nation-state borders—that haunt our contemporary moment and produce undocumented refugees who must navigate the wreckage.

Captain of a Dictator-ship

Paul Gilroy has famously theorized the ship as "a living, microcultural, micro-political system in motion," and this insight helps illuminate the way *The Ordinary Seaman* depicts the ship as a micropolitical system, with its traditionally rigid hierarchy of power, and as a microcultural transisthmusian system (4). I argue that the *Urus* is a floating dictator-ship that symbolically functions as a microcosm of authoritarianism. It is floating in the double sense: literally, it is a boat afloat in the Brooklyn waterfront, and figuratively, it is a liminal figure adrift between U.S. and Latin American spaces and histories. The *Urus* is a floating signifier for histories of oppression and exploitation and for the violation of human and labor rights. I strategically harness the ship as a symbol of authoritarianism, highlighting how ships are incredibly hierarchical spaces and deeply imbricated in the histories of slavery and imperialism.

I want to meditate first on the idea of the *Urus* as a dictator-ship, riffing on the "ship" in "dictatorship" by focusing on the micropolitics of the ship. A ship is a compelling metaphor for a dictatorship, given the rigid power hierarchies aboard ships. The strict hierarchy of authority and status is manifest most strikingly in the figure of the captain, who is often described as a figure of absolute power in historical accounts, contemporary ethnographies, and literary narratives. For example, Markus Rediker describes the slave ship captain as "the monarch of his wooden world" (*The Slave*, 58), and a number of Americanist literary critics have read Captain Ahab in Herman Melville's novel *Moby-Dick* as an authoritarian figure, including C. L. R. James, who calls Ahab "an American totalitarian" who "is by nature a dictatorial personality" (34, 15). Captains are at the top of the hierarchy of power and authority, and their orders must be followed without question.[6] The figure of the captain is a useful analog for political power, and the captain is often referred to as a god, a king, and a dictator.[7] Like a dictator, the captain has supreme power and is immune from accountability. Captains of slave ships in particular wielded their absolute authority violently so as to ensure that their orders were followed at all times. The captain used exemplary violence—ranging from corporal punishment and torture to death—to maintain shipboard discipline among sailors and slaves alike, for "terror was essential to running a slave ship" (Rediker, *The Slave*, 197). Terror as a tactic of disciplinary power used by the captain, a figure who is both sanctioned by and above the law, finds its contemporary instantiation in the authoritarian figure of the dictator (and military junta), also infamous for torturing, terrorizing, disappearing, and murdering national subjects en masse.

Yet Elias, unlike a traditional totalitarian captain or dictator, does not have to resort to spectacles of violence to make the ship an authoritarian space. He does not have to employ physical abuse or brute force, because his power comes from the economic and legal systems he uses to limit the sea laborers' agency and avoid persecution for his crimes. Historically, mariners have lacked legal protection and have been subject to the dictates of the captain; this vulnerability to structural violence continues today, as they can be fired indiscriminately, can be denied their wages if a ship's owner runs out of money, and can be abandoned at sea with impunity.[8] *The Ordinary Seaman* lays bare the macrolevel external structures—flags of convenience and immigration laws—and microlevel hierarchies of power and working conditions on the *Urus*. At both the macro and micro levels of this "structured space," the Central American seamen are vulnerably positioned at the bottom of the hierarchy without protection (Sampson, 7). The lack of international shipping regulations and on-board accountability, exacerbated by the crew's isolation at the Brooklyn pier, allows Elias to violate the crew's human and labor rights by imposing terrible living conditions and unsafe working conditions on them, withholding their pay, and keeping them trapped aboard the *Urus* without valid work and travel visas.

Elias keeps the crew disciplined through the loopholes and anonymity built into the flag of convenience system and threats of deportation. He takes advantage of the Panamanian flag of convenience[9] to manipulate the crew's sense of national location and corresponding legal status, thereby dictating their immobility and their inability to protest the conditions on the *Urus*. On their first day on the ship, Elias explains, "*onboard* they were in Panama, contracted seamen protected by that country's sovereign laws. *Onshore* they were in the United States, where, of course, for the next four days, until their seamen's transit visas expired, they were perfectly legal. But they all knew what rough places port cities could be, and this was one of the most dangerous, especially when they left the port yard and entered the streets around 'los proyectos'" (25–26). Elias initially coerces the crew to stay on board, frightening them with the threat that they will be murdered and later with the threat they will be deported if they are caught in the United States, since they no longer have visas. Later, when Esteban asks if he can go visit Bernardo in the hospital, Elias wields his power as captain and U.S. citizen over Esteban: "I've told you over and over, you are an illegal alien whenever you set foot ashore.... You're not going there. That's an order from your captain" (323–324). Unbeknownst to the crew, Elias lets their shipping articles lapse, rendering the ship "a stateless vessel" and the men unauthorized aliens in the United States (154). However, ironically and perversely, this is insignificant because Elias and Mark never had the crew sign shipping articles in the first place, so not only are the crew never paid, they are "unlicensed seafarers" and "have never been a legally employed crew," meaning that at no point were they ever protected by Panamanian law (155, 350). In other words, though the crew were technically initially on Panamanian territory on the ship, as Elias explained to the men, they were never legally laborers in either Panama or the United States. These legal ambiguities reveal how flag of convenience registries represent a "hypertransnationalism, whereby, paradoxically, a contracting state becomes a traveling, floating signifier that is not bounded by territory and is emptied of its protections"; in the case of the *Urus*, the ship becomes a floating dictator-ship that subjects the crew to social death (Shemak, 189).

Elias is a dictatorial captain without having to be violently dictatorial because the structures of power created by imperialism, capitalism, and the nation-state (symbolized by the flag of convenience and immigration authorities) provide him with immunity for his crimes. He uses the authoritarian position that the captain possesses to direct the crew's work, and he gains the men's trust by working alongside them and by strategically lying and blaming the owners for all the workplace deprivations and financial problems. His fluency in Mexican vernacular Spanish facilitates his communication with the crew, as does his ruse that he is "a regular dude" and that they are all, figuratively speaking, in the same boat, needing to repair the ship so that it can set sail and they can all earn their promised money from the supposedly mysterious owners (305). Elias also does not have to be a traditional dictatorial figure because conditions of war and poverty—which are partly the result of U.S. support for military dictatorships and brutal counter-insurgency campaigns and death squads in the crew's home countries of Nicaragua, Guatemala, and Honduras—have made the men seek out work on the ship, and the fear of deportation makes them too afraid to leave. The *Urus* functions as a de facto dictator-ship that keeps the crew trapped in conditions of limited agency, deprivation, and impoverishment.

In one of the novel's deeply ironic moments, Elias portrays himself as the antithesis to Anastasio Somoza, Nicaragua's dictator from 1967 to 1979, and on the side of revolutionary fighters like Esteban.[10] Elias is working on the ship with the crew when a report comes across the radio of "a short burst of nasal-fulminating English, the U.S. president...requesting full renewed-funding-arming-training of the

Nicaraguan Freedom Fighters" (80). In reaction to President Reagan's request, Elias decries U.S. military support of the Contras in Nicaragua, fulminating:

> "That fucking idiot! Wants to start the war up again. I don't see why we can't leave Nicara-goo-wah alone. Such a fucking tiny country!"... And el Capitán was asserting that the United States caused the betrayal of the revolution's ideals by suffocating it with an illegal war, saying, "That's the problem with the fucking Americans, can't deal with being an imperial power and so they fucking deny they are one, just don't fucking want to know, do they?" And now el Capitán looking down at Esteban again and saying that back in '79 during the insurrection against Somoza he'd really wanted to join the Sandinista International Brigades fighting on the Southern front but he'd had a business in the Amazon going. (80)

Elias imagines himself an aspiring left-wing revolutionary as he sympathizes with the Sandinistas and with Esteban, disidentifying with the United States' foreign policy. The United States backed the right-wing dictatorship of Somoza and later funded the Contra (counter-revolutionary) forces that fought against the Sandinista government. Elias voices his desire to have been part of the Sandinista struggle, but this impulse is rooted less in anti-imperialist politics and more in fulfilling the "romantic ideas about an adventurous life" he had as a youth (281). The passage is telling, pointing to the contradiction of politically identifying with an anti-authoritarian socialist struggle and living a life that belies those politics. No decolonial revolutionary, Elias, like Ahab before him, worships "the religion of his age—material progress," evident in his choice to pursue a capitalist business venture in the Amazon over a revolutionary collectivist struggle (James, 9). Elias attempts to disavow his privilege and his power to the very men he is exploiting and will later abandon. Tellingly, he lives in a building in Manhattan called Imperial Loft, and while he denies his privilege he simultaneously exercises it to the detriment of the Central Americans trapped on the *Urus*. Rather than a ruthless political dictator, Elias is a manipulative and unscrupulous neoliberal capitalist who tries to extract as much as he can from his workers without regard for their human and labor rights. Yet the novel precisely invites us to see the links between these different forms of domination.

As both captain and owner, Elias uses the ship as a vehicle or technology to exploit people for monetary and narrative profit—for economic and cultural capital. He fetishizes Latin America as an inherently pure, spiritual, and medicinal place and sees himself as a modern-day adventurer: "a man of adventure, of jungle and sea, a risk taker, a shipping and timber magnate, an eco lodge owner with his own medicinal plant business down in the Amazon" (277). Elias embarks on a venture, in the senses of both adventure and business endeavor, which is a way for him as a middle-class white man to gain capital as he participates in the enduring "capital fiction"—to use Erika Beckman's term that names "fiction of and about capital"—that Latin America is the United States' (economic) backyard (x).[11] The novel is a fiction about a capitalist venture at the same time that it depicts the enduring fiction, rooted in Manifest Destiny and the Monroe Doctrine, that Latin America is a source of capital for the United States. Elias plans to use the repaired ship to go into the timber trade in the Amazon, which gestures toward the hemispheric history of the United States extracting raw material goods from Latin America for profit. As an aspiring "shipping and timber magnate," Elias pursues the quintessential American frontier fantasy (277).[12] His nostalgia and exoticization highlight the enduring capital fiction of Manifest Destiny as well as the enduring fiction of "Central America as a wild site of masculine fantasy and renewal" in the U.S. imaginary (Friedman, 262).[13] Elias evokes two kinds of intervention in Latin America—the United States' capitalist enterprises of filibustering and of using the countries of Central America as "banana republics"—at the same time that the backdrop of the novel evokes a third kind of intervention: the United States' covert support of right-wing counter-insurgents.

In addition to physical exploitation, the white men in the novel use the Central American crew and Latin America in general for their narrative labor, exploiting their stories to impress friends and charm lovers. Elias constantly tells stories at parties, "reliving his Amazon exploits for a very captive audience" (294). He uses Latin America as fodder for his narrative exploits, with the emphasis here on exploits as exploitation, not as heroic feats. His stories about his adventures in the exotic Amazonian jungle recycle colonialist tropes and function as a form of narrative capital that gives him cultural capital in his bourgeois social circle. More insidiously within the economy of the novel's plot, Elias's stories are another means by which he exploits Latin America(ns) for his own capital gain. For his part, John the Ship Visitor uses the story of the *Urus*'s abandoned crew to woo and entertain his lover, Ariadne. "I've sure as hell got a story for her tonight," thinks John, "and he'll feel glad about that, arranging himself on his long evening journey home to Ariadne around his anticipation and relief at having a story to bring her (if not an ice-encased leaf)" (133). As if the Central Americans' plight is a gift and their story is a material object of exchange for Ariadne's affection, the novel figures the men as goods or cargo of sorts in John and Ariadne's romantic relationship.[14] As a ship visitor, John works for the port chaplain, boarding ships, advocating for seafarer's rights, and ministering to their needs, so he is in a position to help the exploited and abandoned crew of the *Urus*; yet he is oblivious to the politics of his own narrative acts. The crew of the *Urus* work for free repairing the ship but are also unwittingly put to work in the stories told about them for the entertainment and wooing of others. The crew are not compensated for either their physical or narrative labor. Like the characters whose lives are commodified in Salvador Plascencia's *The People of Paper*, which I consider in chapter 2, the characters in *The Ordinary Seaman* are exploited for their narrative labor as Elias and John traffic in the commodity of their stories. Elias and John suffer from what Diana Taylor has elsewhere termed "percepticide," as they willfully refuse to see the contradiction between their own liberal politics and their complicity in economic and narrative systems that subjugate the very peoples with whom they claim to be in solidarity (*Disappearing*, 119).

Challenging what Stanley Cohen has called a "state of denial," the novel exposes how Elias willfully disavows the ethical implications of his exploitation of the Central American crew for monetary and narrative profit. Like Ahab before him, Elias "has been trained in the school of individualism and an individualist he remains to the end," as he abandons the Central American crew and rationalizes away his selfish actions as honorable (James, 11). Elias plays the victim, blaming Mark for their failed (ad)venture, deluding himself with the U.S. fantasy of new beginnings, the value of hard work, and how it is admirable just to try. Consoling himself with the neoliberal values of individualism and entrepreneurism, he thinks: "Because trying to get ahead, to innovate, to make something of yourself, guey, is honorable. There's an implicit honor in just the bloody fucking effort, that's all. And if that doesn't quite excuse everything, it ties you, binds, connects you to all those who've come before who've made such an effort also, the successes as well as the failures" (374). Indeed, his actions bind him to the hemispheric history of domination and exploitation in the Americas—from Hernán Cortés[15] and William Walker to Anastasio Somoza. Seduced by the imperialist ideology of Manifest Destiny that justifies its exploits and interventions with the notion that it is bringing progress, civilization, and democracy to Latin America, Elias is not the well-meaning hero he believes he is. Rather, he is a ship captain who is another version of the abusive figures hungry for capital and power who have come before him: the slave owner, the conquistador, the filibusterer, the dictator, and the capitalist.

Ships of Death

As a dictator-ship, the *Urus* is the latest in a long and violent history of ships that includes slave ships, ships of colonization, filibustering ships, and ships of economic imperialism. As a "floating anachronism," the *Urus* is a remnant of slavery but also a haunting manifestation of U.S. interventions in Central America (Gruesz, "Utopia," 67). The *Urus* functions metaphorically as a palimpsest that contains the phantom traces of material and literary histories of different kinds of domination. The *Urus* is variously and repeatedly called a "dead ship" (38, 47, 106, 295), a "secret slave ship" (305), a "phantom ship" (97, 362), and a "ghost ship" (105, 107, 108, 116, 340). These descriptions explicitly name the exploitation taking place on the ship at the same time that they link this exploitation to the dark underside of coloniality's maritime history, primarily in the form of human trafficking. The ship is technically dead because its engine does not work and it cannot run, but this is symbolically significant. The mechanically dead ship mirrors both shipwrecks and ships of death (slave ships) at the same time that the *Urus* becomes the space of social death for the characters.

As scholars of the Black Atlantic remind us, ships evoke the Middle Passage "and the half remembered micro-politics of the slave trade and its relationship to both industrialization and modernization," an economic history that a group of African American and Afro-Latina/os who encounter the *Urus* inscribe back onto the ship (Gilroy, 17). "Los blacks"[16] party on the pier, and when they notice the crew furtively observing them, they begin to insult and taunt them. The narrator relates: "Los blacks seemed to know something about the

Urus; it was as if they'd somehow figured out what the crew's situation was. They spray-painted DEATH SHIP on the grain elevator, and skulls over crossed bones, and another night someone even wrote, CAGUERO DE LA MUERTE, which seemed to mean, 'Shitter of Death,' though they probably meant 'Cargo Ship of Death,' leaving out the *r* in *carguero*" (50). As they mark the ship as a "death ship," they recall the history of the Middle Passage and slave ships in the Americas. It is important that "los blacks" make the connection between slave ships as ships of death and the crew's situation on the *Urus*. Their historical consciousness gives them epistemic clarity—it allows them to "know something" about the crew's situation, mainly that the men are trapped in a space of social death. That they are rendered as *los* blacks, rather than *the* blacks, insists on a hemispheric rather than a national (read U.S.) history of slavery. By emphasizing a shared history of slavery in the Americas rather than just a U.S. national history through the term "los blacks," the novel subtly constructs a transnational optic that prods readers to connect seemingly distinct histories, spaces, and forms of power. By labeling the *Urus* as a ship of death, los blacks are not simply labeling the crew's present situation but making a historical linkage as well as a predictive gesture. That is, their graffiti act names the past to warn about the crew's future, so it is oriented toward both the past and the future, an analeptic and a proleptic narrative gesture. The scriptural economy of Elias's speech act of officially naming the ship and writing "*Urus*" on it hides below the layer of paint a palimpsestic history of shipping in the Americas, the legacy of slavery and imperialism that is lurking in the shadows.[17] In contrast, los blacks' illegal and unofficial speech act is a defiant act of reading and interpreting the truth about the ship as a carrier of death (cargo) and as a process that transforms men into waste products (shit), inscribing it visibly in plain sight.

"Caguero" functions as a floating signifier, for its linguistic ambiguity gestures toward both "caguero" and "carguero," toward both "shitter" and "cargo ship." Yet, while "carguero" does, in fact, translate as "cargo ship," "caguero" is not actually a word in Spanish. Coming from the Spanish word "cagar," meaning to evacuate the bowels, "caga" is a colloquial word for "shit," and "cagadero" is a colloquial word for "toilet," like the English vernacular "crapper" or "shitter," as the narrator translates it. While "caguero" does not denote a word in the dictionary, reading the two acts of graffiti together puts "death ship" beside "caguero," generating a bilingual pun of sorts. "Carguero" and "caga" creates a word, "ca(r)guero," that with the absent presence of *r* signifies both ship and shit, a kind of Spanglish equivalent to the child's game where you hold your tongue while saying "ship" and it sounds like "shit." This particular linguistic play, however, tells a serious truth, as all of the words scrawled in graffiti—"cargo," "ship," "death," and "shit"—signal a history of treating humans as cargo and as commodities and of people being shit on and being treated like shit or, to play on another symbolically laden term frequently used in the novel, as (s)crap.[18] The bilingual slippage highlights how the crew have been turned into cargo, their labor becoming the commodity being produced, traded, and consumed in the ship's economy.

The name of the *Urus* is also symbolically significant because linguistically it contains traces of other histories and peoples. The prefix "ur" means original or earliest, highlighting the coloniality of power that originated in colonization and the slave trade, and if the *Urus* is symbolically the "ur" ship of colonialism and slavery, then it is also a repetition with a difference, that difference registering more contemporary forms of domination, such as undocumented labor exploitation, since the seamen are all turned into unpaid, undocumented migrant laborers. The fact that Urus is also the name of an indigenous tribe in Peru and Bolivia recalls how indigenous peoples in the Americas have been shipwrecked by Euro-American imperialism. We can also interpret the name *Urus* in terms of its play on words. We can read it as "u r US," or "you are U.S.," to signal that the crew are both trapped in the United States and, as Central Americans, continually subjected to the United States' imperial designs. We can also read it as "u r us," or "you are us," in relation to racial minorities, which signals how "you Blacks are us Latina/os and Central Americans," groups exploited by the United States through slavery and through socioeconomic inequalities in the present. Interestingly, the etymology of the Indonesian "urus" means to manage, to control, and to be in charge of, which speaks to the power dynamics on the ship. All of these ways of reading the *Urus*'s name capture how it serves as a symbol of domination and exploitation.

As a technology of subjectification, Rediker explains, the slave ship was a factory that produced slaves, labor power, and race (*The Slave*, 10–11). The *Urus* is a twentieth-century version of the slave ship and it functions as a factory, which in this case produces undocumented subjects, undocumented labor power, and racialized Latinos-in-formation. Indeed, Bernardo, who sees the reality of their situation, draws the links, naming what they do as "slave labor" (58) and telling Elias that he treats them as "slaves" (68). The death ship of the *Urus* does not exploit them as slaves in the historical sense of slavery, but the seamen are similarly forced into a "wageless life" as unpaid laborers (Denning, 79).[19] The slave ship produced the condition that Orlando Patterson has called "social death," and the *Urus* produces the status of the "illegal alien," which Lisa Marie Cacho has also deemed a contemporary form of "social death." As Cacho argues, "illegal aliens" have been constructed under immigration law as "permanently criminalized," and their "permanently rightless status" makes them "ineligible for personhood" (6).[20]

By figuring the *Urus* as a death ship, the novel provokes readers to see links between slave ships and dictatorships and between fugitive slaves and undocumented refugees. When the Cuban hairdresser Gonzalo tries to align his asylum status as a Cuban exile with Esteban's—"We refugees from communist countries have to look out for each other, no?" he rhetorically asks Esteban—Esteban maintains his difference, declaring: "The truth is I'm a refugee from a ship" (266). Esteban insists that while he is a refugee, he is a different kind of refugee: he has fled the ship of the *Urus*, not the state of Nicaragua.[21] The turn of phrase makes him into a refugee from a ship of state, which plays on the common and widely used metaphor of the ship of state. Gonzalo persists, insisting on the similarity of their situation with a nautical colloquial expression: "Pues, sí...But you're from Nicaragua and I'm from Cuba. *Same boat*, as they say here, no" (266). Gonzalo's linguistic use of "no" is common in Spanish, as Latin Americans frequently use "no?" rhetorically to affirm the answer to a question; at the same time, Gonzalo manipulates the phrase to impose his anticommunist, anti-Castro politics on Esteban. They are not in the same boat, since Gonzalo fled a state (Cuba), not a ship of state (the *Urus*). Esteban again maintains the distance between their situations and politics, revealing to Gonzalo that he defended the Nicaraguan Revolution fighting for the Sandinistas in an irregular warfare battalion. Gonzalo, aware of the preferential treatment in the United States for refugees from communism, advises Esteban to lie: "It will be much easier for you to get legal status here when you tell them you're fleeing those maldito Sandinistas. If you say the opposite, chico, you won't stand a chance" (267). Unlike Cubans, who were automatically granted asylum when they came to the United States because they were presumably fleeing communism, Central Americans in the 1980s had great difficulty getting asylum, due to the United States' Cold War geopolitics in the hemisphere, as they were considered labor migrants, not political refugees. Central American refugees were squeezed in what Andrew Friedman has described as a "double rhetorical vise" whereby Central American victims of "U.S.-backed governments and military men were cast not as victims of U.S. violence but potential refugees already flooding the country unless the United States continued to support those inflicting the violence" (263, 265).[22] Moreover, the crew's "ambiguous refugee status from a phantom ship" is illegible in the eyes of the law, because the United States does not grant asylum to economic refugees, let alone those who are physically and psychically harmed by labor practices in the United States (362). Esteban is rendered doubly invisible in the eyes of immigration authorities because he is a left-wing Sandinista who is fleeing neoliberal capitalist exploitation and is thus seen as a threat to U.S. interests, not as a victim of them. Esteban's declaration that he is a refugee from a ship, not from a state, positions the *Urus* as a dictatorship that he has fled. Esteban needs protecting from a U.S. citizen and capitalist, not from a Latin American dictatorship.[23]

When Esteban finally decides to leave the ship for the first time, he gazes out to Ellis Island and the Statue of Liberty, which index the problem of legality that he is forced to face as a sailor-turned-undocumented-migrant vulnerable to deportation by the U.S. state if he is caught. C. L. R. James was detained on the same island toward which Esteban gazes, facing a similar threat of deportation for violating visa regulations, when he wrote his study of Melville's *Moby-Dick*. James's reading of Captain Ahab as a totalitarian figure is crucially influenced by his interpretation of the United States' immigration system.[24] He concludes his study with a final extended reflection on his own experience as a "prisoner" on the *Pequod* of Ellis Island (143). He deems his fellow prisoners "aliens, mariners, renegades, and castaways," adding "aliens" to Melville's phrase (145). Francisco Goldman's characters are also aliens without proper visas, mariners who cannot set sail, renegades who are forced to steal food and wood to survive, and castaways who are stranded on a deserted pier in Brooklyn. Documenting how he is not treated as a human being with basic rights but as an "alien" who should be "exterminate[ed]" (143), James declares: "it was at that time that I began to be aware that what was happening to me and the others on Ellis Island was, in miniature, a very sharp and direct expression of what was taking place in the world at large" (127). What takes place on the *Urus* is also a sharp and direct, though exaggerated, expression of what takes place in the United States for undocumented "aliens" like Esteban who are an exploited class. Routed through James, whose prescient study helps us understand authoritarian U.S. power both on the *Pequod* and on Ellis Island, Goldman's novel helps us understand authoritarian U.S. power on the *Urus* and in the United States, not to mention current immigration detention centers, which have moved off Ellis Island to become part of a new detention industrial complex in which abuse and deprivation are rampant.

The death ship of the *Urus* does not only produce undocumented subjects; it also produces the physical death of Bernardo. When Bernardo's leg is badly burned, Elias tries to cure him with homeopathic and herbal medicine, but his leg rots from infection, and eventually Mark dumps him at a hospital. Bernardo dies, and, with no identification, he is buried in an unmarked pauper's grave.[25] Bernardo is disappeared from the ship and from the lives of his family and friends, who never learn his true fate, drawing parallels with the hundreds of thousands of desaparecidos who were disappeared under military dictatorships in Central America and the Southern Cone. When Esteban discovers that Bernardo is missing and there is no trace of him anywhere, the narrative recounts: "trying to comprehend or even imagine this mysterious abyss that swallowed Bernardo, he suddenly realizes that it isn't something that has been done only to Bernardo. It's something that has been done to all of them, and that they never even knew or suspected the truth makes it all the more terrifying. And makes it also too much like what happened to la Marta and to how many compas, everyone he's lost so far, another thing he's never understood until right now" (369). In Rodrigo Lazo's phrasing, *The Ordinary Seaman* "asks what happens to those who are *abyssed*? How many out there are dead without identification or even notification of their next of kin?" ("Hemispheric," 1093). This lack of notification is key, as the disappeared remain in a limbo state of uncertain death. The grammar of the word choice is important because the noun "the abyss" is used as both a verb and a condition (the abyssed in Lazo's formulation and the something that has been done to them in Esteban's formulation). The transitive verb "to disappear" is used similarly in Latin America as a noun and a condition (the disappeared).[26] Through the abyss, the novel draws attention to the larger cruel reality of disappearances in the Americas. Goldman's novel prompts us to widen the category of the disappeared and connect various kinds of disappearance and the range of regimes that have abyssed subjects from slavery and dictatorships to neoliberal capitalism and national immigration laws.[27] At the same time, as part of the Latina/o dictatorship novel tradition, Goldman's novel speaks to how Latina/os are "children of the abyss," inheritors of the ghosts produced by these regimes that continue to haunt our contemporary moment.[28]

While Bernardo disappears into the abyss of an unmarked grave, Elias and Mark disappear from the historical record, escaping detection and persecution for their crimes because their identities are untraceable. Mark boards a flight to the Yucatán to "rent a little place on the beach. Chill until it's all in the past," and Elias escapes into his Imperial Loft, embracing domestic life and paternal duties until he can come up with another moneymaking venture. There is a sharp distinction between those who are disappeared by repressive regimes like a dictatorship (i.e., the sixteen family members of Esteban's Guatemalan friend) or by exploitative regimes like neoliberal capitalism (i.e., Bernardo) and those who have the privilege and power to disappear their crimes from the historical record and evade legal sanctions with impunity. That is, Elias's and Mark's disappearing acts parallel the vast majority of political and military leaders under Latin American authoritarian regimes who have created their own disappearing acts by escaping unprosecuted for their crimes.[29]

As a phantom ship, the *Urus* embodies violent histories that are residually present in their haunting. According to Avery Gordon's formulation, "haunting is one way in which abusive systems of power make themselves known and their impacts felt in everyday life, especially when they are supposedly over and done with (slavery, for instance) or when their oppressive nature is denied (as in free labor or national security).... What's distinctive about haunting is that it is an animated state in which a repressed or unresolved social violence is making itself known, sometimes very directly, sometimes more obliquely" (xvi). The *Urus* is a symbol of the United States' neoliberal economic policies and military counter-insurgency campaigns in Central America floating back to U.S. shores in ruins, the failures of imperialism and its unresolved social violence returning home. The *Urus* paradoxically never sets sail, which is also a critique of teleological notions of history. The *Urus* embodies the lack of real progress in the United States as it moves from an era of slave ships to one of neoliberal dictator-ships. Shifting from a reliance on slave labor to undocumented labor, the *Urus* reminds us that the United States is steeped in a deep history of domination, exploitation, and forced migration. To repurpose the epigraphic words of Rediker, the *Urus* is a ghost ship shipwrecked at the edges of modern consciousness. The history of the United States is scattered with the debris of shipwrecks like the *Urus*.

Navigating the Discourse of a Shipwreck

Shipwreck narratives are widespread in Western cultural, political, and philosophical thought, and Goldman is heir to this long tradition.[30] When the Ship Visitor comes across the *Urus*, he declares, shocked, that it is a "fucking shipwreck, right here in Brooklyn harbor" (154). The *Urus*, oxymoronically, is a shipwreck in port, hidden in plain sight in a global city. Shipwrecks are usually caused by natural disasters at sea—the fault of storms, icebergs, hurricanes—but Goldman's shipwreck is a social disaster caused by the ideological and economic structures of neoliberal capitalism that enable Elias and Mark to exploit their Central American crew. I read the trope of shipwreck in the novel as indexing a material object (the wrecked ship), a state of existence (the shipwrecked sailors), and a metaphor (the symbolic economy of the wreckage), as well as a narrative device (the shipwreck narrative). The shipwreck metaphor in *The Ordinary Seaman* draws connections between different kinds of political, military, and economic domination in the hemisphere, as the ruins of the *Urus* unveil the dark underside of imperial designs.

The shipwrecked *Urus* functions as a narrative device that generates the central conflict in the novel (how to survive the shipwreck and navigate to safety), but the shipwreck is also a "nautical metaphorics of existence" (Blumenberg, 7). Bernardo tells an elderly Argentinian couple who encounter him by chance on the pier washing the crew's ragged clothes: "I think this ship is in violation of every conceivable maritime law and regulation. The truth is, we're stranded here, as much as any shipwrecked sailors on some remote island" (120).[31] Bernardo encapsulates their lack of mobility and their horrendous living and working conditions by using a simile that compares them to shipwrecked sailors. When Esteban first meets Joaquina and tells her about his and the crew's plight, the narrative relates: "'So you're a náufrago, güey,' she says. 'De veras?' A shipwrecked sailor—that's true enough. 'Sí pues,' he says, 'it's true'" (215). Esteban affirms her evaluation; she subsequently introduces him as "a shipwrecked mariner," and the Latin American migrant community in Brooklyn remembers him as "that shipwrecked sailor" (218, 257). Esteban's acceptance of the designation as "true enough" signals that it approximates his condition of existence but does not fully capture it, partly because he has not sailed anywhere and thus is not technically a sailor, but also because he is not a castaway, in the literal sense of someone who has survived the sinking of a ship. Rather, he is a laborer who is exploited and rendered undocumented while onboard a ruined ship, but since it is difficult to find an appropriate term to name his existence, he resorts to nautical language, just as when he says he is a refugee from a ship in attempting to articulate why he is not a political refugee but a refugee from a shipwrecked dictator-ship.

This metaphor of the shipwreck is so central to understanding their circumstances that the men consider inscribing it on their bodies. A group of them discuss tattoos with the Honduran El Tinieblas, whose body is covered in tattoos that represent key moments and people, making his body a text as the tattoos materialize a narrative of his life. His tattooing practices also physically imprint markings of U.S. economic imperialism, since he has tattoos of banana trees and "Chiquita Banana," representing the banana plantation where he grew up, inked on his skin. The men debate whether El Tinieblas should get a tattoo of a ship, given that he has never actually sailed. El Barbie suggests: "'Puta vos, don't tattoo anything, then'... 'Sink the fucking ship. Sink it so no one can ever see it again. Don't tattoo anything, and then you can say, Ve? Underneath here?'— and he tapped his own chest—'there's a sunken ship'" (179). El Barbie's suggestion is arresting and incredibly suggestive. By refusing to inscribe a formative moment in his life alongside the other key moments he has habitually imprinted on his skin, El Tinieblas would be staging an act of mutiny on his skin. That is, El Barbie suggests that El Tinieblas's refusing to tattoo the ship on his body would function as a symbolic act of defiance, sinking the *Urus* and turning him from a mariner into a renegade and a shipwrecker. Moreover, El Barbie suggests that El Tinieblas already carries the ship(wreck) inside himself. As El Barbie performatively taps his own chest, he implies that they can all sink the *Urus* by *not* getting tattoos because they all carry the marking deep within themselves. As I discuss in relation to Héctor Tobar's novel *The Tattooed Soldier* in chapter 4, Guillermo Longoria's jaguar tattoo celebrates his career in the Guatemalan military's Jaguar Battalion and his training in counter-insurgency tactics at U.S. military schools, and serves as a physical and symbolic inscription of his participation in state-sponsored massacres. In contrast, the absent corporeal presence of the *Urus* on the ordinary seamen marks their experience of oppression and signals their defiance of it. The metaphorical tattoo embedded beneath the surface of the skin reverses the shipwrecking. That is, it turns El Barbie and El Tinieblas from victims into resisters of their exploitation, and they become the agents of or the ones causing the shipwreck thereby terminating the owners' business venture that profits off of the bodies of the crew.

Furthermore, reading the novel through the genre of the shipwreck narrative illuminates how the nautical metaphor symbolizes the failures of U.S. economic and military imperialism. Josiah Blackmore argues that eighteenth-century Portuguese shipwreck narratives break, disrupt, and contest dominant historiographic discourses of the Portuguese Empire.[32] Though writing about and from a different time, place, and imperial power, Goldman's shipwreck narrative has a similar disruptive socially symbolic function: it breaks hegemonic narratives of the United States to reveal the ruins of imperial economic ventures and military interventions. I thus read the irreparable *Urus* as symbolizing the destruction produced by U.S. imperialism in the hemisphere and the never-ending work of repairing its disasters. With the sinking of the *Pequod*, C. L. R. James declares, Ahab "will bury himself in the wreck of American industrial civilization" (56). Unlike Ahab, Elias and Mark escape the shipwrecked *Urus*, but Goldman's revision of the shipwreck narrative likewise comments on the wreck of industrial civilization, updating it to depict the wreck of U.S. imperialism and neoliberalism in the Americas and the exploitation of subjects for their physical and narrative labor.

The shipwreck is also a mode of narration. Though discourse entails forward movement and progress, the novel focuses on stasis, on being trapped, and then on the forced movement to survive.[33] Blackmore argues that shipwreck narratives are not simply narratives that recount a shipwreck; they are also a "practice of prose writing" that entails a link between "calamity and writing" (xxi). Blackmore uses the term "discourse" to underscore the relationship between seafaring, disaster, and narration: "discourse (*discurso*) [is] a keystone in both nautical and narrative practice. A *discurso* is the route of the ship, its itinerary, and it is also the route a writer creates and a reader follows. *Discurso* is the path of the ship and the path of the narrative, and is even synonymous with narrative itself" (29).[34] Discourse aligns the forward movement of a ship that successfully navigates its predetermined voyage and arrives at its designated destination with the forward movement of a plot that progresses through various conflicts to a successful resolution at the end of the narrative voyage. The nautical and narrative discourses in *The Ordinary Seaman* are at odds with one another: the owners have one route plotted for going on a lucrative nautical venture, but the ship never undertakes its discourse, as it never sails. Instead, it is wrecked on the dock and subsequently wrecks the lives of the ordinary seamen. Despite the endless repairs they do to the ship, the men never make real progress, and the ship never sets sail. To move forward, the Central Americans have to figuratively hijack the ship and plot a new course.

If a discourse implies a linear advancement through time, the novel's discourse is fractured or shipwrecked. In terms of its formal structure, the novel is divided into six distinctive parts ("Miracle," "Desastres," "As Is, Where Is," "A Haircut," "But Luck Is Not for Everybody...," and "Scraps"), and each part is divided into numbered chapters. The novel begins with the part titled "Miracle" and a typical forward progression of plot: a man named Esteban gets a job and migrates to engage in the work—until he boards the *Urus*, which alters the plot of his life and of the novel. This first part has no numbered chapter designation, which seems insignificant until you begin the second part, "Desastres," which starts with a chapter numbered "1" and opens "one hundred and eleven nights later" with Esteban lying awake in "two rank T-shirts and jeans and rotted socks," symbolizing how the crew's hopes have been stranded (33).[35] Read against each other, the first part's title, "Miracle," gestures with dark irony toward the men's optimistic hopes that their jobs will pay well and they will return to Central America having progressed economically. In part 1, the crew arrive in Brooklyn, and when Bernardo first sees the *Urus*, he insists: "This isn't a miracle. It's a disaster" (27). Bernardo immediately recognizes that their situation is not a miracle that will help them economically improve their lives but a disastrous shipwreck. He materializes his critique in part 2 by naming the stray cat he adopts Desastres, a resistant act that dialectically opposes

Mark's naming of his dog Miracle. The novel begins with hope (the miracle) and quickly shifts to despair (the disaster), and rereading the former in dialogue with the latter reveals that the part 1 is an ominous preface that foreshadows the wreckage of the crew's lives aboard the *Urus*. In other words, when you start reading, it appears that you are simply beginning the novel rather than reading a foreboding preface, and unless you pay attention to the numeral *1* that begins the next part and indicates that it is the novel's first chapter, you drift along not realizing that the story contains at its initiation a breakage, a rupture in its very narrative framing.

The crew's predicted economic progress and the novel's presumed narrative progress are both stranded. The opening paragraph of part 1 ends by invoking the "wide-awake war dead" (3) in Nicaragua, while the opening paragraph of part 2 begins with Esteban, who "lies awake shivering," wearing rotting clothing, and fantasizing about escaping the ship (33). This parallel structuring between both parts' first paragraphs draws a link between Esteban's two lives, implying that he is among the sleepless and haunted war dead whether he is in Nicaragua or on the *Urus*, because both are embattled sites.[36] The novel also opens with Esteban's arrival at Managua's airport only to find it closed, foreshadowing how his movement will be limited. The novel thus starts out with the theme of foreclosed mobility, of mobility thwarted both on the thematic level and on the formal level, both gesturing toward a wreckage.

The ship is a chronotope, a fusion of time-space, but as a shipwreck the *Urus* is a fractured or marooned chronotope. As theorized by Mikhail Bakhtin, "in the literary artistic chronotope, spatial and temporal indicators are fused.... Time, as it were, thickens, takes on flesh, becomes artistically visible; likewise, space becomes charged and responsive to the movements of time, plot and history" (84). With respect to *The Ordinary Seaman*, time thickens and takes on the metallic flesh of the ship, and the palimpsestic descriptions of the *Urus* are layered with various histories of domination and exploitation. Likewise, the space of the *Urus* is charged with these histories, and its dilapidated disrepair symbolizes the destructions wrought by them. The space of the ship is falling apart, and time stands still, with no working clocks on the vessel. Since neither ship nor time can move forward, the crew are trapped in a static shipwrecked temporality and spatiality. Indeed, the narrative scripts this stranded temporality in terms of a ship: "the future is here and, hijueputa, look at it: a ship that doesn't move" (177). The crew's future is shipwrecked as long as they remain on the *Urus*, and so is the novel itself, since the ship is not responsive to the movement of the plot.[37] That is, the plot precisely cannot advance through the chronotope of the shipwreck. Just as the engine on the ship is dead, the novel's plot cannot propel itself forward if the setting remains the immobile ship, because all the men do is work on repairing the ship and slip into frustrated boredom, which is not enough narrative action to sustain the four-hundred-page novel.

Each of the novel's six parts begins by marking the passage of time, but mixed verb tenses narrate the novel's ambiguous sense of sleeplessness, lost time, and liminality.[38] The novel's overall treatment of temporality—frequently rendered in analepsis and prolepsis—provides a vague time frame, giving the reader a sense of being adrift, having to piece together the scraps of temporal clues the novel provides to understand precisely when events happen, while simultaneously implying that the exact order of events is less important than capturing the stagnant condition of the trapped crew, which is similar to that of people trapped in a drawn-out "low-intensity" civil war and of undocumented migrants trapped in a cycle of poverty. Moreover, time in the novel is palimpsestic because Esteban's memories of the war are constantly underneath the surface, disrupting his thoughts and experiences in the present day.[39] The novel rarely differentiates these memories by placing them in separate paragraphs or noting the shift in time and location, instead moving between the present, the past, and even the future, quite seamlessly. Esteban's interruptive memories are signs of trauma, but they also formally capture the way he attempts to navigate past and present embattlements and to repurpose the scraps from the shipwrecks of his life in order to write an alternative future.

Scraps, Holes, Ruins

As a shipwrecked vessel, the *Urus* has scraps of debris everywhere and holes all over it, and it is docked at a pier that is in ruins.[40] Scraps are a central trope in the novel—indeed, the title of the novel's final part is "Scraps" (331). Four denotations of the word "scrap" are particularly salient in relation to the novel: the material left over from manufacturing and consumption; the remains of a meal; a piece of the whole; a fragment of a narrative. By the end of the novel, Elias and Mark have scrapped their plans, and the United States Marshals Service plans to seize the ship and auction it for scrap. While the unsalvageable condition of the ship—evident in the expression to sell something for scrap—is key in the novel, it is important that the novel's final part's title is the plural "Scraps," highlighting the ways scraps occupy opposing functions in the novel. Elias and Mark treat the crew like the discarded scraps of their envisioned capitalist feast, a mere leftover burden that can be tossed aside when plans go awry. Scraps are that which is discarded and thrown away; yet they can also be repurposed or reused creatively for survival. The crew collect "weathered scraps of wood" and eat scraps of food that they find on the ship and that Esteban later steals during his nightly forays into Brooklyn (333). Moreover, in the hope of attaining aid, Esteban tells the Latino Americans he meets in Brooklyn scraps or bits and pieces of his situation, and the crew recount their own narrative scraps to the Ship Visitor. Scraps, then, signal both relations of exploitation and strategies of survival.

The Statue of Liberty looms on the horizon, visible from the *Urus* and symbolizing the limitations to their horizon of future possibilities. As Bernardo constantly repeats like a refrain, "When that statue walks, chavalos, this ship will sail," metaphorizing their own physical immobility and the impossibility of their economic mobility (45).[41] The inscription at the base of the statue is an absent presence in the text; the crew cannot see it, but it is always there, haunting their situation. Emma Lazarus's poem "The New Colossus," engraved on the bronze plaque, ends with the stanza containing its infamous lines that imagine Liberty, "the Mother of Exiles," crying out:

> Give me your tired, your poor,
> Your huddled masses yearning to breathe free,
> The *wretched refuse* of your teeming shore.
> Send these, the homeless, *tempest-tost* to me,
> I lift my lamp beside the golden door! (emphasis added)

Refuse is that which is worthless and discarded, such as scraps and trash. Esteban, Bernardo, and the rest of the crew are "wretched refuse" in the *Urus* who are "tempest-tost." The Statue of Liberty does not walk and does not provide liberty or protection to the Central Americans in the abyss of the *Urus*. She is a specter, another haunting in the novel—the ghost of unattained liberation. The invocation of the Statue of Liberty, as Kirsten Silva Gruesz has revealed through her reading of José Martí's writing about the Statue of Liberty, renders visible the crew's inability to attain liberty at the same time that it holds out a prophetic flash of a possibility of liberation in a utopian future on the horizon ("Utopia," 78). With Liberty immobile, the men must create their own kinds of refuge, rather than relying on the state or the Ship Visitor for protection.

Toward the end of the novel, Esteban thinks about his dead lover, la Marta, and how intimately he feels her absence, despite having fallen in love again with Joaquina. The scene, focalized through Esteban, reads: "We even have children, he thinks one day, feeling stuck on the ship.... So who are their children? And he thinks, They're orphans. They're everything that's invisible but still more enduring than a fucked up iron pirate ship that's made a bunch of poor men even poorer. Everything that gets lost, that never gets a chance to learn what it was going to be" (363). The novel poses the problem of futurity, more specifically that of an orphaned futurity. Esteban feels as if their love and their future have been killed or orphaned by the war. The focalization of Esteban's thoughts is vague and begs the question of who are the orphans and what causes their abandonment. On the one hand, the wording suggests that Esteban's and la Marta's nonexistent but imagined children—who would have been born in an alternative timeline in which la Marta survived the war and she and Esteban built a future together—are orphans. They are orphaned precisely because la Marta, a fellow Sandinista, was killed by the U.S.-supported Contras. Esteban's and la Marta's children are invisible, are the unrealized future that never gets the chance to exist but endures nonetheless, haunting the present. An impossible life is also an impossible narrative, and the novel is invested precisely in recuperating those stories and lives.

On the other hand, the ambiguousness of the wording also suggests that the "they" who are orphans are the men on the *Urus*. This makes sense given that, in the figurative sense of orphan, the crew have been abandoned and deprived of protection. Indeed, Esteban acts as a kind of caregiver for the orphaned crew, bringing them food and supplies. Rather than sending remittances of money back to his family in Nicaragua, he brings aid to his improvised family on the ship. As Caminero-Santangelo puts it, Esteban's "support for the crew is, in fact, a metaphorical 'remittance' paid to support those at 'home' on the *Urus*" ("Central Americans," 182). He establishes an alternative kinship structure with the crew when he cares for them and later when he helps those who want to remain in the United States by connecting them with a Latina/o American migrant community. The novel suggests that communities of mutual aid and testimonial storytelling open the possibility of new futures for the men.

In a Salvadoran restaurant in Brooklyn, Esteban finds a community of affect and aid, and he establishes a network of shared grief and solidarity. He meets many survivors of the dictatorships and civil wars in Latin America and, as what April Shemak terms an "asylum speaker," he shares his testimony with them (206).[42] Many of those who listen, "when they learn of Esteban's ambiguous refugee status from a phantom ship on the Brooklyn waterfront, offer him a temporary place to stay, a couch or floor to sleep on," and he documents their names, addresses, and phone numbers into a notebook (363). He literally calls on this network when the crew are going to be evacuated from the *Urus*, contacting everyone to find shelter for those who want to stay in the United States. This migrant solidarity network constitutes a transisthmusian and trans-American community that functions as an alternative to the model of white aid and deportation offered by the Seafarer's Institute and the United States government. It also suggests a way for economic refugees to access unofficial aid networks, given that the ordinary seamen would not be granted the aid offered by the church in the Sanctuary Movement, a political-religious movement in the 1980s that sheltered Central American political refugees and imagined itself as a contemporary Underground Railroad.[43] The novel implicitly refers to the Sanctuary Movement when it briefly mentions that Esteban "met refugees from the Salvadoran and Guatemalan wars and death squads there [in the Salvadoran restaurant], including a doe-eyed, skinny chapala chapina who'd had sixteen members of her family disappear, and until recently had been living with a group of nuns on Coney Island" (361). The nuns "helped her get out of Guatemala and were extremely kind to her," much in the same way that Esteban's many contacts kindly help the crew escape the *Urus* so they do not get deported and return home penniless (361). The ordinary seamen are refugees seeking sanctuary or safe harbor.

Yet it is important to note that Esteban refuses to help the men who are addicted to sniffing glue escape the ship. Though, practically speaking, it makes sense that Esteban would not want to ask his friends to take in drug addicts, the men were not addicts when they boarded the *Urus*. They coped with the trauma of the ship through sniffing paint fumes, and though they are now considered degenerate, Esteban's refusal to help them points to the limits of his network of aid as an alternative model. Esteban discards them from the new imagined community of Central American refugees in New York. Given the novel's revalorization of scraps, integrating the discarded fragments into a new whole, the drug addicts unsettle this paradigm of sanctuary. They foreground others who likewise disappear into the abyss—the abyss of a pauper's grave, the abyss of the unmarked graves of the desaparecidos, and even the abyss where the impossible lives of unborn children have been left. In this case, the abyss is substance abuse and other nonlegible, non–socially sanctioned modes of coping with trauma that exclude people from accessing sanctuary. While Esteban learns to be scrappy and to resourcefully repurpose the crew's situation when they are discarded like scraps and abandoned like orphans, the drug addicts do not.

Scraps are the discards, but they are also the remains. Jacques Derrida theorizes that scraps are remains that should not be thrown away but should be taken into account because they are disruptive and provide the potential to think otherwise, to show the future directions of philosophical thought that are currently unthinkable.[44] Esteban and the crew, and other refugees of U.S.-supported imperialist ventures (whether economic or militaristic), are also scraps in this sense, in that they portray the limits of U.S. interventionism and structures of aid for refugees. These characters evoke questions about alternative futurities, about the futures that are currently foreclosed under contemporary paradigms of governance and affiliation, and about futures that can be opened if social relations are transformed. Perhaps the drug addicts are the most disruptive of the remains in Derrida's sense, because they show the limits of solidarity and incorporation, left as they are at the social margins.

The novel stitches together various narrative scraps, but holes remain. The crew's testimonies to John the Ship Visitor come in bits and pieces: "they tried to give the Ship Visitor as clear a picture as they could of el Capitán and el Primero, and about everything that had happened to them since June, trying to get it all in order, interrupting each other, everyone wanting to give his own version of certain events so that the Ship Visitor sometimes had to hear the same story told over and over" (339–340). Attempting to relay their experiences in chronological terms, the crew struggle to fill the holes in their stories and suture together the different scraps of events to provide a coherent, whole narrative. The telling is intersubjective and competitive as they interrupt each other in their desire to retell things from their own perspectives. Yet they all implicitly agree not to tell the Ship Visitor a key piece of information: that Esteban has escaped the ship, has acquired a job, and is caring for them. In a parenthetical aside in the middle of a section narrating how the Ship Visitor comes to learn about the crew's fate when he queries the men about their knowledge of the ship's captain, first mate, and mysterious owners, an embedded narrative reveals another hole in Esteban's and the crew's story. "(El Capitán also asked, Where does Esteban go all the time? And they answered, No sé. Saber. Quién sabe, mi Capi? And when el Capitán asked Esteban directly where it was he was always going off to, Esteban just answered, Nowhere. Though none of this was part of the story they told the Ship Visitor.)" (342). In three different Spanish-language iterations of "I don't know/who knows," the crew declare that they do not know and, implicitly, do not have access to knowledge about Esteban's activities. On one level, the literal level, this is true, because Esteban does not share all of his journeys with the crew. But on a more strategic, rhetorical level and on the level of power relations, the crew know about and survive off of Esteban's aid, so they tactically refuse to share any of this information with the Ship Visitor. This serves as a means of fracturing their reliance on his white aid and thus their dependency.

Moreover, Elias and John are the heroic protagonists of the adventure stories they tell their lovers and friends as they use the crew for their narrative labor, but the testimonial scene on the *Urus*, as well as the novel's overall character-system, works against this narrative exploitation. It subverts the power dynamic of white narrator and brown subject/object of narration. *The Ordinary Seaman* turns the Central Americans from minor characters in Elias's and John's stories into major characters laboring to rewrite the narratives of their lives, rather than simply doing the narrative labor of making the white characters interesting. That is, though the Central American crew are exploited for their narrative labor, the majority of the novel is focalized through the titular ordinary seaman, Esteban, and functions as a testimony against their exploitation, as well as a narrative of their attempts to escape the shipwreck and survive.[45]

For his part, Esteban tells Elias that he is going "nowhere," as if he has not left the ship or is going to a place called nowhere. This is an interesting response, because Elias traps the crew on the *Urus* with fears of the disciplinary violence of what was then called the United States Immigration and Naturalization Service (INS) and of the urban violence of the surrounding working-class neighborhood, giving the crew nowhere to go on a ship that is going nowhere, disappearing them into the hole of the ship. Esteban's response highlights the lack of mobility of the crew and of the ship at the same time that it hides his activities. Holes in their narratives, thus, are also tactical ellipses. They are a means of withholding information strategically. The crew withhold Esteban's economic activity from the Ship Visitor and Esteban withholds it from Elias, purposefully doing so as a means of asserting agency, protecting Esteban's mobility, and maintaining a strategic silence or secret when faced with those in power. This kind of narrative hole or gap is similar to the coded, under-the-radar kind of communication I discuss in chapter 1 in relation to *The Brief Wondrous Life of Oscar Wao*, but instead of getting rendered formally in footnotes and the trope of blank pages, in *The Ordinary Seaman* it gets rendered formally in parentheses, evasive ellipses, and deliberate silence.

In the novel's oddest and most suggestive use of the trope of holes, Joaquina is fascinated by and collects any kitchen item that contains holes. Bewildered, Gonzalo exclaims, "Any kitchen thing with holes in it, she has to have it. What do you think a psychologist would say about that? She doesn't even cook!" (258). Gonzalo tries to trap Joaquina into the economic logic of the domestic sphere; according to his patriarchal rationale, a woman should only collect kitchen items for the utilitarian purpose of producing food to consume. Moreover, he hints that her desire for holed objects is a crazy obsession with an underlying psychological meaning, surely betraying some sort of deviance. When Joaquina takes Esteban shopping, he sees the sheer variety of perforated kitchen items and is charmed by her attempts to convince him of the "perfect...beauty" of the single utensil she has chosen from among endless options (353). Joaquina teaches Esteban to appreciate "the challenge of recognizing what makes one utensil more beautiful than the other, and the pleasure of orchestrating your own collection, one where all these utensils with holes in them, all different sizes and colors, become their own ordered little world, one without any other justification" (353). Joaquina places the colorful objects on display to brighten up the room she shares with her brothers in an overpopulated building where mainly Mexican imigrants live. Joaquina is a collector who repurposes the hole-filled kitchen objects to decorate this domestic migrant space. Moreover, Joaquina's revaluing of holes is a form of what Angela Naimou has called an "aesthetic of salvage." Naimou explicates how, in stark contrast to Elias and Mark's neoliberal imperial "economic salvage of the *Urus*," the novel functions as an "artistic practice and a mode of reading that responds to the histories of legal personhood" (51). Joaquina's aesthetic pleasure as an undocumented migrant signals a desire for something of her own, something she can order and control according to the logic of her own individual aesthetic preference.

While on the surface this seems steeped in the market logic of individualism and consumption, when read alongside the narrative holes in *The Ordinary Seaman* and all of the damaging holes in the novel, it offers an alternative model of reading and narrating.[46] Joaquina's act of loving holes serves as a model for repair, for revaluing holes. She finds the holes that populate our everyday lives and mundane possessions, holes that most people do not notice, and turns them into objects of beauty. A hole, which is traditionally read as signaling something missing or lacking, becomes in Joaquina's aesthetic vision a thing of beauty and of value. Given that Joaquina is a working-class undocumented migrant, we can also read her love for things with holes as an aesthetic means of surviving and navigating the holes in the immigration system. Joaquina's aesthetic act teaches us to be simultaneously conscious of the holes that steal agency, making subjects into discarded scraps, and the way subalterns take advantage of and repurpose holes to assert their own value and agency.

Holes and scraps are the markers of the bleak conditions locally on the *Urus* and hemispherically under coloniality, but the scraps of food and wood the crew gather from among the ruins and the holed objects of beauty Joaquina collects are also precisely the means through which the novel's characters find sustenance, refuge, and pleasure. For their part, the seamen refuse to give Elias and the Ship Visitor a key scrap of their story in not telling them about Esteban's employment. Esteban and Joaquina take advantage of the holes in the system to build a network of aid among the Latina/o American exile and undocumented migrant community in New York City.

These holes and scraps are strategic refusals and hidden transcripts that recall the means of fugitive escape and survivance enacted historically by subaltern communities in the Americas.[47]

The Brooklyn waterfront is in ruins, as is the *Urus* docked there. It is "hard to believe nothing more apocalyptic than just time has happened here," observes the narrator (132). While ruins are archives of historical violence and economic abandonment, ruins are also sites of revelation. In his essay "Apocalypse: What Disasters Reveal," Junot Díaz uses the occasion of the earthquake that devastated Haiti to meditate on the signification of "apocalypse." Explaining that "apocalypse" comes from the Greek word *apocalypsis*, which means "to uncover and unveil," Díaz argues that an apocalypse "is a disruptive event that provokes revelation." As a revelatory event, an apocalypse reveals the underlying hierarchies of power and forms of inequality and oppression that are too often veiled or disavowed. Catastrophe gives us the opportunity to be what Díaz calls "ruin-readers," or interpreters of the underlying structures and conditions that enable or bring about the disaster. *The Ordinary Seaman* provides a means of reading (and writing) the revelations in the ruins, unveiling the abuses of authoritarianism and imperial interventions and their haunting afterlives.

The Ordinary Seaman, like the other novels I examine in this book, suggests that transhistorical, transnational, and transracial comparisons are key to reading the ruins left by oppression and exploitation. How is the ruin-reading done, though, and how can a novel structure it? *The Ordinary Seaman* suggests that intersectional comparisons are integral to this process of ruin-reading. As Esteban fantasizes early on about one of los blacks who is drinking and dancing on the pier, he becomes angry when she, too, participates in their taunting, as they all throw beer bottles at the *Urus*. He thinks: "but look, there she is screaming and laughing at us too, I could drop a wrench right down her mouth, smash those white teeth like glass too. In Nicaragua we end up not just screaming and throwing bottles, we slaughter each other. And they give us the best weapons on earth to do it. Y qué? What does any of that have to do with this?" (49). This is the primary question posed by the novel. The issues of relationality and comparability are at the heart of the novel's project—they are the central perceptual, epistemological, and formal problems posed by *The Ordinary Seaman*. What does a ship have to do with a dictatorship? What does the "death ship" or "ghost ship" of the *Urus* have to do with a slave ship? What does one form of exploitation have to do with another? What does being a refugee of a U.S.-owned ship have to do with being a refugee of U.S. economic and military imperialism? What does a shipwreck have to do with narration? What does one plot line have to do with another? What do material holes and scraps have to do with narrative holes and scraps? What does economic exploitation have to do with narrative exploitation? What does the past have to do with the present? Answering these questions is a form of ruin-reading. And the more we can learn to read the ruins, to fill in the holes and stitch the scraps together to make comparisons, the more we can see what José Martí once termed "the truth about the United States," or, in Goldman's case, the truth about the *UrUS* (329).

{ 4 }

Plotting Justice

Nobody deserves terror.
Justice.
What we deserve, all of us, is some measure of justice.
—ARIEL DORFMAN, "Love Letter to America"

Historically, the most terrible things—war, genocide, and slavery—
have resulted not from disobedience but from obedience.
—HOWARD ZINN, *The Zinn Reader*

And I know that in order for me to be a full human being
I cannot forever dwell in darkness
I cannot forever dwell in the idea
of just identifying with those like me
and understanding only me and mine.
—TWILIGHT BEY, *in Anna Deavere Smith,*
Twilight: Los Angeles, 1992

Impunity for the crimes of authoritarian regimes is the norm in postdictatorship Latin American countries; very few of the perpetrators of mass injustice under the region's many dictatorships are ever convicted and punished through the judicial system for terrorizing, torturing, murdering, and disappearing civilians. Ariel Dorfman wrote the play *La muerte y la doncella* (*Death and the Maiden*; 1990) precisely to imagine putting dictatorship on trial. Set at a moment of transition in "a country that is probably Chile but could be any country that has given itself a democratic government after a long period of dictatorship," the play stages a tension-filled encounter between Paulina Salas, a woman who was brutalized, raped, and tortured as a political prisoner, and Roberto Miranda, the doctor she believes helped torture her (*The Resistance Trilogy*, 88). She decides to hold him captive in her house and put him on trial in order to exact a confession, convict him, and sentence him to death in her improvised courtroom where she serves as both prosecutor and judge. This fantasy of justice ends ambiguously as the audience is led to believe that Paulina chooses not to take her revenge, instead allowing the doctor to go free.

In contrast, *The Tattooed Soldier* (1998), by Guatemalan American Héctor Tobar, foregoes the improvised courtroom and carries the scenario of exacting justice to its deadly conclusion as Antonio Bernal, a Guatemalan leftist, kills Guillermo Longoria, the soldier responsible for murdering Antonio's wife, Elena, and child, Carlos. When their friends begin to disappear, rumored to be maimed and tortured by the military dictatorship, Antonio and Elena, university student activists in Guatemala City, flee to a rural village. The couple are later targeted for abduction and questioning after Elena writes a letter to the local government complaining about unsanitary conditions in a slum adjacent to the village. While Antonio is at work, Elena and Carlos are killed by an anticommunist civilian brigade headed by Guillermo Longoria, a military death squad member who received part of his training in U.S. military schools. As Antonio is about to board a bus to flee into exile after the murder, a neighbor indicates to him that Longoria, who is nonchalantly eating an ice cream in the park, is the killer of his wife and child. Years later when he is a refugee in Los Angeles, Antonio accidentally encounters Longoria in MacArthur Park and identifies him through his tattoo. Antonio decides to punish the ex-soldier in the name of all fellow aggrieved Guatemalans who suffered gravely under the military dictatorship. Antonio ultimately takes advantage of the chaos of the 1992 Rodney King uprisings to shoot and kill Longoria.[1] In contrast to *Death and the Maiden*, which stages its struggle for truth and justice in the domestic sphere, *The Tattooed Soldier* depicts fantasies of retributive justice as they erupt on the stage of the public sphere and plays out the deadly logic of their fulfillment. Yet Tobar's novel, like Dorfman's play, invites us to grapple with the difficult processes of attaining justice and of laying to rest the haunting specter of authoritarian rule at the personal, national, and transnational levels.

The novel stages the ethical dilemmas surrounding transnational military training, human rights violations, and impunity through a hemispheric framework that brings together two conflict-ridden sites—Guatemala and Los Angeles—plagued by military violence and police brutality. This trans-American geography aligns social justice for oppressed populations, constructing an imagined solidarity of insurgent minorities who dissent against the states that fail to protect them. At the center of the novel are two explosions: the firing of Antonio's gun at Longoria, who synecdochally stands in for the Guatemalan military dictatorship, and the three days of uprisings that erupted in Los Angeles partially as a result of the acquittal of the four white police officers whose brutal beating of an African American man named Rodney King was caught on video. These diverse acts of anger against impunity are crossed in the novel so as to illuminate one another, as each is made to resonate with the other. The novel portrays the impact of the United States' "hydra-headed, repressive apparatus that include[s] armies, police forces, paramilitaries, training centers, arms manufacturers, and think tanks," both hemispherically in Guatemala and locally in Los Angeles (Gill, 234). The novel's transnational imaginary interrogates the abuses and human rights violations that subalterns suffer at the hands, machetes, batons, and guns of the repressive state apparatuses in the Americas.

This chapter considers how a novel can plot out trans-American fantasies of justice. *The Tattooed Soldier* uses individual characters and their life stories to stand in for and dramatize national and transnational traumas, for, as Ana Patricia Rodríguez and Ileana Rodríguez remind us, "countries, like individuals, carry specific genealogies of violence, which are rooted in larger global systems of power and control enforced through local forms of (neo)colonialism, imperialism, racism, war, genocide, and impunity" (*Dividing the Isthmus*, 104). I begin by examining Longoria's training at the School of the Americas to demonstrate how the novel exposes hemispheric operations of repression dependent on problematic discourses of order and contamination. I then analyze how the two explosions at the heart of the novel—the retributive violence against the Guatemalan military apparatus enacted symbolically through Antonio's gun and the three days of uprisings that erupted in Los Angeles after the acquittal of the white police officers—articulate various grievances against institutionalized and state-sanctioned violence, both in Guatemala and in the United States. Finally, I mobilize the formal valences of plot in terms of an assassination plan and a literary sequence of events to trace how the novel's narrative structure is at odds with the two main protagonists' desires for order and just vengeance. I end by asking how the foreclosed plot of Elena's life and her collectivist-oriented activism, which challenge the sociopolitical order and insisted on structural change, offer a different model for generating social transformation and attaining justice than Antonio's individualized act of retribution. Overall, Tobar's insertion of the Rodney King uprisings into his Latino dictatorship novel asks us to read state-perpetrated violence transnationally and to imagine different intersectional, cross-racial configurations of solidarity in struggles against impunity.

Ordering Disorder

The Tattooed Soldier centers on the U.S.-funded military dictatorship and civil war and their aftereffects on traumatized and displaced Guatemalans, depicting what happens when U.S. "intervention comes home to roost," this time in a Los Angeles deeply divided by hierarchies of race and class (Juan González, 129). The novel represents this imperialist intervention and serves as a fictional counterpoint to it, functioning as a form of what Ariana Vigil has called "narrative intervention" that contests U.S. military intervention in Guatemala (*War Echoes*, 65). Guillermo Longoria, a poor, and indigenous Guatemalan campesino who was abducted by the army and forced into military service at the age of seventeen, is a member of the Jaguar Battalion, a death squad responsible for disappearing, torturing, and assassinating presumed political dissidents and for eradicating entire villages.[2] As part of his training, Longoria attends the United States' infamous School of the Americas (SOA) in the Panama Canal Zone as well as the U.S. Army John F. Kennedy Special Warfare Center and School (SWCS) in Fort Bragg, North Carolina.[3] As an agent in the larger U.S.-controlled hemispheric military apparatus, Longoria's career highlights the complicity of the United States with Central American authoritarian regimes. "Military bases, weapons, and strategic alliances with local security forces constitute the cutting edge of the U.S. empire," as historian Lesley Gill explains in her study of the School of the Americas, "and the security forces—militaries, paramilitaries, militarized police forces constitute one of the most basic forms of imperial intrusion and control" (3–4). Sergeant Longoria, a minor player in this network, serves as a cipher through which the novel represents the Guatemalan authoritarian state apparatus as well as its links to U.S. military training and imperial violence.

Longoria first visits the United States as part of a group of ten other Central American soldiers who train at Fort Bragg. Here he learns not only the counter-insurgency and torture tactics used by U.S.-backed authoritarian regimes throughout Latin America but also the underlying ideology used to justify the mass violence perpetrated against hundreds of thousands of campesinos, workers, union organizers, human rights activists, students, and indigenous peoples. A Puerto Rican soldier teaches the Central Americans "Psyops" or "psychological operations" (220).[4] In this form of warfare, he explains, "we fight terror with terror.... We fight confusion by creating more confusion"; he goes on to extol "the value of terror, the beauty of terror as a weapon.... Violence and randomness, that's the recipe. If the people believe death can come from anywhere, anytime, they will be paralyzed by fear" (221–222). As the army indoctrinates him in anticommunist ideology and counter-insurgency tactics, Longoria comes to believe that the tactical use of violence, chaos, fear mongering, and terror—in other words, the violation of human rights—is justifiable in the government's war against those who dare challenge the status quo. Many of the Cold War ideologies and counter-insurgency warfare tactics that wreaked violence across Guatemala and the rest of the continent's dictatorships are homegrown in the United States, for "under the tutelage of the United States, beliefs about professionalism, human rights, just wars, and subversion are crafted" (Gill, 11). Longoria is trained to generate disorder with violence under the premise that it will bring peace and order to the nation, and he internalizes the military doctrine that terror is beautiful, even aestheticizing it on his own skin with a tattoo.

The novel uses the trope of the diseased body to dramatize how the United States and Guatemala disseminate a transnational Cold War discourse that pejoratively paints anyone who challenges the status quo as a communist and as an infectious agent. The "enemy" is deemed "a virus, a plague. An infection spread by ideas, a disease carried on by the spoken word" that can spread and contaminate others (Tobar, 170). This discourse enables Longoria to rationalize obeying his military orders to kill civilians: "this thing they were fighting was a cancer, and sometimes the children were contaminated with it too. You killed the cousins and the uncles to make sure the virus was dead. That's what the officers said, and you had to believe it.... Guatemala was like a human body...and if you didn't kill these organisms the body could die" (64). The nation-state is imagined as an able body that is in danger of being permanently disabled by the disease of communism; therefore, like an infectious agent, the enemy must be eliminated to restore the health of the country. As Julie Avril Minich observes, "this image reveals how the use of disease as a metaphor for social decline or political crisis can reinforce totalitarian power, which brutally polices the shape and contours of the national body" ("Mestizaje," 220). These discourses of disease and cleansing that privilege certain bodies and ideologies over others to establish "order" were precisely what justified the genocidal campaign in Guatemala that killed and displaced hundreds of thousands of indigenous people, leftist students, union laborers, and campesinos.[5] Innocence is no longer possible with the metaphor of disease because anyone can catch the virus, so every murder ordered by the army is necessary. To be able to accept his new identity as a Jaguar soldier, Longoria must repress hesitation and remorse and fully internalize the discourse of the healthy nation-state that the hemispheric military apparatus disseminates.

Longoria's training at the School of the Americas and the Special Warfare Center and School fundamentally alters his worldview, and this change in worldview motivates him—indeed forces him—to shift identities. Enamored with the "insistent orderliness" (215) he finds at Fort Bragg, he develops an obsession with "order and cleanliness" (216) that correlates with the military cleansing of dissidents in the name of making Guatemala a civilized and healthy country. Longoria is thus indoctrinated into the ideology of "civilization" produced and perpetuated by modernity/coloniality: "*civilization.* What the officers back in Guatemala meant when they said they didn't live in a civilized country. Being here in the United States for the first time, he could grasp the concept. This was a country where order and cleanliness reigned supreme" (216).[6] Longoria accepts the hemispheric hierarchy of power and believes that the United States is the paragon of progress, and through his training, he learns the so-called American way and espouses the ideology of American exceptionalism.[7] The orders he receives at the SOA and SWCS, as well as in the Guatemalan army, interpellate him into a subject of empire and the Guatemalan military dictatorship. His sense of self is effectively reordered as he comes to believe that Guatemala is backward and has not fully entered modernity.

Embracing his role in bringing "order" to Guatemala, Longoria marks his skin with a jaguar tattoo when he is training at Fort Bragg, a permanent visual inscription of his service in the Jaguar Battalion. The tattoo is brightly colored, "a jaguar with a sleek yellow pelt and fierce eyes, sharp and resplendent, its mouth wide open, exposing a pink tongue rendered with such skill that you could almost see the saliva glistening" (241). The coloring of the tattoo is both vivid and ominous and is in stark contrast to the eradication of color from Longoria's personal space, whether in the barracks or later in his apartment in Los Angeles. The aggressive visual aesthetic of the jaguar, red mouth open and dripping saliva, is threatening, and the animal's "fierce" eyes parallel the "cara de matón" (face of a killer) that Longoria puts on to intimidate the civilians he preys on, both when he is a soldier and when he is retired and working in Los Angeles (25). Longoria thinks of it as "an American tattoo," and though he uses the misnomer "American" to signify the United States, in a sense it is an American tattoo since it marks Longoria's transition into a U.S.-trained Guatemalan soldier (242).[8] As Longoria imagines it, the jaguar "was born a North Carolina jaguar, but as it breathed in the tropical air it became a real Guatemalan jaguar," taking on new life and a new national subjectivity and following Longoria's reverse migration home to Guatemala after having been molded into a military subject in the United States' transnational military training center (242). Longoria sees the jaguar as tying him inextricably to the Green Berets who tattoo their signature insignia on their chests, for he, like them, is a "soldier who carried his loyalty in his skin" (242). The epidermal politics of identification creates a sense of solidarity and connectedness between military men across national-origins. The tattoo physically and symbolically inscribes Longoria's acceptance of the "civilizing" projects of U.S. and Guatemalan counter-insurgency tactics.

The figure of the jaguar he dons has links to Longoria's Mayan ancestry and the country's Mayan past, which he attempts to explain to Jake, his tattoo artist: "jaguars were feared even way back in Guatemala's history.... The Mayans built temples to the jaguar god. The Jaguars had spots that were like the camouflage uniforms the battalion wore. The jaguar stood for the new Guatemala the army wanted to build, a country of warriors and strong men, an empire like the one the Mayans had, except now they would carry submachine guns instead of spears" (241). The passage is telling because it reveals how little historical and cultural knowledge Longoria has about his Mayan heritage and the complex significations of the jaguar in the Mayan worldview and cosmology.[9] Longoria collapses the past with the present, eliding the distinction between the jaguar's spiritual significance for the Mayans and the army's use of the jaguar as a technique of intimidation and social control and as a part of the larger spectacle of terror the military stages in the theater of war.[10] The jaguar's spots function as crypsis, a natural form of coloration that allows the jaguar to blend into its environment to facilitate predation; the simile Longoria uses to connect the jaguar's spots to his military uniform, though, also functions as a form of camouflaging in that it hides the vast differences between natural biological predation and the army's hunting down of those it deems a threat. Moreover, the simile is telling because it demonstrates how the army naturalizes its rhetoric of war, deeming anyone who challenges the status quo a deadly virus that threatens national security and the natural order, enforcing this at gunpoint. Longoria's identification with U.S. imperialism is also present below the surface as he imagines that the Guatemalan nation-state has aspirations for empire.

Though Longoria sees the jaguar as part of the Mayan imperial past and as a prophetic predictor of Guatemala's imperial futurity, ironically, he is forced to disavow his Mayan heritage and espouse an affectless and hypermasculine demeanor, or a "stony masculinity," in order to become a member of the Jaguar Battalion (175). Indeed, the tattoo "announced the new species of man Longoria had become," signifying his rebirth as a ruthless military man and his new corresponding social location, which pits him against his fellow indigenous people and campesinos (241). The disavowal is a violent one as his military operations instantiate his altered role in the social order. In one scene, the Jaguar Battalion brutally hacks villagers to death with machetes, and Longoria is assigned the task of burning down a church where half-dead villagers are trapped, their ears sliced off as trophies for the Jaguars.[11] In another, they raze a village, shooting the campesinos at the market, and Longoria is ordered to execute one of the campesinas the Jaguars have spared to cook for them. In both cases, Longoria is initiated into the bloodshed that will mark his military career by means of his fear that he will be considered unworthy of his jaguar tattoo due to his subordination in racial and class hierarchies. The sergeant of his battalion "made sarcastic remarks about Longoria's trip to Fort Bragg, asking who this peasant was to receive such an honor" (248), and later the sergeant gives him a look that implies "this Indian is not worthy of the beautiful jaguar tattoo on his arm" (251). To deny his indigenous campesino roots and prove his masculinity and strength, Longoria lights the match that sets off the burning of the church and pulls the trigger that kills the indigenous campesina, who reminds him of the market women he knew and loved as a child. In these acts of violent military masculinity, he effectively kills his past self and becomes a "new species of man"; in doing so, he ceases to speak Quiché and discards his childhood name: "in the army he became 'Longoria'" (63).[12]

When Longoria leaves Guatemala and moves to Los Angeles as a retired army sergeant, he hopes to live in a country that is free of conflict and that embodies the kind of society he thought he was helping to build in Guatemala. "Order was what he was looking for when he came to Los Angeles. Order and peace, a respite from so much fighting and confusion" (214). What he finds is not the idyllic ordered cleanliness of the Fort Bragg military base, which he imagined was a microcosm of the United States, but a city divided by hierarchies of race and class. He struggles to make sense of the poverty and racial tensions he witnesses in working-class Los Angeles, given that he once considered the United States the paragon of civilization. He uses the discourses of order and contamination he learned in the army to interpret his new surroundings. "There were days when Longoria thought the same kind of infection was spreading here in Los Angeles, although the symptoms might be different from the ones in Guatemala. Los Angeles could use a thorough cleaning" (64). Reading the United States through Guatemala, as he once judged Guatemala through the lens of his experience at the military base in the United States, Longoria sees the need for a violent imposition of order, a "cleansing" of Los Angeles.

Since he can no longer engage in military operations, Longoria attempts to impose order on his new surroundings by transferring the military rhetoric of cleansing onto his domestic space and his own body, both of which he keeps "meticulously clean" (20). He lives in a colorless apartment pared down to the essential furnishings and a weight bench, with no decorations whatsoever. He obsessively scrubs his room to keep it clean of any dust or dirt, thereby engaging in a different kind of warfare, "a war of attrition" against the city he sees as filthy and contaminated (20). Marked by what cultural theorist David Batchelor has called "chromophobia," Longoria's bare and colorless domestic space symbolically represents his fear of the ideological and racial Other, of both the revolutionary dissident he was taught to exterminate and his own racial identity, which he was forced to expunge.[13] Moreover, the sterile blankness of his Spartan lifestyle is telling, as it exemplifies his desire for whiteness and how his attempts at assimilation have killed his indigenous self.

Longoria also reproduces his role as a Jaguar in civilian form, demonstrating how operations of repression cross national boundaries and how Central Americans in the United States do not fully escape the military dictatorships they have fled. He works at a mail service company, El Pulgarcito Express, for a Salvadoran named Duarte, who has his employees spy on the people who use his mail service to discover if they are engaged in any subversive activities.[14] As a member of the Salvadoran right-wing party, Duarte considers his work an extension of the army in monitoring the actions of Central Americans abroad: "Once in a great while we organize a little action to let them know we're here. A little letter, a phone call, sometimes something more serious. The newspapers get all excited and call us a 'death squad,' but it's nothing like that. Just little things. *Acciones*" (29). When customers complain about the mail service, Longoria stares at them with his "soldier's gaze, his *cara de matón*.... Anyone from Central America recognized the look.... Dead dictators and demagogues lived on in these cold brown eyes" (25–26). Perpetuating military intimidation tactics, Duarte functions as a synecdochal specter of the repressive right-wing parties, much as Longoria functions as a synecdochal specter of the military dictator. The violence of Central American dictatorship continues in the United States.

The broader context of hemispheric military repression that undergirds the novel draws parallels between military brutality in Guatemala and police brutality in Los Angeles. Longoria admires the LAPD's treatment of Rodney King, wondering if the officers were trained at Fort Bragg in Psyops because he recognizes their tactics of domination (243). As he witnesses the urban warfare that follows the acquittal of the police officers who beat Rodney King, Longoria is reminded of his counter-insurgency campaigns in Guatemala.

> What was happening on the screen was a battle bigger than anything Longoria had ever seen. It was being fought all over the city, by huge crowds, masses of people. Fire and laughter. Violence welling in the eyes of the crowd, the march of police forming battle lines. He could feel it now, this resurfacing of animal instincts. So much like the taste of blood that passed through the Jaguars when they entered a village,

when not even the doe-eyed children and the farm animals were safe from their machetes and machine guns. Longoria, agent of disorder, carrying a lighter and a little can of fluid with a smell he really liked. To see this here in Los Angeles, fire dancing from house to house, singeing everything in its path, was to remember the names of villages turned to ash: San Miguel, Nueva Concepción, Santa Ana. (272)

And, then, at a distance, emerging on the smoky horizon as if from a dream, he saw what was instantly recognizable to him as an armored vehicle of the United States Army, a desert brown Humvee. At last! Longoria began to laugh. The U.S. Army had come to save him, one of their own, a soldier trapped behind enemy lines.... Longoria looked at their faces and saw himself in the moments after his forays in the villages, smoke and flame and chaos all around him. Soldiers rolling into battle, men setting fires. Longoria playing with his cigarette lighter, the Jaguars marching through the dance of ash in the hot wind. It seemed that the demons of his memory had taken flight and were loose on the streets of L.A. A trick of his mind, a hallucination. Everything spilling from his head onto the street. (292–293)

Longoria relives the military operations in Guatemala that eradicated villages as he witnesses events unfold in the Los Angeles. The past collapses into the present through his memories of the massacres. Guatemala flickers in the background, haunting the events and framing, even overdetermining, the ways Longoria interprets the events. Longoria sees the events through the military optic he acquired as a soldier in the Guatemalan army.[15] This optic plays a trick on his mind and skews his reading of the situation because he attributes the source of the violence to the crowd and not to the state and because in Guatemala he and the army set the fires, whereas here in Los Angeles aggrieved people of color are setting the fires.

As Longoria's memories of Guatemalan dictatorial violence mix almost inseparably with present-day Los Angeles, the narrative demands we to read various forms of state repression at different times and places together as the U.S. army mirrors the Guatemalan army. Mike Davis explains that the 1992 uprisings were "accompanied and followed by massive repression coordinated, for the first time, by the federal government and involving the INS, ATF, FBI, as well as the Army and the Marines," arguing that "this official violence" is integral to characterizing the events ("Burning," 2). When the U.S. Army arrives to quell the uprisings, provide security, and establish order, Longoria feels joy and a deep sense of identification with these official state-sponsored forms of violence. His emotional investment in the hemispheric repressive state apparatus, in this case represented by the U.S. Army and its Humvees, is followed by a fleeting sense of disillusionment and futility. Feeling as if "the infection had followed him to Los Angeles," Longoria is overwhelmed by "an inchoate feeling that he had been tricked in some way he didn't understand" (292). What has "tricked" him is the transnational military apparatus and the Cold War discourses of order and illness that justify the repression of subaltern dissent against oppression and the military's false promise that by being an "agent of disorder" he can create a just and civilized society (272).[16] Longoria does not have the vocabulary to interpret what he senses emotionally; the modern/colonial ideology of civilization and barbarism and the Cold War ideology of communist threat and counter-revolutionary military protection into which he has been interpellated prevent him from understanding that injustice cannot be wiped away by injustice. Indeed, the order he longs for can never exist as long as the disorder of coloniality's inequalities structures society.

Individual Retribution against Collective Impunity

In *The Tattooed Soldier*, Los Angeles is a site for imagining and physically dissenting against different kinds of impunity in an attempt to attain a measure of justice. Ana Patricia Rodríguez posits that "impunity serves as the cultural logic that gives shape to postwar cultural production in Central America and informs the production of posttraumatic literature across the isthmus, even in those locations that did not experience war" (*Dividing the Isthmus*, 104). Tobar's novel is structured by the cultural logic of impunity in Central America, but because the text is set in a location that did not experience the Guatemalan civil war (i.e., Los Angeles), the novel is also shot through with the problem of impunity in the United States for police officers who enact violence against African American subjects. Los Angeles and popular uprisings by aggrieved people of color serve as the narrative vehicle through which Tobar's novel plays out the possibility of enacting justice and memorializing the victims of Central American dictatorships and U.S. counter-insurgency campaigns.

Distraught after encountering Longoria in MacArthur Park, Antonio tracks the tattooed soldier's movements for multiple days until he breaks into Longoria's apartment and learns that he was a member of an elite death squad responsible for many more assassinations than those of Elena and Carlos. In the bottom drawer of Longoria's dresser, Antonio discovers Longoria's most treasured possession: a photo album full of certificates and diplomas from Longoria's military training at the School of the Americas and Fort Bragg, newspaper clippings about his battalion's military engagements in Guatemala, and photographs that commemorate his involvement in the counter-insurgency campaigns. The "pictures of corpses" he keeps tucked in the back of the album feature murdered men, women, and children in a variety of postures and positions, most of them violated or dismembered, with Longoria and the men in his unit posing proudly over these dead bodies (175). Kirsten Weld has argued that the once-secret National Police archives discovered in Guatemala, which provide evidence of the crimes perpetrated by the state's repressive security apparatus during the civil war, are "paper cadavers" (3). What Antonio discovers in the tattooed soldier's room are photograph cadavers. Longoria's album is a "morgue," in the term's denotations both as a place where bodies are kept and as an archive of records in a newspaper office (175).[17] The photos serve as material evidence that captures Longoria's military past and as a disturbing chronicle of how "dead bodies come from the labyrinths of the interlocking systems of empire and state violence" (Gómez-Barris, *Where Memory Dwells*, 17). On a broader level, Tobar's novel serves as a memorial space and burial site for the victims of the dictatorship. It is a literary excavation of the mass atrocities perpetrated by the Guatemalan state with the United States' support that soldiers like Longoria attempt to literally and figuratively bury. Despite the apartment's immaculate cleanliness, Antonio is sickened by what he finds in this apartment "filled with disinfectant and perversions," for no matter how hard Longoria scrubs with disinfecting products, he cannot cleanse his life of the stain of death, as he is permanently soiled by his death squad's actions (176).

In seeing the photos Longoria keeps as war trophies, Antonio becomes a witness to the mass atrocities of the military apparatus. While he does not witness them firsthand, he feels a responsibility to bear witness to the material evidence he has seen and to the stories he heard secondhand in Guatemala about his tortured friends.

> Antonio had seen all those pictures in the soldier's rooms, those anonymous cadavers. They had passed through his hands, all the peasants and students and revolutionaries and sons and daughters hacked and shot to death with no living witnesses. He knew the people only as photographs, but he could feel that they all died alone, like Elena and Carlos, in their homes and villages and fields, without anything or anyone to protect them. Now Antonio could act for them. He could act for the massacred who had been left without fathers, husbands, or brothers to avenge them.... *I did not bury my wife and child, but I can stand and seek vengeance, for them and for the many, for the anonymous dead.* (182–183)

Antonio comes to believe that even though he cannot speak for the dead, he can "act" for them. He frames his assassination of the tattooed soldier as being done in memory of all those who have been disappeared and murdered and as a means of personally defying the military dictatorship's crimes. Moreover, given that he thinks that only men can avenge these deaths, his act is a hypermasculine means of attaining justice. He cannot name or bring back to life the "anonymous dead," but he can serve as their patriarchal protector and avenger.

Antonio vacillates between thinking about his plan to kill Longoria as a personal act of revenge and as a heroic political act. He feels the burden of the "responsibility of bringing [Longoria] to justice...because there was no one else to do it. They lived in an interval of history without courts, without the passionless procedures of official justice" (229). Knowing that "official justice" will not punish Longoria, Antonio decides to take matters into his own hands, using a gun to enforce a conviction. He has trouble deciding how and when to put his plan into action, and it is not until the Rodney King verdict is handed down and the city erupts around him that Antonio decides the time is ripe to find Longoria and exact justice. As he witnesses the masses of minorities in Los Angeles rise around him, he believes he is living a "municipal day of settling accounts, a day for all vendettas, private and public" (283). He takes advantage of the temporary reversal of power during the uprisings to attain the justice he so eagerly desires. In contrast with Longoria, who identifies with the police and the military during the Los Angeles uprisings, Antonio identifies with the masses. He envisions himself *"walking with the multitudes"* and killing Longoria *"for the unknown thousands"* (208). The crowd expresses Antonio's hunger for justice, and he decides that he can channel everyone's outrage, kill Longoria, and bring a measure of justice into an unjust world. Antonio interprets his individual act as a communal act. He fantasizes that his solitary act of retribution can re-establish justice and help end the impunity, effectively conflating individual vengeance with collective justice.

The uprisings serve as a model of action for Antonio as he sees fearless people of color demanding what they feel they are due. The events of 1992 in Los Angeles consisted of "three days of mass action—across a spectrum that includes debate, peaceful protest, and self-defense as well as looting, arson, and street warfare" (Davis, "Burning," 2). However, the events, popularly known as the Rodney King "riots," are indelibly marked in the national consciousness as race riots characterized by looting and arson rather than this spectrum of dialogic, political, and criminal activity.[18] While many people in the crowd, as the novel acknowledges, take advantage of the chaos in the streets to loot and burn, Antonio identifies with those who express a sense of grievance that they seek to rectify. When he arrives at El Pulgarcito Express in search of Longoria, the Central Americans and Mexicans attacking the building are complaining about the fact that the mail service company has cheated and robbed them; their looting and destruction of property function as a form of protest against their exploitation as well as, indirectly, against their surveillance, since Longoria and the owner, Duarte, have spied on them as well. As a reaction to "intolerable conditions," affirms Martin Luther King, Jr., "a riot is the language of the unheard" (qtd. in Goodman, 291).

It is crucial to note that Antonio does not only take advantage of and inspiration from the uprisings; his conversations with homeless Black men are also a catalyst for his actions. After unexpectedly spotting Longoria in MacArthur Park, Antonio recounts his personal history with Longoria to his new homeless Black friends, Frank and the Mayor. As he tells Frank and the Mayor about Longoria and the fact that in Guatemala "there is no one to punish the army for their *barbaridades*. No court will do it," the two men imagine what they would do if their family members were murdered and "the cops don't do shit" (177–178).[19] Outraged at the thought, the two men encourage Antonio to kill Longoria in an attempt to help him imagine attaining justice against the jaguar soldier. For his part, Antonio knows little about the Rodney King case but "wishe[s] he knew more about it so that he could understand the rage and hurt that seem[s] to overtake his two black friends" when they learn of the acquittal (273). The novel reflects and refracts Antonio's own "rage and hurt" over the impunity in Guatemala through the African American community's own sense of injustice over the impunity in the United States, where white police officers can severely beat (and even kill) a Black man and not face legal consequences. The Central Americans and African Americans express solidarity with each other in their outrage at policing and legal systems that do not protect the innocent and punish the guilty. Marta Caminero-Santangelo argues that the Los Angeles uprisings do not establish panethnic alliances between Latina/os and Blacks; rather, she suggests, "Tobar's representation of the uprisings, far from suggesting a minority coalition and cooperation, highlights the distances—indeed the deep cleavages—between ethnic groups in Los Angeles and, in some sense, the grave obstacles to any formulation of panethnic community in the United States that might successfully claim cultural citizenship" ("Central Americans," 190). While the cleavages are certainly evident, the novel is also less focused on imagining fully realized cross-racial solidarities. Instead, the novel prompts us to look at each community's grievances in light of the other's and to understand them as distinct inflections in a larger system of militarized violence, racial discrimination, class inequality, and impunity. The novel prevents us from reading police brutality and counter-insurgency warfare as entirely separate and distinct problems, asking us to understand them as part of a continuum of authoritarian domination and a larger network of state repression and militarized violence that oppresses people of color and poor people.

Different, local grievances against the repressive state apparatuses and deep-seated frustrations about injustice and impunity converge in the novel. Antonio, a displaced refugee of the Guatemalan military dictatorship and U.S. imperialism in the region, aligns himself in the homeless camp with other people displaced by modernity/coloniality, especially his two Black friends and his undocumented Mexican friend, José Juan. The homeless camp in the underbelly of the urban Global North is filled with "refugees" hunched over "like walking question marks" (41). This evocative figuration questions the celebratory and exceptionalist rhetoric of the United States as a place of "vibrant promises," which is how Antonio imagined the United States back in Guatemala (41). Moreover, Eric Vázquez, interpreting this "embodied entreaty of the question mark," argues that it gestures toward what he calls an "interrogative mode of justice," which is markedly more expansive than Antonio's formulation of revenge as justice and than the uprisings in Los Angeles that failed to address systemic inequality and impunity. For Vázquez, "the questionmark people allude to an expansive opening for claims to redress in which justice must be imagined" ("Héctor Tobar's"). Their bodies pose the question of how to rectify structural inequality and oppression locally and transnationally.[20]

Central American and African American experiences of injustice, though different in their local iterations and applications, have broader ramifications for the long, dark history of coloniality and the "civilizing" project of modernity in the Americas. As I demonstrate in chapter 3, Francisco Goldman's *The Ordinary Seaman* draws linkages between African American and Central American histories through the trope of the ship; Héctor Tobar's novel uses the Los Angeles uprisings as a conjuncture of these histories, bringing together Blacks and Latina/o Americans who express grievance through dissent. Historically the 1992 uprisings in Los Angeles were, according to Mike Davis, "a 'conjuncture' in the classical Leninist sense: an explosive, over-determined convergence (but not necessarily synthesis) of separate grievances and community histories" ("Burning," 1). The Rodney King case was not an isolated incident but part of a long history of slavery, segregation, lynching, disenfranchisement, housing inequality, unemployment, deindustrialization, environmental racism, racial profiling, and other institutionalized oppression leveled against African Americans and other minority groups in the United States. Likewise, Antonio's and Longoria's individual experiences with the murderous violence of the transnational military apparatus must be placed in the context of colonialism, banana republics, dictatorship, racial genocide, displacement, and U. S. imperial interventions in Latin America.[21] The novel's parallel between racism, poverty, and violence in Guatemala and in Los Angeles does not collapse the specific and separate local conditions of each community; rather it converges them and lets them resound off of one another. The distinct but intersecting traumatic histories that converge in Los Angeles expose the "stretched-out spatial networks of imperial violence" (Friedman, 266). Reflecting each other, they outline a transnational problem of inequality and repression that must be acknowledged and addressed.

The explosive anger in Los Angeles over police brutality and unequal justice under the law expresses and amplifies hemispherically the anger of aggrieved and displaced Central Americans, asking us to see each community's plight as a mirror image of the other. The novel's Latino counter-dictatorial imaginary "infuses the clamor for civil rights with a claim to sovereignty on an international scale; retribution involves reversing the history of conquest and subordination" (Flores, 200). Yet the novel does not imagine solidarity between insurgent minorities so much as it imagines the insurgency of minorities as being in solidarity. That is, it imagines there is a shared experience of disenfranchisement, displacement, impoverishment, repression, and impunity. The intersections of resistance represented in the novel give voice to the repressed dissent and underrepresented rage against the authoritarian practices and racialized police brutality employed in Central America and, under the aegis of "democracy," in the United States.

Narrative Scales of Justice

The Tattooed Soldier has a multiperspectival, multitemporal, and multigeographic narrative structure. This structure, with its shifting points of view and fractured chronology, positions Los Angeles as a reflection of Guatemala and fractures the binary between Antonio's and Longoria's two opposing ideological positions and social locations. Antonio believes that he and Longoria are foils of one another. "*We are opposites balancing a scale, we are mathematics. I am tall, he is short. I live under the sky, he lives under a roof. He has a girlfriend, I am alone. He has a job, I do not. He is the killer, I am his victim*" (229). Antonio and Longoria are "opposites balancing a scale" in another sense, for as characters they are weighted equally in the novel, since both of their life stories and perspectives are given equal narrative space. In the novel's larger character-system, each has a roughly equivalent amount of character-space. The novel's overall structure of narration challenges any simple binary between good and evil. Longoria is not wholly evil, while Antonio is not wholly good. As readers, we are drawn into Antonio's desire for revenge and identify with his sense of injustice. At the same time, we read the world from Longoria's point of view and understand the socialization processes that forged his identity and the institutions that shaped his worldview. Though Longoria symbolically embodies the genocidal acts of authoritarian violence perpetuated by the U. S.-supported Guatemalan government, he is a also victim of circumstance who struggles to make sense of the world with an ideology that obscures relations of domination and leaves him with a confusing, inaccurate reading of his own social location.²² Like Antonio, we crave justice and an end to the impunity, but we also recognize that Antonio's individual assassination of Longoria cannot seamlessly function as a form of collective justice for those who were killed, disappeared, and displaced by the military dictatorship. The novel thus refuses a facile demonizing of Longoria and a corresponding romanticizing of Antonio.

The novel's form shows how individual motives and sociohistorical conditions are complex and radically entangled. In chapter 5, I focus more at length on the use of foil characters as a literary strategy in Cristina García's *King of Cuba*; while García's novel also fractures constructed binaries, her novel rotates between opposing points of view. In contrast, Tobar's novel rotates between opposing characters at the same time that their points of view directly interrupt each other and the past frequently interrupts the present. This novel formally models how to see from another's point of view. Antonio and Longoria, as well as Elena, focalize the narrative and recount events from their individual and diverging worldviews. These alternating perspectives offer a more complicated portrait of the unfolding events than would be possible if the novel were focalized through only one of the characters. As I will demonstrate, the shifting focalization and intersecting plot lines rupture the novel's revenge plot and beseech other visions of justice and means of ordering society.

The novel's tripartite structure imitates the crisscrossing of lives through intertwining focalizations, and its repeated flashbacks formally instantiate how the past violence lingers in and even shapes the present. Part 1, "Antonio and the Sergeant," focuses on Antonio's and Longoria's individual lives in Los Angeles while intermittently flashing back to their pasts in Guatemala. Antonio and Longoria alternate focalizing the events: Antonio focalizes the first and third chapters; Longoria focalizes the second and fourth chapters. In chapter 5, this rotating structure is interrupted when Antonio and Longoria cross paths for the first time in MacArthur Park. When Antonio spots Longoria's jaguar tattoo, the novel stylistically imitates the way Longoria's appearance disrupts Antonio's life and jumps abruptly to Longoria's vision of events, as he looks up from his game of chess, sees Antonio, and thinks to himself that Antonio has "una cara que da lástima" (a face to be pitied) (78). Just as Longoria's physical presence interrupts the forward trajectory of Antonio's life, Longoria's point of view abruptly interjects itself into Antonio's focalization. The encounter sends Antonio into a tailspin of memories and terror until he realizes that he need not fear because Longoria does not remember him and is no longer an armed soldier. With poetic irony, Longoria's chess opponent declares "Checkmate," and part 1 ends with this reversal of power dynamics, foreshadowing how Antonio will kill Longoria and figuratively topple the king or, in this case, the dictator-figure. Antonio and Longoria's physical meeting alters the construction of the novel, as a long flashback sequence ensues and part 2 of the novel begins.[23]

In contrast to part 1, part 2, "Antonio and Elena," has a very traditional chronological plot structure. It recounts the development of Antonio and Elena's romantic relationship, their flight to San Cristóbal, and the murder of Elena and Carlos. Unlike the chapters in part 1, those in part 2 are focalized by Elena, and the action takes place entirely in Guatemala. The narration follows their courtship and Antonio's increasing involvement in politics but focuses most heavily on Elena's activist entanglements and their "*internal exile*" in the interior of the country after their political activities as students make them targets of the state, forcing them into hiding (108). Unlike Antonio, Elena does not settle easily into her exile and is increasingly disenchanted with their middle-class domestic lifestyle and her own pregnancy. Feeling trapped, she decides to take action and investigate what is causing the high infant mortality rate in Colonia La Joya, discovering that the city's garbage dump and the local residents' excrement are contaminating the river's water supply and poisoning the colonia, which lies along the riverbank. The tropes of contamination and sanitation link this scene to the discourses of disease, order, and cleansing that permeate the novel, which opens with Antonio and José Juan getting evicted from their apartment in Los Angeles, thereby becoming homeless undocumented migrants. Searching for a place to bathe, the pair discover that the Los Angeles River, which runs through the city, is "not a river, [but] a sewer," infested with trash, chemicals, and excrement (73). The city's undocumented migrants and homeless population bathe here, as it is the main source of natural public water. This contaminated river resonates with the one in Guatemala. The rivers in each country mirror each other, as both pose health hazards to impoverished communities that lack access to clean water. When Elena investigates the "source of the infection," she discovers that while the immediate source of the deaths may be microbes, the real killer is environmental racism (58). Contrary to what Longoria has been led to believe, the source of the "infection" he is trained to fight is not the "cancer" of communism but a symptom of institutionalized inequality and oppression (64).[24] Material filth threatens the physical bodies of the poor, revealing that the real danger is not demands for social justice—in the form of either Elena's protest letters or urban uprisings—but the inequitable distribution of resources and wealth. While part 2 stylistically differs from the rest of the novel because it is focalized by Elena, proceeds chronologically, and does not jump between nation spaces, the recurring tropes lead the reader to make these structural analyses and transnational connections.

As in part 1, Longoria again interrupts their lives and the narrative structure. The final chapter of part 2 recounts the events leading up to and culminating in the murder from both Longoria's and Elena's perspectives. In an abrupt switch, the final chapter of part 2 begins with Longoria's point of view, not Elena's, emphasizing formally how Longoria will soon silence the plot of her life with his gun. For his part, Longoria is leading a brigade to "apprehend the two subversives," Antonio and Elena, in order to subject them to "interrogation and clandestine execution," after her investigations and letter of protest have caused suspicion about their real identities and political orientation (140, 147). Antonio survives because he is not home, but one of the men accidentally kills Carlos, and Longoria deliberately kills Elena when the other two members of the brigade attempt to rape her. Part 2 concludes with Longoria, having successfully completed another political assassination, stopping for an ice cream break in San Cristóbal, and the novel replays the scene where Antonio spots Longoria eating ice cream, which ended the first chapter of the novel, but this time it focalizes the events through Longoria's perspective. While Longoria's face is burned indelibly into Antonio's memory, Longoria barely registers Antonio staring at him, an entirely forgettable moment in his life. The novel's "iterative narrative"—to use Gérard Genette's term for repeated incidents seen from a different character's perspective as well as present events that remind the characters of past events—highlights how life altering the murders are for Antonio and how common executing an assassination is for Longoria (189).

The novel leaps forward temporally and northward geographically as it begins part 3, "Antonio and Guillermo," by returning to the present time in the United States, with Antonio having crossed paths with Longoria in the park. Part 3 recounts the events that lead to Antonio's killing of Longoria, as well as Antonio's and Longoria's experiences of the Los Angeles uprisings; the novel ends with Antonio pondering the significance of the uprisings and of his actions. Unlike the previous two parts, part 3 does not follow a set pattern. In five of the nine chapters, Antonio and Longoria rotate between focalizing a chapter, and in the other four chapters, they both focalize events but there is no set rotational pattern. In part 3 the organization is much more irregular than in parts 1 and 2, and flashbacks occur erratically and more frequently.

Shifting between temporalities, nation spaces, character perspectives, and plot lines, the novel formally reflects how the specter of traumatic pasts haunts the present. Time and space interject, collapse, morph, and repeat throughout the novel. A characteristic sense of in-betweenness permeates *The Tattooed Soldier*: "Antonio spun in the flux between decades and countries, time and space distorted. He was in a park in Guatemala, a park in Los Angeles. The present, the past, somewhere in between" (79). If the novel had been written as a linear narrative with one singular perspective narrating the events, it would not have captured the feelings of in-betweenness and the violent pasts that haunt both Antonio and Longoria. The novel's form plays out the ways the past constantly interrupts the present and shapes conditions of possibility. The novel's use of disruptive chronologies registers the afterlife of memories of atrocities and reflects the paradox of trying to move forward while addressing the wrongs of the past. Using a repetitive chronology that I analyze in chapter 1, Junot Díaz's *The Brief Wondrous Life of Oscar Wao* depicts how the trauma of dictatorship affects the postmemory generation and how the cyclical nature of violence gets visited upon this generation through Oscar's death in the cane fields. Using a disruptive chronology, *The Tattooed Soldier* formally registers how traumatic memories interrupt the present; at the same time, it establishes similitudes between geographical sites, temporal events, and national discourses and practices of repression.

Integral to these formal politics is the way the novel plays with the various significations of "plot" in its overall design of exploring transnational justice and impunity.[25] Antonio's revenge is plotted in that he plans it and mulls over how to get away with murder and that it is the main plot development in the novel and the central conflict to be resolved.[26] In *Reading for Plot: Design and Intention in Narrative*, Peter Brooks theorizes about "plots and plotting, about how stories come to be ordered in a significant form, and also about our desire and need for such orderings" (xi). *The Tattooed Soldier* mobilizes plot both in terms of the architecture that structures and gives an order to the narrative—that thread that allows the basic plot to be summarized on the back of a book jacket even as the events and emotional landscapes sketched out are much more complex—and in terms of the need and desire for order and meaning—that narrative desire for comprehensibility and for a just social order expressed by the characters in the novel as well as the desire for narrative cohesion that we as readers also crave. The novel is shot through with multiple kinds of "order": there is the narrative order or sequential arrangement of the novel, there is the desire to maintain order or discipline that Longoria learns in the military, there are the military orders or directives that Longoria follows, and there is Antonio's desire to restore order or justice and end impunity. Plot functions as a means of tracking the intersection between these various kinds of orders and desires.

The novel employs "desire as a narrative thematic" and "desire as a narrative motor," using the desire for justice as the central theme of the book as well as the motor that drives the plot to its resolution (Brooks, 54). Importantly, though, the narrative form is at odds with the two main protagonists' yearnings and fantasies. The novel disrupts both characters' differing desires for order by foiling Antonio's desire to restore order to an unjust world and Longoria's desire to impose order through a "cleansing" of society. The novel portrays how Longoria's desire for order stems from his counter-insurgency training at U.S. military schools and reveals how this indoctrination resulted not only in genocide but also in the death of Longoria's indigenous self and the colonization of his mind. The novel interjects Longoria's life story throughout, which humanizes him and unsettles readers' sympathies with Antonio's hatred of Longoria and Antonio's plot to rectify injustice. The novel's emplotment through multiple focalizers, frequent flashbacks, and a transnational geography prevents a simple resolution to a complex ethical dilemma. Longoria is held accountable for his actions, but the novel leaves open-ended the question of how to attain just accountability. In other words, though the novel's revenge plot is resolved with the murder of Longoria, the novel does not resolve the larger plot for justice that is at the root of both kinds of violent dissent in the novel, whether enacted by Antonio or by the Mayor, Frank, José Juan, and the other people of color involved in the Rodney King uprisings. The search for justice and the quest to repair community remain unfinished at the end of the novel, disrupting the characters' and readers' desires for closure.

Despite punishing the tattooed soldier for killing Elena and Carlos, which symbolically represents holding the Guatemalan military dictatorship accountable for its crimes, Antonio realizes as the novel concludes that the reversal of power is only temporary. Like Longoria, who is left trying to grasp why he feels he has been deceived, Antonio is left grasping for how precisely to understand the ethics of the "beautiful disorder" he witnesses in Los Angeles (305).[27] With the city in postuprising ruins, he wonders about the righteousness of his act. "*The revolutionary is guided in all his actions by great feelings of love.* . . . Antonio wondered if throwing a rock was an act of revolution and thus also an act of love. José Juan running off to set a fire, Antonio pulling a trigger. Ten thousand people taking things and breaking windows because they were angry. . . . No, it was absurd to mistake rock throwing and looting for an act of love, but Antonio was willing to allow for the possibility" (306). Antonio ponders whether destruction and the toppling of hierarchies of power, however briefly, can be revolutionary. He fantasizes that ruins can be a catalyst for renewal and that new forms of solidarity can emerge in the light of the new day. The novel, focalized through Antonio, imagines a very different kind of cleansing from the kind of political and racial cleansing that Longoria subscribes to: "All the brooms on the streets now—they were definitely an act of love. The sweeping and the sweeping, strangers meeting to collect a treasure of shimmering shards. We are cleaning now. Here is the true brotherhood of the city" (306). Throwing a rock and cleaning shards of glass are acts of destruction and of rebuilding, and they complement each other. They are, Antonio hopes, part of the same process of revolutionary love, a precious treasure of shards broken in defiance that can now be collectively pieced back together to form a new future.

Antonio is unsure, however, whether killing Longoria has been in service of the revolution to topple authoritarian regimes and end impunity. The novel's closing lines depict Antonio remembering Elena and wondering how she would responded to his actions: "If only

Elena were here in Los Angeles.... If she were alive, Elena would put her arms around him and whisper all the answers in his ears" (307). The specter of Elena invoked at the end of the novel is compelling, especially given that Antonio met Elena when she was "reading *Nicaragua Avenged*, an account of the assassination of Anastasio Somoza, thinking that the bastard got what he deserved. Immersed in the gory details of the dictator's demise—he was blown up by bazooka-wielding guerillas" (83).[28] Engrossed in the political history of dictatorship in Nicaragua, Elena does not notice Antonio, the future avenger of her death, approaching her for the first time. The encounter foreshadows Antonio's assassination of a soldier in the military apparatus that upheld Guatemala's dictatorship. Yet when Elena later witnesses firsthand the disappearance of a working-class protester in Guatemala who is surely going to be tortured, she imagines not the killing of those in power but their imprisonment: "one day there would be prisons for these men. A zoo for gorilla generals who ordered silence. Iron cages for the ape soldiers who grabbed people from the street in broad daylight" (95). When she takes action, Elena does not opt for armed revolution or for individual retribution; instead, she dissents against the injustices she sees through peaceful protests and letter writing. Her motto is: "the revolutionary is guided in all his actions by great feelings of love," an ideal she associates with one of her heroes, Ernesto "Che" Guevara, after seeing these words painted on a mural with his image (90). How precisely to define revolutionary action and love is what Antonio grapples with at the end of the novel as he invokes Elena and considers the enduring significance of the events that have transpired in Los Angeles. How Elena might have imagined justice in more restorative and loving rather than retributive terms is left dangling in the air with the image of a collective cleaning that is very different from Longoria's violent vision of cleansing. Indeed, the novel does not answer the question as to whether Antonio's actions are just because it leaves open-ended the definition of revolutionary love.

The novel's scale of justice, or the way the novel calibrates justice, takes into account the victimization of both Antonio and Longoria, thereby leaving readers to debate how to heal the wounds caused by dictatorship and how to achieve justice, given the restraints of impunity and of structural racism and inequality in the Americas. "How can those who tortured and those who were tortured co-exist in the same land? How do we keep the past alive without becoming its prisoner? How do we forget it without risking its repetition in the future?" ponders Ariel Dorfman (*The Resistance Trilogy*, 146).[29] The possibility of a different solution from the one offered by Antonio's gun, a future of just coexistence, flashes up momentarily through the spirit of Elena, who participates in leftist student organizing, attends mass demonstrations, and writes letters of protest against structural oppression. Her nonviolent forms of challenging the sociopolitical order and her insistence on structural change contrast sharply with Antonio's individualized act of retributive justice.

Before Antonio and Longoria cross paths in MacArthur Park, the novel depicts a moment of peaceful dissent that highlights the path not taken by Antonio and a possible alternative plot that can never unfold because it is foreclosed by Elena's murder. A massive number of people from Central America and the United States gather in MacArthur Park carrying banners that read "SOLIDARIDAD CON LA REVOLUCIÓN SALVADOREÑA / ALTO A LA REPRESIÓN EN EL SALVADOR Y GUATEMALA / APOYO TOTAL A LA LUCHA ARMADA" (Solidarity with the Salvadoran Revolution / Stop the Repression in El Salvador and Guatemala / Total Support for the Armed Struggle) (67). Calling for the end to military repression in El Salvador and Guatemala and peacefully expressing support for the revolutionaries seeking to topple U.S.-supported authoritarian regimes, the hundreds of demonstrators in the Los Angeles amphitheater and the hundreds more on the surrounding embankment "sang out in a chorus: '¡Presente!'" (68). They assert their presence and voice their resistance to the military dictatorships and U.S.-supported counter-insurgency forces that attempt to disappear them from the national stage as viable political actors (68). On the podium leading the chants, Longoria sees a small woman with "thick eyebrows and flat peasant face" and fantasizes "stuff[ing] his fist in her throat," using violence to silence their cries of "¡Mientras haya pueblo, habrá revolución!" (68). Their act of expressing collective solidarity with the people of Central America, so different from the disorganized rage against the system that is depicted during the Rodney King uprisings, offers a brief glimpse at alternative means of social transformation, at the same time that the posters express support for armed revolutionary struggles. The fact that they are in the United States and able to protest without fear of being massacred or disappeared, a privilege that baffles and enrages Longoria, is certainly at work in the scene.[30] We can read the unnamed female leader as a stand-in for Elena. She embodies Elena's collectivist and activist-oriented ideals. Had the plot of Elena's life not been foreclosed by Longoria's gun and had Elena gone into exile abroad, she might have emerged as a leader in this diasporic social justice movement.[31]

Trans-American alliances emerge in the diaspora as urban cities provide an opportunity for solidarity between Central American migrants and U.S. people of color, reconfiguring the contours of the "pueblo." Rather than having "el pueblo" signify the people of one individual nation-state, the imaginary of "el pueblo" at this protest is transnational and rooted in political and socioeconomic struggles in Central America and in the United States that, though similar and different, share a common desire for radical equality. The scene ends as "a thousand brown-skinned fists rose simultaneously in the air, surrounding [Longoria] like a forest of bare, knobby tree trunks" (68). The mass of people rooted to the earth in a park in Los Angeles expressing their dissent against military dictatorships, death squads, and U.S. military aid and interventionism, as well as their solidarity with leftist and working-class struggles, challenges Longoria and his worldview.[32] Throwing a single fist in the air, this embodied gesture of political resistance resonates with Brown Power and Black Power movements. Yet this protest is a foreclosed political imaginary and collectivity in the novel because Longoria, not Antonio or Elena, encounters the rally. Bereft of an activist community, Antonio resorts to violence instead of banding in solidarity with other aggrieved refugees, undocumented migrants, and people of color.

The novel asks us to consider what happens when an individual takes justice into his own hands and uses a gun to exact retribution against a member of the military apparatus who murdered his family. The novel simultaneously presents an intimate and complex emotional portrait of Longoria as an indigenous campesino who is forcibly conscripted into the army. The novel contextualizes this within the broader hemispheric context of military training and ideological indoctrination, as well as destitute poverty, structural racism, and police brutality in both Guatemala and Los Angeles. The Los Angeles uprisings are, in Min Hyoung Song's words, "a literary-cultural event, an important source of tropes for imagining the seemingly endemic social problems plaguing the United States and the country's possible futures" (3). In Tobar's novel, these events are an occasion for highlighting endemic structural oppression in both the United States and Central America and therefore also a means of reflecting on other possible futures in the Americas. This trans-American scope reveals how local and transnational hierarchies of power and inequality must be dismantled if lasting justice is to be achieved.

Overall, the novel offers multiple paradigms through which to interpret the ethics of Antonio's killing of Longoria. Reflecting on her own theatrical production about the uprisings in Los Angeles, *Twilight: Los Angeles, 1992*, Anna Deavere Smith explains the importance of a sustained creative examination of people's reactions to injustice: "sometimes there is the expectation that in as much as I am doing 'social dramas,' I am looking for *solutions* to social problems. In fact, though, I am looking at the *processes* of the problems" (xxiv). Similarly, *The Tattooed Soldier* does not offer a solution; instead, it explores the processes of the problems of violence and impunity in various forms. Confronted with the reality of the historical transition to democracy in Chile and the trial of former dictator General Augusto Pinochet, Ariel Dorfman cannot imagine a way out of the impasse facing the country that so desperately needs to reveal the truth about the atrocities of the dictatorship while rebuilding under the ominous shadow of very powerful armed forces poised to retake control if they are brought to court to answer for their human rights violations. So in *Death and the Maiden*, Paulina does not get to exact her revenge and feel a sense of justice attained.[33] By situating his novel outside Guatemala and the constraints of a nation transitioning out of authoritarian rule and into democratic rule, Tobar frees the literary imagination to fully play out the fulfillment of Antonio's desire for retribution, which is unimaginable in another time and place. While the novel resolves Antonio's revenge plot, it leaves the larger plot for justice unresolved.

Antonio hopes that his act of retributive justice can function as restorative justice, but the novel refuses to endorse this fantasy.[34] At the level of story, the novel's events follow a revenge plot, but at the level of discourse, the novel plots a different course. The novel's story plays out the events of retributive justice, whereas the novel's discourse sets the conditions for restorative justice.[35] The novel creates a dialogue between Antonio's, Longoria's, and (to a lesser extent) Elena's worldviews and desires, in addition to revealing the conditions that shape their different worldviews and desires. Antonio and Longoria never dialogue about, let alone come to a shared understanding of, the harm done, but the novel's multiple perspectives and its empathetic backstories do account for the harm done to Antonio and Elena, as well as Longoria. In other words, thematically, the novel is about revenge and punishment through retributive justice, but formally, the novel models the process of dialogue essential for restorative justice and illuminates the need for reparation and healing over retribution.[36]

As *The Tattooed Soldier* suggests, the questions of how to achieve a more just world and whose vision of justice should prevail are very much up for debate. Viet Thanh Nguyen's articulation of what he calls "just memories" of atrocities provides one useful model for moving forward. Nguyen conceptualizes a "doubled model" that entertains both "the ethics of recalling one's own and the ethics of recalling others." "In a doubled ethical memory," posits Nguyen, "remembering is always aware of itself as being open-ended and in flux, rather than being satisfied with fixity and conclusiveness" ("Just Memory," 151). *The Tattooed Soldier* grants narrative space and narrative voice to complex experiences of violence in which victim and victimizer sometimes occupy both positions. This narrative act of remembering domination is rooted in a process that establishes linkages between and accounts for the specific kinds of state violence in Guatemala and the United States.

Like the other Latina/o novels I have examined thus far, *The Tattooed Soldier* does not offer a prescriptive model for ending impunity; rather, it taps into our deepest desires for justice and invites us to grapple with past trauma and present forms of structural violence in the hope that we can imagine a radically different postdictatorship future. As I demonstrate in chapter 2, Salvador Plascencia's *The People of Paper* asks us to consider the militarization of the U.S.-Mexico border and the surveillance of undocumented migrants by federal migration authorities in our conceptualization of dictatorial power; *The Tattooed Soldier* asks that we consider the policing of racial minorities by local and federal law enforcement as well. Tobar's novel centers on the Rodney King uprisings, but the text also gestures backward toward the civil unrest in Watts, and, given our contemporary moment, the novel continues to be relevant to recent examples of racial profiling and police brutality as well as the civil unrest across the country inspired by these events. After a white police officer gunned down and murdered an eighteen-year-old Black teenager named Michael Brown in Ferguson, Missouri and the city erupted in civil unrest and mass protests, Héctor Tobar penned a column in the *Los Angeles Times* titled "Reading Ferguson: Books on Race, Police,

Protest and U.S. History." Tobar offers a list of books to help contextualize the civil unrest in Ferguson within other examples of racial unrest provoked by white police and mob violence, from arrests and beatings to murders and lynchings. Attentive to the history of violence against people of color and the problem of the color line, Tobar includes the Zoot Suit Riots in 1943 as well as the Watts Riots in 1965 and the uprisings in Los Angeles in 1992, thereby insisting that we read Mexican American history alongside African American history alongside Guatemalan history and that we not disaggregate racialized state repression and dissent by studying only individual racial groups. Tobar creates an intersectional reading list that insists on reading violence against Black and Brown people as part of the larger history of the operations of white supremacy in the United States and across the Americas. Ending the list with a creative production, Tobar recommends Anna Deveare Smith's *Twilight Los Angeles*, noting that, for him, the highlight of the play is the Black former gang member Twilight Bey's meditation: "Twilight is that time of day between day and night....I call it limbo....So sometimes I feel as though I'm stuck in limbo, the way the sun is stuck between night and day in the twilight hours." The notion of being in limbo, betwixt night and day, at the cusp of a new day when darkness begins to recede to give way to first light, captures the twilight of the Los Angeles uprisings represented in the closing pages of *The Tattooed Soldier*. In the crepuscular light, Antonio is left without a solution, and the novel is left without an ethical resolution, stuck in the twilight of justice, searching for answers and for a different, more just world.

{5}

The Fall of the Patriarchs

> *Las mujeres reconocemos, constantamos, que nuestra experiencia cotidiana concreta es el autoritarismo.*
> As women we recognize, constantly, that our concrete everyday experience is authoritarianism.
> —JULIETA KIRKWOOD, *Ser política en Chile*
> (Being Political in Chile)

> *Feminism is not simply the struggle to end male chauvinism or a movement to ensure that women will have equal rights with men; it is a commitment to eradicating the ideology of domination that permeates Western culture on various levels.*
> —BELL HOOKS, *Ain't I a Woman*

> *If revolution incorporates feminism it will transform itself.*
> —MARGARET RANDALL, *Gathering Rage*

In Cuban American Achy Obejas's short story "We Came All the Way from Cuba So You Could Dress Like This?" (1994), the unnamed narrator relates in a wry tone that her father, a right-wing exile, believes that their family members "are living, breathing examples of the suffering Cubans have endured under the tyranny of Fidel Castro" (113). Counter to her father's opinion, the story works to align the two men. The narrator relates how her "father will stand up in Miami and cover his heart with his palm, just like Fidel, watching on his own TV in Havana," the two men mirroring each other's actions as the Cuban national anthem plays because a Cuban boxer has won an Olympic medal (120). When the narrator tells her father about a rumor that the boxer "practiced his best boxing moves on his wife," her father retorts, "Yeah, well, he's a Communist, what did you expect, huh?," blaming the boxer's physical abuse of women on political and economic ideology rather than on gender ideology (120). The story puts pressure on this narrative by delinking the exile's construction of communism as the source of violence and oppression, drawing attention instead to heteropatriarchy. When the narrator challenges her father about his self-declared reasons for migrating to the United States to give her a better life by suggesting that his motivations were instead rooted in class-based aspirations and masculinist competition, her father, infuriated, physically censors her accusations. "And then my father will reach over my mother's thin shoulders, grab me by the red bandanna around my neck, and throw me to the floor, where he'll kick me over and over," recalls the narrator (121). As he beats his daughter, the story creates a connection between the father and the Olympic boxer, revealing that patriarchy, not communism, is at the root of domestic violence.

What interests me about Obejas's short story is how it draws parallels between the dictator figure and the exile figure, suggesting that the Cold War binary that constructs Cuba as a site of communist oppression and the United States as a site of democratic freedom is both false and obfuscating. Cristina García's novel *King of Cuba* (2013) likewise draws connections between exile politics, heteropatriarchy, and authoritarianism. Set in the near future of 2015, the novel follows the final days of Goyo Herrera, an eighty-six-year-old embittered Cuban exile, and El Comandante, the eighty-nine-year-old unnamed dictator ruling over Cuba.[1] The novel switches between the narrative perspectives of these antithetical octogenarians who reflect on their ailing bodies, their disillusionments, and their potential legacies. For over half a century, Goyo has dreamed of killing El Comandante and becoming a hero for the Cuban exile community, and the novel culminates with Goyo shooting at El Comandante while he is giving a speech at the United Nations. Interspersed between the main narratives about the exile and the dictator are a series of vignettes and notes narrated by Cuban men and women from a variety of social locations and occupations.

This novel provides an interesting case study because it shares a number of the formal conventions of Latin American and Latina/o dictatorship novels. García follows the Latin America boom generation's technique of centering the dictator as a main character and focalizing consciousness; at the same time, she employs a number of the formal techniques I have analyzed thus far in other Latino dictatorship novels, such as notes at the bottom of the page (employed by Junot Díaz), the metafictional appearance of the author (employed by Salvador Plascencia), an aesthetic concern for the resourceful repurposing of scraps (employed by Francisco Goldman), and the juxtaposition of two politically opposed perspectives and an assassination plot (employed by Héctor Tobar).² Despite its formal alignments, as I discuss in the introduction, *King of Cuba* fits awkwardly into the Latina/o tradition because of its critical depiction of the Cuban Revolution and because Cuba under and after Fidel Castro is categorically different from the right-wing dictatorships that are the objects of critique in the other Latina/o dictatorship novels I have examined. My attention to dictatorship novels by Latina/o writers from a number of different national-origin groups reveals how Latina/os have differing experiences of and even conceptualizations of dictatorship while sharing a commitment to challenging authoritarian hierarchies. *King of Cuba*'s depiction of heteropatriarchy as an authoritarian social system thus provides an important case study that enriches our understanding of the conceptual work and formal politics of Latina/o dictatorship novels.³

This chapter examines *King of Cuba*'s transnational critique of heteropatriarchy in Greater Cuba. The term "Greater Cuba" moves beyond the Cold War rhetoric that ossifies a strict binary between Cubans on the island and Cubans in exile, instead foregrounding the "extended and somewhat pretended geography" of Cuba that encompasses various sites of Cuban cultural production on and off the island (Muñoz, "Performing Greater Cuba," 402). I begin by examining how the novel breaks down the binary between El Comandante and Goyo by positioning the dictator figure and the exile figure as foil characters whose many similar character traits foil their imaginations of themselves as polar opposites, exposing their similar investments in hypermasculinist hero narratives. I contend that the novel stages the death of these two priapic patriarchal subjectivities to articulate the desire for an alternative option for Greater Cuba. I then unpack the ways the vignettes and notes that interrupt El Comandante's and Goyo's narratives generate what I call a "resolver" aesthetic, that formally captures the strategic negotiations of power hierarchies and the resourceful and creative means of survival amid scarcity. Though Goyo's left-wing daughter Alina is a minor character, I end by demonstrating how a "resolver" interpretive practice attends to the scarce narrative attention she is granted and resourcefully read her alongside several other defiant daughters of the counter-revolutionary exile generation in U.S. Cuban fiction to reveal an alternative vision of liberation and art in Greater Cuba.

Foiling Hypermasculine Hero Myths

King of Cuba follows the model of the Latin American dictatorship novels that explore the consciousness of the dictator figure through free indirect discourse; at the same time, it expands on that model by crossing the Straits of Florida to explore the consciousness of the exile figure, likewise through free indirect discourse. The dictator figure *and* the exile figure are both the main objects of critique in this Latina dictatorship novel. García thereby adapts the genre of the dictatorship novel so as to critique exile politics more specifically and more broadly to critique entrenched political binaries and heteropatriarchal ideology in Greater Cuba. The two main characters, Goyo and El Comandante, are locked in a mutual hatred for each other across the "clichéd ninety miles of bitterness" (Quiroga, 10). El Comandante considers exiles like Goyo "gusanos" (4), the revolution's invective for traitors, and Goyo considers El Comandante a "tyrant" (10) and "despot" (16) who has destroyed the nation of Cuba and Goyo's own life. Each is invested in what José Quiroga calls the "fully developed scripts" with which Cubans on the island and in exile frequently interpret each other. "From the political point of view of the Cuban state, allegiance to the social project of the revolution is the mark of *cubanía*, just as from the political point of view of exile, opposition to the project is the essence of what being Cuban is all about," and Cristina García structures her novel around this oppositional stance (xii).

The dictator and the exile are antagonists, and the novel's structure reflects their antagonism. Sections and chapters rotate between focusing discretely on El Comandante and on Goyo.[4] The inter- and intra-chapter rotations between El Comandante's plot line and Goyo's plot line are interrupted by short vignettes narrated by various characters.[5] The two men's lives are separated by geography, and their narrative sections are separated by vignettes; this marked division of narrative action and character-space mirrors how these two figures espouse different political and economic ideologies.

Yet Goyo and El Comandante are not as different as they believe or as the novel's basic structure suggests, for they are foil characters. In the narratological sense, the term "foil character" refers to "a character in a work who, by sharp contrast, serves to stress and highlight the distinctive temperament of the protagonist" (Abrams, 225). García's representation of Goyo and El Comandante tweaks this narratological formulation of foil characters to draw similarities despite their presumed contrasts, revealing their similar temperaments and character traits. Their shared characteristics include: they are octogenarians who are suffering from a number of illnesses and are shrinking, they are plagued by solitude, they are obsessed with their manhood and virility but suffer from bouts of impotence, they are philanderers who believe that their wives should be faithful and subservient, they are power and status hungry, they are illegitimate sons of rich men, they are disappointed by their children, and they have a predilection for Latin maxims, the writings of José Martí, and cigars.[6] The literary device of foil characters does more than simply draw out the similarities between the two characters, though. The nonnarratological denotations of the noun "foil" and the verb "to foil" help articulate how foil/foiling functions as a multivalent narrative strategy. The multiple significations of the noun and the verb that apply to the novel include the following: a sheet of metal that produces a mirror reflection; a person or thing that serves as a contrast; a defeat or failure; to ruin a plan; to frustrate; and to overthrow. Despite their *contrasting* political ideologies, El Comandante and Goyo *mirror* each other in their similarities, *reflecting* each other's mutual investment in the authoritarian regime of heteropatriarchy. Goyo plans *to overthrow* El Comandante and become a celebrated exile hero, but the assassination attempt is a *failure*. El Comandante orders a grand historical re-enactment of the triumphs of the revolution, but his *plan is ruined* by the theatrical production *Bay of Pigs: The Musical!*. The novel ultimately *frustrates* the political leader's and the exile's desires to die heroically as symbols of revolution and freedom, as both characters are *defeated* by heart attacks. By scripting El Comandante and Goyo as foils and then foiling their quests to be heroes, the novel demythologizes their celebratory narratives—of the successful revolution and of the "freedom fighters" who will save the victims of exile—which have dominated in Cuba and in Miami, respectively, and exposes the ways they both espouse the dictatorial form of heteropatriarchy.[7]

Having "cojones," or the colloquial "balls," as in guts or bravery, is central to both characters' notions of heroism. Cojones yokes heroism and masculinity, exposing how the mythos undergirding both exile politics and the revolution is steeped in heteropatriarchy.[8] Depicting the men in decidedly unheroic terms, the novel satirizes the hypermasculinist vision of heroism and power that both characters espouse. In doing so, the novel demythologizes "[el] mito de la masculinidad latinoamericana" (the myth of Latin American masculinity) that Gabriela Polit Dueñas identifies as at the center of dictatorships in Latin America and of Latin American dictatorship novels, while simultaneously demythologizing the myth of exile masculinity (53).

The bodies of women serve as the stage on which Goyo exercises his masculine hero fantasies. Given Goyo's predilection for infidelity and his reliance on sex for validating his sense of self, it is not surprising that part of the origin of his nemesis narrative between him and El Comandante has to do with a woman. Goyo was smitten with a pianist named Adelina Ponti whom he took on three dates until, according to Goyo, she "fell under the tyrant's spell" (69). Adelina becomes pregnant, but El Comandante does not recognize the child as his son, and when she later commits suicide, Goyo blames El Comandante. Though he tells himself that he is avenging his father and brother and all other exiles, in the final minutes of his life as he stands in the United Nations, the only person he thinks about is Adelina, making his attempted assassination less an act of political defiance and more the act of a spurned and jealous lover. The fact that Goyo's and El Comandante's dueling masculinities are fought over the memory of a woman's body generates a "double social critique: of the patriarchal sexual economy as well as authoritarianism" (Tierney-Tello, 11).

El Comandante is obsessed with the virility of power, which the novel parodies through various phallic episodes. In a key moment in El Comandante's childhood gender formation, El Comandante's mother reassures him: "Ay, mijito, your pinga will be the greatest in the land, in all the Americas, perhaps in all the world" (8). She assuages her young son's insecurity by telling him he will have the "greatest" (as in the biggest and the most important) penis. Exaggerating for narrative effect the association of the phallus with power, the image is laden with undertones of domination and imperialism as it moves from the level of the nation to the hemisphere and then to the globe. This is also a disturbing account of how a mother responds to her son's curiosity about his genitals, which implicates women in perpetuating patriarchy.[9] With this childhood socialization in hypermasculinity, the little boy starts to dream about his foretold grandiose penis: "he imagined his pinguita growing and growing until it floated high in the skies, a massive flesh-toned dirigible draped with parachute huevones and a proud snout that served as the control room for the whole impressive operation and that nobody—not even the Yankees, with their warships and gun batteries—would ever dare shoot down" (9). The exaggerated image of a massive airship penis is grotesquely hilarious. The image is telling as it connects the penis to the warship and the phallus to war, tying masculinity to power and then to military prowess, capturing virile military power. With its "proud snout," the penile airship embodies the ego-driven arrogance of military revolutionary leaders such as El Comandante. At the same time, the dirigible is an anti-imperialist airship resisting "Yankee" military power, which metaphorizes the "revolutionary masculinity" that undergirds El Comandante's sense of self (Saldaña-Portillo, *The Revolutionary*, 77). The ambivalent negative valences of phallic power and positive valences of anti-imperialist defiance in the descriptions of the penile airship symbolically capture the failures and the successes of the revolution. Given that this scene occurs in the novel's first chapter, it also sets the stage for the novel's satirical critique of heterosexism and its depiction of El Comandante as, to pun on a colloquial term, a dicktator.[10]

In addition to phallic imagery, both Goyo and El Comandante identify with stellar imagery, which provides a fitting metaphor for linking the two kinds of domestic dictatorship the men represent. Goyo nostalgically recalls his relationship with his daughter Alina when she was a child: "once he'd been her sun and she a tiny, eager planet in his orbit" (20). As the patriarch of the family, Goyo relishes being the sun around which his young daughter orbits because it places him as the central figure in her life and because she eagerly seeks his attention and approval.[11] Goyo laments that his daughter no longer worships him and now is markedly critical of his politics. The sun, at the center of the solar system around which all the planets revolve, exerts a gravitational pull on the planets that is centripetal. The novel depicts patriarchy as a centripetal discourse, that, like authoritarianism, seeks monovocality, centrality, and dominance. Goyo not only longs for a position of unchallenged authority, he also uses disciplinary force to maintain his household rule, violently enforcing patriarchal notions of deference. Pressured by Luisa to use physical violence to discipline their son for using drugs when no other tactics work, Goyo blackens Goyito's eye, dislocates his jaw, breaks his arm, and finally puts a gun to his head (105). Subjected to corporeal punishment for breaking his father's household rules, Goyito becomes the victim of his father's gun, the very weapon Goyo will later fire at El Comandante. The gun serves as a symbolic means of connecting the violent acts Goyo commits in the private, domestic space and in the public, political space with his phallic weapon. Moreover, the only other description in the novel of physical violence as a form of punishment and disciplinary correction occurs in relation to the tortured hunger strikers in La Cabaña prison. Domestic violence in the United States and penal violence in Cuba are of course different kinds of violence, but the novel suggests that both are authoritarian and are rooted in the exercise of patriarchal authority.

For his part, El Comandante imagines he is both the sun and the brightest star in the sky, thinking he is the most stellar, so to speak, of Cubans and of leaders. As he tries to mentally break the hunger strikers in La Cabaña prison, he flaunts his disciplinary power by slowly relishing a lavish multicourse meal as they suffer the anguish of hunger. Midway through the meal, he declares, "But remember this: you won't create a new solar system in which I am not the sun. Even after I'm gone, the heat of my presence will be felt" (137). El Comandante imagines he is the sun and the citizens are planets who revolve around him because of the inescapable pull of his gravitational force.[12] The dictator-as-sun is an apt metaphor for the centripetal nature of authoritarian power, as well as a strikingly egocentric analogy. As he thinks "glumly" about the state of the country, he claims that "nobody wanted to buckle down and do the hard, anonymous work of building the Revolution brick by brick. Every last cubano craved the limelight, but there simply wasn't enough room for eleven million stars. Just one" (167). In this version of the stellar metaphor, El Comandante wants to be the most revered person, the brightest star in the sky. While he believes that the revolution has been, is being, and will be built out of the communal and anonymous work of the people, the novel reveals that he is above this socialist, collectivist paradigm, as he is the star on the stage of politics.

When read together, Goyo's and El Comandante's mutual identifications with the sun highlight the patriarchal construction of power in which the dominant father figure is at the head of the household or nation, at the top of gendered hierarchies of power, and at the center of everything. In her study of experimental fiction written by women under the dictatorships in the Southern Cone, Mary Beth Tierney-Tello observes that feminist writers and activists "came to see authoritarianism as an expression and outgrowth of patriarchal oppression" (6). *King of Cuba* likewise points to the patriarchal foundations of authoritarian power as it introduces the image of the male figure of power as the sun around which all others should revolve. Importantly, this sun metaphor first appears in relation to the patriarch of the house, not the patriarch of the nation; the novel later connects the metaphor to the figure of the dictator, thereby moving from the domestic familial dictatorship of Goyo to the domestic national dictatorship of El Comandante. At the root of these two differing kinds of domestic dictatorship—one occurs in the domestic sphere of the house and the other in the domestic sphere of the nation—is heteropatriarchy. Richard T. Rodríguez has demonstrated the necessity of "interrogating kinship configurations wedded to masculinity, nationalism, and heteropatriarchy" (18). Goyo's and El Comandante's visions of heroism and of power are rooted in this triad of masculinity, nationalism, and heteropatriarchy. The two different domestic dictators at the center of *King of Cuba* provide an occasion to interrogate the underlying logic of the heteropatriarch as the dictatorial head of the family and of the nation.

The novel's alignment of patriarchal and revolutionary rhetoric highlights what Margaret Randall has identified as the "fundamental error" of the Cuban and Nicaraguan revolutions: "their inability—or unwillingness—to develop a feminist agenda" (16). The so-called New Man was the model for the new human being that the Cuban Revolution propagated, but as various scholars have exposed, the model was flawed because it was not rooted in an agenda that valued and prioritized the experiences of women, queer folks, or people of color. As Randall charges in her study, "in all the socialist experiments there has been an emphasis on constructing a model human being: socially responsible, generous, internationalist, healthy in mind and body. But what is the message, if this new model is male, heterosexual, light skinned, and with conservative personal values?" (86).[13] El Comandante is a light-skinned, heterosexual male who is socially conservative because he believes women should be subservient and that he can treat women as disposable commodities with his numerous affairs. This points to the failures of the revolutionary left, represented by El Comandante in the novel, to divest from heteropatriarchy and from phallic conceptualizations of power and thus begs the question of how to build a truly transformative or decolonial revolution without first ending heteropatriarchal ideologies and structures of power.

By representing the dictator and the exile as foil characters, the novel also highlights the dictatorial politics of the conservative Cuban exile community. As María Cristina García puts it, "the exile community was often as repressive and authoritarian as the government they sought to overthrow" (121). Cuban exile groups in South Florida have historically used slander, harassment, intimidation, vandalism, boycotting of businesses, political blacklisting, and at times even bombings and murders. The combination of paramilitary tactics, propaganda, political action committees, and economic pressure created a monolithic political position that repudiated Fidel Castro, supported the embargo, and attempted to marginalize anyone who questioned that stance or was even neutral about Castro or the embargo.[14] Constituting what Alejandro Portes and Alex Stepick have called a "moral community" (137) characterized by a "ferocious right-wing frame" (139), the Cuban exile community in South Florida has created a hegemonic outlook and a close sense of we-ness.[15] It has also frequently been accused of "encouraging political intolerance, racial bigotry, and sexism" (M. C. García, 202). Goyo is intimately a part of this exile community with his network of personal friends, his economic success, and his constant use of exile websites that rail against the Cuban government.

After receiving an anonymous email with only a map of the Everglades, Goyo decides to find "the band of Freedom Fighters" he is convinced are in the mangroves training to overthrow El Comandante. In doing so, Goyo follows the legacy of his brother who fought and died in the Bay of Pigs invasion (66). Cuban American paramilitary actions, intermittently and clandestinely supported by the U. S. through the Central Intelligence Agency (CIA), were most active in the 1960s and 1970s, but given the setting of the novel in 2015, Goyo's journey into the mangroves in search of armed counter-revolutionaries is anachronistic.[16] The "theatricality of the Everglades" stages Goyo's investment in a hypermasculine narrative in which he will wield a gun and fulfill the dreams of the right-wing exile community (69). His quest is a delusional one, though, for the armed men in fatigues whom he encounters in the mangroves turn out to be figments of his imagination. The novel thereby suggests that this counter-revolutionary fantasy is no longer historically viable or desirable.

Goyo journeys into the mangroves in search of the past and a way to live out his exile fantasy of being a successful counter-revolutionary fighter; for his part, El Comandante seeks to commemorate the revolution's victories and reconnect to his glory days as a revolutionary fighter. El Comandante requests an epic multiday historical re-enactment of the Bay of Pigs invasion; instead, he is presented with a piece of musical theater starring "amphibians toting toy machine guns" who defend their island against "mercenary pigs" who invade with "cardboard cutout[s]" of bomber planes (177).[17] Hilariously defying the genre of historical re-enactment, *Bay of Pigs: The Musical!*—complete with the over-the-top exclamation point to declare its enthusiasm for military history in song—celebrates the infamous Cuban victory at the Bay of Pigs while simultaneously flouting El Comandante's desire for a masculinist performance of anti-imperialist prowess and military solemnity.[18] The program cover features "a vintage photo" of El Comandante looking quite dashing at the height of the Bay of Pigs invasion: a megaphone in one hand, a pistol in the other, the ubiquitous cigar in his mouth" (176). The photo captures the iconic "barbudo" in military fatigues, with cigar in hand, who symbolized revolutionary and anti-imperial defiance, inspiring leftist struggles across the Americas.[19] El Comandante, however, is played by "Commander Frog," a bearded frog in fatigues who chews on a cigar and shouts orders while intermittently bursting into song. The megaphone in the photo indicates that El Comandante is directing the show, just as Commander Frog is directing the battle plans, and the phallic symbols of the pistol and the cigar symbolize military prowess and Cuban masculinity. "The Revolution had fashioned itself a male affair, a matter of strong, tough, long bearded guerillas expelling the island's invaders," which is precisely how the musical re-enacts the history under El Comandante's orders (Hodge, 629). Yet placed in the body of a frog and played by an actor who has a lisp and "woodenly" recites his lines, Commander Frog is far from the dashing hero and preeminent orator whom El Comandante imagines himself to be and seeks to memorialize (178). Moreover, as José Quiroga notes, "the romance of the bearded revolutionaries produced the early images of the revolution, the photographic register of the golden years." Analyzing the performance artist Ana Mendieta's *Facial Hair Transplant*, in which Morty Sklar shaved his beard and Ana Mendieta attached it to her face, Quiroga argues that Mendieta's barbudo signals "the end of the *barbudo* as historical star, the death knell of its symbolic significance in the present" (181). The disjuncture between the photograph of El Comandante as a defiant anti-imperialist hero, his representation as the bearded singing frog on stage, and his now eighty-nine-year-old self watching the play elicits a similar effect. It highlights the romance of the barbudo that, according to El Comandante's orders, the play is supposed to commemorate as a historical hero and relevant symbolic model for Cubans in the present. Yet this romantic representation, in the form of a bearded frog with poor acting skills, elicits laughter and amused entertainment more than revolutionary fervor or renewed dedication to the vision of the New Man put forth by the revolutionary barbudos, suggesting the need for a new model to orient the future of revolutionary struggles.[20]

Both El Comandante and Goyo spend the end of their lives worrying about being heroes lauded by history and fearing no longer being the sun at the center of the family and the nation. They cling desperately to the centrality of their heteropatriarchal positions of power. The novel ends by staging the fall of its twinned patriarchs at the levels of both plot and narrative form. The theme of autumnal decline is temporally structured into the novel's tripartite division. Each part is labeled as a three-day time period: July 26–28, August 13–15, September 8–10.[21] The temporality of the novel's organization moves from summer to fall, structurally mirroring the autumnal decline of the two generational political positions that the octogenarian main characters represent.[22] The third part's date is significant because of a female figure, which symbolically calls for the displacement of the Cuban revolutionary and counter-revolutionary imaginaries that place men and masculinity at the center of their memorialized hero narratives.

The novel's last chapter is entitled "Exeunt," a stage direction that indicates actors should exit the stage (229). As a kind of metafictional indication of the end of the novel, "exeunt" sets the stage, so to speak, for the exit of the characters from the story-world of the novel. "Exeunt" is Latin for "they go out" and gestures toward El Comandante's and Goyo's predilection for quoting Latin phrases, a point reinforced by the Latin epigraph to the final chapter: "Sic transit gloria mundi" (Thus passes the glory of the world) (231). The phrase captures the passing of their heteropatriarchal and hypermasculinist dreams of glory.

The trope of the foiled and failed hero is structured through autumnal decline as the novel ends by killing both characters' desires to die immortalized as heroes.[23] Goyo, believing he has shot and killed El Comandante, falls to the ground and dies of a heart attack while thinking, "a hero. Sí, he would die a hero" (234). The novel trails off with ellipses as Goyo expires but then continues with the dramatic irony that El Comandante has not fallen because of Goyo's bullet but because he too is suffering from a heart attack. Mirroring Goyo's foiled dream of a hero's death, El Comandante thinks, "Damn it, he should've taken the fucking bullet. He'd wanted to die in battle, on horseback, like the great Martí. Or like Caesar, looking his killers in the eye, the blood between them the last word" (234).[24] El Comandante wants a masculinist death in battle or at least from an assassin's bullet; instead he dies in a decidedly unheroic manner, his body having broken down from mere old age. The scene is also humorously ironic because throughout the novel El Comandante believes he is exceptional yet he succumbs to a common killer, a heart attack. The novel's central conflict between the octogenarian revolutionary and counter-revolutionary figures is resolved in the denouement. And the resolution is quite final: death. Through twin deaths, I suggest, the novel attempts to kill the myths attached to both the old conservative exile generation and the generation that unquestionably celebrates the revolution.[25] *King of Cuba*, then, dramatizes the fall of the patriarchs, in the sense both of their physical deaths and the deaths of their relevance and their ability to represent models of futurity.

A Resolver Aesthetic

Twenty vignettes and twenty-five notes are interspersed throughout the novel, interrupting and sometimes challenging El Comandante's and Goyo's narratives. Though they are much shorter than El Comandante's and Goyo's sections, typically running one or two paragraphs in length, the vignettes are titled, so they constitute discrete individual sections in each chapter. Placed next to asterisks at the bottom of the page and in slightly smaller font, the notes are also short, ranging from one to eight lines of text.[26] The notes and vignettes are inserted between Goyo's and El Comandante's narratives, mimicking how Cubans find the means to build a life in between or create a life out of the cracks in power and the economy. The vignettes and notes formally instantiate the ways people survive and exist in between the two hegemonic positions the old men represent—the revolutionary state and the counter-revolutionary exiles—that have dominated political discourses in Greater Cuba. The vignettes and notes fracture the main focus on the dictatorial old men and interject other stories, perspectives, commentaries, and experiences into the novel.

The artist Zaida del Pino's vignette about building a space of her own and the corresponding note on "resolver" metaphorically captures the formal function of the vignettes and notes in the novel. "I waited years for an apartment in Havana," explains Zaida, until, fed up, she decided to take matters into her own hands: "I built my own place in between these two old mansions in Vedado. It's gloomy and narrow, but I shift a spotlight around to where I'm painting y me resuelvo" (39). Undaunted, Zaida makes due with the poor lighting and the limited amount of space between the two enormous houses, once markers of upper-class wealth, that loom over her makeshift home.[27] Zaida's space-claiming is an act of asserting agency and an attempt to survive and thrive in a country where resources are scarce. An asterisk next to "me resuelvo" leads to a note at the bottom of the page that reads:

> *Resolver*, to resolve, is Cuba's national verb. This could mean anything from "resolving" a cake for a niece's quinceañera to "resolving" the Revolution's overreliance on imports.
> —*Fulgencia Correa, grammarian* (39)

Indeed, "resolver" is a common word that Cubans use to articulate how they survive by "resolviendo" or inventing a solution to a difficult situation. Though the translation of "resolver" would be "to resolve" in the sense of to solve, to decide, or to settle in the English denotations of the word, the word has a variety of connotations and usages in Cuban Spanish, including to resolve, to solve, to make do, to figure something out, to survive with what you have, to reinvent, and to resourcefully get by. I posit that resolver in *King of Cuba* is a strategic act and an aesthetic practice that entails a creative solution when faced with limited options.

As the novel's note suggests, resolver is an important practice of survival, negotiation, and reinvention. Resolver came into common usage in the early 1990s during the so-called Special Period in Time of Peace that designated the severe economic crisis that followed the collapse of the Soviet Union and the resulting disappearance of the subsidies it provided Cuba. The word became a widely used verb to describe how people creatively found solutions to the Special Period's attendant economic challenges, and it remains in use today despite the formal end of the Special Period because of continuing limited access to certain material goods and services.[28] Resolver is a mode of strategically working within or around the system to fix a problem, to gain an advantage, or simply to get by, using ingenuity to make do with what is available.[29]

Resolver is a communal practice on the island, and the notes and vignettes capture the means by which everyday people resolve situations.[30] Each note and vignette ends by listing the characters' names and occupation. Naming them calling attention to their professions suggests that to understand what the characters recount we must know how they labor to live amid the scarcity of material goods. In one vignette, the arborist Eusebio López recounts how during the Special Period some street vendors covered "scummy mop threads with batter and bread crumbs" and sold them as "fried steaks" while others "melt[ed] Chinese condoms as 'cheese' for pizzas" (31). Eusebio opens his vignette with an interrogative sentence construction that begins "Did you hear the one about...," making it difficult to discern whether he is relating a story, a rumor, or even a dark joke. His anecdotes resonate with those of the celebrity chef Hortensia Ramos, who relates in a note how "at the sentimental behest of El Comandante," she hosted an episode of a cooking show during the Special Period that taught people how to make "palomilla steaks" out of "pounded grapefruit rinds" (42). Whether the novel is recounting practices that occurred historically, inventing these incidents, or exaggerating them, their presence in the Cuban popular imaginary speaks to the intertwined discourses of scarcity and inventiveness that García draws on for the multiple voices in her novel.[31] Used with humor in the novel, her "resolver" aesthetic draws attention to the scarcity of resources alongside the abundance of creativity in response.

Resolver is a marker of resourcefulness as well as illicit activity. The notes and vignettes chronicle a number of illicit practices, but as the factory tour guide Yevette Aguirre posits rhetorically in a note, "*stealing* is an ugly word, Papito, but I ask you this: when I steal your entry fee from the state, why do you call that 'theft'? Everyone here works for slave wages so I ask you: who's robbing whom?" (91). Yvette resists the stigmatizing designation of her actions as stealing, questioning what constitutes theft in the context of poverty. Similarly, the vignette by the chambermaid Idealia Ferrer relates how tourists do not leave them tips, not even "as much as a miserable peso for cleaning their rooms"; in response, the maids pretend a tourist's towel is lost so that the hotel charges the tourist a fee, and then they "find" the towel and receive a couple of pesos for doing so (93). The towels are a strategic way to make extra money and to redistribute wealth on a small scale. In referring to these kinds of activities as resolver, the term and the actions function as a means of addressing, or resolviendo, the challenges of living in Cuba with scarce resources; thus "the use of the word becomes itself a way of *resolver*, for the word covers and legitimizes the struggle for survival" (García-Alfonso, 7). The notes and vignettes formally give voice to modes of resolver while simultaneously legitimating them.

The artist Zaida is working on a series of paintings called "Buscando Carne en La Habana" (Looking for Meat in Havana), a title that gestures toward the dual meaning of meat in the sense of food and in the colloquial sense of physical bodies (40). The paintings comment on the inaccessibility of meat for most people in Cuba at the same time that they gesture toward illicit economies of sexual desire there, including sex tourism and prostitution. Indeed, strategically selling one's body for money is another resolver strategy. Zaida's art exposes the contradiction between the state discourse about the black market and the reality that the black market provides meat, not only in the form of the commodities of food and sex but also as a means of survival for those who engage in its illicit economy (40). As Sujatha Fernandes observes in relation to Cuban visual artists, "it is widely acknowledged that the black market is necessary for survival but, officially, of course, it doesn't exist.... Official rhetoric continues to promote a fantasy of the benevolent, providing state, and black-market activities transgress revolutionary morality.... Visual artists aim to expose these contradictions and provoke public acknowledgment of the black market" (156–157). Zaida's art aestheticizes everyday people practicing resolver amid the shortages, capturing what it is like to live without pigs after the Bay of Pigs incident and the U.S. embargo.

Zaida's figurative search for meat represents the resolver tactics she uses to be able to paint. The dialogic relationship between Zaida's vignette and the note on resolver appended to it draws a connection between the vernacular expression "me resuelvo" and aesthetic production. In her discussion of "resolver" and "inventar" in Special Period fiction, Esther Whitfield notes that these verbs represent "practices for survival whose structural proximity to artistic creation, or to making something of nothing, haunts the period's literature," much as Zaida's resolver strategy for building a space of her own haunts her art. Both the theme and the aesthetic of Zaida's paintings are shaped by having to produce her paintings in limited light with limited materials. Because she is forced to paint with a "medieval palette" because of the shortage of art supplies (García, 40), Zaida's art is characterized by "an aesthetic that has its basis in material lack" (Whitfield, 37). Zaida creatively navigates her circumstances in order to produce art and inserts this experience into her painting series, which makes her artistic practice simultaneously a resolver aesthetic practice.

The queer theater director Orestes Mejías likewise relies on resolver tactics to stage *Bay of Pigs: The Musical!* given the dearth of resources to fulfill El Comandante's extravagant request for a multiday historical re-enactment and the fact that he is forced to direct the production. After denouncing the regime, Mejías goes into hiding and is found "surviving on crabs" in the swamps near the Bay of Pigs (148). Mastering the art of resolver to stay alive, Mejías subsists on what is available in his immediate environment. An asterisk after "crabs" marks one of the novel's most explicitly confrontational notes, in which a crab catcher, Gumersindo Pérez, relates how he hunts the island's massive crustaceans. Portraying them as dangerous, Gumersindo ends with this confession: "sometimes I fantasize that the crabs will rise up and fight back—an army of them, claws waving, refusing even us" (148). This note is inserted underneath a discussion between Orestes and El Comandante about the musical, which Orestes assures El Comandante will "be a showcase for both El Líder and the Revolution" (148). The note, attached to the information that Mejías has been resourcefully surviving on crabs, aligns the dissident crabs with the queer theater director who, El Comandante notices with reservation, has "something wrathful in his expression" (148). El Comandante warns Mejías to be careful or he will be "sleeping with the fishes," an allusion to Mejías's personal history of persecution and the collective persecution of queers and dissenting artists in Cuba (148). If we recall that crabs move horizontally and that the expression "crabwise," which plays off of the sideways movement of crabs, is an adverb that means "in a sidling or cautiously indirect manner," then the note and *Bay of Pigs: The Musical!* both work crabwise as indirect critiques of El Comandante's dictatorship.[32] They function discursively and formally as critiques from below, whether from the bottom of the page, like the note, or from the "low" genre of the musical. Mejías uses a resolver aesthetic, making do with the situation at hand by writing crabwise and working under the threat of violence.

The range of resolver tactics depicted in the novel serves as a stark counterpoint to the Herreras' overconsumption of food, drugs, and material products. Goyo is a rich landlord who refuses to fix the buildings he owns, and his "considerable fortune" finances his wife's accumulation of goods and his son's debauchery (10). Luisa accumulates an astonishing amount of material possessions in her life. When she dies, Goyo sorts through "a mountain of her personal belongings: crocodile handbags, designer suits, . . . a thousand tubes of lipstick" (162). The list shows how Luisa's life is defined by conspicuous consumption. Moreover, crocodile bags are illegal in the United States because crocodiles have been overhunted, which imbricates Luisa in a different kind of black market from the one in Cuba, a black market that is not about economic survival or resolver strategies but about class status and profiting off of the overpoaching of vulnerable populations. Both Goyito and Luisa are obese and participate in the dieting industry, especially at the Rice House, where "Luisa [spends] many months and thousands of dollars shedding extra pounds" (129).[33] For his part, Goyito goes "on a jag of father-son-debauchery" with Goyo before enrolling in the Rice House (127). In stark relief to the lack of goods on the island, Luisa and Goyito have easy access to and over consume food as well as material possessions. Goyito wants "a fast-track fortune" (36) and goes on many "crime spree[s]" (185). The fact that he does not turn to crime out of necessity or dire economic circumstances highlights how privileged and resource rich the Herreras are in the United States and how, in contrast to those on the island, they do not have to rely on resolver strategies. While the characters in the vignettes and notes explicitly critique the economy of scarcity in Cuba under socialism, the vignettes and notes also implicitly critique the exiles' lifestyle of excessive consumption under neoliberal capitalism in the United States. The novel challenges the victim narrative of the conservative exiles, given their investments, both literal and figurative, in class hierarchies.

The novel's notes and vignettes are rooted in a resolver aesthetic that values the strategic acts and practices that constitute creative solutions to limited options and agency. In chapter 1, I interpret the footnotes in Junot Díaz's *The Brief Wondrous Life of Oscar Wao* as mimicking underground forms of storytelling and evasive modes of communication under the Trujillato and as postmemory strategies for reconstructing a history of the dictatorship from below and from afar. I argue that the footnotes are integral to the novel's zafa aesthetic, which formally resists the Trujillo dictatorship as well as entrenched hierarchies of power in postdictatorship Dominican Republic and the United States. With references to historical figures who have actively resisted colonialism and dictatorship—such as the Taíno chief Anacaona and the Spanish intellectual Jesús de Galíndez—the footnotes in *The Brief Wondrous Life of Oscar Wao* are positioned within a history of active resistance; in contrast, the notes and vignettes in *King of Cuba* are situated within a history of creative and strategic negotiation and survival amid economic obstacles.[34] In other words, rather than functioning as a formal embodiment of the zafa, the notes and vignettes function as a formal embodiment of resolver. A similar literary device of inserting information at the bottom of a novel's page takes on different meanings and purposes, given the particular historical context of the Dominican Republic and of Cuba.

The notes also formally fracture El Comandante's and Goyo's heteropatriarchal domination of the character-system. El Comandante and Goyo monopolize the majority of narrative attention in the novel's character-system, such that a scarcity of narrative space is left for other characters. With every note, an asterisk indicates that readers should look at the explanatory text at the bottom of the page. In the majority of cases, each asterisk is inserted after a particular word or sentence in El Comandante's or Goyo's narrative. The asterisk draws the reader's eyes down to another voice and interpretive perspective. "Asterisk" comes from the Greek *asteriskos* (little star).[35] The little stars at the bottom of the page disrupt El Comandante's and Goyo's thoughts and assert the agency and stories of other subjects whom El Comandante and Goyo eclipse with their fantasies of being the central heroes of revolutionary nationalism and counter-revolutionary exile. Both men want to be the sun or the brightest star around which everyone else revolves, but the little stars interrupt and undercut them, establishing alternative narratives underneath El Comandante's and Goyo's narratives.

Moreover, the notes and vignettes are nearly all narrated in the first person singular or plural, in contrast to El Comandante and Goyo's sections, which are narrated in third person free indirect discourse.

The use of "I," "we," and "our" grants the characters the authority to speak, despite being allocated limited character-space in their brief cameos. The characters provide the "Radio Bemba" perspective—the Cuban colloquial term for the word on the street or word-of-mouth news—which contrasts with the official and dominant discourses vocalized by El Comandante and Goyo in the main body of the novel (89). In one sense, the notes and vignettes democratize the narrative by bringing in more perspectives, but we can also read this redistribution of narrative attention as a socialist practice that allocates voice and space more equitably, if still unevenly. Using analogies to both democracy and socialism is another way the novel's form interrogates entrenched binaries. The notes and vignettes dramatize the state of being constantly caught between the diametrically opposed island and exile communities and serve as a means through which the novel structurally tries to break down this binary.

The notes and vignettes function centrifugally in fracturing El Comandante's and Goyo's dominance. At the same time, the voices represented in the notes and vignettes are largely critical of and bitter about life on the island and come from a more unified perspective than their multicharacter multivoicedness suggests. Thus, they simultaneously function centripetally by being almost unanimously negative in their presentation of Cuba as a corrupt state and stagnant society.[36] The tone is one of singular disillusionment and a yearning for the fall of El Comandante and the end of socialism rather than a desire to salvage its benefits and rectify its failures. In her study of contemporary arts in Cuba, Sujatha Fernandes finds that "even in the despairing circumstances of the present, many Cubans continue to believe that the revolution was important and that elements of its values and institutions can be salvaged" (4); the arts provide a vital avenue for "a weary and contemplative population questioning and searching for the value of their revolution in the midst of hardship, defeat, and new possibilities" (43). Garcia's notes and vignettes do not give voice to these Cubans, instead silencing their affects, their despair coupled with resourceful hope. Fernandes examines how film, rap, and visual and performance art constitute what she calls artistic public spaces, which function as critical spaces for discussion and debate about the current and future state of Cuba. All of the characters in *King of Cuba*'s notes and vignettes who are artists, writers, and intellectuals only complain about repression and blacklisting, with no suggestion of the rich dialogue going on in the arts in Cuba.

Despite the dialectical and multivoiced structure of the novel, its depiction of the social landscape does not represent the vibrancy of cultural production in Cuba or the range of affective affiliations with the revolution. The notes and vignettes resolve, so to speak, the dilemma of El Comandante and Goyo dominating the narrative, and they embody the resolver aesthetic, which García introduces into the Latina/o dictatorship novel to chronicle and give formal shape to creative resourcefulness amid adversity. But the novel, which ends in the death of El Comandante and Goyo, does not resolve the problem of how to move forward or how to creatively imagine a more egalitarian world.

Defiant Daughters

To return to Achy Obejas's "So We Came All the Way from Cuba So You Could Dress Like This?," which I open this chapter discussing, the unnamed narrator is invested in liberatory politics while her father is invested in an authoritarian heteropatriarchal order.[37] Like the narrator of Obejas's story and the character of Pilar in Cristina García's first novel, *Dreaming in Cuban* (1993), Goyo's daughter Alina is the child of a virulently conservative, anticommunist, procapitalist exile parent. Yet Alina, unlike the other two female characters, is a minor character who is apportioned little character-space and is never allowed to focalize the narrative. I employ a resolver reading practice to interpret Alina's significance, making do with this scarcity of narrative attention and resourcefully turning to some of the other defiant daughters of the conservative exile generation who appear in Cristina García's and Achy Obejas's fiction. I thereby demonstrate how, when read in conjunction, these defiant daughters' narratives gesture toward other kinds of political subjectivities and other possible futures.

Alina is first introduced through her father's point of view and only appears in a few scenes in the novel, and her perspective is entirely filtered through Goyo and the narrator. She has recently come to live with her father to help care for Goyo, but he is suspicious of her motives, believing that she is after his money. Her photographs have been featured in *National Geographic*, but her profit- and status-minded father does not value her artistic career. He most resents having to rely on his daughter and internalizes her help as "humiliat[ing]" (21); he "would rather crack his skull than endure her assistance," so he tries hard to avoid her help (79). This is a realistic depiction of an old man who still wants to feel independent at the same time that it reflects how Goyo's sense of himself as a man is tied to being in control of his body, his surroundings, and his family.

In contrast to her father, who espouses normative machismo, Alina does not abide by normative femininity. She is six inches taller than her father, with "manly shoulders" (13) and "burly arm[s]" (23), and when she returns from exercising she is described as "wolfing" down meat and "attack[ing]" the cupboards in search of canned tuna (20–21). Her long-distance swimming and her diet of animal protein make her more muscular. In contrast, Goyo is increasingly frail, and his daughter can carry him with one arm to the bathroom. Instead of feeling grateful that he has a daughter who cares for him, Goyo sees his daughter as overly masculine and threatening. He even others her by thinking of her "as a species [he] barely understood" (20). Since she does not abide by the social conventions of femininity, Goyo believes "she had no regard for her safety, was indifferent to appearances, and was incapable of harnessing language to any socially appropriate use" (20). Rather than see her as fearless, brave, strong, confident, outspoken, and not obsessed with superficial appearances, Goyo takes the signs of her empowerment and turns them into defects. Alina does not abide by patriarchal norms for proper female behavior or subscribe to standards of feminine beauty. Her athleticism and her artistic personality differentiate her markedly from her mother, Luisa, who used an excessive amount of makeup, was obsessed with plastic surgery, and was a social climber. Alina's supposed lack of manners and refusal to pay deference to her father or to patriarchal social norms of behavior and dress all imply that she queers gender norms.

Alina is a photographer who has documented a range of experiences, has traveled extensively, and is not afraid to take risks, challenge norms, or break the rules both in her life and in her art. She has photographed the Penitentes, a secret all-male religious sect that reenacts the crucifixion in New Mexico; the wildlife reserves in the Serengeti in Africa; and the endangered waterfowl in Florida. For one of her recent projects, she photographed the naked bodies of senior citizens, scandalizing her father. The novel also documents the aging bodies of Goyo and El Comandante and their entrenched antagonisms, but Alina provides a useful alternative to the two old men who dominate the narrative. As a photographer, Alina has a wide frame of reference, which captures how she is not boxed in ideologically like her father and El Comandante, who have very narrow vision.

Alina's progressive politics are at odds with her father's worldview. "To Goyo's dismay, his daughter was a blatant liberal who argued against the 'futile' trade embargo. Every utterance of hers was an apologia for a moribund regime long sustained by the depth and breadth of ignorance. Alina, like so many others, supported the oppressor while deriding the oppressed" (19). Narrated from the counter-revolutionary and condescending perspective of Goyo, Alina's critique of the United States' long-standing embargo of Cuba is silenced. Alina would likely argue that the exiles are supporting the oppressors and deriding the oppressed with their celebration of the United States' imperialistic foreign policy toward Cuba and their nostalgic desire for the prerevolutionary Cuba where her family had wealth and power. Seeing Cuba as a country struggling to make its own path in a world-colonial system dominated by global capitalism, she refuses to call El Comandante by the expletives that her father frequently uses and instead refers to him by the neutral "El Comandante" (21, 80). Alina names Goyo's tirades against Cuba "crazy exile vitriol" (21) and a "militant psycho act" (102). Twice she awakens her father, once when he is unconscious in the swamp, dreaming he has found the freedom fighters, and again when he is in a car crash, dreaming he has died and is flying through the sky. This act of waking up her father positions Alina as a voice of reason and suggests that Goyo's consciousness needs to be raised.

Alina is critical of her father's actions and his mentality, yet her views are merely alluded to and never fleshed out. Goyo's dismissal of her from the hospital room—she is "waved...off with a flutter of his wrist"—mirrors the way she is dismissed from the overall narrative so that Goyo and Goyito can share intimate father-son moments, which develops the male son Goyito as a rounder character with a fuller backstory (104). The novel does not linger on Alina's personal thoughts and feelings as it does on Goyito's, and her lack of substantive presence in the narrative is an elision. We are left to piece her opinions and her sexual orientation together out of a few scattered comments and out of Goyo's alternatively annoyed, dismissive, and paternalistic reactions to her. In a sense, we have to use a resourceful "resolver" interpretive practice to access Alina's significance as a character and see the way she counters the domestic dictatorship of heteropatriarchy.

Focusing on the art of another one of Cristina García's defiant daughters of the hard right exile generation, Pilar Puente, helps establish a literary genealogy for Alina, whose perspective, artistic vision, and character development are foreclosed in *King of Cuba*. Symbolically, these Latina characters provide alternate perspectives and possibilities for liberation than the dominant heteropatriarchal narratives propogated by both the Cuban exiles and the Cuban revolution as exemplified by Goyo and El Comandante. Pilar Puente is one of the main characters in *Dreaming in Cuban*, which chronicles the lives of three generations of women, including Pilar's grandmother Cecilia, who lives in Cuba and actively supports the revolution; Pilar's mother, Lourdes, who owns Yankee Doodle bakeries in New York City and is an adamant counter-revolutionary capitalist;[38] and Pilar, who is an artist and self-identifies as a punk.[39] By examining Pilar's artistic productions, I in turn recuperate Alina from her minor role in *King of Cuba* and reposition her alongside Pilar as one of several defiant daughters and artist figures in Cuban American literature who strive toward a more socially just world.

When Pilar's mother, Lourdes, asks her daughter to paint something patriotic to commemorate the grand opening of her second Yankee Doodle bakery, she decides to make a painting of Lady Liberty in "her full punk glory" (144). Pilar paints the background of the canvas in an "iridescent blue gouache—like the Virgin Mary's robes in gaudy church buildings" so that it will "look irradiated, nuked out" (141). Then Pilar describes how she paints the statue:

> When the paint dries, I start on Liberty herself. I do a perfect replication of her a bit left of center canvas, changing only two details: first, I make Liberty's torch float slightly above her grasp, and second, I paint her right hand reaching over to cover her left breast, as if she's reciting the National Anthem or some other slogan.... The next day, the background still looks off to me, so I take a medium-thick brush and paint black stick figures pulsing in the air around Liberty, thorny scars that look like barbed wire. I want to go all the way with this, to stop mucking around and do what I feel, so at the base of the statue I put my favorite punk rallying cry: I'M A MESS. And then carefully, very carefully, I paint a safety pin through Liberty's nose. (141)

The painting is striking. By decentering Lady Liberty from the middle of the canvas, Pilar offers an alternative perspective on liberty. Using the iconic iridescent blue of the shroud of the Cuban La

Virgen de la Caridad de Cobre (and even the Mexican La Virgen de Guadalupe), Pilar makes Lady Liberty look as though she has been exposed to radiation, subtly evoking the United States' waging of war on other countries, including Cuba, in the name of liberty. The use of "nuked out" by a U.S. Cuban American is haunted by the trace of the history of possible nuclear warfare in the Cuban Missile Crisis. The famous torch that lights the way for migrants and offers a symbolic ray of hope in the darkness of their situation as they seek safe harbor is just out of Liberty's grasp, implying that liberty is aspirational and not yet achieved in the United States. Pilar gestures toward the national holiday marking the occasion of her commissioned painting by posing Lady Liberty in a patriotic gesture with her hand over her heart pledging her allegiance to the United States. Yet the occasion is marred by thorny scars that resemble the barbed wire used to cage animals or people and that recall the thorns around Jesus Christ's head as he was martyred to bring salvation to the world. The image implies that the discourses of salvation and liberty undergirding U.S. nationalistic and hemispheric projects do not bring democracy and progress but instead leave wounds and scars. The thorny scars are made out of black stick figures, recalling the people who have been scarred by U.S. nationalism and imperialism. Lady Liberty has a safety pin through her nose, and the word "safety" in "safety pin," combined with the other images of violence and the language of war, questions whether the United States provides safety or refuge either at home or abroad.

Pilar's painting, "SL-76," is a defiant critique of the United States and its discourse of liberty. The punk slogan, written in emphatic capital letters, charges that the United States is a mess and makes a mess of things elsewhere and so is not an ideal site or provider of liberty and democracy. With the rallying cry at her base and the safety pin through her nose, Lady Liberty is a punk. Pilar thus tries to punk, so to speak, her mother's unquestioning patriotic devotion to the United States, insisting on alternative conceptualizations of liberation.[40]

In an intertextual scene in her novel *Days of Awe* (2001), published almost ten years after García's *Dreaming in Cuban*, Achy Obejas imagines a future piece of artwork that Pilar produces, giving us a glimpse into the possible evolution of Pilar's defiant art. In Obejas's novel, Pilar collaborates with the Cuban Deborah Menach on a piece of transnational performance art. Deborah describes to the novel's narrator,

Alejandra (Ale), how they staged their performance simultaneously, Pilar in the United States and Deborah in Cuba. Both women "wrapped themselves in a Cuban flag and hung by a wire from the apex of a historically important building.... When they touched ground, both women dropped the flags to reveal their naked bodies. Then they walked through the streets until each was arrested" (322). Their arrests were an integral part of the performance, and Deborah goes on to explain the artistic vision behind the work, saying they were

> confronting authority, confronting conformity, confronting the attitudes that say the truth—what is beauty—can only be defined by the imposed order.... The idea was to force another look at ourselves, to reconsider that all of our accomplishments—whether it's the revolution or the success of the Cubans in Miami or whatever—are all meaningless, all illusionary, unless we go back to our true origins, to our unmasked, vulnerable selves, the ones we see in the mirror when we're alone. We wanted to take this image, which is of such magnitude, and confront the institutions of our society, but not in a violent way, not in a disrespectful way, and not in a way that could possibly echo left-right politics, because then everything just gets lost. We wanted it to be universal, but also fresh, also radical. (323)

In hanging themselves like flags from the Freedom Tower in Miami and the cathedral in Havana, shedding the flags they are robed in, walking through public space naked, and getting arrested, Pilar and Deborah confront various discourses and institutions. Each transforms her body into a flag, a patriotic symbol of the imagined community of Cuba and a material object that helps create transnational affective attachments to the nation. They shed this national symbol and expose their nakedness, a dual gesture that enacts their challenge to patriotic and patriarchal nationalisms and that confronts social norms of dress in the public sphere and the taboo around nakedness, in particular around the naked female body.

Pilar hanging from the Freedom Tower in Miami connects this performance to "SL-76," the painting she created in her youth. The Statue of Liberty, which stands on Ellis Island, was the main port of entry and processing center for predominantly European migrants arriving via ships until 1954. Freedom Tower served as the "Ellis Island of the South" for Cuban migrants to the United States from 1962 to 1974; it was both a processing center and an aid center for

Cubans arriving via boats and planes. According to official U.S. history, written in no uncertain terms on the National Park Service's website, "Freedom Tower stands tall as a symbol of hope and freedom, and the firm belief that democracy should be available to all who fight against tyranny and demagoguery.... As a beacon of hope and freedom, the Freedom Tower remains a national system of the liberty sought and found by Cuban refugees."[41] Pilar's performance art puts pressure on this triumphalist narrative of the United States as the site of freedom and invites viewers to reconsider the success of the Cubans in Miami, just as Deborah's performance puts pressure on the triumphalist narrative of the Cuban revolution and its successes. In tandem, the performances resist dominant discourses of the U.S. nation-state, the Cuban nation-state, and the Cuban exile community. While Pilar's painting uses a punk aesthetic to question the meaning of liberty, Pilar's and Deborah's performance uses nudity to question the meaning of liberty in Greater Cuba. In contrast to Lady Liberty, which I point out remains immobile in Francisco Goldman's *The Ordinary Seaman*, Pilar and Deborah are ladies of liberty, which I point out dramatize their freedom through nakedness, at the same time that their mobility is restricted by their arrests.

By contesting authority and conformity on the island and in the United States, Pilar and Deborah continue the anti-institutionalism of punk that Pilar espoused in *Dreaming in Cuban*; at the same time, they strive to move beyond the entrenched binary of "left-right politics" and masculinist notions of political agency and subjectivity by calling for "fresh" or new forms of "radical" aesthetics and politics (323).[42] *King of Cuba* reproduces the binary between left-right politics through the foil characters of El Comandante and Goyo, but it also plays out the collapse of that binary as the two men die at the novel's end. When she was younger in *Dreaming in Cuban*, Pilar believed that art "is the ultimate revolution" (235). Though Pilar and Deborah do not use the words "revolution" or "revolutionary," preferring instead to use the word "radical" to describe their performance, their desire to challenge the political and patriarchal hegemonic orders of the day begs the question of how to define revolution and what the role of art is in a revolutionary imagination. García's and Obejas's novels suggest that a transnational vision that questions political binaries and ideologies is key to revolutionary art.

"Revolution" has two very different significations; it is the overthrowing of a regime in power, and it is a movement around something in a circular path. The word "revolution" holds in tension a complete radical change (liberation) and a continual motion around something (rotation). The second definition is at odds with the first because a rotation, like that of a planet around the sun, is continuous and unchanging, whereas a radical regime change is disruptive and overturns a hegemonic or ossified power structure. In this sense, a revolution that has been institutionalized exists as a contradiction (at least in terms of the first definition). The vignette "Island Blogger 2" in *King of Cuba* points this out: "real revolutions, good citizens, don't last over half a century" (131). The novel's metaphor of Goyo and El Comandante as suns suggests that both figures are patriarchal and authoritarian, each desiring a centripetal notion of revolution in which his offspring or his citizen subjects are planets and he is the sun around which they revolve.

The opening of Achy Obejas's *Days of Awe* foregrounds the link between political revolutions and the earth's natural revolutions while privileging revolution as an open-ended process. The narrator, Ale, poetically and insightfully declares:

> Revolutions happen, I'm convinced, because intuition tells us we're meant for a greater world.... The word itself is imbedded with a kind of circular logic that has at its core a contradiction. Revolutions are, after all, for the moment. The minute they cease to be the outside challenge, the moment they become the power inside, they shift more than their balance. They demand another upheaval, another ensanguined engagement.... And they're regular as the seasons.... Indeed, we measure time by the constant and sluggish turn of our own watery orb; nothing could be steadier and more predictable than these collective, planetary revolutions. (1)

King of Cuba and *Days of Awe* both suggest with their feminist and counter-dictatorial critiques that revolutions cannot be fully revolutionary if they revolve around the patriarch as the central site of power and if they have been institutionalized. The denotation of revolution as a circular orbit highlights the limiting binary entrenched in the logic of left versus right or pro versus anti politics in Greater Cuba, suggesting that we instead need to imagine new utopias and new futures. José Esteban Muñoz writes that there is a Cuban American left made up of those who "do not demonize the revolution but instead view it ambivalently" ("Performing Greater Cuba," 401). He goes on to explain: "this ambivalence is not a passive ambivalence. It is more nearly a passionate investment in Cuba that sees the promise of the revolution, its potential, and its various failures and shortcomings" (415). This kind of productive ambivalence acknowledges failure and potentiality and holds in tension its disenchanting errors of the past, such as the persistence of heteropatriarchy in the revolutionary imagination, and its utopian struggle for a more egalitarian world.

Ale's meditation and Pilar's and Deborah's performances define "radical" and "revolution" as constantly confronting authority, challenging conformity, and rising up against authoritarian forms of power, which is integral to the process of decolonization and what I have termed the counter-dictatorial imaginary. García and Obejas, as well as the other Latina/o novelists I have examined, insist that a revolution that does not break down all forms of dictatorship and authoritarian hierarchies is an incomplete revolution or a revolution that requires another revolution to build on its gains. Alina, Lola, Little Merced, Joaquina, Elena, Pilar, and Deborah are all minor characters in the novels I have analyzed, but they all articulate deep critiques of power and model alternative ways of grappling with oppression. Recall Lola, who asserts that we are all Trujillos; Little Merced, who learns to block Saturn's dictatorial gaze; Joaquina, whose aesthetic appreciation for objects with holes symbolizes how undocumented migrants can both experience pleasure and take advantage of holes in the system; Elena, who desires a transnational social movement against impunity; and Pilar and Deborah, who expose the incomplete projects of liberation domestically and hemispherically. In doing so, they implore us to continue to use our imaginations in the project of decolonization.[43] Latina/o dictatorship novels interrogate various manifestations of dictatorial power while their valorization of ambiguity and their ambivalent endings leave us torn between hope and despair, finding beauty yet seeking justice amid the violence, exploitation, repression, and injustice. They suggest that the counter-dictatorial imaginary is not just a critical stance toward dictatorial power but a continual struggle, ever desiring and striving toward the perhaps unreachable horizon of that "greater world" that Ale believes lives in our revolutionary intuitions.

{ CODA }

Violence will keep changing in name, but violence will always remain as long as there's no change at the root, from where all these horrible things are sprouting.
—ARCHBISHOP ÓSCAR ROMERO, *quoted in Oscar Martínez,* A History of Violence

La solidaridad es la ternura de los pueblos.
Solidarity is the tenderness between peoples.
—GIOCONDA BELLI, *quoted on a mural in Managua, Nicaragua*

Culture contains the seed of resistance which blossoms into the flower of liberation.
—AMÍLCAR CABRAL, *quoted on a mural in Balmy Alley San Francisco, United States*

The work: To make revolution irresistible.
—TONI CADE BAMBARA, *This Bridge Called My Back*

In 2003, a group of Latina/o children of Chilean exiles created an art exhibit, "Two 9/11s in a Lifetime: A Project and Exhibit on the Politics of Memory," that brought the haunting past of Chile's dictatorship into San Francisco's Mission District and generated a dialogue about histories of political terror and oppression.[1] The scholar Macarena Gómez-Barris explains that one of the goals of the exhibit, which she and the other members of the 9/11 Collective curated, was "to reflect the violence in Chile, as well as the disruption, aggression, and trauma that many US-based Latina/os confront, either directly or indirectly" ("Two," 102). The members of the collective—having grown up in the United States and lived beside and collaborated with Latina/os from other national-origin groups, as well as non-Latina/os—view political repression in Chile in light of the oppression experienced by Latina/os in the United States, and vice versa. The Latina/o dictatorship novels I have examined depict the afterlives of Latin American authoritarian regimes on Latina/o communities alongside various forms of authoritarian power that racialized minorities face in the United States; the "Two 911s" exhibit likewise does this, using other genres.

The 9/11 Collective showcased various kinds of aesthetic modes, media, and performance to generate linkages between past and present violence. Roberto Lagos's photodocumentary juxtaposes untitled photos of "dictatorship brutality" in Chile with photos of "police brutality" in the United States ("Two," 109). The lack of titles on the photographs and the use of the same medium—black and white photography—make it difficult to differentiate the locations of these documented scenes of state-perpetrated violence. The photographs prompt viewers to see connections between "the increased surveillance and violence on civilian populations that is a result of both [9/11] national tragedies" (109). This tactic of rendering indeterminate the location of institutionalized brutality so as to produce a comparative reading of violence draws attention to congruent and contiguous modes of oppression across the Americas. Likewise, to close the opening night of the exhibit, the organizers publically named Chilean activists and victims of the dictatorship; after doing so, they asked the audience who they wanted to commemorate. Among those memorialized, audience members named Salvadorans, Guatemalans, and Argentinians as well as local San Francisco activists. "The process of publicly naming and thus linking victims and activists from around the Americas produced a connected memory about seemingly disparate events. In many ways, the performative act by the 9/11 Collective was a form of cultural memory, enacting the terror imaginary of dictatorship and other forms of systematic violence.... What began as testimony by Chilean exiles and sons and daughters of exile was transformed into an embodied scenario of political alliances across national and historical experiences," recalls Gómez-Barris ("Two," 149). The geopolitics of memorialization enacted through the act of collective remembering yokes together disparate experiences of state violence in the Americas. Out of these linkages emerge "connected memories" that enable disparate groups to see themselves in solidarity across time and space, producing a powerful version of what I have termed the Latina/o counter-dictatorial imaginary.

Over the course of this book, I have tracked the myriad ways Latina/o authors strategically utilize narrative form and literary tactics to critically represent histories of dictatorship and oppressive hierarchies of power. In this coda, I offer some conjectures on how cultural producers visualize the Latina/o counter-dictatorial imaginary using non-print-based artistic forms. I focus in particular on murals in Balmy Alley in San Francisco's Mission District and consider how their depictions of authoritarian repression in Central America coexist alongside depictions of repressive structures and discourses in the United States. While the 9/11 Collective used the history of the U.S.-supported Pinochet dictatorship in Chile as a catalyst for producing connected memories, I use the murals' representations of the history of U.S.-supported military dictatorships and counter-insurgency campaigns in Central America to illuminate how the murals enact this kind of memory work. The murals forge linked histories of violence at the same time that they are material testaments to interracial solidarity and the collective struggle for social justice. Analyzing the visual polyphony in Balmy Alley provides another texture and layer to the counter-dictatorial imaginary I have traced over the course of the preceding chapters.

On Placas and Palimpsests of Paint

Lining a narrow one-block street in San Francisco's Mission District, historically a working-class Latina/o and Latin American migrant community, a number of murals memorialize the violence perpetrated by U.S.-supported authoritarian regimes in Central America. Amid the layers of paint, other histories of violence are layered on the walls, fences, and garage doors of Balmy Alley. A number of images and topics crisscross the murals; depictions of militarization, colonialism, the AIDS epidemic, gentrification, and environmental destruction appear side by side with artistic and popular cultural icons, indigenous imagery, and spiritual figures, as well as colorful representations of nature and cultural traditions. The murals function as space-making and space-claiming practices that also memorialize political histories.

Though Chicana/o artists began painting murals in Balmy Alley in the 1970s, it was not until the mid-1980s that it became a full-fledged mural environment, and this consolidation of mural production is linked to the history of the United States' support for brutal military regimes and counter-insurgency warfare in Central America.

Angered by what was occurring in Central America, Chicana/os Patricia Rodríguez and Ray Patlán responded when a New York City–based group of artists put out the Artists' Call Against U.S. Intervention in Central America.[2] They organized an interracial group of thirty-six artists who produced, over nine months in 1984, twenty-five murals in Balmy Alley that denounced state-sponsored violence, stood in solidarity with revolutionary struggles, and celebrated indigenous peoples and cultures in Central America.[3] The mural project was called PLACA. As Patlán explains, "we used the word 'placa' because it is so flexible. In Spanish, especially street Spanish, it can mean cops [and] it can mean your mark" (Wojczuk and Rowand); "we wanted to leave a mark" (Lizarraga, 103).[4] Through their murals, the artists inscribed the "placa" or mark of Central American dictatorships and U.S. imperialism onto the cityscape of San Francisco. Thirty years later, some of the markings of this project remain materially in the paint on the walls of Balmy Alley, and the project is marked more ephemerally but indelibly in the consciousness of the new generation of artists painting murals in Balmy Alley and in the memories of the Mission community.

Though the majority of the PLACA murals have deteriorated and been replaced, and more murals have since been added to the alley that depict a rich range of themes, the different layers of mural production in Balmy Alley testify to histories of violence in Latin America and the United States. Just as I have read disparate Latina/o dictatorship novels as part of a collective tradition, the space of the alley invites us to read an individual mural in conversation with and as part of the mural tradition of that particular streetscape. Balmy Alley is an example of a mural environment, or what Guisela Latorre describes as a "series of murals in close proximity to one another and within a defined and limited space."[5] As such, "these murals are not supposed to be seen as single works of art, but rather, their position and iconography should be understood in function of the surrounding murals and in relation to the space in which they reside" (142). Reading the murals in relation to each other illuminates a collage-like dialogue between numerous murals in Balmy Alley. To trace the visual dialogues in the mural environment, I first examine the only extant PLACA mural left in the alley, and then I consider a pair of murals where the palimpsestic layering of more current murals over the PLACA ones is still visible. I end by focusing on how two recent murals carry on the activist-oriented mission of PLACA by adapting it to contemporary social justice struggles. These murals collectively exhibit a tension between disappearance—caused by war, gentrification, undocumented migration, and weathering over time—and presence—created through art, memorialization, resistance tactics, and the superimposition of one mural atop another. These murals visualize the Latina/o counter-dictatorial imaginary on the walls of the cityscape and construct transhistorical and transnational public sites of memory.

The themes of military violence and cultural resistance are at the center of the only fully intact PLACA mural left in Balmy Alley, Miranda Bergman and O'Brien Thiele's "La Cultura Contiene la Semilla de la Resistencia que Retoña en la Flor de la Liberación / Culture Contains the Seed of Resistance which Blossoms into the Flower of Liberation" (1984; fig. C.1).[6] This mural, which was restored in 2014, stretches across two garage doors. The left door shows a group of people holding photos of murdered or disappeared loved ones. The image memorializes the frequent use of photos of disappeared

FIGURE C.1 *Miranda Bergman and O'Brien Thiele, "La Cultura Contiene la Semilla de la Resistencia que Retoña en la Flor de la Liberación / Culture Contains the Seed of Resistance which Blossoms into the Flower of Liberation," 1984 and repainted 2014. Photograph by Manuel Vargas López*

loved ones as a form of protest and as a human rights claim against state impunity by groups such as the Mothers and Family Members of El Salvador (Comité de Madres y Familiares de El Salvador; COMADRES) and the Mothers of the Plaza de Mayo (Asociación Madres de Plaza de Mayo) in Argentina. While photos are a technology of reappearing the disappeared; present here on the walls of San Francisco, the photos also demand that the United States be held accountable for the torture and death its interventions have wrought. Amid crops labeled "for exportation only" and two people looking defensively beyond our sightline toward invading armed forces that have set the village on fire, a young boy has just painted "RESISTE" (RESIST) in bold red letters on a wall. Written in the imperative mood, the word is an imploration to resist state-sponsored terror and imperialism. A metapainting moment, the child's placa literally marks resistance on the wall, drawing attention to the memory work of the mural that makes visible the violence of U.S.-backed counter-insurgency groups, which are symbolized in the faces of the military figure and President Ronald Reagan who hover above the entire scene within the smoke from the flames of a burning building. The boy's graffiti is inscribed on a wall that also doubles as the wing of a dove of peace that flies above the painting. The palimpsest of the wing superimposed over the wall suggests that mural-making is simultaneously an act of resistance and a utopian imagining of a more peaceful future. The young boy's close-fisted gesture of holding the paintbrush is echoed by a young girl on the right door of the mural who holds aloft a pencil in her fist and carries a book with "Nuestra Historia" (Our History) printed on the cover. In front of her are joyful, vibrantly colored images of people harvesting crops and enjoying the fruits of their labor, which are feeding the community rather than supporting an export-based economy. Emerging from a man's guitar, a rainbow extends into a basket of fruit held by a smiling woman. The words of Cuban protest singer Silvio Rodríguez are written on the rainbow in English and Spanish.[7] If we read the mural from left to right just as we would the pages of a book, we see that images of war and exploitation give way to images of peace and cultures of resistance and resilience.

When we look at the remains of the PLACA murals amid the murals that replaced them, we see within the palimpsestic layers of paint a palimpsestic history of authoritarian violence. Two side-by-side murals, Juana Alicia's "Una ley inmoral, nadie tiene que cumplirla / No One Should Comply with an Immoral Law" (1996) on the left and Joel Bergner's "Un pasado que aún vive" (A Past That Still Lives) on the right (2004), materialize state-sponsored military violence in El Salvador (fig. C.2). The mural by Chicana visual artist Juana Alicia memorializes Archbishop Óscar Romero, whose assassination by a right-wing death squad was ordered by an army major who was trained in the United States' School of the Americas. The mural is dominated by Romero's face and piercing gaze, and the quote that provides the mural's title surrounds his head in decorated block letters, styled after traditional Salvadoran folk painting. In this same spot, Juana Alicia originally painted a PLACA mural, "Te oímos Guatemala" (We Hear You Guatemala) (1984), which depicted an indigenous woman wailing over a dead body draped in a white sheet, grieving over the genocide of indigenous people in Guatemala

FIGURE C.2 *Juana Alicia, "Una ley inmoral, nadie tiene que cumplirla / No One Should Comply with an Immoral Law," 1996 (left); Joel Bergner, "Un pasado que aún vive" (A Past that Still Lives)," 2004 (right). Photograph by Jennifer Harford Vargas*

perpetrated by the military dictatorship supported by the United States. Above the wailing figure, in the Mexican tradition of retablo painting, the dedication "Te oímos Guatemala" was painted in red letters on a banner that unfurled to display the blue outline of San Francisco's rooftops and skyline. When this original mural became too weathered, Alicia decided to paint the new mural in homage to Óscar Romero, "Una ley immoral...", rather than restoring the PLACA mural. Shifting from depicting the death of a nameless Guatemalan and marking anonymous grief to vivifying an icon of resistance mourned by many and prominently marking his words on the walls of San Francisco, Alicia's mural asserts the lasting presence not only of grief but also of resistance, for the military could take Romero's life but not his symbolic afterlife. Moreover, the palimpsestic layering of one Alicia mural painted over another reinflects the declaration that we hear Guatemala's grief into the entreaty that we not comply with immoral laws.

Adjacent to Alicia's mural, Bergner's mural, rich in detail and imagery, visualizes spectral histories of violence. It contains scenes of a mountain village in the background; in the foreground a woman sits in the bed of a truck, clutching her child and a letter from her husband, who has migrated to California in search of work. Her husband's face appears on the blanket on her lap, haunting her thoughts, just as the spectral bodies of the victims of state atrocities appear throughout the mural. Ghost-like soldiers shoot people whose blood turns the river that runs down the side of the mural a deep and swirling red. On the walls of the village's buildings, silhouettes of soldiers line up in a firing squad to shoot a group of people; suggesting that El Salvador's past lives in the cityscape of El Salvador (and of the United States, where the mural itself is located). The faces of absent victims appear in the mountain peaks, haunting the background of the mural with their ghostly presence.

Above both Bergner's and Alicia's murals are the barely visible outlines of pink mountain peaks and blue silhouettes of military soldiers. These fading images, which frame both murals, are the remains of the top portion of Brooke Fancher's PLACA mural "My Child Has Never Seen His Father" (1984), which depicted over two dozen Central American soldiers in blue walking across the wall of the building with pinkish-purple mountains in the background. The main section of Fancher's mural, which was replaced by Bergner's mural, featured indigenous women with a baby and a young man. The more time that passes, the more indistinguishable the traces of this previous PLACA mural are, as the brown wood beneath the chipped painting increasingly emerges with each passing season. Read together, the existing murals (by Alicia and Bergner) and the PLACA-era murals (by Alicia and Fancher) create a link between U.S.-supported state-sponsored violence in El Salvador and in Guatemala, both of which destroyed villages and split up families.

The murals' multiple layers of paint and the multiple histories of violence in Central America that the murals collectively invoke generate, to use Max Silverman's term, a "palimpsestic memory" (4). When read together, the murals form a "composite structure" that "is a combination of not simply two moments in time (past and present), but instead a number of different moments, hence producing a chain of signification which draws together disparate spaces and times" that are "profoundly connected" (3). The murals function as a palimpsestic memory by bringing together the past and the present and differing national spaces and histories of oppression simultaneously, exposing a larger pattern of authoritarian violence and impunity. Collectively, these murals, in their presence, absence, and haunting traces of presence, create a rich transnational dialogue about military violence and displacement. Indeed, as Berger's mural title suggests, the past still lives on, not just in this pair of murals but beneath and across the surfaces of Balmy Alley.

Silhouetted soldiers, skeletal death squad members, skulled border patrol agents, and baton-wielding police appear across a number of the murals produced from the 1980s to the present, marking Balmy Alley with state-perpetrated forms of repression and death. While "placa" refers to leaving a mark, "placa" also denotes a badge of identification, such as a police badge, as well as an object inscribed with identifying information. These two other meanings of placa capture how many of the murals chronicle the abuses of repressive state apparatuses and inscribe the concerns of each generation of activist-oriented muralists painting in Balmy Alley.

The PLACA aesthetic project of chronicling U.S. imperialism and memorializing histories of violence in Latin America has been reinflected and adapted to current social justice projects. Two murals about undocumented migration and gentrification by artists raised in the Mission but with origins in El Salvador and Mexico exemplify this. The murals cast the Mission and San Francisco as prominent settings rather than background landscapes and cast policing as ominous forces dictating the lives of the Latina/o citizens and migrants.

"Enrique's Journey" (2014),[8] by Salvadoran American artist Josúe Rojas, critiques the violent effects of U.S. immigration policy and the militarization of the border (fig. C.3). The mural depicts a young boy standing atop a train with his eyes closed and arms outstretched as an angel hovers over him. Rural villages with white houses and red roofs appear in the landscape behind him, and the train is marked with the words "La Bestia Express" (The Beast Express); La Bestia is the colloquial name for the trains that pose grave physical dangers, including dismemberment and death, for the undocumented migrants who ride atop them. A series of greenish-blue skulled figures labeled "I.C.E." (Immigration and Customs Enforcement), "Fear," and "La Migra" (The Border Patrol)," with "Unjust Immigration Policies" written below them, reach their creepy hands toward the migrant child. The skulled figures symbolize the "social death" that marks the condition of being an undocumented subject (Cacho, 6), as well as the "landscape of death" created by the militarization of the U.S.-Mexico border and the growing border enforcement apparatus that funnels migrants into more deserted and dangerous areas of crossing (Nevins, 174). The skulled border patrol agents are also positioned in

FIGURE C.3 *Josué Rojas, "Enrique's Journey," 2014. Photograph by Nancy Gapasin Gnass*

an intertextual dialogue with the skulled military and police enforcement officers in the other Balmy Alley murals.⁹ Other children and adults are perched atop the train that runs across the mural and below the San Francisco cityscape. Due to their prominent positioning, it appears as if the undocumented migrants are already in the space of San Francisco, and indeed, they are present in Balmy Alley. The words "Nuestra Mission" (Our Mission) are painted on one of San Francisco's white-walled and red-roofed buildings, which look exactly like the buildings in the Central American countryside, defying the border fence that separates the two geopolitical spaces. The sign is a space-claiming and community-building gesture, a means of laying a collective claim to the neighborhood of the Mission on behalf of migrants and their children. At the same time, the sign suggests that it is "our mission" to welcome undocumented Central American migrants and give them sanctuary, just as San Francisco provided sanctuary to those fleeing the violence in Central America in the 1980s.¹⁰

Expanding over and above two garage doors is "Mission Makeover" (2012), which Chicana Lucia Ippolito designed in collaboration with her Mexican migrant father, the printmaker and muralist Tirso Araiza. This mural indicts policing, gentrification, and their attendant displacements in the Mission District (fig. C.4). On one door their mural depicts two police officers arresting two young men of color and on the other door a police officer enjoys a "Starsucks" coffee beverage with a white woman who shops at "Wealth Foods," "Trader Foes," and "Mallie Clones," allusions to big corporations like Starbucks, Whole Foods, and Trader Joe's, as well as local high-priced markets like Mollie Stones. The scenes' critique of gentrification and the policing of youth of color links economic displacement with mass incarceration. Above one garage door, a skulled figure sits in front of a laptop with a large letter *F*, invoking how Facebook and the local dot-com and startup booms have drastically driven up housing prices in the area. The increased wealth in the neighborhood brings economic death to its working-class residents of color, particularly longtime Latina/o residents who can no longer afford to live there, including some of the artists who painted murals in Balmy Alley. Above the other garage door, a group of police in riot gear, with a "Foreclosure" sign behind them, drive a couple out of a lush island-like landscape that resembles Eden. Behind the foreclosure

FIGURE C.4 *Lucia Ippolito and Tirso Araiza, "Mission Makeover," 2012. Photograph by Nancy Gapasin Gnass and Sergio Herrera*

sign is a sign advertising "Luxury Hipster Community / For techies with lots of cash," with the words "Alta Impunidad" hovering above the luxury condos. The use of "alta impunidad" (end impunity) inserts the discourse of human rights into this depiction of gentrification, suggesting that housing is a fundamental right. It also provides a sign for how we can read gentrification in dialogue with the other kinds of human rights violations memorialized across the Balmy Alley murals, which together expose a long continuum of violence in the Americas that rests on political and economic impunity.

The murals I have analyzed thus far insist that we see wars abroad in dialogue with wars at home.[11] Two large, expressive eyes at the center of one of the murals gaze back at those who walk down Balmy Alley; one pupil contains the dove of peace, the other a skulled soldier with a rifle. Susan Kelk Cervantes's "Indigenous Eyes: War or Peace" (1991) is framed within what remains of the original PLACA mural, "Indigenous Beauty" (1984), by Nicole Emanuel (fig. C.5). "Indigenous Beauty" still exists on the walls surrounding the garage door that contains "Indigenous Eyes"; its pastoral Central American setting flows into the hills surrounding San Francisco, making the Central American villagescape and San Francisco cityscape merge into one overall landscape. The penetrating

FIGURE C.5 *Susan Kelk Cervantes, "Indigenous Eyes: War or Peace," 1991 (center); Nicole Emanuel, "Indigenous Beauty," 1984; restored 1991 (surrounding). Photograph by Jennifer Harford Vargas*

eyes and their hopeful vision of peace amid the traumatic memory of war look out at the other murals in Balmy Alley and at the viewer, imploring us to see the spectrum of violence caused by dictatorship, imperial interventionism, institutionalized racism, gentrification, policing, and immigration policies. The mural environment of Balmy Alley is a material manifestation of how authoritarian regimes and policies have left their marks on the political and cultural imaginary of multiple generations of muralists, who have left their own placas marking the space in defiant acts of memory and activism.

The novels I have examined forge links between dictatorship, imperialism, white supremacy, heteropatriarchy, neoliberalism, and border militarization.[12] The murals in Balmy Alley help us visualize these linkages. Rather than see isolated incidents, when we view them together in one mural environment, the patterns and connections between the murals become more apparent. They generate what the Holocaust scholar Michael Rothberg has conceptualized as "multidirectional memory." Rothberg notes how too often the remembrance and memorialization of one social group's history of extreme violence gets framed in terms of a competition for recognition that pits the severity of one group's victimization against another's. He proposes that we instead understand "memory as *multidirectional*: as subject to ongoing negotiation, cross-referencing, and borrowing" (3). To do so, he explains, "a certain bracketing of empirical history and an openness to the possibility of strange political bedfellows are necessary in order for the imaginative links between different histories and social groups to come into view; these imaginative links are the substance of multidirectional memory. Comparison, like memory, should be thought of as productive—as producing new objects and new lines of sight" (18–19). Rothberg's insights crystallize the productive memory work of Balmy Alley. The multidirectional memory produced by the murals creates new lines of sight by challenging viewers to recognize the separate struggles depicted in the murals as interrelated. New lines of sight emerge from positioning gentrification, policing, and displacement in the Mission in relation to, and inflected by, the history of counter-insurgency campaigns in Central America, for example. The murals enact the cultural work of the Latina/o counter-dictatorial imaginary by visualizing various forms of authoritarian power and memorializing the struggles against violence and disappearance. One of the payoffs of this multidirectional memory is that it can lead to "unexpected acts of empathy and solidarity; indeed multidirectional memory is often the very grounds on which people construct and act upon visions of justice" (19). The cultural mission behind the PLACA murals was to raise consciousness and to generate solidarity, and the new post-PLACA murals carry on this mission, as Balmy Alley continues to offer a comparative and anti-authoritarian vision of justice.[13] The Latina/o counter-dictatorial imaginary is rooted in these linked struggles for social justice and helps illuminate the linkages themselves, as it draws attention to the spectrum of domination that dictates people's ability to be fully free.

The multidirectional memory of the murals does more than visualize larger patterns of authoritarian power. The murals' physical, material presence also works against historical amnesia. As Alejandro Murguía puts it, "every mural is a challenge: a gauntlet against forgetting, an attempt to recover the memory and history... of our continent" (98). Even if a mural fades or another mural is painted over it, its presence remains as a layer embedded in the historical palimpsest of this muralistic site of memory. The murals collected in Balmy Alley document varying historical moments and are produced in different historical moments. Balmy Alley's mural environment is an ever-changing dialogical process, as murals are variously recovered, replaced, and added, creating a shifting landscape of transhistorical and transnational connections. Balmy Alley's mural environment juxtaposes different social conditions and forms of systemic violence, and it will continue to adapt to reflect new sociohistorical conditions and modes of oppression and exploitation. When new murals get painted in the future in response to the sociopolitical, socioeconomic, and environmental justice concerns of the future, they will exist in dialogic relationship with our present moment and with the atrocities of the past in Central America that PLACA marked across the walls.

While I have focused on the mural production in Balmy Alley, a single mural that is not part of a mural environment can also function as a polyphonic space and engage in similar cultural and memorial work. For example, Juana Alicia (the Chicana PLACA muralist who painted "Te Oímos Guatemala" and then replaced it with "Una ley inmoral...") expands her focus from Central America to include anti-authoritarian and social justice struggles in the Caribbean, the Southern Cone, and Greater Mexico in "The Spiral Word: El Codex Estánfor" (2012; fig. C.6). At the center of one panel, "Resistance and Revolution" (shown on this book's cover), is legendary Argentine folk singer Mercedes Sosa, who went into exile as result of the brutality of the Argentine military dictatorship. Superimposed on Sosa's sarape is a collection of Latin American and African American faces, including those of José Martí, the Zapatistas, Violeta Parra, Asata Shakur, Gabriela Mistral, the Mirabal sisters, the mothers of the disappeared women in Juarez, John Carlos and Tommie Smith, and Comandante Ramona (Alicia, "Narrative for Murals"). Alicia's inclusion of the Dominican revolutionary sisters who fought against the dictator Rafael Trujillo alongside figures who symbolize Black Power, indigenous sovereignty, and anticolonialism, as well as the movement against feminicide, generates an image of multilayered struggles that are distinct but part of the tapestry of hemispheric history.[14] With Sosa at the center of the panel and multiple people embedded in her image, the usual spatial division between different individual people depicted in a mural is collapsed as the viewer sees both the individual people and the collective simultaneously. The trans-American vision of revolutionary resistance that emerges spans generations and racial groups. As a stand-alone mural, "Resistance and Revolution" exhibits a palimpsestic and

FIGURE C.6 Juana Alicia, "Resistance and Revolution," from *The Spiral Word: El Codex Estánfor*. ©2012. Image Courtesy of Juana Alicia

multidirectional memory similar to the murals in Balmy Alley and exemplifies how the counter-dictatorial imaginary can appear in various mural forms.

Creating Political Memory

Murals are just one example of the ways U.S. cityscapes and aesthetic productions are visually marked with the histories of Latin American dictatorships and U.S. military interventionism in the region. While this book has focused on the genre of the novel as one case study in the formal features of the Latina/o counter-dictatorial imaginary, and this coda has opened outward to consider the aesthetic form of the mural, there is more work to be done on other forms of Latina/o cultural production, such as music,[15] film,[16] and Day of the Dead altars.[17] I offer the framework of the Latina/o counter-dictatorial imaginary in the hope that more scholars will examine other kinds of creative production and other genres of Latina/o literature that remember Latin American authoritarian regimes and that use the trope of dictatorship to interpret the sociopolitical landscape of the United States.[18] Artistic productions contain the marks of these histories, and documenting and analyzing their placas will enrich and extend the contours of the Latina/o counter-dictatorial imaginary that I have sketched in this book. Latina/o cultural production—whether in the form of a novel, mural, altar, film, or music—is a material reminder of the afterlives of the dictatorial past and contemporary dictatorial forms of oppression that shape our cityscapes, our rituals of remembrance, our activist projects, and our creative endeavors. These haunting pasts continue to be aesthetically, affectively, and politically resonant in the present.

I began the introduction to this book with an epigraph by Gloria Anzaldúa in which she asserts that Latina/os and Latin Americans must know each others' histories and struggles. Anzaldúa's coeditor of *This Bridge Called My Back*, Cherríe Moraga, expands on the value of this panethnic, transnational, and intergenerational historical consciousness. "I watch how desperately we need political memory, so that we are not always imagining ourselves as the ever-inventors of our revolution; so that we are humbled by the valiant efforts of our foremothers; and so, with humility and with a firm foothold in history, we can enter upon an informed and re-envisioned strategy for social/political change in decades ahead," Moraga relates in her recent preface to the book's fourth edition ("Catching Fire," xix).[19] Latina/o dictatorship novels and the murals in Balmy Alley offer the kind of political memory that Moraga asserts we so desperately need.[20] Their counter-dictatorial imaginary gives us a framework to make connections not only between different forms of authoritarian power and oppression but also between different movements for justice and decolonization. The need for "revolutionary solidarity" continues unabated (xvi). As does the necessity of exposing the forms of authoritarian power that dictate our ability to build a more just future.

{ NOTES }

Introduction

1. Julia Alvarez begins her novel about the Rafael Trujillo dictatorship in the Dominican Republic, *In the Time of the Butterflies*, with the image of a tree. The Dominican survivor Dedé draws a tree on an envelope as she attempts to give directions to the "gringa dominicana," who stands in for the Latina author-testimonial collector (3). Dedé "watch[es] the tree come apart and back together again" as she folds and unfolds the envelope, which symbolically sets up from the beginning of the novel the divisions and connections between Dominicans on the island and in the United States (4).

2. In *Graphs, Maps, Trees* Franco Moretti examines Latin American dictator novels as "the final branching of the tree" of free-indirect style (89). Moretti's tree offers an abstract model for the literary history of free-indirect style in world literature, positioning the Latin American dictator novel within the style's development over the last two hundred years. My use of the family tree to describe the development of the dictatorship novel in the Americas is more metaphorical and is not based on one particular narrative style but instead is focused on capturing a genre tradition shared by Latin Americans and Latina/os.

3. Among others, consider Ana Castillo's *Sapagonia* (1990); Julia Alvarez's *How the García Girls Lost Their Accents* (1992) and *In the Time of the Butterflies* (1994); Cristina García's *Dreaming in Cuban* (1992), *The Lady Matador's Hotel* (2010), and *King of Cuba* (2013); Francisco Goldman's *The Long Night of White Chickens* (1992) and *The Ordinary Seaman* (1997); Graciela Limón's *In Search of Bernabé* (1993); Demetria Martínez's *Mother Tongue* (1994); Héctor Tobar's *The Tattooed Solider* (1998); Edwidge Danticat's *The Farming of Bones* (1998) and *The Dew Breaker* (2004); Loida Maritza Pérez's *Geographies of Home* (1999); Sandra Benítez's *The Weight of All Things* (2001); Angie Cruz's *Let It Rain Coffee* (2005); Junot Díaz's *The Brief Wondrous Life of Oscar Wao* (2007); Daniel Alarcón's *Lost City Radio* (2007) and *At Night We Walk in Circles* (2013); Sylvia Sellers-García's *When the Ground Turns in Its Sleep* (2007); Carolina de Robertis's *The Invisible Mountain* (2009) and *Perla* (2013), and Michael Nava's *The City of Palaces* (2014). I include Edwidge Danticat, a Haitian American writer, in this list, even though Haitian Americans usually do not identify and are not identified as Latina/os. I do so not to impose an identity category but because Haitian Americans challenge Latina/o studies to extend its scope and parameter of analysis and consider countries like Haiti that get restricted to Caribbean studies or to studies of the African diaspora when there are many shared geographic, racial, and imperial histories. Moreover, her fiction exhibits a number of the narrative tactics and themes that I explore in this book. See Ricardo Ortiz's "Edwidge Danticat's *Latinidad*" for an elaboration on how Danticat's *The Farming of Bones* puts pressure on our constrained conceptualizations of Latina/o identity, and see my "Novel Testimony" for an analysis of how *The Farming of Bones* testifies against the Trujillo dictatorship's 1936 massacre of Haitians and Haitian Dominicans in the Dominican Republic. For a moving meditation on how the Duvalier

dictatorships have haunted Danticat's writing and molded her sense of her role as a writer, see the titular essay in *Create Dangerously: The Immigrant Artist at Work.*

4. Charles Taylor defines the social imaginary as "the ways people imagine their social existence, how they fit together with others, how things go on between them and their fellows, the expectations that are normally met, and the deeper normative notions and images that underlie these expectations" (23).

5. José Martí's notion of "Nuestra América" envisions a Latin America united against U.S. imperialism; at the same time, Martí was deeply critical of the different forms of white supremacy enacted against African Americans, Native Americans, and Latina/os in the United States, so "Our America" invokes a broader interracial and transnational solidarity against U.S. domination. Martí is now a foundational figure in Latina/o and trans-American studies whose work has inspired and served as a basis for literary histories of the Americas. See, for example, Susan Gillman, Michael Hames-García ("Which America Is Ours?"), Laura Lomas, and José David Saldívar (*The Dialectics of Our America*).

6. This is not an exclusively South-to-North process. Just as migratory routes are circular, so are generic routes. We can consider, for example, how in 2007 Latinos Junot Díaz and Daniel Alarcón were both named to the highly prestigious and selective Bogotá 39, a list of the top thirty-nine Latin American authors under the age of thirty-nine. See Milian and Riofrio for a discussion of the implications of the Bogotá 39's list in terms of how we conceive of Latina/o literation in relation to Latin American literature.

7. While I tend to use "trans-American" and "hemispheric American" studies throughout the book, scholars use a variation of terms for this work, including "transamerican," "pan-American," "comparative American," and "transnational American" studies. For scholars who have tracked how Latina/o and Latin American writing overlap and who have excavated the transnational nature of Latina/o literature, see the work of scholars such as Debra A. Castillo, Raúl Coronado, Juan Flores, Kirsten Silva Gruesz, Monica Hanna, Rodrigo Lazo, Laura Lomas, Marissa K. López, Claudia Milian, Ricardo L. Ortíz, Yolanda Padilla, Ana Patricia Rodríguez, John "Rio" Riofrio, María Josefina Saldaña-Portillo, José David Saldívar, Ramón Saldívar, Alicia Schmidt Camacho, Maya Socolovsky, Diana Taylor, and Ariana Vigil.

8. Most critics agree that the genre has its roots in colonization but that its modern trajectory began with Domingo Faustino Sarmiento and caudillo literature.

9. Though I have named some of the most prominent writers, there are a vast number, range, and variety of dictatorship novels in the Latin American tradition. The genre is extensive and varies nationally and by region. Scholars are prone to offering long lists of dictatorship novels; see Carlos Pacheco, Gabriela Polit Dueñas, and Adriana Sandoval, as well as Julio Calviño Iglesias's elaborate schematic renderings.

10. See Juan Carlos García, Roberto Gónzalez Echevarría, Carlos Pacheco, Gabriela Polit Dueñas, and Ángel Rama (*Los dictadores*). See Mary K. Addis for a study of the dictator novel as a genre, building on Fredric Jameson's notion of genre criticism.

11. Some typical themes and tropes associated with the Latin American novels include the monopolization of power and authority, supernatural or messianic power, omnipotence, megalomania and egocentrism, cruelty, barbarism, repression (i.e., censorship, terror, jail, torture, death, disappearance), paranoia, dependency on the United States, the dictator's lack of class and education, the dictator as a bastard child, the dictator's solitude (i.e., lack of friendship and of love), the dictator's double or doppelgänger, the dictator's homosocial acolytes, the dictator as an archetype or myth, the failing body of the dictator, the demise of the dictator (through assassination, exile, or natural death). Some frequently used narrative

techniques include marvelous realism, satire, parody, ridicule, exaggeration, myth, interior monologue, free-indirect style, multiple voices, fractured texts, and temporal fragmentation.

12. I use "afterlife" in the sense in which Macarena Gómez-Barris defines it: "the *afterlife* of political violence [is] the continuing and persistent symbolic and material effects of the original event of violence on people's daily lives, their social and psychic identities, and their ongoing wrestling with the past in the present" (*Where Memory Dwells*, 6).

13. This is a good place to note that throughout the book I deliberately do not translate the code-switching in my quotations from the novels. If a Spanish word or phrase is not translated in the novel, I do not offer a translation, so as to give readers the same effect they would have if they were reading the novel and to honor the author's linguistic decisions. In addition, I do not italicize the Spanish words I use, so as not to mark them as foreign and Other. If a Spanish word is italicized in a novel or scholarly work, I retain those italics.

14. Most critics writing in Spanish, such as Juan Carlos Garcia and Conrado Zuluaga or Juan Antonio Ramos, respectively, use the terms "la novela del dictador" (the novel of the dictator) or "la novela de la dictadura" (the novel of the dictatorship), while Carlos Pachecho prefers "la narrativa de la dictadura" (narratives of the dictatorship). Some scholars use broader terminology; for example Julio Calviño Iglesias uses "la novela del poder personal" (the novel of personal power) to encompass various types of authoritarianism historically, from *caciquismo* to military juntas, and Gabriela Polit Dueñas uses "la novela del caudillo" (the novel of the strongman) to emphasize local and national male authoritarian leaders. Domingo Miliani distinguishes between "las novelas de una dictadura" (novels of a dictatorship), "las novelas de un dictador" (novels of a dictator), and "las novelas del dictador" (dictatorship novels); the subtle linguistic shift is difficult to translate, but he uses the first two terms to distinguish between novels where the object of narration is a real historical dictator or dictatorship and the third term to refer to novels where the object of narration is a symbolic, abstract, or syncretic dictator/dictatorship that stands in for a continental conditional rather than a single historical regime. Publishing in English, the critics Ignacio López-Calvo, Mary K. Addis, and Gerald Martin generally use the "dictator novel" or the "novel of the dictator," while Magalí Armillas-Tisyera prefers "dictator-novel" and Roberto González Echevarría switches between "dictator-book" and "dictator-novel." Raymond Leslie Williams vacillates between the terms "dictator novel," "novel about dictatorship," and "novels on the dictator theme."

15. Cuba fits awkwardly into the dictatorship novel tradition, in terms of both Latin American and Latina/o literatures. I will discuss the reasons for the latter later; here I want to note the reasons for the former. Latin American literary critics rarely include novels that depict Fidel Castro as a dictator in their studies of dictatorship novels. This is in part due to the conflicted relationship between Latin American writers and the Cuban Revolution; many novelists enthusiastically supported the revolution and then came to have more complex and varyingly critical attitudes toward the Cuban government. This is also in part due to Latin American literary critics tending to implicitly define the anti-dictatorial stance of the dictatorship novel as a stance against right-wing authoritarian regimes.

16. My project's more expansive use of dictatorship is similar to Ariana Vigil's more expansive approach to militarization and war. Vigil explains that her book "considers institutionalized violence and militarism not just on the battlefield but also within the family, the nation, and the community. This questioning of the spatial and temporal parameters of war acknowledges how individuals and communities far removed from the front lines are nonetheless impacted by armed conflict. In this way *War Echoes* calls

attention to the space in which the majority of individuals experience violence while insisting that we recognize the myriad of ways in which war 'comes home,' particularly for women and communities of color in the United States. The book thus...illustrates how U.S. Latina/o texts offer a unique perspective on the intersections of race, gender, sexuality, and militarization" (2–3). Moreover, like Vigil, "rather than make a causal claim" between different forms of dictatorial domination, my book "makes a correlative one, emphasizing the prevalence of violence" across the Americas (6).

17. Carlos Pacheco writes that "la primera relación entre la narrativa y el dictador es bélica" (the primary relationship between the narrative and the dictator is antagonistic) (29), while Juan Carlos García observes: "el texto literario de todas las épocas coincide...en configurar un personaje que el lector tiende a despreciarlo, a combatirlo, a querrer derrocarlo....La literatura puede seguir teniendo un espacio para el compromiso social sin disminuir su imprescindible valor estético...su capacidad de ser, simultáneamente, arte y compromiso" (the literary texts of all periods agree...in the configuration of a character who the reader despises, would like to fight, would like to depose....Literature may continue to provide a space for social commitment without losing its essential aesthetic value...its capacity for being, simultaneously, art and politically committed) (18–19). For an exception to this line of thinking, see Armillas-Tisyera, who has recently accounted for the tangled and complex politics of resistance and complicity and the ambivalence at the heart of the Latin American genre. Unless otherwise noted, this and all subsequent translations in this book are mine.

18. Miliani distinguishes between texts that denounce dictators/authoritarian regimes and those that exalt them, but critics generally only study denunciatory texts under the rubric of the dictatorship narrative.

19. Such claims are frequent. See Pacheco, who cites writers and scholars who see the dictator as "la única creación política del mundo hispanoamericano" (the only political creation of the Hispanic world), "un arquetipo latinoamericano" (a Latin American archetype), and "una figura clave" (a key figure), as well as those who consider dictator novels "mitos necesarios" (necessary myths) for understanding "la realidad hispanoamericana" (Latin American reality) (31). See also Polit Dueñas (30).

20. This also problematically ignores the long history of dictatorship in Europe extending back to Roman times, as well as dictatorships in other parts of the world.

21. Gene Bell-Villada points out, in relation to political discourse, that Latin America is "notorious for its military dictatorships, so much so that certain words from its procedures and its ethos—'junta,' 'incomunicado,' 'politico,' 'número uno'—have infiltrated the sidelines of the U.S. political lexicon" (481). Ignacio López-Calvo likewise notes: "Latin America has been typically misrepresented in the U.S. news media through a sensationalist prism that basically limits the information to drug trafficking, natural disasters, and dictators" (3).

22. This also forecloses fruitful global comparisons. There is a rich tradition of dictatorship novels in world literature ranging from Salman Rushdie's *Shame* and Mohammed Hanif's *The Case of the Exploding Mangoes* to Ngugi wa Thiong'o's *Wizard of the Crow* and Nuruddin Farah's *Variations on the Theme of an African Dictatorship* trilogy, not to mention novels dealing with Stalin's, Hitler's, and Franco's authoritarian regimes. For a comparative study of Latin American and African dictator novels, see Armillas-Tiseyra.

23. What is now called symptomatic reading or a hermeneutics of suspicion has been dominant among ethnic literary scholars who, to use Fredric Jameson's famous term,

unearth the "political unconscious" of a text through ideology critique. Critics such as Stephen Best and Sharon Marcus argue that we need to "attend to the surfaces of texts rather than plumb their depths" and move away from a symptomatic reading of literary form and toward a "surface reading" of aesthetic form (1–2). While I agree with their view of the importance of attending to the surface of a text, their dismissal of identity politics and the important work done by critics (and artists) to expose how race, ethnicity, gender, sexuality, class, and ability shape subject formation and inform one's social location is troubling. Instead, my method is more closely aligned with the work of Paula M. L. Moya and Ralph E. Rodríguez. Moya theorizes a method of close reading that combines surface and symptomatic readings of literature; her method "model[s] a form of close reading that interprets a literary work's themes, structure, plot, and symbolism in terms of the ideas and practices that reflect, promote, and contest the pervasive sociocultural ideals of the world(s) with which the work engages" (36). Rodríguez moves away from but does not dismiss symptomatic readings with his "neo-formalist reading of race," which develops a method for "reading race on and off the page" that thus "affords us an opportunity to pause and question the very racial logics that govern our lives and reading practices" ("In Plain," 88).

24. Latina/o literary critics such as Mary Pat Brady, John Alba Cutler, Marcial González, Monica Hanna, Julie Avril Minich, Ernesto Javier Martínez, William Orchard, Paula M. L. Moya, Yolanda Padilla, Ralph E. Rodriguez, Elda María Román, Ramón Saldívar, and Jayson Gonzalez Sae-Saue have variously articulated the critical payoffs of formalist analysis, close reading, genre criticism, and an attention to narrative structures and character types in interpreting Latina/o literature.

25. See Alex Woloch and Paula M. L. Moya for additional explications of socioformal analysis. Levine terms her methodology "strategic formalism." Her strategic formalism is similar to socioformal analysis and allows for ideology critique and formalist analysis to coexist methodologically. It is beyond my scope here to parse the differences between these formalist approaches, but I heed their insistence that we attend to the sociopolitical dimension of literary form in analyzing Latina/o dictatorship novels.

26. See also Coleen Lye, who argues that we need to understand "race as form rather than as formation," especially for ethnic literary criticism (97).

27. Michael Hames-García expounds a theory of "multiplicity" that accounts for how social identities mutually constitute one another (*Identity*, ix–xi, 4–14). The influential and important term "intersectionality" captures the intersection of separate identities, but as Hames-García explains, it is also necessary to "account for multiplicity, understood as the mutual constitution and overlapping of simultaneously experienced and politically significant categories such as ability, citizenship, class, ethnicity, race, gender, religion, and sexuality. Rather than existing as essentially separate axes that sometimes intersect, social identities blend, constantly and differently, expanding one another and mutually constituting one another's meanings" (13).

28. Ramírez's image also personifies the past migrating in the guise of "fantasmas mojadas," which could be translated as "wet ghosts" but, given that the ghosts are compared to other "clandestine migrants," is more accurate as "wetback ghosts"—problematically using a pejorative term (mojado) for undocumented migrants. Yet I want to shift the focus from the illicit and clandestine ghost-migrant to the epistemologically undocumented, for we have not sufficiently accounted for the dictatorial pasts that subtly mark or abruptly interject themselves into Latina/o literary narratives and thus shape Latina/o literary history. This book seeks to document these texts.

29. Armillas-Tisyera uncovers the archival history of the correspondence that the "Los padres de la patria" generated between multiple writers; most importantly, she unpacks the varying conceptualizations of political commitment that the correspondence reveals to illuminate new readings of the formal narrative politics of Carpentier's, García Márquez's, and Roa Bastos's novels. Her formalist analyses and her attention to the international political and economic forces that support dictators align with the concerns of this book.

30. For example, many Latin American critics have focused on mourning in postdictatorship cultural and intellectual production. Two prominent examples are Idelber Avelar and Alberto Moreiras. Avelar investigates the centrality of allegory in postdictatorship writing in Chile because he sees it as the trope that voices mourning and considers mourning "the postdictatorial imperative par excellence" (3). Moreiras, meanwhile, believes "that political rethinking in the postdictatorship regime is done in the condition of mourning" (Franco, *The Decline*, 259). The dead are being mourned, as is the death of the belief in the socialist revolutionary ideals of the Cold War moment. Jean Franco posits that contemporary literature "can still hold out the possibility if not of alternatives, of the possibility of thinking beyond mourning" (259). Latina/o postdictatorship cultural production, in particular the novel, fulfills this possibility and provides the occasion for thinking alongside and beyond mourning because the cultural work that it does is not primarily focused on mourning.

31. For additional pertinent conceptual meditations on the "post," see Kwame Anthony Appiah, Elda María Román ("'Post' Ethnic Forms"), and Ella Shohat.

32. In this sense, we could think of them as doing similar work to the neo-slave narratives of the African American tradition. While African American literature and scholarship is highly attuned to the trauma of slavery and to the residual elements of slavery in the present, Latina/o literature and scholarship has not had a specific genre that is dedicated, like the neo-slave narrative, to thinking intergenerationally about the afterlife of trauma. I propose that the Latina/o dictatorship novel is such a genre.

33. Though scholarship has tended to focus on one national-origin group (and mainly on Chicana/os or Puerto Ricans), comparative Latina/o literary studies is a growing field. For other studies configured around pan-Latina/o groupings of authors and cultural producers, see Frederick Luis Aldama (Latina/o Caribbean), Raphael Dalleo and Elena Machado Sáez (Latina/o Caribbean), Lyn Di Iorio (Latina/o Caribbean and Chicana), Laura Halperin (Latina Caribbean and Chicana), Juanita Heredia (Latina Caribbean, Chicana, Latina South American), Ylce Irizarry (Latina/o Caribbean and Chicano), Ellen McCracken (Chicana, Latina Caribbean, Latina Central American), John "Rio" Riofrio (Chicana/o and Latina/o South American), Maya Socolovsky (Latina/o Caribbean and Chicano), David J. Vázquez (Latina/o Caribbean and Chicano), and Ariana Vigil (Latina/o Central American and Chicana/o). For transnational Latina/o literary scholarship, see note 7.

34. I take these two terms from Juan Flores's "Pan-Latino/Trans-Latino" chapter (141). As Flores observes, "pan-ethnicity only stands up as a reliable group category if it is recognized that each group making up the aggregate is at the same time participating in a transnational community" (157).

35. Scholars vary widely in the ways they designate various Latino subgroups. For example, scholars will use "U.S. Central American" or "Central American American," or "Latino-Caribbean" or "U.S. Caribbean Latino," for regional identities and "Dominican American," "Dominican-American," or "Dominican diaspora" for national identities. I use

"Latina/o Caribbean," "Latina/o Central American," and "Dominican American," etc., in order to distinguish U.S. Latina/os from Latin Americans. Yet I do so recognizing that these distinctions can sometimes be difficult to make, and depending on the context and purpose, we may want to consider them together as Latina/o Americans. As Frances R. Aparicio puts it, "when does a Latin American become a U.S. Latina/o?" ("(Re)constructing," 39). This is an unresolved question, as some scholars, such as Marissa K. López, Juan Poblete, John "Rio" Riofrio, and María Josefina Saldaña-Portillo, assert that Latina/o (and more specifically Chicana/o in the case of López's work) identities begin their formations in Latin America. I vary my usage throughout this book—between, for example, "Latina/o Dominican," "U.S. Dominican," "Dominican American," "Latina/o Caribbean," "Latina/o", and "Latina/o American"—depending on what I intend to highlight. To quote Aparicio, my "use of labels is contingent, fluid, and relational, used strategically and structurally depending on the context" (43).

36. For example, U. S. Dominican novels have been considered part of what Ignacio López-Calvo calls the Trujillo cycle of novels, and he and others have drawn comparisons between Junot Díaz's and Julia Alvarez's work and other Dominican and Latin American novels. Meanwhile, Ariana Vigil and Ana Patricia Rodríguez richly examine representations of the Central American civil wars in U.S. Central American and Chicana/o literature. Yet these two Latina/o Caribbean and Latina/o Central American literary and scholarly traditions are not in conversation. I am precisely interested in pulling these disparate strands together into a broader comparative framework. Ricardo L. Ortíz provides a comparative consideration of Latina/o literature to identify what he terms "a post–Cold War Latina/o literary project" ("The Cold War," 87). Ortíz uses the Cold War as an organizing framework for his study, whereas I use the category of the dictatorship novel. Providing an overview of the central thematic concerns in twenty-first-century Latina/o literature, Theresa Delgadillo notes: "war spills across the pages of twenty-first-century Latina/o fiction in unprecedented ways" (600). Her use of "war" broadly encompasses Latin American independence struggles and the civil wars in Central America, as well as the U.S. wars in Asia and the Middle East. This book is also interested in tracking civil wars and authoritarian regimes across Latina/o literature but begins a decade earlier, in the 1990s, and focuses on Latin America.

37. For overviews of the historical development of the terms "Hispanic" and "Latino" by the government, social movements, the media, and academics, see, among others, Cristina Beltrán, Marta Caminero-Santangelo, Arlene Dávila, Suzanne Oboler, and Juan Poblete.

38. Unlike English, Spanish is a gendered language; for example, the *o* in Latin*os* can refer to male Latinos or can encompass both men and women, whereas the *a* in Latin*as* refers only to women. Rather than use the gender "neutral" term "Latino" to encompass men and women, feminist scholars, activists, and artists, developed "Latina/o" to be more gender inclusive. "Latin@" is now also used by scholars and activists, and "Latinx" has recently gained a great deal of visibility and traction; both terms seek to trouble constructed and normalized gender binaries. For articulations of the term "Latin@," see Juana María Rodríguez and Claudia Milian. J. M. Rodríguez explains that the @ arose in cyber communities and reads it as "sign of positionality" that orthographically "impacts the semiotic, the metaphorical, the phonetic, and categorizing function of a word" (126). Milian meditates on the @ as "Latin-at" (153) and "Latin-*at*-ness" (152), noting that it pushes us to consider seriously "where the Latins were really *at* in U.S. Latinoness and Latinaness and in other ambits" (153). She also points out that even though it is not clear how to pronounce the @ in "Latin@," it is also not clear how to pronounce the slash in "Latina/o" (153). Rather than pronounce the @ as "at," I prefer to pronounce it as "ao"—based on the Caribbean

vernacular tendency to drop the *d* in "ado" and pronounce it as "ao" (for example, "pelado" is pronounced "pelao")—so as to trouble gender dynamics phonetically. While I personally prefer this pronunciation because, unlike "at," it is rooted in Spanish (and because my family is from the Caribbean coast in Colombia, so it sounds very familiar), I am conscious that it does not reflect the linguistic patterns of other Latin American groups, and in a book centrally concerned with comparability, I am wary of Caribbean pronunciation dominating. So I opt for the currently more common and conventional usage of Latina/o as shorthand for "Latina and Latino." I agree with Milian that we need a "theoretical undertaking of topos and praxis of the *meaning* of the slash" in Latina/o studies (156, emphasis in original), but this note is not the place to theorize the slash, the arroba, or the *x* in Latina/o, Latin@, or Latinx.

39. Other frameworks for thinking through the category of Latina/o include Cristina Beltrán's and Juana María Rodríguez's articulations of Latina/o as rhizomatic; Marta Caminero-Santangelo's suggestion that we consider Latina/o as "a contradictory totality" (*On Latinidad*, 19); María Elena Cepeda's coining of "imagiNation" to highlight how identity narratives function as "both noun *and* verb" (8); Raúl Coronado's proposition that Latina/o is not a subject position but a "literary and intellectual culture that emerges in the interstices between the United States and Spanish America" (30); Carmen E. Lamas's idea of the "Latina/o continuum"; Marissa K. López's use of Chicana/o as "historical process" and "evolving project" (12); José Esteban Muñoz's theorization of "feeling Brown" ("Chico"); David J. Vázquez's concept of the "matrixed subject" (*Triangulations*, 6); and Juan Flores's explication of "differentiated site of intersecting social identities" (202).

40. For an examination of how Chicana/os were inspired by revolutionary movements in Latin America in the 1970s, see Alan Eladio Gómez's *The Revolutionary Imaginations of Greater Mexico*.

41. Other Latina/o dictatorship novels that depict more positive representations of the Cuban Revolution include Julia Alvarez's *In the Time of the Butterflies*, Junot Díaz's *The Brief Wondrous Life of Oscar Wao*, and Demetria Martínez's *Mother Tongue*.

42. Like other Cuban American writing, García's novel "tentatively negotiate[s] a precarious relationship with a larger body of Latino literature that has become identified in much literary criticism with left-wing and third world politics" (Caminero-Santangelo, 167).

43. Throughout this book, I use the terms "migrant" and "migration" rather than "immigrant" and "immigration" because they accommodate a number of different trajectories, goals, and statuses, rather than the fixed destination with the eventual acquisition of citizenship implied by "immigration." When it is relevant to the novels and characters that I examine, I draw attention to migrants' different statuses—for example, as exiles, refugees, or undocumented migrants.

44. See Ricardo L. Ortíz for a brief overview of U.S. Cold War foreign policy from George Freeman to Jean Kirkpatrick and how it shaped support for brutal dictatorships and military juntas across the Southern Cone and Central America from the 1950s to the 1980s and indeed even earlier with its support of Trujillo and the Duvaliers in the Caribbean from the 1930s to the 1980s ("The Cold War," 72–75).

45. Lillian Guerra articulates the distinction: "besides the allegations offered in counter-revolutionary rhetoric, there is little known evidence that the Cuban government has continually used violence and wide-scale terror as a means for maintaining rule or drowning dissent. U.S.-backed military dictatorships in Chile, Argentina, Guatemala, El Salvador, Brazil, Paraguay, Uruguay, and surrogate armies like the Contras annihilated hundreds of thousands of people seeking economic equity and political rights from the 1960s through

the 1980s, and into the mid 1990s, in some cases. During this time, Cuba apparently remained a haven from both right-wing and left-wing violence.... The country's record on human rights abuses then and today pales by comparison with the excesses of capitalist military regimes operating with full U.S. support in the same decades" (206).

46. This ideological construction of Castro in the U.S. imagination is evident when El Comandante enjoys a hot dog on the streets of New York City and the "image of the oldest living dictator eating a hot dog went viral and ended up on the front page of the next day's *New York Post* with the headline TYRANT WANTS THE WORKS!!!" (222). The three exclamation points add humor to the depiction and emphasize how vociferously El Comandante is perpetually represented as a tyrannical dictator in the U.S. imagination.

Chapter 1

1. In Díaz's novel, an additional similarity is that both the dictator and the writer are machistas and philanderers, since Yunior and Trujillo share this investment in heteropatriarchy, though Yunior is self-critical about this whereas Trujillo is not. Cristina García satirizes this commonality in her novel *King of Cuba* as the dictator, El Comandante, and the writer, Babo, who are friends, compete over women and El Comandante "pull[s] a revolutionary droit du seigneur," seducing a woman to whom Babo is also attracted and infuriating him (57).

2. Indeed, Magalí Armillas-Tisyera observes, "anxiety about the possible similarities between the writer and dictator is built into the dictator-novel and is, in fact, a question that lies only partially hidden at the heart of the genre" (*Dictator-Novel*).

3. In chapter 2, I focus on how Salvador Plascencia's *The People of Paper* collapses the difference between the two by depicting the writer as a dictator, in effect reversing Asturias's formulation by imagining that every novel is always a dictatorship.

4. For histories of the Trujillo dictatorship, see Robert Crassweller, Lauren Derby, Jesús de Galíndez, Eric Paul Roorda, and Richard Lee Turits.

5. See Ignacio López-Calvo's examination of "the key conventions, shared concerns, and recurrent *topoi*" in literary and cultural representations of Trujillo, which he terms "Trujillato narratives" (xi).

6. Vargas Llosa's novel differs from the other novels published in the 1970s because it splits narrative focalization between three main perspectives—Trujillo, the men who assassinated him, and Urania Cabral, the daughter of an ex-minister of the regime who is raped by Trujillo when she is a teenager. Despite this technique of split focalization, the dictator remains a major character and an organizing perspective, hence my placement of Vargas Llosa with his boom generation contemporaries and their explorations of dictators' consciousnesses, despite *The Feast of the Goat* having been published twenty-five years later. Moreover, Junot Díaz's character Abelard Cabral and his moral dilemma of his daughter's beauty attracting Trujillo's desire are allusions to *The Feast of the Goat*, and Yunior foregrounds this intertextuality at the same time that he criticizes Vargas Llosa's novel (80, 234).

7. When the dictator as protagonist is at the very center of the character-system, he monopolizes the narrative perspective, and the interiority and agency of minor characters are subordinated to that of the dictator as protagonist and narrator or focalizer. Woloch makes similar observations about the relationship between narrative centrality and totalitarian political centrality in relation to *King Lear*: "if the protagonist in certain forms of narrative has absolute centrality—controlling the narrative's structural dimension—so the monarch qua monarch has an achieved form of political centrality: the state as a whole,

as well as *each* individual subject within the state, takes on an identity only vis-à-vis the king" (283–284).

8. In *Story and Discourse* Seymour Chatman defines story as the "what" of the narrative and the content of narrative expression, splitting story into events (actions and happenings) and existents (characters and settings). Discourse, for Chatman, is the "how" of the narrative, the form of narrative expression, and the structure of narrative transmission. For Woloch, story is the content (the *events* in the novel) while discourse is the form of the telling (the *rendition of* the events in the narrative). While Chatman places character in the story part of narrative, Alex Woloch's notion of character-space refuses the split, illuminating the interrelation between story and discourse when representing character.

9. An example of this is the use of the word "Trujillo" to stand in for abusive power. When the band discovers Beli beaten nearly to death outside the cane-field, they wonder what has happened to her. "*Trujillo*, she whispered" (151). The comment references the Gangster's wife, who is *a* Trujillo but introduces herself as "Soy Trujillo" (141). These uses of "Trujillo," common in the novel, do not denote Rafael Trujillo, the minor character in the story; instead, they evoke Rafael Trujillo, the symbol and embodiment of authoritarian repressive power. As a result of his pervasive presence in the novel's discourse and his minor presence in the novel's story, Trujillo does not fit neatly into the two kinds of minor characters Woloch lays out.

10. For a long list of Trujillo's titles, see Juan Carlos García, and for discussions of Trujillo's use of titles and the various narratives put forth by the regime to justify its existence, see Derby, Horn, López-Calvo, and Galíndez.

11. "Culo" means "ass," and the suffixes *-cracy* and *-crat* denote a form of government and a member of government, respectively, so the humorous bilingual neologisms *culocracy* and *culocrat* ("asscracy" and "asscrat") indicate a regime ruled by hypermasculine sexuality.

12. Maja Horn demonstrates how Trujillo's "own pervasively hypervirile discourse was, at least in part, a strategic response to the imperial and racialized notions of masculinity that accompanied the U.S. presence in the country, especially during the U.S. military occupation" of the island, thereby contesting the typical reading of Trujillo's masculinity through the Latin American caudillo tradition (1). As I have briefly discussed, Díaz satirizes Trujillo's predatory hypermasculinity, but the novel's references to U.S. imperial occupation and Spanish imperialism and its structural positioning of Trujillo in the narrative discourse ask us to make the type of deeper structural linkages that Horn points out. Horn also demonstrates the way "Trujillo's performance and discourse of masculinity were clearly in part informed by the U.S. military values that he had internalized from the U.S. marines," which is similar to the way the Guatemalan character of sergeant Guillermo Longoria in Hector Tobar's novel *The Tattooed Soldier* is socialized into violent masculinity through his military training in the United States in counter-insurgency tactics, which I discuss in chapter 4 (34).

13. In his reading of Domingo Faustino Sarmiento's foundational text *Facundo*, Roberto González Echevarría claims "the modern dictator-novel is born" when Sarmiento declares "I am Facundo Quiroga" and recognizes that his power as writer is "analogous" to that of the dictator (207). It is interesting to think of Sarmiento's identificatory claim in relation to Lola's claim in Díaz's novel. Lola's claim is not based on an individual identification—I am Rafael Trujillo—but on a collective identification—we, all Dominicans and Dominican Americans, are Rafael Trujillo. This switches the emphasis away from writing and authority and toward the ways people exert dictatorial power or reinforce it. Marissa K. López

examines Sarmiento's travel writing within "a nascent Chicana/o national imaginary"; here in Junot Díaz's work we get a glimpse into how the Latina/o counter-dictatorial imaginary is heir to Sarmiento's *Facundo* as well (27).

14. Praising Trujillo was part of the "political economy of discourse" in Dominican society, and "military epithets such as 'Capitán' were adopted as popular male forms of address" (Derby, 5). By naming his character "the capitán" and giving him the job of a military police captain who engages in brutal political repression under Joaquin Balaguer's presidency, Díaz links the past to the present. Oscar is killed for "overstepping the scripts of hegemonic masculinity… in Dominican military culture," where military officials continue to have impunity (Horn, 128). The capitán thus symbolizes the post-Trujillato era and its unbroken connection to militarized violence and U.S. imperialism. As Torres-Saillant puts it in relation to Balaguer's rule, "the Trujillo power structure had returned with the backing of the United States and wearing the guise of a democracy" (*An Intellectual History*, 230). See Christopher González's relevant discussion of Balaguer as an authorial figure in the novel who "manage[s] to write with impunity, and write prolifically" (66).

15. Reflecting on her titular phrase "where memory dwells," Gómez-Barris relates: "I have come to think about the 'dwelling' of the memory of torture, disappearance, and forced exile… as a double entendre: as a literal 'living with' and inhabitance of bodies, psyches, and spaces; and as a lingering presence, one that persists, insists, resists, and exceeds the containment of these bodies and of the nation's boundaries, the afterlife of the event of violence" (28).

16. Oscar's life story begins and ends the novel, but he is the focus of the events on only 145 of its 335 pages.

17. Elena Machado Sáez argues that Yunior is a dictator in the text because he narrates "a foundational fiction about Oscar's progression from inauthentic diasporic male to an assimilated, unsentimental un-virgin" (538) and thereby silences "Oscar's points of queer Otherness" and suppresses hints of a "homosocial romance" between Yunior and Oscar (524). Yunior the character certainly exhibits authoritarian tendencies as he criticizes and seeks to discipline Oscar into the prototypical Dominican male. An additional reading arises as well when we foreground the formal features of the novel. I highlight Trujillo's demoted and Oscar's elevated positions in the novel's character-system, and I contend that parody and exaggeration are key critical modes in the novel, whether they are used to deflate and denigrate Trujillo or subtly criticize Oscar's social marginalization.

18. For more on narrative transculturation, see Ángel Rama's *Writing across Cultures*.

19. See the varying uses *to say* ("they say," 1, 154; "it was said," 107, 120, 145, 141, 241, 251), *to believe* ("was believed," 3, 17, 83, 111, 125, 243; "believed to be," 151, 226; "if the stories are to be believed," 233), *to claim* ("there are those alive who claim," 139; "the family claims the first sign," 248), *rumor* ("rumor had it," 106, 255, 266; "was rumored," 91, 110, 120, 121, 145; "if the rumors are to be believed," 78), *legend* ("legend has it," 97, 212; "so goes the legend," 155), *whisper* ("the whispers," 80, 245; "it was whispered," 226), *secret* ("a secret history," 245; "in a secret report," 99; "one of the Island's best known secrets," 217; "our parents are still so damn secretive," 227), etc.

20. In addition, "it is said" is a transmogrification in English of the Spanish phrase "se dice," used to indicate something discussed orally among a community.

21. See historian Richard Turits, who describes "the state's oppressive control over speech, its elaborate mechanisms of surveillance, and the potentially horrific consequences for even the smallest slip of the tongue" (228).

22. The tropes of silence, evasive narration, secrets, gaps, and disappeared histories appear in a number of Latina/o dictatorship novels, including Daniel Alarcón's *Lost City Radio*, Carolina de Robertis's *Perla*, Francisco Goldman's *The Long Night of White Chickens*, Demetria Martínez's *Mother Tongue*, and Sylvia Sellers-García's *When the Ground Turns in Its Sleep*.

23. This is a significant number if we think of Oscar as a martyr figure who, like Jesus Christ, died young. It is additionally compelling if we consider the number's signification of truth and the triumph of good, which resonates with Yunior's declaration that he will craft a zafa against the fukú and my argument that the zafa occurs through the form in which in the story is told.

24. This includes the prologue, which deals heavily with the Trujillato; thus, only three footnotes are found in the sections dealing with Oscar's life.

25. Most of the existing critical work on the paratextual device of footnotes in fictional novels focuses on either European or U.S. postmodern novels. Díaz's work is in the vein of other footnoted novels by Latina/os and Latin Americans, including Sandra Cisneros's *Caramelo*, Patrick Chamoiseau's *Texaco*, Manuel Puig's *El beso de la mujer araña*, and Augusto Roa Bastos's *Yo el supremo*. Both Puig's and Roa Bastos's novels are dictatorship novels.

26. Given that many readers are unaccustomed to reading these paratexts, the footnotes also force the reader to pause and follow a different but related line of thinking, actively engaging with the text. The breaks in traditional patterns of reading that the footnotes produce are a structural mechanism for consciousness-raising about the oppressions recorded in the footnotes.

27. See Benstock and Grafton for a discussion of academic footnotes vis-à-vis fictional ones.

28. To put it in Monica Hanna's terms, the footnotes also stage a "historiographic battle royal" between Yunior's and Trujillo's different "historiographic models" ("Reassembling," 504).

29. According to Pierre Bourdieu, a linguistic habitus is the subset of dispositions one acquires through speaking in particular contexts. It is shaped by the linguistic field—the structured system of sanctions, censorships, and linguistic relations of power based on unequal distribution of linguistic capital. The field of dictatorship shapes linguistic practices, I argue.

30. "Signifyin'," as Henry Louis Gates, Jr., terms it, "is the figurative difference between the literal and the metaphorical, between surface and latent meaning" and "presupposes an 'encoded' intention to say one thing but to mean quite another" (82).

31. *The Brief Wondrous Life of Oscar Wao* is also embedded in the tradition of social justice characteristic of the U.S. ethnic novel. Ramón Saldívar theorizes that *The Brief Wondrous Life of Oscar Wao* and *The People of Paper*, which I analyze in chapter 2, are part of a new turn in twenty-first-century, postrace-era ethnic fiction toward "historical fantasy," which "indicates desires for forms of social belonging that link the realm of public political life to the mysterious workings of the heart's fantastical aspirations for substantive justice, social, racial, poetic, or otherwise" (596).

Chapter 2

1. Revolutionary movements against and assassination attempts to defeat the dictator appear as a trope in Latina/o fiction as well; see, for example, Julia Alvarez's *In the Time of the Butterflies*, Cristina García's *King of Cuba*, and Daniel Orozco's "Somoza's Dream."

2. Plascencia's novel is one of a number of Chicana/o texts in the dictatorship novel tradition. Consider Ana Castillo's *Sapagonia*, Sandra Benítez's *Bitter Grounds* and *The

Weight of All Things, Graciela Limón's *In Search of Bernabé,* Demetria Martínez's *Mother Tongue,* and Michael Nava's *The City of Palaces,* the majority of which focus on representations of military dictatorships in Central America. See also short stories, plays, and comics such as Helena María Viramontes's "The Cariboo Café," Benjamin Alire Sáenz's "Alligator Park," Castillo's *Psst...,* and Oscar 'the Oz' Madrigal's "Los Borrados."

3. In Augusto Roa Bastos's *Yo el supremo,* for example, El Supremo dictates the narrative of his regime, along with his directives, to his scribe. The novel represents language as power, but the words the dictator dictates signify endlessly, eluding his control; and the text he narrates is full of errata, notes made by others, and a scribe who copies down his directions and leaves intact passages that he orders him to strike from the text. In *The People of Paper,* it is not language that betrays the dictator but the novelist's own characters, since the writer is the dictator.

4. Though Gabriel García Márquez's *El otoño del patriarca* is not a metafictional novel and does not figure the writer as a dictator, García Márquez once remarked that his novel is "almost a personal confession, a totally autobiographical book, almost a book of memoirs.... If instead of seeing a dictator you see a very famous writer who is terribly uncomfortable with his fame, well, with that clue you can read the book and make it work" (qtd. in Martin, *Gabriel García Márquez,* 354).

5. "Saturn" is the fictionalized author figure's nickname throughout the novel. His girlfriends, Liz and Cameroon, occasionally call him by another nickname, "Sal." In this chapter, I use "Saturn" when referring to the storyline about the war between the characters and the figure they call Saturn, and I use "Sal" when referring to the storyline about the fictional character of the author. I refer to the real-life author as Plascencia.

6. The novel was first published by McSweeney's Books in hardback; in this edition, the name is cut out, but in the paperback edition, published by Harcourt Books, the name is scratched out. See p. 117 in both editions.

7. See Frederick Luis Aldama ("Magical Realism") for a reading of Plascencia's use of magical realism in relation to other Latina/o fiction.

8. Coined by Américo Paredes, "Greater Mexico" refers to the collection of Mexican-origin people and culture that extends beyond the boundaries of the nation-state of Mexico. Labor diasporas as well as economic and political structures and cultural and symbolic forms are all part of Greater Mexico. As Ramón Saldívar theorizes it, Greater Mexico is "an imaginary social space consisting in transnational communities of shared fate," and its extension beyond the site of the nation-state "represents a far more complex imaginary site for the emergence of new citizen-subjects and the construction of new spaces for the enactment of their politics outside the realm of the purely national" (*Borderlands,* 59).

9. Like Junot Díaz and Héctor Tobar, Salvador Plascencia completed an MFA in creative writing, and we can read these writers as part of what Mark McGurl has called the "Program Era," pointing to the proliferation of degree-granting creative writing programs in U.S. universities after World War II. Interestingly, Francisco Goldman and Cristina García, the two other novelists I examine at length, though they have taught in MFA programs, do not have MFAs; they have both had lengthy careers as journalists, and García holds a master's in international relations.

10. For example, William Faulkner declares: "I think that any writer worth his salt is convinced that he can create much better people than God can" (qtd. in Olson, 341); Gustave Flaubert affirms: "the author in his work should be like God in his universe, everywhere present but nowhere visible" (qtd. in Miller, 24); and John Barth advises: "The novelist,

whose trade is the manufacture of universes, needs ideally to know everything, or else he's liable to do an even odder job than God did" (qtd. in Stonehill, 690).

11. Olson is responding to Jonathan Culler's charge that the concept of narrative omniscience and the corresponding analogy of an omniscient author-narrator to an omniscient God is inaccurate and therefore useless for analyzing the narrative techniques it is meant to describe. Culler partly finds the author-as-God analogy inappropriate because literary criticism does not presuppose the perfection of the author or the freedom of the characters. Yet the characters in *The People of Paper* precisely demand their freedom from narrative control, and the minor character Smiley critiques the imperfect author, who cannot even remember that he created Smiley.

12. Salvador Plascencia is not the first creative writer to have characters who speak back to challenge the author or who even rebel against the author. Consider Luigi Pirandello's *Six Characters in Search of an Author*, Denis Diderot's *Jacques the Fatalist and His Master*, Bret Easton Ellis's *Lunar Park*, O'Brien's *At-Swim-Two-Birds*, Gilbert Sorrentino's *Mulligan Stew*, John Fowles's *The French Lieutenant's Woman*, or Ronald Sukenick's *The Death of the Novel and Other Stories*. The difference between these novels and Plascencia's novel is that it is the only novel in which the author is figured as a dictator and the only novel in which all-out revolution is waged against the author.

13. "Tyrant" (46, 95, 101, 232, 228), "dictator" (232, 235), "master" (216), "despot," (212, 232), "emperor" (240).

14. Interestingly, Federico de la Fe assumes they are in a novel that has a traditional plot arc, but this basic plot diagram does not hold true for many modernist and postmodernist novels. Given his claims to a deterministic plot, the diagram plays most heavily on the naturalist novel, where fate is not in a character's hands but in the hands of an overdetermining force, be that nature or heredity or the social environment. In this sense, it is appropriate that Federico de la Fe imagines narration and plot as an element of nature, i.e., the planet Saturn.

15. This is not to say that the characters cannot make their own decisions—clearly they can, since in the world of the novel they wage a war against the novelist—rather, decisions are overdetermined by the plot written by the author. It is also important not to fall into the trap of the fallacy of authorial intention. Rather, the novel asks us to participate in a thought experiment about what, from characters' perspectives, it feels like to be in a novel's plot. We suspend disbelief and pretend that the author is not writing the characters' emotional responses. John Fowles's comment in *The French Lieutenant's Woman* is appropriate here: "The novelist is still god, since he creates (and not even the most aleatory avant-garde modern novel has managed to extirpate its author completely)" (qtd. in Olson, 343).

16. Here I am adapting Mary Pat Brady's observation that Chicana authors "write with urgency about the power of space, about its (in)clement capacity to direct and contort opportunities, hopes, lives" (9).

17. We as readers are placed in the position of Saturn because we read the characters' thoughts on the pages of the novel. The characters' critiques of Saturn violating their privacy also apply to us. We are guilty of peering into their inner thoughts merely by virtue of reading the novel.

18. "The major effect of the Panopticon: to induce in the inmate a state of conscious and permanent visibility.... Power should be visible and unverifiable.... [In] the peripheric ring, one is totally seen, without ever seeing; in the central tower, one sees everything without ever being seen" (Foucault, *Discipline and Punish*, 201–202).

19. I deliberately use the phrase "border patrol state" from Leslie Marmon Silko's "The Border Patrol State (1997), not only because it is an accurate descriptor but also because of the way her essay makes connections with dictatorships in Latin America. In this essay, Silko relates how she is detained by the border patrol and points out the ways her experience intersects with border patrol violence against undocumented migrants, people of color, and people who might look like they would help political refugees coming from El Salvador, Guatemala, or Nicaragua to escape the U.S.-funded military regimes and civil wars occurring in those countries. Moreover, she makes a provocative and relevant analogy between the U.S. border patrol and the military dictatorship in Argentina. Silko writes, "I will never forget that night beside the highway. There was an awful feeling of menace and violence straining to break loose. It was clear the uniformed men would be only too happy to drag us out of the car if we did not speedily comply with their request (asking a question is tantamount to resistance, it seems). So we stepped out of the car and they motioned for us to stand on the shoulder of the road. The night was very dark, and no other traffic had come down the road since we had been stopped. All I could think about was a book I had read—*Nunca Más*—the official report of a human rights commission that investigated and certified more than 12,000 'disappearances' during Argentina's 'dirty war' in the late 1970s. The weird anger of these Border Patrolmen made me think about descriptions in the report of Argentine police and military officers who became addicted to interrogation, torture, and the murder that followed. When the military and police ran out of political suspects to torture and kill, they resorted to the random abduction of citizens off the streets. I thought how easy it would be for the Border Patrol to shoot us and leave our bodies and car beside the highway, like so many bodies found in these parts and ascribed to drug runners" (116–117). Given the recent escalation of deaths due to the hypermilitarization of the U.S.-Mexico border and the high number of disappeared and unidentifiable undocumented migrants, Silko's evocation of the disappeared and her application of it to the borderlands is prescient.

20. Given the parameters of this book, it is important to connect this militarization of the U.S.-Mexico border with the United States' support of military dictatorships in Central America. See Timothy J. Dunn's study of how the militarization of the U.S.-Mexico border is linked to the low-intensity conflict strategies that the United States developed in Central America in the 1980s.

21. Like Francisco Goldman's *The Ordinary Seaman* and Héctor Tobar's *The Tattooed Soldier*, as well as Benjamin Saenz's *Flowers for the Broken* and Demetria Martínez's *Mother Tongue*, *The People of Paper* examines undocumented migration to the United States and authoritarian regimes in Latin America in relation to each other but in a more symbolic fashion.

22. Federico de la Fe's and EMF's last battle strategy is to "envelop Saturn, to surround him, forcing him to concede *territory*" (210, emphasis added).

23. With regard to the characters' war against Saturn and the idea of the page as territory or land, the New York millionaires Ralph and Elisa Landin state: "We came to see the war we had funded. We read the field reports; with our fingers we followed the path of Saturn over maps that illustrated the topography of land and the perilous terrain of love" (219). The Landins' funding of Saturn in the war recalls the U.S. funding of dictatorships and right-wing counter-insurgency groups in Latin America.

24. There are allusions to Napoleon Bonaparte in both Latin American and Latina/o dictatorship novels, as well as globally. The dictator of Mexico, Porfirio Díaz, was an admirer of Napoleon and a dedicated Francophile, and the novel also alludes to the French presence in Mexico with a reference to Napoleon III.

25. Malintzín or Malinche was an indigenous translator and the lover of conquistador Hernán Cortés. She is seen as a traitor of the Mexican people because she reputedly gave Cortés information about her people that enabled the Spanish to conquer the Aztecs. Malinche traditionally symbolizes treachery in Mexican and Chicano culture, but Chicana artists and critics, such as Norma Alarcón, Gloria Anzaldúa, and Cherríe Moraga, have recovered her to symbolize the strategic negotiations of patriarchal sexual exploitation.

26. The transhistorical comparisons trace the arc of coloniality in the Americas back to European imperialism, with colonizers like Columbus and Cortés, who are also referenced in the novel, in addition to fictional characters, such as Merced's British lover, who is described as a colonizer (197), and Cardinal Mahoney's lover Ida, who is the descendant of a colonizer and a slave (223). Subcomandante Sandra remarks that "Federico de la Fe had showed us that we were not free people, that we were enslaved and serving Saturn" (216). The slave analogy connects to the Napoleonic allusions in the novel. The reference invokes the centrality of the successful Haitian Revolution to the Americas in establishing the first free Black nation and in defeating the French Empire, inflicting a devastating blow on Napoleon. In rising up against Saturn, then, the characters battle for their liberation against the tyranny of slavery, imperialism, and dictatorship, all symbolically embodied in Saturn.

27. For more on this rupture between fiction and reality, see Ramón Saldívar's interpretation of the novel as a "border novel riven by the trope of *parabasis*" ("Historical Fantasy," 581).

28. This resonates with the Latin American dictatorship novel, which often depicts the solitude of power and parodies the abject body of the dictator.

29. Smiley, who has been instructed in their guerilla warfare tactics, has been charged with slitting Saturn's throat with his carnation knife and "letting his ink drip" or, if that is not possible, stealing all the pages of the novel that have been written up to that point and writing on the title page, "'You are not so powerful'" (105). This humorous description shows how the characters imagine turning the violence of writing against the writer, spilling his blood and his ink as they assassinate him, and how they literally attempt to take back their own stories by stealing the pages of the novel that contain their narratives.

30. In the film *Stranger Than Fiction*, the main character, Harold Crick, seeks out the literary critic Jules Hilbert in an attempt to figure out what to do about the voice in his head narrating his life that has proclaimed he is going to die. The first task Hilbert assigns Harold is to determine the genre of story he is in. "The only way to determine the story you are in is by determining the stories you are not in," Hilbert explains, as he uses examples from various novel genres ranging from myths and fairy tales to murder mysteries and gothic fiction. Playing on generic conventions, the film asserts that to understand his narrative predicament—the fact that his life is being narrated and perhaps even authored by another person—Harold must understand the genre he is living out. Each genre carries a series of conventional moves and, more important for Harold, a certain expected resolution. The literary professor and the protagonist presume that by deducing the genre they may be able to strategically interrupt its plot conventions and foil Harold's predicted death. Ironically, while the characters in *The People of Paper* similarly rebel against their narration, unlike Harold they have no idea what kind of book their lives are composing, nor do they seek to discover the genre.

31. In *Stranger than Fiction*, Harold Crick describes his empty life to Professor Hilbert when they first meet; brutally honest with him, Professor Hilbert declares: "I'm not an expert in crazy. I'm an expert in literature theory. And I gotta tell you, thus far there doesn't

seem to be a single literary thing about you. I don't doubt you hear a voice. But it couldn't possibly be a narrator because, frankly, there doesn't seem to be much to narrate." The comment, full of dramatic irony, is telling, for it points to our aesthetic predilection for complexity, interesting characteristics, and dramatic life episodes. Harold, whose life seemingly contains nothing of interest to an outside observer, appears to be antiliterary because nothing interesting happens to him, since he works for the Internal Revenue Service and does the same thing every day. The episode is interesting given Federico de la Fe's conclusion that to ward off Saturn's surveillance they need only remove all cause for narrative interest, hiding their interior lives beneath the endless mundane details of their existence. While Hilbert advises Harold "don't do anything that will move the plot forward. Instead let's see if the plot finds you," Federico de la Fe assumes that if they simply do nothing Saturn will lose interest and the plot will find a different set of characters to move it forward. This tactic of evasion presumes a realist or modernist novel where characters are unique individuals whose consciousnesses will be explored and that plot is driven by character interiority and dramatic action.

32. Given the novel's concern with the toxic effects of pesticides on farm workers and on the environment, we can also read it as fitting into "a distinctive Chicano/a environmentalism, one that drew on Mexican American traditions and that joined ecological concerns with social concerns," which Randy J. Ontiveros has termed "Green Aztlán" (88).

33. See David J. Vázquez's "Toxicity and the Politics of Narration" for a reading of the significance of this lead poisoning in terms of environmental racism and internalized racism.

34. For the theorization of dialogized heteroglossia and centripetal and centrifugal forces, see Bakhtin.

35. See Alicia Schmidt Camacho's theorization of migrant melancholia; for a reading of the melancholic Mexican American figure in *The People of Paper*, see Guadalupe Carrillo.

36. Implicit in her criticism that he is a sellout is the accusation that he has assimilated into white middle-class "American" culture. What John Alba Cutler identifies as "the specter of assimilation that looms over Chicano/a literature" thus also looms over Liz's accusation (1).

37. Elda María Román has tracked "the way upward mobility has been correlated with cultural betrayal" in Chicana/o literature and culture, and this accusation of cultural betrayal is evident in Liz's critique of Sal as a sellout (102). Liz's accusation stings, and the novel uses metafiction to explore the author's anxiety about his class status and the possibility that as a novelist he is exploiting his characters. We can therefore read the novel as an example of what Román identifies as "the sellout narrative," in which, she explains, "characters may pass white, act subservient to whites, Anglicize their names, define themselves in opposition to the racialized or immigrant working class, and deny their cultural heritage—all in an attempt to improve their socioeconomic status" (12). Román demonstrates the way in which ethnic upward mobility narratives dramatize a need for group solidarity by either punishing these figures who stand in for betrayal or by attempting to reintegrate them back into an affective community for political purposes, which she calls "sellout redemption narratives" (195). The fact that Sal ends up heartbroken and alone suggests that he is punished by the narrative for his oppressive behavior toward his characters and the women in his life. On the level of plot, he remains a sellout and an outsider. On the formal level, however, the novel reinforces a commitment to a working-class ethnic collective through the author's self-critique and through its formal and thematic interrogation of exploitation and the policing of undocumented migrants.

38. In addition to Santa Anna, see Leo R. Chavez study of this stigmatizing discourse, which is encapsulated in his term the "Latino threat narrative" (21).

Chapter 3

1. The Patriarch provides refuge to the deposed dictators of Latin America, allowing them to live in a "casa enorme que parecía un transatlántico encallado en la cumbre de los arrecifes" (big house that looked like an ocean liner aground on the top of the reefs) (16–17; Rabassa, 33). This figuration of the former dictators' residence as a shipwreck parallels how the Patriarch's presidential palace is described as a "naufragio" (shipwreck) (86; Rabassa, 50), and just as the former dictators are covered in "la rémora del exilio" (the barnacles of exile) (62; Rabassa, 36), by the end of the novel the Patriarch's body is also lined with "remora" (barnacles), and he looks like an "ahogado" (drowned man) or a shipwreck victim (378; Rabassa, 242).

2. Rodríguez theorizes "the ever-shifting literary, cultural, and historical configurations of the Central American isthmus as an in-between discursive space linking regions, peoples, cultures, and material goods. I offer the trope of the *transisthmus*—an imaginary yet material space—as a spatial periodizing term and as a 'cultural provision' for reading Central American literatures and cultures outside of categories that up to now have elided larger regional complexities" (*Dividing the Isthmus*, 2).

3. For an overview of the emergent field of U.S. Central American studies, see Arturo Arias and Claudia Milian.

4. See Ariana Vigil's *Understanding Francisco Goldman* for analyses of both of these texts and for an overview of Goldman's journalistic and literary career. Produced for the Understanding Contemporary American Literature series at the University of South Carolina Press, Vigil's book demonstrates how Goldman is an "American" writer "in the broad, hemispheric, multi-lingual sense of the term," accounting for his contributions to both U.S. and Latin American literatures.

5. Idelber Avelar, Naomi Klein, and David Harvey, among others, argue that the violence of military dictatorships (particularly that of Augusto Pinochet in Chile) made the transition to the free market possible, ushering in neoliberalism. In the words of Jean Franco: "drawn into the deadly logic of the Cold War, the military of the Southern Cone and Central America became engaged in a war on communism that would not only destroy civil society but also facilitate the transition from welfare states to the porous neoliberal state by removing certain obstacles—the bargaining power of workers, the dreams of a liberated society. This epochal change was brutal" (*The Decline*, 12). See Klein and Harvey for an overview of the history of neoliberalism and of its basic tenets.

6. See anthropologists Michael Orbach and Helen Sampson for ethnographic explanations of strict shipboard hierarchies and the captain's dominant position on the ship.

7. If, as I discuss in chapter 2, the political analogy of the author-as-dictator and the divine analogy of the author-as-god in Salvador Plascencia's *The People of Paper* offer different conceptualizations of narrative power, the political analogies of the captain-as-king and captain-as-dictator are also suggestive in terms of narrative power dynamics. If the trope of the captain-as-king indicates that captains inherit absolute power from the structural position they occupy, the trope of the captain-as-dictator redirects attention to

issues of surveillance and repression and captures how captains are granted impunity to wield their power. In other words, while the monarchical equation imagines a captain with absolute authority, the political equation imagines an abusive and surveilling captain. The slippage between dictator and king is often exploited for parodic effect in the Latin American dictator novel, as is most evident in Enrique Lafourcade's *La fiesta del rey Acab*, which translates as "King Acab's Party" (though the published English-language translation of the novel is *King Ahab's Feast*). In *King of Cuba*, Cristina García plays on this association of the dictator with a king and extends it by also applying it to the conservative Cuban exile.

8. For historical studies of mariners and the exploitation and abuses they suffer, see Fink, Linebaugh and Rediker, and Rediker (*Between the Devil*); for contemporary studies, see Chapman and Sampson.

9. International law requires that a ship be registered in a sovereign state. A flag of convenience is what is used when owners register their merchant ship in a different sovereign state from their own. The incentive for U.S. shipowners like Elias and Mark to purchase a flag of convenience in another country like Panama is to evade laws, regulations, and taxes, thereby reducing operating costs and increasing profits. Shipowners and shipping operations use flags of convenience the way manufacturing companies use maquiladoras and free trade zones, making merchant ships "sweatshops at sea" (Fink). Goldman's choice of Panama for the flag of convenience gestures toward Panama as a site of U.S. imperial designs to control a passage across Central America via canal and train (which the United States also attempted in Nicaragua). See Carlisle for a detailed historical account of the United States' direct role in creating Panama's flag of convenience, whereby Panama offered its "sovereignty for sale." See Shemak and Naimou for more extensive explanations and analyses of the flag of convenience system, especially as it pertains to *The Ordinary Seaman*.

10. The Somoza family dictatorship, which ruled Nicaragua from 1939 to 1979, was headed first by Anastasio Somoza, then by his son Luis, and finally by his son Anastasio.

11. Beckman uses the term "capital fiction" "to designate two overlapping discursive arenas: first the fictions generated by capital . . . and second, the specific expressions of those fictions within an assembled corpus of images and texts" (x).

12. Elias is a modern-day successor of the filibusterers and business tycoons, from Cornelius Vanderbilt and William Walker to the United Fruit Company, whose imperialist ventures scarred the history of Central America, in particular of Nicaragua, Panama, Honduras, and Guatemala (the home countries of the men on the *Urus* and of its flag of convenience). Given that Walker invaded and declared himself president of Nicaragua, we can also think of Walker as a dictator. The United Fruit Company flourished by fostering relationships with Central American dictatorships and exploited the open shipping registry to create the Honduran registry and flag all of its ships in Honduras.

13. For more on this, see Greenburg's *Manifest Manhood and the Antebellum American Empire*.

14. Like Elias, the Ship Visitor also espouses a romantic, masculinist fantasy that he is a man of adventure, as he envisions himself a brave and tough "American" following in the footsteps of the frontiersman or oldtime seaman. Ariadne is seduced by the stories he tells her about his "strangely fantastical yet heroic occupation" (147), which she thinks make him a "real American guy, not office bound but free," with a "romantic, manly aura" (145).

15. Mark sarcastically thinks that they are "Capitán Elias Cortés and First Mate Mark Pizarro" (305).

16. Elias calls them "los blacks," and the crew take to calling them this as well (45).

17. Elias paints the name of the *Urus* on its prow and stern and then later paints over the name before abandoning the ship. This act of erasure, coupled with the flag of convenience registry and the pier's isolation, visually highlights how the *Urus* functions as a covert site in which Elias and Mark both secretly hide and actively cover over their exploitation of the Central Americans as their actions render the men unauthorized migrant laborers who are never paid and have no legal recourse to claim compensation. The *Urus* functions as a covert site of empire. "Covert" evokes a secret that is both kept and covered over through the active involvement of people and the psychological involvement of disavowal, which echoes how Elias and Mark use the *Urus* as a covert site to enact their imperial venture and deny their unethical actions (Friedman, 19–20). The novel provokes us to see the *Urus* as a symbolic microcosm of U.S. imperial actions both at home and abroad, as both a setting for and trace of U.S. empire. The painting-over of the ship's name also recalls Herman Melville's "Benito Cereno," another text about a slave ship in the Americas. For an intertextual reading of *The Ordinary Seaman* in relation to "Benito Cereno," see Gruesz, Lazo, and Naimou.

18. This humorous bilingual wordplay that simultaneously reveals a truth about relations of power recalls Junot Díaz's bilingual wordplay with the fukú or "fuck you" curse generated by coloniality, which I analyze in chapter 1.

19. The ship also encapsulates David Graeber's argument that "modern capitalism is really just another form of slavery" (61).

20. Also see Cacho's discussion of the links between social death and neoliberalism; of particular pertinence here is how employers (like Elias and Mark) take advantage of neoliberal ideology and the rightlessness of their undocumented employees to bypass laws and regulations (18–22).

21. See Shemak for a discussion of how this also ties to the category of "refugee seaman" created by the United Nations in 1957.

22. The preferential treatment given to Cubans also reflects the United States' contradictory pro-democracy foreign policy vis-à-vis dictatorships; that is, the United States supported many right-wing dictatorships and military juntas (including Anastasio Somoza in Esteban's home country of Nicaragua and Fulgencia Batista in Gonzalo's home country of Cuba) but purportedly was defending democracy with its embargo of Cuba and its repeated attempts to topple Fidel Castro. The Cuban Refugee Program was the most comprehensive refugee assistance program in the history of U.S. immigration. María Cristina García relates an interesting but little-known piece of Cold War history in which the United States supported secret military training camps for Nicaraguan and Cuban exiles in South Florida to help support the Contras (155).

23. The novel figures the seamen simultaneously as veterans of the civil wars in Central America, refugees from a dictator-ship, and exploited undocumented migrants. The linkages are prescient, given that there are currently many undocumented migrants, especially unaccompanied minors, from Central America coming to the United States, and the contemporary migratory push factors are rooted in the U.S. support for Central American authoritarian regimes and funding of brutal counter-insurgency military campaigns and the aftermath of this violence.

24. Donald E. Pease explains: "James confirmed the prevailing understanding of Ahab as a 'totalitarian type.' But after arguing that the [U.S.] security state had put into place the authoritarian rule it purported to oppose, he also generalized this type to include Ishmael,

whom he described as 'an intellectual Ahab,' as well as the members of the McCarren committee and the administrators of the national security state" (xiv).

25. See Naimou for a reading of the pauper's grave in relation to the history of African Americans in New York City.

26. In *A Lexicon of Terror* Feitlowitz's explains the "unprecedented, obscurant usage of a single word: *desaparecido*. It was coined by the Argentinian military as a way of denying the kidnap, torture, and murder of thousands of citizens. Then-commander of the army Roberto Viola put it this way: A *desaparecido* was someone who was 'absent forever,' whose 'destiny' was to 'vanish.' Officially, a *desaparecido* was neither living nor dead, neither here nor there. The explanation was at once totally vague and resoundingly final" (49). In *Cruel Modernity*, Jean Franco relates how disappearance is a "triple deprivation—of a body, of mourning, and of a burial" (192–193).

27. The theme of state-sponsored disappearances runs through Latina/o dictatorship fiction and is part of the postmemory attempt to use narrative as a form of reappearance; see, for example, Julia Alvarez's "Disappeared Does Not Take a Helping Verb in English," Daniel Alarcón's *Lost City Radio*, Graciela Limón's *In Search of Bernabé*, Demetria Martínez's *Mother Tongue*, and Carolina de Robertis's *Invisible Mountain* and *Perla*. While traditionally referring to state-sanctioned disappearances under Latin American authoritarian regimes, Goldman's novel is also one of a number of Latina/o fictional and documentary texts expanding the definition of los desaparecidos to include new forms of violence that produce disappearance, such as the feminicide in Juarez and the thousands of deaths of undocumented migrants who disappear on the migrant trails as they cross through harrowing conditions atop trains or on foot through Mexico and the southwestern United States.

28. In a 2012 discussion organized by the *Barnes and Noble Review*, close friends Francisco Goldman and Junot Díaz spoke about their writing processes and the particular traumatic histories they bear witness to in their work. Díaz relates: "For a people like mine, children of the abyss, of apocalypses without end—from slavery to dictatorship to immigration—bearing witness is sometimes all we had, like firing a flare up into the dark vault of the universe. Bearing witness in order (to quote you Frank [Francisco Goldman]) to put something back into the abyss so that it won't only be silence and loss" (Messer). Díaz's deliberate use of the word "abyss" recalls this scene in *The Ordinary Seaman*; at the same time, in Díaz's formulation, the abyss is not just something that happens to Bernardo and the crew on the *Urus*. It is passed down to the postmemory generation of U.S. Latina/os, as I outline in the introduction. Goldman's and Díaz's writings are both haunted by their inheritance of the histories of slavery, imperialism, dictatorship, and forced migration in Central America (Goldman) and in the Caribbean (Díaz).

29. I take the phrase "disappearing acts" from Diana Taylor's *Disappearing Acts: Spectacles of Gender and Nationalism in Argentina's "Dirty War."*

30. Shipwrecks are a common event in literature across time periods, from the Bible and Homer's *Odyssey* through William Shakespeare's *The Tempest*, Jonathan Swift's *Gulliver's Travels*, Daniel Defoe's *Robinson Crusoe*, Herman Melville's *Moby-Dick*, Gabriel García Márquez's *Relato de un náufrago* (*The Story of a Shipwrecked Sailor*), and Charles Johnson's *Middle Passage*; and shipwrecks continue to be popular in the U.S. cultural imaginary, evident in high-grossing and award-winning films such as *Titanic*, *Cast Away*, and *Life of Pi*. As is evident from this list, the shipwreck novel, like the dictatorship novel, is predominately written by men and focuses on male protagonists, and the ship functions both as a means

of throwing off the yoke of civilization and of masculine self-making. For a range of essays on shipwreck across time periods and cultures, see Carl Thompson's edited volume *Shipwreck in Literature and Art: Images and Interpretations from Antiquity to the Present Day*.

31. The Argentinian couple evokes the specter of the right-wing military dictatorships in Argentina that disappeared thousands of people.

32. Blackmore expounds: "the shipwreck narratives are stories of lived failure given that any voyage undertaken for the purposes of material acquisition or conquest that does not achieve these goals is one of defeat. In this, shipwreck represents on a first symbolic level the breaking apart of the ship of state as an economic entity and as an agent of imperialism and colonization. But, more disturbingly and significantly, the shipwreck narratives are evidence of the disruption of what might be termed an order of empire, both as a praxis and as a flow of hegemonic and authoritative texts" (44).

33. The *Oxford English Dictionary* defines "discourse" as "more generally: the onward course of something in space or time; succession or sequence of time, events, actions, etc."

34. Narrative theorists distinguish between story as the content of a novel (the events) and discourse as the form of the telling of a novel (the rendition of the events).

35. Thompson says that shipwreck narratives have a "tripartite structure—*threat, disaster,* and *aftermath*" (5). *The Ordinary Seaman* fractures this structure with its aftermath narrative, for it begins in the aftermath—119 days after their arrival to the wrecked ship—and the threats and disasters are scattered throughout the novel. Moreover, the novel ends with some of the crew trying to sail the *Urus* and instead wrecking it against the pier.

36. The narrative also depicts the crew's situation as if they were under fire or in a low-intensity conflict, drawing associative connections between Esteban's experiences battling the Contras in the Nicaraguan civil war and his experiences on the *Urus*.

37. This is also part and parcel of the novel's critique of linked histories of exploitation and domination, which wreck future progress. As Ariana Vigil points out in her analysis of this scene, the novel "explicitly *questions*...the relationship between futurity, progress, and movement," since it "simultaneously invoke[es] the futility of war as well as of capitalist development, economic expansion, and global integration" (*Understanding*).

38. For example, "Desastres" begins: "Now, one hundred and eleven nights later, Esteban lies awake shivering in two rank T-shirts and jeans and rotted socks under his thin blanket on his mattress on the floor, thinking, Oye? What if he takes the lifeboat? Rows away somewhere. Row where? Row away or run away. Where?" (33). "As Is, Where Is" begins: "In another six weeks, in December, after a night of freezing rain, the Ship Visitor will find them. He'll board a ship whose name and port of registration will have recently been painted off the prow and the stern" (129). "A Haircut" begins: "Grief stays hidden like an alarm clock with no hands set to go off at the bottom of sleep. But desire lies awake next to the boredom, doing everything it can to keep depression and deepest worry out of bed" (159).

39. There are more than sixteen short interruptions where Esteban's war memories surface in the present-day narrative, and there are a few episodes that recount for several pages or more his experiences in the war.

40. The seemingly postapocalyptic landscape is marred by "collapsed skeletons of piers and smashed terminals" (23). Docked on a "long, broken pier," the *Urus* is in a "deserted and apparently defunct end of the port" filled with "abandoned looking" buildings (19).

41. Bernardo's other refrain is to call the ship a "floating eggshell" and a "broken eggshell" (28). The broken floating eggshell also foreshadows Bernardo's dreams of economic stability

being shattered and of him not surviving the *Urus*, which, rather than nurturing him like an incubator for eggs, will serve as an incubator for his own economic exploitation and the empty abyss into which he will disappear.

42. Mexicans, Colombians, Salvadorans, Cubans, Guatemalans, Nicaraguans, Argentinians all help Esteban. The novel mentions Cuba, the Dominican Republic, Puerto Rico, Mexico, El Salvador, Nicaragua, Honduras, Guatemala, Panama, Ecuador, Colombia, Peru, Argentina, Brazil. This list of countries functions as a list of sites of dictatorship and U.S. imperialism in Latin America.

43. For histories of the Sanctuary Movement, see Golden and McConnel as well as Crittenden.

44. See Anais Spitzer's discussion of Derrida's *Glas* (2).

45. This foregrounding of the Central Americans' perspectives normalizes the Central Americans' point of view, such that we view the events through the eyes of the exploited rather than the exploiter, and when we do get the white perspective, it is filtered through the brown perspectives; for the Ship Visitor is not introduced as a character and does not focalize the novel until part 3 or page 129, Mark does not focalize the events until page 275, and Elias does not focalize the novel until 323.

46. The damaging holes in the novel include the holes on the damaged *Urus*, legal loopholes in the shipping industry that Elias and Mark use to escape accountability, the hole in the system that Bernardo disappears into as he is buried in an unmarked pauper's grave, emotional holes of despair, sexual holes, and bullet holes.

47. See James C. Scott's *Domination and the Arts of Resistance: Hidden Transcripts*, Gerald Vizenor's *Survivance: Narratives of Native Presence*, and Doris Sommer's *Proceed with Caution, When Engaged with Minority Writing in the Americas*.

Chapter 4

1. Héctor Tobar was part of the *Los Angeles Times* reporting team that covered the uprisings and won a Pulitzer Prize for their journalism.

2. Such death squads were prominent all over Central America, as we are reminded by William Duarte, Longoria's Salvadoran boss in Los Angeles, who tells him: "we have a battalion like yours in El Salvador. They're called the Atlatacl [sic] Battalion. Yes, yes, of course, you've heard of them. I forget, I'm talking to an expert here! The American training is simply the best, isn't it?" (29). The Atlacatl Battalion was a Salvadoran counter-insurgency unit trained, like Longoria, at the United States' School of the Americas; the battalion was responsible for massive human rights violations, including the famous El Mozote massacre. *The Tattooed Soldier* contains subtle references to El Salvador, Honduras, and Nicaragua, gesturing toward the United States' broader Cold War counter-insurgency operations in Central America.

3. Tobar's descriptions of Fort Bragg echo historian Lesley Gill's descriptions of Fort Benning and the counter-insurgency training at the School of the Americas, which began in the Panama Canal Zone in 1946 but was moved to Fort Benning, Georgia, in 1984. The School of the Americas is now called the Western Hemispheric Institute for Security Cooperation. Since its establishment it has trained over 64,000 soldiers. The U.S. Army John F. Kennedy Special Warfare Center and School, located in Fort Bragg, North Carolina, also specializes in training soldiers in counter-insurgency. Many of the most prominent

military officials who have been accused of the worst human rights violations under Latin American dictatorships have been graduates of the School of the Americas and have been trained with the infamous "Torture Manuals" used there. This training is important because, according to "numerous truth commissions reports from the 1980s and 1990s, state security forces were responsible for the vast majority of the massacres, murders, disappearances, and extrajudicial executions that characterized the twentieth-century Latin American 'dirty wars,' when many countries suffered under the boot of military dictatorships" (Gill, 11).

4. Latinos were frequently used to train the Latin Americans because of their Spanish proficiency and cultural background. That the lieutenant is Puerto Rican serves as a reminder of the United States' other imperial and militaristic operations in the hemisphere, and of how the United States sets Latina/os and Latin Americans against one other to prevent unity.

5. The CIA-orchestrated 1954 coup against the democratically elected president Jacobo Árbenz Guzmán instigated a brutal four-decade civil war, and by its official end in 1996, "the state killed two hundred thousand people, tortured tens of thousands more, drove hundreds of thousands into exile, and committed more than six hundred massacres" (Grandin et al., 5). Official reports by both the Recuperación de la Memoria Histórica (Recovery of Historical Memory Project; REMHI) and the Comisión para el Esclarecimiento Histórico (Commission for Historical Clarification; CEH) attribute approximately 90 percent of the deaths and disappearances to the Guatemalan government and its armed forces, which were supported by U.S. military training and economic aid. For more detailed official accounts, see the reports produced by the REHMI, which was led by the Catholic Church, and the CEH, which was administered by the United Nations. The REHMI released a four-volume, fourteen-thousand-page report in 1998, which has been published in English as *Guatemala: Never Again!*, and the CEH released a twelve-volume report in 1999, which has been published in English as *Memory of Silence* (ed. Daniel Rothenberg). For a terrific journalistic investigation of the assassination of Bishop Gerardi, who headed the REMHI project, see Francisco Goldman, *The Art of Political Murder: Who Killed the Bishop?*

6. This discourse of civilization and barbarism is central to the Latin American dictatorship novel tradition, evidenced by Domingo Faustino Sarmiento's foundational text, *Facundo: Civilización y barbaridad* (*Facundo: Civilization and Barbarism*). Moira Fradinger's observation that "the dictator is a 'barbaric' nucleus within the structure of the modern state, which uncovers the modern as 'barbaric,' instead of presenting just a modern failure to tame the barbaric," pertains here in relation to Longoria and his indoctrination into a discourse of civilization that results on barbaric deeds done in the service of the modern state (197).

7. See Lesley Gill for a detailed account of the numerous ways the United States military schools indoctrinate Latin American soldiers in the "American way of life" and American exceptionalism.

8. "America" designates both North and South America, but the United States has appropriated "American" much as it has historically taken territorial, political, and economic control of various parts of the Americas, including Guatemala.

9. See Ana Patricia Rodríguez's explanation of the jaguar's symbolic and spiritual significance to the Maya and her reading of the significance of the jaguar cult and bloodletting in relation to Longoria's and Antonio's positions in the novel (*Dividing the Isthmus*, 123–128).

10. See Diana Taylor's work on the spectacle of dictatorship in *Disappearing Acts*.

11. "This was hard work, raising the machete to cut and hack. They chopped and grunted like men trying to clear a sugarcane field" (247). The scene recalls Edwidge Danticat's *The Farming of Bones* in which Haitians and Haitian Dominicans are butchered by the Trujillato, often with machetes, a historical event known as the Parsley Massacre, to which Junot Díaz also makes reference in *The Brief Wondrous Life of Oscar Wao*.

12. When he first hears Longoria speak, Antonio is surprised that "the killer spoke like a peasant" (162). *"God knows what led this peasant to join the army, to become one of the army's hired killers,"* Antonio wonders (163), but he then dismisses the image of Longoria as a peasant, rationalizing that "if the solider was a Jaguar then he was the negation of what Antonio had just imagined him to be [a peasant]. He was a professional killer of peasants. Whatever he had been before, he now wore a jaguar tattoo. The tattoo was the key to everything" because "the Jaguars were synonymous with the terror the army spread through the countryside. They burned houses and left decapitated heads at the entrances of the villages they destroyed. The Jaguars had carried out a holocaust in the mountains" (164). Unlike Antonio, over the course of the novel readers learn what made Longoria the campesino into a killer of campesinos.

13. Chromophobia is the fear of color, especially the fear of being contaminated or corrupted by color, which Batchelor connects to the Western fear of and hatred for the Other.

14. Longoria reads a letter from a woman who is bored working as a housekeeper in Los Angeles; she requests that her family send her books in Spanish, especially by Guatemalan Miguel Ángel Asturias, mentioning that she has found his *El señor presidente* in Los Angeles. Ironically, Longoria is tempted to go "rescue" her from her dreary life, completely oblivious to the fact that *El señor presidente* is a renowned Latin American dictatorship novel and was originally unpublishable in Guatemala because of its critique of Jorge Ubico's dictatorship (159).

15. For his part, Antonio reads the events through the political optic he acquires participating in civil protests in Guatemala with Elena. "Elena would have loved to see the throngs of nannies taking over the streets of an American city, like the garbage workers they had joined in Guatemala all those years ago" (306).

16. Lesley Gill identifies this contradiction when she writes: "The consolidation of what became known as neoliberal capitalism required broad impunity for the powerful, and it depended on the maintenance of strong security forces to maintain 'order'; in the midst of increasing social decomposition and disorder that were themselves the result of the state's own policies. Order and disorder were thus closely connected in the state-sponsored, political and economic violence that plagued Latin America" (15).

17. "Scattered all over the green linoleum, everywhere, were pictures of corpses. A morgue had fallen from the album and spilled around his feet. Corpses with their eyes open" (175). The narrative goes on to repeat numerous times the phrase "corpses with" followed by detailed descriptions of the positions of the corpses and how they have been mutilated (175–176).

18. Moreover, the Rodney King uprisings are remembered as Black-on-white and Black-on-Korean violence, erasing the presence of Latina/os and Mexican and Central American migrants, who were also present as actors. Various scholars have done media analyses of the coverage of the riots, demonstrating how the media racialized the riots as predominantly African American actors and Korean American victims, despite the fact that the demographics of the riot zone neighborhood had shifted significantly and half of the residents were Latina/o Americans; moreover, half of the people who were arrested had

Spanish surnames, and 80 percent of these were recent migrants. See Davis (*Magical Urbanism*), Pastor, and Valle and Torres.

19. Tobar published the novel in 1998, two years after the signing of peace accords in 1996, and the novel's literary present is in 1992, two years before this official end to the civil war. Yet Antonio's words, and Tobar's novel, are prescient, as impunity has been nearly total. The most recent renewed effort to prosecute former military dictator General José Efraín Rios Montt on charges of genocide and crimes against humanity was not successful. Under Rios Montt's rule, the Guatemalan army waged a scorched-earth campaign that resulted in the genocidal massacre of indigenous communities similar to the ones we see Longoria participate in Rios Montt, like Longoria, received training at the School of the Americas.

20. The question-mark people exemplify the central question of the novel about how to conceptualize the transnational connections between different local manifestations of violence and impunity. This question about relationality and comparability is also central to Goldman's *The Ordinary Seaman*, which, as I argue in chapter 3, is posed in the form of the question "Y qué? What does any of that have to do with this?" (49). As I advance in the introduction, the Latina/o counter-dictatorial imaginary establishes linkages between different forms of domination.

21. These pasts appear subtly in the novel, for example, when Antonio is reminded of the ruins of the Mayan civilization as he looks at the traces of the razed neighborhood beneath the homeless camp and when Frank reminds him of San Martín de Porres, the Black patron saint of social justice in Peru who was the son of a slave. As Jean Franco puts it and as the novel suggests with its depictions of Longoria's brutal counter-insurgency campaigns, "atrocity has changed little since the sixteenth century. Las Casas's descriptions of Indians being thrown into the holes they dug…is eerily similar to accounts of the massacres documented in the Guatemalan report of the Commissions on Truth and Reconciliation, *Memoria del Silencio*" (*Cruel Modernity*, 6).

22. Similar to minor dictator figures in Latina/o novels such as the Gangster and el capitán in Díaz's *The Brief Wondrous Life of Oscar Wao* or Pico Duarte in Danticat's *The Farming of Bones*, Longoria functions as a stand-in for the dictatorship. Yet, different from these characters, Longoria is also given a much more elaborate backstory and is shown to be a victim of the dictatorship as well as a perpetrator of its abuses.

23. According to Marta Caminero-Santangelo, "the long narrative digression presented by Antonio's memories of his wife and son signifies the interruption of a new U.S. ethnic community in progress by the haunting reappearance of the (former) nation" ("Central Americans," 188).

24. Minich explicates this contradiction: "even as metaphors of disease, cleanliness and hygiene are mobilized metaphorically to justify armed warfare against the racialized poor, contaminated drinking/bathing water is used as a literal weapon. The metaphorization of illness, then, conceals how disease is mobilized against the very people accused of contaminating the body politic" ("Mestizaje," 223).

25. Looking at the *American Heritage Dictionary*, Peter Brooks notes that there are four basic definitions of "plot": a piece of land, a ground plan, the events that outline the action of a narrative, and a secret plan. Recognizing the "subterranean logic connecting these heterogeneous meanings," Brooks explicates how they are linked by an overall sense of boundedness and order (12). *The Tattooed Soldier* uses "plot" in four ways: as a "plot of land" (192, 193), as a "burial plot" (223), as a genre (the "plot of wartime drama," 238), and as a plan ("plot his revenge," 298). The homeless men are also displaced from their hillside plot of

land by the bulldozer that razes their encampment. These various uses of plot link war, death, displacement, and revenge, all key themes in the novel.

26. As Brooks points out, "the organizing line of plot is more often than not some scheme or machination, a concerted plan for the accomplishment of some purpose which goes against the ostensible and dominant legalities of the fictional world, the realization of a blocked and resisted desire" (12).

27. "An insurrection had taken place in these streets, a beautiful disorder. It was the window he stepped through to kill the tattooed solider. And now it was shut" (306).

28. I have not been able to find a book by the name of *Nicaragua Avenged*, so it appears that Tobar made up the title, which is interesting given that the novel refers to Miguel Ángel Asturias's *El señor presidente*. Daniel Orozco's short story "Somoza's Dream" is a Latino dictatorship short story about the assassination of Somoza.

29. Edwidge Danticat explores this dilemma beautifully in *The Dew Breaker* (2004), opting not to stage the conflict between victim and victimizer in the public sphere as in Tobar's novel, instead moving it into the domestic sphere and the intimate space of the family as Ka struggles to come to terms with the knowledge that her father was a torturer under the brutal Duvalier dictatorship in Haiti. Like Tobar's novel and Dorfman's play, Danticat's novel refuses to offer a resolution to the complex dilemma of how to attain restitution and reconciliation.

30. When Longoria encounters the protests, he is furious and laments: "*In Guatemala we knew how to handle these people. In Los Angeles, they are allowed to operate freely. In Los Angeles we cannot stop them*" (68). The repressive military dictatorship that kept Longoria's intimidation tactics and human rights abuses immune to legal ramifications no longer protects him in the United States. Power has shifted, and Longoria's position of domination in the social order can be challenged by Antonio and others. In fact, an old woman recognizes the tattoo on Longoria's arm as the mark of a death squad and implores him to tell her the location of the body of her disappeared son.

31. The foreclosed plot line of Elena's activism commences not with Longoria's gun but with her internal exile in San Cristóbal, which closes down her connections with the student activist movement. Her subsequent domestic and maternal duties, coupled with Antonio's demand that she not challenge the status quo, prevent her from being an active agent in the struggle to end the military dictatorship. This foreclosed feminist-activist plot line sets in motion the masculinist violence-revenge plot line between Antonio and Guillermo. Elena's foreclosed plot line likewise highlights the very delimited amount of character-space given to Esteban's girlfriend la Marta, a Sandinista revolutionary who is killed by U.S.-supported Contra forces in *The Ordinary Seaman*, which I analyze in chapter 3. In Goldman's novel, however, la Marta remains an undeveloped minor character; she is only depicted in terms of being Esteban's lost love. La Marta's dreams and political views are not voiced in the novel, in contrast to Elena, who functions as a kind of a political consciousness for Esteban.

32. See Erik Vázquez for a detailed discussion of this scene in relation to the grassroots activism that Central American migrants engaged in, especially around anti-interventionism and labor exploitation, during the 1980s and 1990s in Los Angeles.

33. Reflecting on why *La muerte y la doncella* ends with victim and victimizer continuing on with their lives, Dorfman writes: "even as my imagination ran rampant, even as I savored a society turned upside down and inside out, where the hunted of yesterday before the hunters of today, even in a play where the author supposedly can write whatever

he wants, I found myself prodding Paulina toward an ending she did not want and I did not want and yet was there, waiting for her and the people of Chile: My protagonist, having tried to bring some personal measure of justice to the world, sits down, when all is said and done, in a concert hall in close proximity to the doctor she thinks damaged her irreparably, both of them sharing the same space, the same music, the same peaceful and miserable and lying land. In *Death and the Maiden*, I could not, Paulina could not, fantasize another ending" (*Exorcising Terror*, 48). See Sophia A. McClennen for an analysis of Dorfman's literary-political project in relation to what she theorizes as his "aesthetics of hope."

34. Retributive justice is based on the idea of just desert, that is, that punishment is the acceptable response to crime and that the severity of the punishment for wrongdoing should be proportionate to the severity of the crime; this form of justice is meted out through the criminal justice system. Restorative justice, in contrast, is based on the idea that perpetrators should take responsibility for their crimes and express regret and that victims should have a space to express their views and emotions; this form of justice can occur via a range of approaches from truth and reconciliation commissions to community-based organizations. Models for restorative justice seek solutions that promote repair, reconciliation, and the rebuilding of social relationships; fostering dialogue between perpetrator and victim in order to attain healing is key. For a useful overview of these two different conceptions of justice, see Wenzel, et al.

35. Russian formalists distinguished between "fabula" and "sjužet"—what subsequent narrative theorists have called "story" and "discourse"—to respectively describe the order of events in a narrative versus the narrative's presentation of the order of events. Brooks argues that plot cuts across this distinction: "to speak of plot is to consider both story elements and their ordering. Plot could be thought of as the interpretive activity elicited by the distinction between *fabula* and *sjužet*, the way we *use* the one against the other (13). In this sense, the novel's plot for justice uses a restorative discourse to put pressure on a retributive story.

36. We can also read the novel as another example of what Julie Avril Minich elsewhere calls "narrative remediation." See "Disability, Losers, and Narrative Remediation."

Chapter 5

1. I will hereafter refer to the historical figure of Fidel Castro as Castro and to the fictional characterization of him in García's novel as El Comandante. Though the novel has numerous allusions to Cuban history, from the wars for independence to the Special Period, and though it explicitly names the U.S.-backed, right-wing dictator of Cuba, Fulgencia Batista, as well as Che Guevara, the novel never uses Fidel Castro's name. The novel does not disclose El Comandante's first or last name, using a series of titles and invectives instead to refer to him. Though technically El Comandante has recently "handed the reins of power" to his brother, Fernando, the novel represents him as the dictator of Cuba (30).

2. García also fictionalizes one of the great Latin American writers of the dictatorship novel, Gabriel García Márquez, whom she renames Babo, which gestures toward García Márquez's affectionate nickname in Latin America, Gabo, but also functions as an intertextual reference to Herman Melville's "Benito Cereno" with its signifying slave character of Babo.

3. While I focus on *King of Cuba* because of its formal similarities to and differences from Latin American boom-era dictatorship novels and contemporary Latina/o dictatorship novels, Cristina García's other novels are also interesting to consider, especially because they bring in the history of military dictatorships and U.S. imperialism in Central America.

See Ricardo L. Ortíz for an analysis of García's *A Handbook to Luck* and *The Lady Matador's Hotel* ("The Cold War," 84–87).

4. In my examination of Héctor Tobar's *The Tattooed Soldier* in chapter 4, I argue that the novel's rotational structure of narration grants equal narrative weight to its two main opposing characters to account for how each character has been victimized, albeit differently. I also argue that the rotational structure of narration grants equal narrative weight to its two main opposing characters to foil Antonio's and Longoria's respective plots (as in plans and desires) for vengeance and order, thereby challenging readers to debate how to imagine justice given the restraints of impunity and systemic inequality. In the case of *King of Cuba*, the novel's rotational structure of narration underscores the similarities between Goyo and El Comandante to account for their mutual investment in hero narratives rooted in heteropatriarchal masculinity. Their plots to be immortalized as heroes are likewise foiled, thereby calling for a redefinition of revolutionary action and heroism.

5. To be more specific, twelve of the eighteen chapters use intrachapter rotation within a single chapter. The other six chapters have an interchapter rotation: when one chapter focuses exclusively on only one of the two men, the next chapter immediately opens with the other man, which maintains the rotational pattern.

6. The prominent theme of solitude in *King of Cuba* is structured around the two kinds of fear that Juan Antonio Ramos observes that dictators suffer from in the Latin American dictatorship novel: physical fears (i.e., fears of assassinations, coups, and death) and existential fears (i.e., fear of one's power and adulation declining and of being forgotten by history) (140). In García's Latina dictatorship novel, both the dictator figure and the exile figure suffer from solitude and from physical and existential fears. The novel employs a number of the tropes common to the Latin American dictatorship novel that I outline in the introduction.

7. The term "freedom fighters" for the exile counter-revolutionaries based in South Florida was popularized during the administration of U.S. president Ronald Reagan.

8. El Comandante's and Goyo's visions of heroism are linked both to a celebration of José Martí and to hypermasculinity. Eduardo Aparicio's photo series, "Entre Miami y La Habana / Between Miami and Havana," which María de los Angeles Torres intersperses throughout *In the Land of Mirrors: Cuban Exile Politics in the United States*, highlights this foil as well. The photo pairings "Masculinidad y Nacíon: La Habana 1994 / Masculinity and Nation: Miami 1995" (44–45) and "Martí: La Habana, 1994 / Martí: Miami, 1996" (86–87) in particular showcase the ways hypermasculinity and the image of Martí as a revered hero are used by Cuban exiles and the Cuban state.

9. It shows how women mother, so to speak, patriarchy, as when Luisa mothers patriarchal violence by encouraging Goyo to beat Goyito. Mothers are sometimes also portrayed as dictatorial figures in Latina/o novels, such as Lourdes in García's *Dreaming in Cuban* and Beli in Díaz's *The Brief Wondrous Life of Oscar Wao*.

10. The scene is also exemplary of the novel's overall humorous and satirical style, which is rooted in the Cuban vernacular tradition of choteo. José Esteban Muñoz describes choteo as "a form of mockery and joking that systematically undermines all authority" (*Disidentifications*, 136), and Laura Lomas defines choteo as "merciless, playful ridicule" (26).

11. Goyo is like the narrator's father in Obejas's "We Came All the Way from Cuba So You Could Dress Like This?"—he "cannot endure" a world in which he is not the primary male figure in her life (Obejas, 117).

12. The denotations of "planet" align with the kind of self-conceptualization that the patriarchs have. A planet is: a person of great importance; a controlling or fateful power; a

source of light or power or influence. Goyo and El Comandante are invested in the image of planetary power. Though in scientific terms they identify with stars, because the sun is a star and not a planet, in more general usage and in ancient beliefs the sun is considered a planet.

13. Or, as Ileana Rodríguez captures it, the New Man model was flawed because "the masculine 'I' wants to represent the collectivity" (xvii). See Saldaña-Portillo for a critique of the gender politics and development discourse of the revolution (*The Revolutionary*).

14. As Lillian Guerra explains, "if criticism and contestation of the political authority of Fidel Castro has elicited visceral condemnation or overt repression within Cuba, expressing cynicism about the intentions of exiled Cuban leaders, promoting dialogue with the Castro regime, or endorsing the re-establishment of relations with the United States, could have similar or far worse consequences among exiles abroad. During the 1960s and 1970s, counter-revolutionary activities and U.S. intelligence forces launched a well-documented campaign of psychological warfare, overt violence, economic sabotage, selective assassinations, and terror tactics" directed both at those in the Cuban exile community in the United States who did not follow the strict right-wing, pro-embargo, anti-Castro exile party line and at those on the island (218).

15. The hard-line conservative, right-wing orientation of exiles was not a historical inevitability, since initially many of the counter-revolutionary leaders were left-leaning and rallied under the narrative of the "revolutionary betrayed." As Portes and Stepick, among others, explain, the Bay of Pigs, the Cuban Missile Crisis, and the CIA's repeated betrayal of the exiles allowed the right wing to become dominant. Moreover, Portes and Stepick observe, "the Cuban liberal discourse...always had a difficult time reconciling its progressive claims with the militant opposition to the Cuban Revolution. For left-leaning intellectuals and politicians in Latin America and for liberal academics in the United States, Fidel Castro symbolized the anti-imperialist struggle. His defiance in the face of Yankee hostility gained him much sympathy, which exiled liberals were hard put to counteract" (143).

16. In addition to funding the so-called freedom fighters, the Reagan government also funded the counter-revolutionary forces in Nicaragua. In fact, there were secret U.S. military training camps for the Contras in the Everglades. See M. C. García for more on this history.

17. For another Latino dictatorship novel that stages a theatrical production, see Daniel Alarcón's *At Night We Walk in Circles*, which contains a play critical of the dictator titled *The Idiot President*.

18. Staged by the queer theater director Orestes Mejías, the musical uses camp and choteo aesthetics to both celebrate and parodically make fun of the Cuban Revolution; these two forms of humorous critique (camp and choteo) function as modes of what José Esteban Muñoz calls "comedic disidentification," which strategically generate "important cultural critique while at the same time providing cover from, and enabling the avoidance itself of, scenarios of direct confrontation with phobic and reactionary ideologies" (*Disidentifications*, 119).

19. Because of their ragged beards, Fidel Castro and the rest of the Cuban revolutionaries were frequently called "barbudos" (the bearded ones). The revolutionary barbudo was an inspirational figure for the Latin American revolutions in Central America, for civil rights struggles of people of color in the United States in the 1960s and 1970s, and for the development of the New Left. In the words of Van Gosse, "the ragged *barbudos* led by Fidel Castro, chomping their cigars and darting down green mountain slopes to ambush Batista's

garrisons, were every [U.S.] teenage boy's dream of gun-fighting, personal heroism, and nose thumbing at received authority" (527). Later in the novel, El Comandante meets with a group of Black activists who praise the revolution for inspiring their civil rights struggles. This event at the fictional Hotel Marisa in *King of Cuba* alludes to the Hotel Theresa in Harlem, where Malcolm X invited Fidel Castro to stay and the two figures of liberation met. At the same time, the male-to-male fraternity between the Black activists and El Comandante in the scene and among the barbudos at the center of *Bay of Pigs: The Musical!* begs the question of the historical marginalization of the role of women in the various liberation movements in Cuba (and the United States).

20. While, as I am suggesting, the novel productively critiques heteropatriarchy as an authoritarian social institution, its free indirect discourse also problematically scripts El Comandante as always already a tyrant. In one illustrative example, El Comandante "planned to set the record straight, to put an end to the creeping amnesia regarding the glories of his revolution. He'd ordered Fernando to develop a program that would re-enact the regime's most illustrious days: the attack on the Moncado barracks; the 'History Will Absolve Me' speech during the despot's 1953 trial for treason; the landing of the *Granma* on the shores of the Oriente; the triumph of the Bay of Pigs" (6). As we follow El Comandante's thoughts about key events in the struggle against dictatorship and imperialist interventions, the narrator's injection that reminds the reader that the character thinking about these events is a "despot" elides the fact that in 1953 the despot was the U.S.-backed dictator Fulgencio Batista, not the revolutionary Fidel Castro or his fictional counterpart, El Comandante. The frequent and subtle interruption of epithets into El Comandante's focalization betrays a narrator who disavowals the historical importance of him as a revolutionary hero, and the epithets reproduce the discourse used by Goyo and the right-wing exile community.

21. The dates correspond to the dates of the actions and events that occur in the present time period of each section, but the dates also hold important significance for Cuban history. July 26 refers to the Movimiento 26 de Julio (26th of July Movement), the name of the revolutionary forces Fidel Castro led to overthrow Fulgencia Batista's dictatorship. August 13 is Fidel Castro's birthday, and his fictional counterpart El Comandante celebrates his birthday in this section of the novel. Finally, September 8 is the feast day for la Virgen de la Caridad de Cobre (the Virgin Mary, Patroness of Cuba).

22. The novel also uses natural metaphors of the sun and of autumn to show the decline of constructed and entrenched political binaries. Ylce Irizarry's and Cristina García's discussion of the natural/unnatural binary in García's novel *The Agüero Sisters* applies to *King of Cuba* as well. Irizarry observes: "it seems like there is a definition of the natural that you are working against. There are certain politics for Cubans—whether it is the politics of the Cubans on the island or the politics of exiled Cubans—which people want to seem natural or inevitably correct," and García elaborates: "there is nothing natural about any of these politics; they are all constructs. So, yes, I'm interested in the wildernesses in between. For me, what is considered natural is usually really, really unnatural" (Interview, 181). The vignettes and notes in *King of Cuba* are part of the "wildernesses in between" the politics of the revolution and the exile community, which each side considers naturally heroic.

23. The fact that both Goyo and El Comandante are obsessed with being heroes is ironic in a novel that lacks a clear hero. Depending on one's political orientation, one may be more inclined to identify with either the exile figure or the Cuban leader, but the novel frustrates one's ability to like or identify with either character because they are both portrayed so unfavorably and their quests are portrayed as egomaniacal. In a sense, the

novel does not really have a clear protagonist—rather, it has two antagonists, which also foils the reader's desire for heroic protagonists and enacts the death of the hero narrative.

24. Both El Comandante and Goyo want to be remembered as national heroes who continued the legacy of the nineteenth-century anticolonialist and intellectual José Martí. Historically, the leaders of the Cuban Revolution and the Cuban exiles community both revered José Martí and saw themselves as furthering the nineteenth-century struggle for Cuban independence. See Louis A. Pérez for a discussion of how the leaders of the revolution used "nationalism as an affirmation of independence, self-determination, and sovereign nationhood" to resist U.S. imperial designs on Cuba, memorializing José Martí and linking the revolution to the events of 1898 in that process (22). See María Cristina García for a discussion of how the exiles "tried to establish a symbolic continuum between their experience and the nineteenth-century revolutionary heritage" by also memorializing Martí (84).

25. By being critical of both El Comandante and Goyo, or the institutionalized revolutionary state and the counter-revolutionary exile community that each character respectively represents, the novel also implicitly calls for a different option for Cuban Americans, who, as José Muñoz explains, are too often "smothered by the two overdetermined options or paths that seem available to Cuban Americans: joining the ranks of white Marxists who fetishize the island in an uncritical fashion, or following the path of reactionary right-wing Cubans" ("*No es fácil,*" 80).

26. I call them notes because they are attached to asterisks, unlike the numerical footnotes in Junot Díaz's *Brief Wondrous Life of Oscar Wao*. Asterisks are a pertinent choice for a dictatorship novel because, unlike numbers, asterisks are also used to mark censorship—that is, to mark what cannot be stated outright.

27. The old looming houses are like the old men, El Comandante and Goyo, who loom over the majority of the novel's the narrative space.

28. The Special Period in Time of Peace officially began in 1990 and unofficially ended in 2005; its most severe effects occurred in the mid-1990s. With the loss of economic support from the Soviet Union, Cuba's imports were drastically reduced, and with the loss of fuel, industry and agriculture suffered immensely. To cope, Cuba used austerity measures, turned to tourism and foreign investment, and decriminalized the U.S. dollar (which shifted the economy from an agricultural-industrial to a service-oriented one), in addition to asking citizens to make sacrifices and ration. Community and individually led initiatives like grassroots organizations and private restaurants increased, and there was more freedom in the arts as the Cuban government allowed artists to enter the global market and travel abroad (especially writers, since there was very little paper for publishing) in order to collect taxes on their profits. Though some critics see this period as Cuba's shift to capitalism (and thus evidence that socialism had failed), the Cuban government framed its measures as saying yes to capital but no to capitalism. As Eckstein points out, the government weathered the Special Period by using a combination of socialist, precapitalist, and capitalist strategies, and as Sujatha Fernandes explains it, Cuba became a pragmatic state in relation to the international market but nationally remained a populist state with socialism as its policy and ethos. The major problem, which *King of Cuba* frequently references, was that the new tourism industry resulted in a two-tiered economy in which those with tourism-related jobs had access to dollars and were better off financially; it also reintroduced prostitution.

29. Scholars in various disciplines, from literary studies to religious studies and anthropology, have defined and detailed the uses of "resolver." Their definitions vary and often overlap with "conseguir," "defenderse," "inventar," and "luchar." These verbs are part of what Weinreb calls the "Special Period lexicon" (65). They are variously used across literature and scholarship, with similar applications, though "resolver" is the most frequently mentioned and analyzed.

30. The verb "resolver" covers a range of activities, including bartering, growing food in one's backyard, figuring out a way to make something work that is rundown or broken, participating in informal economies or the black market, and stealing goods in order to sell them.

31. The anthropologist Amelia Rosenberg Weinreb cites two popular Cuban jokes: "What is a Cuban steak? A grilled grapefruit skin. What is Cuban melted cheese? The free condoms distributed by international organizations" (77). Achy Obejas related the "apocryphal" story about the condom pizzas in order to recount how cooking in Cuba had been changed by the scarcity of goods, while the *New York Times* reported that "a television chef" taught people how to make grapefruit steaks (Obejas, "What Anthony Bourdain"; Golden, "Castro's People"). Given the widely circulated rumors that were often started in the Cuban exile community, it is difficult to distinguish truth from fiction in the U.S. press coverage.

32. Mejías uses animals, including crabs, in his musical to represent the Cubans defending the revolution. The symbolic association of the crabs with the revolution is not maintained throughout the novel. After seeing the play, El Comandante has "nightmares from that goddam play—mostly of giant, imperialist crabs running amok in Havana" (208). And on the day when Goyo attempts to assassinate El Comandante, he falls "crab-like" onto his bed out of weakness (226). Crabs are slippery political signifiers in the novel, as they symbolize the revolution, counter-revolutionary exiles, and imperialism at different points. This again draws links between the trenchant politics of the Cuban state and that of the Cuban exiles.

33. In addition, Luisa is addicted to plastic surgery; she has been "cut, snipped, tucked, nipped, and sucked so often that her body looked stitched together from disparate parts" (33–34).

34. I heed Fernandes's caution about using the term "resistance" to refer to García's novel, because the discourses of resistance, rebellion, and revolution have been usurped by both the Cuban state and the Miami exile community. As Fernandes expounds, "I am cautious about speaking of 'resistance' in the Cuban context. On the one hand, notions of 'rebellion' and 'revolution'... have been co-opted by the state in Cuba. Official discourse continually refers to 'resistance' to colonialism, U.S. imperialism, and global capitalism. On the other hand, for decades politically influential and wealthy sectors of the Miami exile community have talked about 'resistance' to the Cuban government and donated millions of dollars to the Republican party in return for legislation such as the Helms-Burton Act, which magnified the difficulties faced by ordinary Cubans during the special period" (185).

35. There is also a vignette titled "Star," in which a Cuban actress asks if writers have a "little monologue" for her (167).

36. García inserts herself into one of the notes and one of the vignettes, in the former declaring "the Revolution is in its last gasp" (108) and in the latter exhibiting how she had to rely on a resolver attitude with the old car she rented to travel around the island (163–164). These are the only two metafictional moments in the novel in which García references

herself, and together they capture the way the notes and vignettes bring in a resolver aesthetic at the same time that they mainly voice a disillusioned perspective.

37. Julia Alvarez's *How the García Girls Lost Their Accents* also depicts the father as dictatorial; Demetria Martínez's *Mother Tongue* and Loida Maritza Pérez's *Geographies of Home* both figure domestic dictatorship through sexual abuse.

38. Lourdes is depicted similarly to Goyo as a fierce critic of the Cuban regime, but rather than channel her counter-revolutionary activities into an assassination plot like Goyo, she becomes an informal member of the New York Police Department and patrols local neighborhoods with baton and handcuffs in hand. Meanwhile, she suffers from an eating disorder, she binges on her baked goods, and she is obese, which literalizes her addiction to consumptive capitalism. Goya's wife, Luisa, is similar to Lourdes: she has an eating disorder, undergoes multiple plastic surgery, is addicted to shopping, and showcases her patriotism for the United States by making Goyo dress in the colors of the U.S. flag.

39. Lola in *The Brief Wondrous Life of Oscar Wao* is another defiant Latina daughter who goes through the phase of being a "punk chick" (44).

40. Pilar's "SL-76" is useful to read in dialogue with the etching "Libertad," by Chicana artist Ester Hernández. The unabbreviated title of Pilar's painting would be "Statue of Liberty-1976," and Hernández produced "Libertad" in 1976 for the U.S. bicentennial. Both Pilar and Hernández create oppositional representations of the Statue of Liberty precisely when the United States is celebrating its founding. In Hernández's black and white etching, a Chicana sculptor stands before Lady Liberty; Aztec gods are carved on the body of Lady Liberty, and the word "Aztlan" is carved at the statue's base. It is unclear whether the sculptor standing on the outstretched hand of a female goddess is chiseling the Aztec images into the body of the statue or uncovering the images from beneath the statue's robes. The Chicana artist is both archeologist and historian, excavating the Aztec images beneath the Statue of Liberty and documenting the way the United States was built on colonized indigenous lands and the way it erases the violence at the base of its nation-building project by relegating indigenous peoples in the national imaginary to the past. The Chicana artist in Hernández's etching reclaims Lady Liberty by inscribing the name of the mythical homeland of the Aztecs on her base; in a similar form of tagging, Pilar reclaims the Statue of Liberty with her inscription of the punk motto at its base. Ester Hernández produced her etching when she was an undergraduate at the University of California, Berkeley, and part of the Chicana/o civil rights arts movement and the Third World liberation movement; Pilar is a Latina Cuban in New York City who is being emotionally manipulated by her counter-revolutionary and capitalistic mother to paint a "patriotic mural" (139). Their respective acts of defiance appeal to different audiences—Hernández's to ethnic nationalism and civil rights–era collectivist-oriented social justice movements and Pilar's to the anti-authoritarian ethos of punk rebellion and individual freedom—but both their artworks uncover the violence hidden by nationalist discourses and patriotic celebrations of the United States' bicentennial.

41. National Park Service, description of Freedom Tower, http://www.nps.gov/nr/travel/american_latino_heritage/Freedom_Tower.html, accessed June 27, 2017.

42. Punk in the Cuban context was seen as counter-revolutionary and as an imperialist influence and was banned on the island by the Cuban state, but in the U.S. context, punk was seen as revolutionary and anti-establishment. For an interesting episode in the history of punk in Cuba, see the Radio Ambulante episode "Cuando La Habana era friki" or the

longer English-language version of the story that Radio Ambulante produced in collaboration with RadioLab entitled "Los Frikis." The founder and executive producer of Radio Ambulante is Daniel Alarcón, author of the Latino dictatorship novels *Lost City Radio* and *At Night We Walk in Circles*.

43. In a sense Cristina García is also a defiant daughter of the boom-era generation of Latin American dictator novelists. Her fictionalization of Gabriel García Márquez as Babo both satirizes the heteropatriarchal underpinnings of the genre and celebrates its investment in the liberatory power of the imagination. While on his deathbed, Babo declares that he wants "to leave behind something imagined, not simply recalled," because "imagination frees us" (59). El Comandante disagrees, preferring action to ideas, but Babo counters, "Words *are* action, mi amigo, as compressed and devastating as any bullet—or caress" (59).

Coda

1. The title and exhibit commemorate the U.S.-supported military coup on September 11, 1973, that ended the life of President Salvador Allende and the project of democratic socialism in Chile and inaugurated Augusto Pinochet's seventeen-year brutal dictatorship. Gómez-Barris characterizes the organizers as part of the "second generation of Chilean exiles [who] came of age in the United States with strong emotional, familial, and political bonds to the traumatic memories of their parents' generation and stories" ("Two 9/11s," 150). Gómez-Barris uses the term "exile" to "reference the ongoing experience of dislocation, trauma and identity construction that began in 1973 and continues today" (98). Gómez-Barris is more interested in positioning exile as an inherited identity category, whereas I use the identificatory term "Latina/o" for those who grew up in the United States because I am more interested in highlighting pan-Latina/o affinities and alliances.

2. Patricia Rodríguez was a founding member of Las Mujeres Muralistas, a group of Latina muralists who challenged the masculinist and Chicano nationalist aesthetics of muralists in the early 1970s. Chicana artist Ester Hernández relates: "the *mujeres* in the collective forced us to get real about what Latino community really meant because they were not all Chicanas. They were from a lot of different backgrounds. They were South American, Puerto Rican. They were Afro-Latino, Euro-Latino, you name it, and they made us deal with our diversity" (Cortez, 68).

3. The artists were a multiracial group. Though the project was led by Chicana/os and many of the muralists were Latina/os, not all of them were.

4. "Placa" has a number of meanings in Spanish, including inscription, nameplate, plaque, badge, license plate, and graffiti tagging. The documentary *These Walls Speak* shows their original mission statement, which reads: "PLACA: to make a mark, to leave a sign, to speak out, to have image call for a response. PLACA: a group of artists who are determined to speak out against U.S. intervention in Central America through imagery on the walls of San Francisco. As artists and muralists, PLACA members aim to call attention to the situation that exists today in Central America, as a result of the current Administration's policies. The situation in El Salvador, the situation in Nicaragua, the situation in Guatemala, the situation in Honduras. PLACA members do not ally themselves with this Administration's policy that has created death and war and despair, and that threatens more lives daily. We aim to demonstrate in visual/environmental terms, our solidarity, our respect, for the people of Central America" (Wojczuk and Rowand).

5. Of interest, given the focus of this book, Latoree explains in her epilogue that she is a Chilean migrant who lived part of her life under Pinochet's dictatorship and was attracted to the Chicana/o murals she analyzes in *Murals of Empowerment* because of their confrontational nature and the spirit of courage they embody, which she found especially inspiring after having lived under Pinochet's repressive regime (244). Ray Patlán recounts how he and other Mission muralists were inspired by Chilean artists who had to paint murals incredibly quickly to avoid being shot during the Pinochet dictatorship (Cortez, 76).

6. The title, written in both Spanish and English on the mural, is a quotation from the African anti-colonial thinker and revolutionary Amílcar Cabral, a testament to the global revolutionary consciousness of the PLACA project. See http://www.sfmuralarts.com/neighborhood/mission/balmy-alley/1.html for color photographs of the murals I discuss.

7. The rainbow reads: "Te Doy una Canción como un Disparo, como un Libro, una Palabra, una Guerilla, Como Doy el Amor / I Give you a Song like a Tribute, like a Book, a Word, a Freedom Fighter, Like I Give You Love." The translation of "disparo" as "tribute" is incorrect because a disparo is a gunshot. Perhaps this mistranslation is a deliberate attempt not to celebrate armed resistance in the public space of the Mission, instead paying tribute to the power of resistance in music and art. This mural and its words about revolutionary love resonate with a mural of Ernesto "Che" Guevara that Elena sees in Guatemala in *The Tattooed Soldier*, which I reference in chapter 4. That mural contains a "string of words that ran underneath Che, painted on a long white ribbon held aloft by a crudely drawn dove: 'The revolutionary is guided in all his actions by great feelings of love'" (90).

8. One of Rojas's inspirations for the mural was Sonia Nazario's *Enrique's Journey*, a nonfiction chronicle of an undocumented Honduran teenager who makes the dangerous journey to reunite with his mother in the United States by riding on top of the trains that run across Mexico.

9. The mural to the right of "Enrique's Journey" is "Tribute to Archbishop Oscar Romero," by Jamie Morgan (2001), which also contains the skull of a helmeted soldier hovering above flames. Morgan painted a PLACA mural with the same title in this same spot, but like Juana Alicia, he painted a new mural instead of restoring his original mural. The themes of undocumented migration in Rojas's mural and political assassination in Morgan's mural exist side by side, echoing each other with their skull imagery, challenging us to read the two historical moments together as a "history of violence" created by U.S. interventions in the region and U.S. deportation policies. As Óscar Martínez shows in *A History of Violence: Living and Dying in Central America*, the violence and poverty that many undocumented Central American migrants are experiencing is partly a result of U.S. interventions in the region in the 1980s and partly a result of the United States' mass deportations of Latino gang members back to Central America in the 1990s, which helped create the massive gang violence currently plaguing the region.

10. The 1980s gave birth to the Sanctuary Movement in the United States, and San Francisco declared itself a sanctuary city; thirty years later, a new Sanctuary Movement has recently arisen, and San Francisco has again reiterated its status as a sanctuary city.

11. Juana Alicia relates how the PLACA project in Balmy Alley was filmed and the video was sent to Ernesto Cardenál, the Nicaraguan poet and minister of culture, and she and three other members of the PLACA Collective were invited to Nicaragua to create a mural there. The experience shifted the way she saw her own Mission neighborhood: "The Mission launched us on an incredible journey that would contrast the petty internal turf wars of our own community with the far more tragic and massively violent Contra War on

the Nicaraguan Revolution. But in some ways, the experience of painting 'El Amanecer' in the center of Managua also illustrated to me that we live in a war zone in the Mission, connected by gangs, police violence, immigration, the AIDS epidemic and economic injustice to the millions of our southern cousins in Mexico and Central America" ("Remembering the Mission"). Alicia also tells about marking a mural with the words that appear as an epigraph to this chapter by Nicaraguan Giocanda Belli.

12. While there are certainly murals that interrogate heteropatriarchy in Balmy Alley, the most visually striking and well-known example is "Maestrapeace" (1994), which is located in the Mission neighborhood but not in the alley. This mural, which was designed and painted by seven women muralists, including PLACA muralists Juana Alicia and Miranda Bergman, wraps around two sides of the Women's Building on Eighteenth Street and is a testament to interracial feminist solidarity. Centered prominently at the top of the mural is the Guatemalan Nobel Peace Prize–winning human rights activist Rigoberta Menchú, and the mural is filled with depictions of women of color and children of color. Positioning this Central American activist against a U.S.-funded military dictatorship at the center of the mural brings prominent visibility to these struggles and positions them within the struggle against heteropatriarchy that the female-centered mural represents overall. Menchú also serves as a linking figure in the violence of coloniality directed against African-origin and Native peoples, symbolized by the two goddesses in her outstretched hands.

13. The murals also testify to the rich history of activist solidarities and collaborative art between Latina/os and Anglo Americans and other people of color contesting U.S. imperialism in Central America in the 1980s, as well as engaging together in other local, hemispheric, and global struggles for justice.

14. The banners and photos that insist on presence and the gestures of defiance that run across the panel are linked both among themselves as well as to the murals in Balmy Alley I discussed earlier, especially in relation to the mural by Miranda Bergman and O'Brien Thiele, "La Cultura Contiene la Semilla de la Resistencia que Retoña en la Flor de la Liberación / Culture Contains the Seed of Resistance which Blossoms into the Flower of Liberation" (1984; fig. C.1). For example, the Juarez mothers hold photos of their disappeared daughters, and this type of protest parallels the image of Emiliano Zapata on the dissenting Zapatistas' banner; it is also recalls the photos of disappeared loved ones in the Balmy Alley mural. The fists raised in the Black Power salute by John Carlos and Tommie Smith mirror the raised fist of Mercedes Sosa, visually echoing each other; the gesture of resistance also recalls the boy with the raised fist holding a paintbrush and the girl with the raised fist holding a pencil in the Balmy Alley mural. See https://elcentro.stanford.edu/about/our-murals for color images of Alicia's full mural.

15. Just one example would be Rebel Diaz, the Brooklyn-based hip-hop duo of two brothers who are children of Chilean exiles and grew up in Chicago. Their politically conscious songs, activism, and educational workshops are emblematic of the Latina/o counter-dictatorial imaginary, as they frequently infuse references to Chilean and Latin American revolutionary struggles into their bilingual music and album artwork, situating them alongside pressing social issues important to communities of color and migrant communities in the United States. See, for example, the songs "I'm An Alien," "Libertad," "Radical Dilemma," "Revolution Has Come," "Which Side Are You On?," and the cover of the album *Otra Guerillera Mixtape Vol. 2*, available on YouTube and the duo's website, www.rebeldiaz.com.

16. To offer one example, Rodrigo Dorfman, the son of Ariel Dorfman, produced a documentary film, *Occupy the Imagination: Tales of Seduction and Resistance,* in which he

aspires to "connect with his revolutionary past" in Chile, partly through the Occupy Wall Street movement that began in 2011. To do so, he creates a montage of images and clips and uses his father's anti-imperialist text *How to Read Donald Duck* as a central text throughout the film. If Ariel Dorfman's *How to Read Donald Duck* reveals how capitalist messages encoded in Disney's cartoons are imported into Chile, Rodrigo Dorfman's film does the reverse, importing a consciousness of the Chilean socialist revolution and subsequent brutal neoliberal dictatorship into the United States, reading the Occupy movement through the lens of Chilean history. The linkages and trans-American vision the film generates through its montage aesthetic creates an alternative understanding of Occupy. The film generates a new cultural memory about the struggle against the Pinochet dictatorship by infusing it into the struggle against rapacious capitalism and the wealthy 1 percent who were the target of Occupy with its tagline—"We are the 99 percent"—that highlighted the massive inequitable distribution of wealth. The film opens up an interesting set of questions about how Latina/os' memories of state-sanctioned violence and attendant displacements shape the ways they engage with and interpret more recent struggles for social and economic justice, such as the Black Lives Matter, the migrant rights, and the campus sanctuary movements.

17. El día de los muertos (the Day of the Dead) is a traditional celebration in numerous Latin American countries. The tradition commemorates relatives and loved ones who are no longer alive and functions as a means of honoring one's kin, in part with ofrendas or altars to the dead. Regina M. Marchi contends that Latina/os in the United States have "utilized the holiday's focus on remembrance to criticize dominant power structures by creating installations intended to raise public awareness of the sociopolitical causes of death. In doing so, they expanded a tradition reserved for family members into one that also remembered groups of people not personally known to the altar makers" (47). The Latina/o counter-dictatorial imaginary is also materialized through the ritual of remembrance that is the altar. SOMArts's Day of the Dead in San Francisco, for example, has a different organizing theme each year and an astonishing range of creative altar installations. In addition to altars for the desaparecidos under dictatorships in Latin America, there have been altars to: people displaced by gentrification in the Mission, victims of feminicide in Mexico and El Salvador, Black people murdered by police in the United States, the queer and queer of color victims of the Pulse nightclub shooting in Orlando, students disappeared in Ayotzinapa, people who suffer from lack of healthcare in the United States, victims of Hurricane Katrina in New Orleans and hurricanes in Haiti, undocumented migrants who have died in the desert in Arizona, and victims of the slave trade in the Americas. Each year, new altars are crafted to grapple with recent pressing issues while retaining a sense of historical struggle. The space is a labyrinth-like set of rooms, each of which houses an altar, but as you navigate through the space you are immersed in a nonlinear, multispatial, multitemporal ritual of remembrance. This transhistorical and transnational public site of memory visualizes linked histories of social, economic, political, and environmental death, calling us through the medium of the altar to mourn the violence that haunts the Americas. Like the mural environment, this altar environment encourages individual readings of each altar as well as a more collective, comparative, and dialogic reading of those victims of violence who are mourned with the altars.

18. One recent example is how Latina/o cultural producers and intellectuals use the trope of dictatorship to expose Donald Trump's racist, anti-immigrant rhetoric and the authoritarian threat he poses. Consider, among others, Lalo Alcaráz's various "Bad Hombre"

cartoons, Lourdes Bernard's graphite portrait "Anatomy of a Dictator," Ariel Dorfman's op-ed articles, Lila Downs's song "The Demagogue," Carolina de Robertis's editor's introduction to *Radical Hope: Letters of Love and Dissent in Dangerous Times*, and references to Trump as "El Caudillo del Mar-a-Lago."

19. In both her foreword to the second edition and her preface to the fourth edition, Moraga offers a list of the extensive violence she sees occurring against people of color in the United States and people in the Global South. In 1983, Moraga's list includes the United States' training and funding of the Contra war against the revolutionary Sandinista government in Nicaragua, the mass murders of Guatemalans and Salvadorans, political repression under Pinochet in Chile, and the Reagan administration's rolling back of many of the progressive gains made in the 1960s and 1970s, among other examples ("Refugees," 256). Thirty years later in 2014, Moraga's list once again includes the Contra war in Nicaragua as well as NAFTA, No Child Left Behind, the Patriot Act, and Arizona's anti-immigrant legislation, among other examples ("Catching Fire," xvii). Moraga's lists generate linked histories and multidirectional memory similar to those generated by the murals and novels I have examined, and her list, like the post-PLACA murals that are added to Balmy Alley, is updated and extended to account for each new historical moment. Moraga also includes anti-Vietnam war organizing among the political movements that she says inspired the work in *This Bridge Called My Back* (xxi). In this book, I have focused on links primarily between various Latina/o national-origin groups and between Latina/os and Latin Americans though also, on occasion, between Latina/os and African Americans. Jayson Gonzalez Sae-Saue's *Southwest Asia* provides a comparative ethnic and transpacific model for thinking through the Asian American and Asian presence in the background of Latina/o cultural production about dictatorship, which is a necessary future line of investigation for scholars to pursue.

20. They also serve as examples of what Juan Poblete calls "Latino/a hemispheric citizenship," in which Latina/os exercise political and cultural citizenship in both the United States and Latin America in the service of social justice (xxxiv).

{ WORKS CITED }

Abrams, M. H. *A Glossary of Literary Terms*. 7th ed. Fort Worth: Harcourt Brace College, 1999.
Addis, Mary. "Synthetic Visions: The Spanish American Dictator Novel as a Genre." *Critical Studies* 3.1 (1991): 189–219.
Alarcón, Daniel. *At Night We Walk in Circles*. New York: Riverhead Books, 2013.
Alarcón, Daniel. *Lost City Radio*. New York: Harper Collins, 2007.
Aldama, Frederick Luis. *Formal Matters in Contemporary Latino Poetry*. New York: Palgrave Macmillan, 2013.
Aldama, Frederick Luis. "Magical Realism." In *The Routledge Companion to Latino/a Literature*, ed. Suzanne Bost and Frances R. Aparicio. New York: Routledge, 2013, 334–341.
Alicia, Juana. "Narrative for Murals at El Centro Chicano de Estánfor." https://juanaaliciaatcentro.wordpress.com/narrative-for-murals-at-el-centro-chicano-de-estanfor/.
Alicia, Juana. "Remembering the Mission: A Reflection." http://www.juanaalicia.com/content/remembering-the-mission-a-reflection/.
Alvarez, Julia. "Disappeared Does Not Take a Helping Verb in English." *Syracuse University Magazine* 10.4 (Summer 1994): 33–37.
Alvarez, Julia. *How the García Girls Lost Their Accents*. New York: Plume, 1992.
Alvarez, Julia. *In the Time of the Butterflies*. New York: Plume, 1995.
Anzaldúa, Gloria. *Borderlands/La Frontera: The New Mestiza*. San Francisco: Aunt Lute Books, 1999.
Aparicio, Frances R. "(Re)constructing Latinidad: The Challenge of Latina/o Studies." In *A Companion to Latina/o Studies*, ed. Juan Flores and Renato Rosaldo. Oxford: Blackwell, 2007, 39–48.
Aparicio, Frances R., and Susana Chávez-Silverman, eds. Editors introduction to *Tropicalizations: Transcultural Representations of Latinidad*. Hanover, NH: University Press of New England, 1997.
Appiah, Kwame Anthony. "Is the Post- in Postmodernism the Post- in Postcolonial?" In *Contemporary Postcolonial Theory: A Reader*, ed. Padmini Mongia. New York: Oxford University Press, 2003, 55–71.
Arias, Arturo, and Claudia Milian. "US Central Americans: Representations, Agency and Communities." *Latino Studies* 11.2 (Summer 2013): 131–149.
Armillas-Tisyera, Magalí. *The Dictator-Novel: Writers and Politics in the Global South*. Manuscript in preparation.
Asturias, Miguel Ángel. "*El señor presidente* como mito." In *El señor presidente: Edición crítica*, ed. Gerald Martin. Barcelona: Galaxia Gutenberg, 2000, 468–478.
Avelar, Idelber. *The Untimely Present: Postdictatorial Latin American Fiction and the Task of Mourning*. Durham: Duke University Press, 1999.
Bakhtin, M. M. *The Dialogic Imagination: Four Essays*. Trans. Caryl Emerson and Michael Holquist. Austin: University of Texas Press, 1982.

Bambara, Toni Cade. "Foreword to the First Edition, 1980." In *This Bridge Called My Back: Writings by Radical Women of Color*, ed. Cherríe Moraga and Gloria Anzaldúa. 4th ed. Albany: State University of New York Press, 2015, xxix–xxxii.

Batchelor, David. *Chromophobia*. London: Reaktion Books, 2001.

Beckman, Erika. *Capital Fictions: The Literature of Latin America's Export Age*. Minneapolis: University of Minnesota Press, 2013.

Bellini, Giuseppe. *El tema de la dictadura en la narrativa del mundo hispánico*. Rome: Bulzoni, 2000.

Bell-Villada, Gene. "Pronoun Shifters, Virginia Woolf, Béla Bartók, Plebeian Forms, Real-Life Tyrants, and the Shaping of García Márquez's *Patriarch*" *Contemporary Literature* 28.4 (1987): 460–482.

Beltrán, Cristina. *The Trouble with Unity: Latino Politics and the Creation of Identity*. New York: Oxford University Press, 2010.

Benítez, Sandra. *The Weight of All Things* (2001). New York: Hyperion, 2000.

Benstock, Shari. "At the Margin of Discourse: Footnotes in the Fictional Text." *PMLA* 98.2 (1983): 204–225.

Best, Stephen, and Sharon Marcus. "Surface Reading: An Introduction." *Representations* 108.1 (2009): 1–21.

Blackmore, Josiah. *Manifest Perdition: Shipwreck Narrative and the Disruption of Empire*. Minneapolis: University of Minnesota Press, 2002.

Blumenberg, Hans. *Shipwreck with Spectator: Paradigm of a Metaphor for Existence*. Boston: MIT Press, 1997.

Bourdieu, Pierre. *Language and Symbolic Power*. Translated by Gino Raymond and Matthew Adamson. 7th ed. Cambridge, MA: Harvard University Press, 1999.

Brickhouse, Anna. *Transamerican Literary Relations and the Nineteenth-Century Public Sphere*. New York: Cambridge University Press, 2004.

Brady, Mary Pat. *Extinct Lands, Temporal Geographies: Chicana Literature and the Urgency of Space*. Durham: Duke University Press, 2002.

Brooks, Peter. *Reading for Plot: Design and Intention in Narrative*. Cambridge, MA: Harvard University Press, 1992.

Cacho, Lisa Marie. *Social Death: Racialized Rightlessness and the Criminalization of the Unprotected*. New York: New York University Press, 2012.

Cala Buendía, Felipe. *Cultural Producers and Social Change in Latin America*. New York: Palgrave Macmillan, 2014.

Calviño Iglesias, Julio. *La novela del dictador en hispanoamérica*. Madrid: Cultura Hispánica, 1985.

Caminero-Santangelo, Marta. "Central Americans in the City: Goldman, Tobar, and the Question of Panethnicity." *Lit: Literature Interpretation Theory* 20.3 (2009): 17–195.

Caminero-Santangelo, Marta. *On Latinidad: U.S. Latino Literature and the Construction of Ethnicity*. Gainesville: University Press of Florida, 2007.

Carlisle, Rodney P. *Sovereignty for Sale: The Origins and Evolution of the Panamanian and Liberian Flags of Convenience*. Annapolis: Naval Institute Press, 1981.

Carpentier, Alejo. *El recurso del método*. Havana: Editorial de Arte y Literatura, 1974.

Carrillo, Guadalupe. "Forms of Sentiment in the Twenty-First-Century Latina/o Novel." Ph.D. diss., Stanford University, 2013.

Castillo, Ana. *Psst...: I Have Something to Tell You, Mi Amor*. San Antonio: Wings Press, 2005.

Castillo, Ana. *Sapogonia*. New York: Anchor Books, 1994.

Castillo, Debra A. *Redreaming America: Toward a Bilingual American Culture*. Albany: State University of New York Press, 2012.

Cepeda, Maria Elena. *Musical ImagiNation: U.S-Colombian Identity and the Latin Music Boom*. New York: New York University Press, 2010.

Chapman, Paul K. *Trouble on Board : The Plight of International Seafarers*. Ithaca, NY: ILR Press, 1992.

Chatman, Seymour. *Story and Discourse: Narrative Structure In Fiction and Film* Ithaca, NY: Cornell University Press, 1978.

Chavez, Leo R. *The Latino Threat: Constructing Immigrants, Citizens, and the Nation*. Stanford: Stanford University Press, 2013.

Cohen, Stanley. *States of Denial: Knowing about Atrocities and Suffering*. Malden, MA: Blackwell, 2001.

Coronado, Raúl. *A World Not to Come: A History of Latino Writing and Print Culture*. Cambridge, MA: Harvard University Press, 2013.

Cortez, Jaime. "Beauty Is a Verb: Mission Muralismo 1971–1982." In *Street Art San Francisco: Mission Muralismo*, ed. Annice Jacoby. New York: Abrams, 2009, 59–76.

Crassweller, Robert D. *Trujillo: The Life and Times of a Caribbean Dictator*. New York: Macmillan, 1966.

Crittendon, Ann. *Sanctuary: A Story of American Conscience and the Law in Collision*. New York: Weidenfeld and Nicolson, 1988.

Cruz, Angie. *Let It Rain Coffee: A Novel*. New York: Simon and Schuster, 2005.

Culler, Jonathan. "Omniscience." *Narrative* 12.1 (January 2004): 22–34.

Cutler, John Alba. *Ends of Assimilation: The Formation of Chicano Literature*. New York: Oxford University Press, 2015.

Dalleo, Raphael, and Elena Machado Sáez. *The Latina/o Canon and the Emergence of Post-sixties Literature*. New York: Palgrave Macmillan, 2007.

Danticat, Edwidge. *Create Dangerously*. New York: Vintage Books, 2010.

Danticat, Edwidge. *The Dew Breaker*. New York: Vintage Books, 2004.

Danticat, Edwidge. *The Farming of Bones*. New York: Penguin Books, 1998.

Dávila, Arlene. *Latinos, Inc.: The Marketing and Making of a People*. Berkeley: University of California Press, 2001.

Davis, Mike. "Burning Too Few Illusions." *Left Turn*, July 14, 2002. http://www.leftturn.org/burning-too-few-illusions.

Davis, Mike. *Magical Urbanism: Latinos Reinvent the U.S. City*. New York: Verso, 2000.

Dawson, Paul. "The Return of Omniscience in Contemporary Fiction." *Narrative* 17.2 (May 2009): 143–161.

Delgadillo, Theresa. "The Criticality of Latino/a Fiction in the Twenty-First Century." *American Literary History* 23.3 (2011): 600–624.

Denning, Michael. "Wageless Life." *New Left Review* 66 (November-December 2010): 77–97.

Derby, Lauren. *The Dictator's Seduction: Politics and the Popular Imagination in the Era of Trujillo*. Durham: Duke University Press, 2009.

Díaz, Junot. "Apocalypse: What Disasters Reveal." *Boston Review*, May 1, 2011. http://bostonreview.net/junot-diaz-apocalypse-haiti-earthquake.

Díaz, Junot. *The Brief Wondrous Life of Oscar Wao*. New York: Riverhead Books, 2007.

Di Iorio, Lyn. *Killing Spanish: Literary Essays on Ambivalent U.S. Latino/a Identity*. New York: Palgrave Macmillan, 2009.

Dorfman, Ariel. *Exorcising Terror: The Incredible Unending Trial of General Augusto Pinochet*. New York: Seven Stories Press, 2002.
Dorfman, Rodrigo, dir. *Occupy the Imagination: Tales of Seduction and Resistance*. Melloweb, 2013.
Dorfman, Ariel. *Other Septembers, Many Americas: Selected Provocations, 1980-2004*. New York: Seven Stories Press, 2004.
Dorfman, Ariel. *The Resistance Trilogy: Death and the Maiden, Reader, Widows*. London: Nick Hern Books, 1998.
Dunn, Timothy J. *The Militarization of the U.S.-Mexico Border, 1978-1992: Low-Intensity Conflict Doctrine Comes Home*. Austin: University of Texas Press, 1996.
Eckstein, Susan. "From Communist Solidarity to Communist Solitary." In *The Cuba Reader: History, Culture, Politics*, ed. Aviva Chomsky, Barry Carr, and Pamela Maria Smorkaloff. Durham: Duke University Press, 2004, 607–622.
Feitlowitz, Marguerite. *A Lexicon of Terror: Argentina and the Legacies of Torture*. New York: Oxford University Press, 1998.
Fernandes, Sujatha. *Cuba Represent! Cuban Arts, State Power, and the Making of New Revolutionary Cultures*. Durham: Duke University Press, 2006.
Fink, Leon. *Sweatshops at Sea: Merchant Seamen in the World's First Globalized Industry, from 1812 to the Present*. Chapel Hill: University of North Carolina, 2011.
Firmat, Gustavo Pérez, ed. *Do the Americas Have a Common Literature?* Durham: Duke University Press, 1990.
Flores, Juan. *From Bomba to Hip-hop: Puerto Rican Culture and Latino Identity*. New York: Columbia University Press, 2000.
Forster, E. M. *Aspects of the Novel*. New York: Harcourt, 1927.
Foucault, Michel. *Discipline and Punish: The Birth of the Prison*. Trans. Alan Sheridan. New York: Vintage Books, 1995.
Foucault, Michel. "Of Other Spaces." Trans. Jay Miskowiec. *Diacritics* 16.1 (1986): 22–27.
Fradinger, Moira. *Binding Violence: Literary Visions of Political Origins*. Stanford: Stanford University Press, 2010.
Franco, Jean. *Cruel Modernity*. Durham: Duke University Press, 2013.
Franco, Jean. *The Decline and Fall of the Lettered City: Latin America in the Cold War*. Cambridge, MA: Harvard University Press, 2002.
Friedman, Andrew. *Covert Capital: Landscapes of Denial and the Making of the U.S. Empire in the Suburbs of Northern Virginia*. Berkeley: University of California Press, 2013.
Fuentes, Carlos. *Geografía de la novela*. Madrid: Alfaguara, 1993.
Galeano, Eduardo. *Open Veins of Latin America: Five Centuries of the Pillage of a Continent*. New York: Monthly Review Press, 1997.
Galeano, Eduardo. *Las venas abiertas de América Latina*. Mexico City: Siglo XXI Editores, 1971.
Galíndez, Jesús de. *La era de Trujillo: Un estudio casuístico de dictadura hispanoamericana*. Santiago: Editorial del Pacífico, 1956.
Galíndez, Jesús de. *The Era of Trujillo, Dominican Dictator*. Tucson: University of Arizona Press, 1973.
Gaonkar, Dilip Parameshwar. "Toward New Imaginaries: An Introduction." *Public Culture* 14.1 (2002): 1–19.
García, Cristina. *Dreaming in Cuban*. New York: Ballantine Books, 1993.
García, Cristina. *King of Cuba*. New York: Scribner, 2013.

García, Cristina. *The Lady Matador's Hotel*. New York: Scribner, 2010.
García, Juan Carlos. *El dictador en la literatura hispanoamericana*. Chile: Mosquito Comunicaciones, 2000.
García, Maria Cristina. *Havana USA: Cuban Exiles and Cuban Americans in South Florida, 1959–1994*. Berkeley: University of California Press, 1996.
García-Alfonso, Cristina. *Resolviendo: Narratives of Survival in the Hebrew Bible and in Cuba Today*. New York: Peter Lang, 2010.
García Márquez, Gabriel. *The Autumn of the Patriarch*. Trans. Gregory Rabassa. New York: First Perennial Classics, 1999.
García Márquez, Gabriel. *El olor de la Guayaba: Conversaciones con Plinio Apuleyo Mendoza*. Bogotá: Grupo Editorial Norma, 2005.
García Márquez, Gabriel. *El otoño del patriarca*. Bogotá: Grupo Editorial Norma, 2003.
Gates, Henry Louis, Jr. *The Signifying Monkey: A Theory of Afro-American Literary Criticism*. New York: Oxford University Press, 1988.
Genette, Gérard. "Time and Narrative in *A la recherche du temps perdu*." In *Essentials of the Theory of Fiction*, ed. Michael J. Hoffman and Patrick D. Murphy. Durham: Duke University Press, 1996, 182–199.
Gill, Lesley. *The School of the Americas: Military Training and Political Violence in the Americas*. Durham: Duke University Press, 2004.
Gillman, Susan. "The Epistemology of Slave Conspiracy." *MFS Modern Fiction Studies* 49.1 (2003): 101–123.
Gillman, Susan. "*Otra vez Caliban*/Encore Caliban: Adaptation, Translation, Americas Studies." *American Literary History* 20.1–2 (2008): 187–209.
Gilroy, Paul. *The Black Atlantic: Modernity and Double Consciousness*. Cambridge, MA: Harvard University Press, 1993.
Golden, Tim. "Castro's People Try to Absorb 'Terrible Blows.'" *New York Times*, January 11, 1993. http://www.nytimes.com/1993/01/11/world/castro-s-people-try-to-absorb-terrible-blows.html.
Golden, Renny. *Sanctuary: The New Underground Railroad*. Maryknoll, NY: Orbis Books, 1986.
Goldman, Francisco. *The Art of Political Murder: Who Killed the Bishop?* New York: Grove Press, 2007.
Goldman, Francisco. *The Long Night of White Chickens*. New York: Grove Press, 1992.
Goldman, Francisco. *The Ordinary Seaman*. New York: Grove Press, 1997.
Gómez, Alan Eladio. *The Revolutionary Imaginations of Greater Mexico: Chicana/o Radicalism, Solidarity Politics, and Latin American Social Movements*. Austin: University of Texas Press, 2016.
Gómez-Barris, Macarena. "Two 9/11s in a Lifetime: Chilean Art, Terror, and Displacement." *Latino Studies* 3.1 (April 2005): 97–112.
Gómez-Barris, Macarena. *Where Memory Dwells: Culture and State Violence in Chile*. Berkeley: University of California Press, 2009.
González, Aníbal. *Killer Books: Writing, Violence, and Ethics in Modern Spanish American Narrative*. Austin: University of Texas Press, 2001.
González, Christopher. *Reading Junot Díaz*. Pittsburgh: University of Pittsburgh Press, 2015.
González, John Morán. Review of *Chicano Novels and the Politics of Form*, by Marcial González, and *Translating Empire*, by Laura Lomas. *American Literature* 82.2 (2010): 430–432.
Gonzalez, Juan. *Harvest of Empire: A History of Latinos in America*. New York: Viking, 2001.

González, Marcial. *Chicano Novels and the Politics of Form: Race, Class, and Reification.* Ann Arbor: University of Michigan Press, 2009.

González Echevarría, Roberto. "The Dictatorship of Rhetoric/The Rhetoric of Dictatorship: Carpentier, García Márquez, and Roa Bastos." *Latin American Research Review* 15.3 (1980): 205–228.

Goodman, Amy. *Democracy Now!: Twenty Years Covering the Movements Changing America.* New York: Simon and Schuster, 2016.

Gordon, Avery F. *Ghostly Matters: Haunting and the Sociological Imagination.* 2nd ed. Minneapolis: University of Minnesota Press, 2008.

Gosse, Van. "The Cuban Revolution and the New Left." In *The Cuba Reader: History, Culture, Politics,* ed. Aviva Chomsky, Barry Carr, and Pamela Maria Smorkaloff. Durham: Duke University Press, 2004, 526–529.

Graeber, David. "Turning Modes of Production Inside Out or, Why Capitalism Is a Transformation of Slavery." *Critique of Anthropology* 26.1 (2006): 61–85.

Grafton, Anthony. *The Footnote: A Curious History.* Cambridge: Harvard University Press, 1997.

Grandin, Greg, Deborah T. Levenson, and Elizabeth Oglesby. Editors' introduction to *The Guatemala Reader: History, Culture, Politics.* Durham: Duke University Press, 2011, 1–12.

Greenberg, Amy S. *Manifest Manhood and the Antebellum American Empire.* New York: Cambridge University Press, 2005.

Gruesz, Kirsten Silva. *Ambassadors of Culture: The Transamerican Origins of Latino Writing.* Princeton: Princeton University Press, 2002.

Gruesz, Kirsten Silva. "The Once and Future Latino: Notes toward a Literary History todavía para llegar." In *Contemporary U.S. Latino/a Literary Criticism,* ed. Lyn Di Iorio Sandín and Richard Perez. New York: Palgrave Macmillan, 2008, 115–142.

Gruesz, Kirsten Silva. "Utopia Latina: *The Ordinary Seaman* in Extraordinary Times." *Modern Fiction Studies* 49.1 (2003): 54–83.

Guatemala, Never Again! REMHI, Recovery of Historical Memory Project; The Official Report of the Human Rights Office, Archdiocese of Guatemala. New York: Maryknoll Press, 1999.

Guerra, Lillian. "Beyond Paradox: Counterrevolution and the Origins of Political Culture in the Cuban Revolution, 1959–2009." In *A Century of Revolution: Insurgent and Counterinsurgent Violence during Latin America's Long Cold War,* ed. Greg Grandin and Gilbert M. Joseph. Durham: Duke University Press, 2010, 199–235.

Halperin, Laura. *Intersections of Harm: Narratives of Latina Deviance and Defiance.* New Brunswick: Rutgers University Press, 2015.

Hames-García, Michael. *Identity Complex: Making the Case for Multiplicity.* Minneapolis: University of Minnesota Press, 2011.

Hames-García, Michael. "Which America Is Ours? Martí's 'Truth' and the Foundations of 'American Literature.'" *Modern Fiction Studies* 49.1 (Spring 2003): 19–53.

Hanna, Monica. "Chronicling Contemporary Latinidad." *American Literature* 8.2 (June 2016): 361–389.

Hanna, Monica. "'Reassembling the Fragments': Battling Historiographies, Caribbean Discourse, and Nerd Genres in Junot Díaz's *The Brief Wondrous Life of Oscar Wao.*" *Callaloo* 33.2 (2010): 498–520.

Hanna, Monica, Jennifer Harford Vargas, and José David Saldívar. "Junot Díaz and the Decolonial Imagination: From Island to Empire." In *Junot Díaz and the Decolonial*

Imagination, ed. Monica Hanna, Jennifer Harford Vargas, and José David Saldívar. Durham: Duke University Press, 2016.

Harford Vargas, Jennifer. "Novel Testimony: Alternative Archives in Edwidge Danticat's *The Farming of Bones*." *Callaloo* 37.5 (Fall 2014): 1162–1180.

Harvey, David. *A Brief History of Neoliberalism*. Oxford: Oxford University Press, 2005.

Heredia, Juanita. *Transnational Latina Narratives in the Twenty-First Century: The Politics of Gender, Race, and Migrations*. New York: Palgrave Macmillan, 2009.

Hernández, Ester. "Libertad." March 6, 2010. http://latinopia.com/latino-art/ester-hernandez/.

Hirsch, Marianne. *The Generation of Postmemory: Writing and Visual Culture after the Holocaust*. New York: Columbia University Press, 2012.

Hodge, G. Derrick. "Colonizing the Cuban Body." In *The Cuba Reader: History, Culture, Politics*, ed. Aviva Chomsky, Barry Carr, and Pamela Maria Smorkaloff. Durham: Duke University Press, 2004.

Horn, Maja. *Masculinity after Trujillo: The Politics of Gender in Dominican Literature*. Gainesville: University of Florida Press, 2014.

Hutcheon, Linda. *Narcissistic Narrative: The Metafictional Paradox*. Waterloo, Ontario: Wilfred Laurier University Press, 1980.

Irizarry, Ylce. *Chicana/o and Latina/o Fiction: The New Memory of Latinidad*. Urbana: University of Illinois Press, 2016.

Irizarry, Ylce. Interview with Cristina García. *Contemporary Literature* 48.2 (2007): 175–194.

Jackson, Kevin. *Invisible Forms: A Guide to Literary Curiosities*. New York: St. Martin's Press, 2000.

James, C. L. R. *Mariners, Renegades, and Castaways: The Story of Herman Melville and the World We Live in*. Hanover, NH: University Press of New England, 2001.

Klein, Naomi. *The Shock Doctrine: The Rise of Disaster Capitalism*. New York: Picador, 2007.

Lamas, Carmen E. "Raimundo Cabrera, the Latin American Archive, and the Latina/o Continuum." In *The Latino Nineteenth Century*, ed. Rodrigo Lazo and Jesse Alemán. New York: New York University Press, 2016, 210–229.

Latorre, Guisela. *Walls of Empowerment: Chicana/o Indigenist Murals of California*. Austin: University of Texas Press, 2008.

Lazo, Rodrigo. "Hemispheric American Novels." In *The Cambridge History of the American Novel*, ed. Leonard Cassuto, Clare Virginia Eby, and Benjamin Reiss. Cambridge: Cambridge University Press, 2011, 1084–1095.

Lazo, Rodrigo. *Writing to Cuba: Filibustering and Cuban Exiles in the United States*. Chapel Hill: University of North Carolina Press, 2005.

Levine, Caroline. "Strategic Formalism: Toward a New Method in Cultural Studies." *Victorian Studies* 48.4 (2006): 625–57.

Limón, Graciela. *In Search of Bernabé*. Houston: Arte Público Press, 1993.

Linebaugh, Peter and Markus Rediker. *The Many-Headed Hydra: The Hidden History of the Revolutionary Atlantic*. Boston: Beacon Press, 2000.

Lizarraga, Willy. "PLACA." In *Street Art San Francisco: Mission Muralismo*, ed. Annice Jacoby. New York: Abrams, 2009, 103.

Lomas, Laura. *Translating Empire: José Martí, Migrant Latino Subjects, and American Modernities*. Durham: Duke University Press, 2009.

López, Alma M. "Greater Cuba." In *The Ethnic Eye: Latino Media Arts*, ed. Chon A. Noriega and Alma M. López. Minneapolis: University of Minnesota Press, 1996, 38–58.

López, Marissa K. *Chicano Nations: The Hemispheric Origins of Mexican American Literature*. New York: New York University Press, 2011.

López-Calvo, Ignacio. *God and Trujillo: Literacy and Cultural Representations of the Dominican Dictator*. Gainesville: University Press of Florida, 2005.

Lugones, Maria. "Heterosexualism and the Modern/Colonial Gender System." *Hypatia* 22.1 (2007): 186–219.

Lye, Colleen. "Racial Form." *Representations* 104.1 (2008): 92–101.

Machado Sáez, Elena. "Dictating Desire, Dictating Diaspora: Junot Díaz's *The Brief Wondrous Life of Oscar Wao* as Foundational Romance." *Contemporary Literature* 52.3 (2011): 522–555.

Madrigal, Oscar 'The Oz.' "'Los Borrados': A Chicano Quest for Identity in a Post-apocalyptic, Culturally Defunct Hispanic Utopia (A Reinterpretive Chicano Comic)." In *Velvet Barrios: Popular Culture and Chicana/o Sexualities*, ed. Alicia Gaspa de Alba. New York: Palgrave Macmillan, 2003.

Marchi, Regina M. *Day of the Dead in the USA: The Migration and Transformation of a Cultural Phenomenon*. New Brunswick: Rutgers University Press, 2009.

Martí, José. *José Martí: Selected Writings*. Trans. Esther Allen. New York: Penguin Classics, 2002.

Martin, Gerald. *Gabriel García Márquez: A Life*. New York: Alfred A. Knopf, 2009.

Martin, Gerald. *Journeys through the Labyrinth: Latin American Fiction in the Twentieth Century*. New York: Verso, 1989.

Martínez, Demetria. *Mother Tongue*. New York: One World, 1997.

Martínez, Ernesto Javier. "Shifting the Site of Queer Enunciation: Manuel Muñoz and the Politics of Form." In *Gay Latino Studies: A Critical Reader*, ed. Michael Hames-García and Ernesto Javier Martínez. Durham: Duke University Press, 2011, 226–249.

Martínez, Oscar. *A History of Violence*. New York: Verso, 2016.

Marx, Karl, and Friedrich Engels. *The Marx-Engels Reader*. Ed. Robert C. Tucker. New York: Norton, 1978.

Massey, Douglas S., Jorge Durand, and Nolan J. Malone. *Beyond Smoke and Mirrors: Migration Immigration in an Era of Economic Integration*. New York: Russell Sage Foundation, 2003.

McClennen, Sophia A. *Ariel Dorfman: An Aesthetics of Hope*. Durham: Duke University Press, 2010.

McClintock, Anne. "The Angel of Progress: Pitfalls of the Term 'Post-colonialism.'" *Social Text* 31/32 (1992): 84–98.

McCracken, Ellen. *New Latina Narrative: The Feminine Space of Postmodern Ethnicity*. Tucson: University of Arizona Press, 1999.

McGurl, Mark. *The Program Era: Postwar Fiction and the Rise of Creative Writing*. Cambridge, MA: Harvard University Press, 2009.

Messer, Miwa. "Old Friends Junot Díaz and Francisco Goldman Talk Shop." http://www.csmonitor.com/Books/chapter-and-verse/2012/0914/Old-friends-Junot-Diaz-and-Francisco-Goldman-talk-shop.

Mignolo, Walter. *The Idea of Latin America*. Malden, MA: Blackwell, 2005.

Mignolo, Walter. *Local Histories/Global Designs: Coloniality, Subaltern Knowledges, and Border Thinking*. Princeton: Princeton University Press, 2000.

Milian, Claudia. *Latining America: Black-Brown Passages and the Coloring of Latino/a Studies*. Athens: University of Georgia Press, 2013.

Miliani, Domingo. "El dictador: Objeto narrativo en *Yo el supremo*." *Revista de crítica literaria latinoamericana* 2.4 (1976): 103–119.

Miller, D. A. *The Novel and the Police*. Berkeley: University of California Press, 1988.
Minich, Julie Avril. *Accessible Citizenships: Disability, Nation, and the Cultural Politics of Greater Mexico*. Philadelphia: Temple University Press, 2013.
Minich, Julie Avril. "Disability, Losers, and Narrative Remediation." *Comparative Literature* 66.1 (Winter 2014): 35–42.
Minich, Julie Avril. "Mestizaje as National Prosthesis: Corporeal Metaphors in Héctor Tobar's *The Tattooed Soldier*." *Arizona Journal of Hispanic Cultural Studies* 17 (2013): 211–226.
Moraga, Cherríe. "Catching Fire: Preface to the Fourth Edition." In *This Bridge Called My Back: Writings by Radical Women of Color*. ed. Cherríe Moraga and Gloria Anzaldúa. 4th ed. Albany: State University of New York Press, 2015, xv–xxvi.
Moraga, Cherríe. *Loving in the War Years: Lo que nunca pasó por sus labios*. 2nd ed. Boston: South End Press, 2000.
Moraga, Cherríe. "Refugees of a World on Fire: Foreword to the Second Edition, 1983." In *This Bridge Called My Back: Writings by Radical Women of Color*, ed. Cherríe Moraga and Gloria Anzaldúa. 4th ed. Albany: State University of New York Press, 2015, 255–259.
Moraña, Mabel, Enrique Dussel, and Carlos A. Jáuregui. "Colonialism and Its Replicants." In *Coloniality at Large: Latin America and the Postcolonial Debate*, ed. Mabel Moraña, Enrique Dussel, and Carlos A. Jáuregui. Durham: Duke University Press, 2008.
Moretti, Franco. *Graphs, Maps, Trees: Abstract Models for a Literary History*. New York: Verso, 2005.
Moya, Paula M. L. *The Social Imperative: Race, Close Reading, and Contemporary Literary Criticism*. Stanford: Stanford University Press, 2015.
Moya, Paula M. L., and Ramón Saldívar. "Fictions of the Trans-American Imaginary." *Modern Fiction Studies* 49.1 (Spring 2003): 1–18.
Muñoz, José Esteban. "'Chico, What Does It Feel Like to Be a Problem?' The Transmission of Brownness." In *A Companion to Latina/o Studies*, ed. Juan Flores and Renato Rosaldo. Oxford: Blackwell, 2007, 441–451.
Muñoz, José Esteban. *Disidentifications: Queers of Color and the Performance of Politics*. Minneapolis: University of Minnesota Press, 1999.
Muñoz, José Esteban. "*No Es Fácil*: Notes on the Negotiation of Cubanidad and Exilic Memory in Carmelita Tropicana's *Milk of Amnesia*." *TDR: The Drama Review* 39.3 (1995): 76–82.
Muñoz, José Esteban. "Performing Greater Cuba: Tania Bruguera and the Burden of Guilt." *Women & Performance: A Journal of Feminist Theory* 11.2 (2000): 251–265.
Murguía, Alejandro. "Balmy Alley." In *Street Art San Francisco: Mission Muralismo*, ed. Annice Jacoby. New York: Abrams, 2009, 97.
Nava, Michael. *The City of Palaces*. Madison: Terrace Books, 2014.
Nevins, Joseph. *Operation Gatekeeper and Beyond: The War on 'Illegals' and the Remaking of the U.S.-Mexico Boundary*. New York: Routledge, 2010.
Nguyen, Viet Thanh. "Just Memory: War and the Ethics of Remembrance." *American Literary History* 25.1 (Spring 2013): 144–163.
Obejas, Achy. *Days of Awe*. New York: Ballantine Books, 2001.
Obejas, Achy. *We Came All the Way from Cuba So You Could Dress Like This?: Stories*. Pittsburgh: Cleis Press, 1994.
Obejas, Achy. "What Anthony Bourdain Didn't Tell You about Cuban Food." WBEZ Blogs, July 22, 2011, http://www.wbez.org/blog/achy-obejas/2011-07-22/what-anthony-bourdain-didnt-tell-you-about-cuban-food-89518.

Oboler, Suzanne. *Ethnic Labels, Latino Lives: Identity and the Politics of (Re)presentation in the United States*. Minneapolis: University of Minnesota Press, 1995.

Olson, Barbara K. "'Who Thinks This Book?' or Why the Author/God Analogy Merits Our Continued Attention." *Narrative* 14.3 (October 2006): 339–346.

Ontiveros, Randy J. *In the Spirit of a New People: The Cultural Politics of the Chicano Movement*. New York: New York University Press, 2014.

Orbach, Michael K. *Hunters, Seamen, and Entrepreneurs: The Tuna Seinermen of San Diego*. Berkeley: University of California Press, 1977.

Orchard, William. *Drawn Together: Pedagogy, Politics, and the Latinx Graphic Novel*. Manuscript in preparation.

Ortíz, Ricardo L. "The Cold War in the Americas and Latina/o Literature." In *The Cambridge Companion to Latina/o American Literature*, ed. John Morán González. New York: Cambridge University Press, 2016.

Ortíz, Ricardo L. "Edwidge Danticat's *Latinidad*: *The Farming of Bones* and the Cultivation (of Fields) of Knowledge." In *Aftermaths: Exile, Migration, and Diaspora Reconsidered*, ed. Marcus Bullock and Peter Y. Paik. New Brunswick: Rutgers University Press, 2009, 150–174.

Orozco, Daniel. "Somoza's Dream." In *Orientation and Other Stories*. New York: Faber and Faber, 2011, 59–92.

Pacheco, Carlos. *Narrativa de la dictadura y crítica literaria*. Caracas: Fundación Centro de Estudios Latinoamericanos Rómulo Gallegos, 1987.

Padilla, Yolanda. "The Other Novel of the Mexican Revolution." In *Bridges, Borders and Breaks: History, Narrative, and Nation in Twenty-First-Century Chicana/o Literary Criticism*, ed. William Orchard and Yolanda Padilla. Pittsburgh: University of Pittsburgh Press, 2016.

Pastor, Manuel, Jr. *Latinos and the Los Angeles Uprising: The Economic Context*. Claremont, CA: Tomas Rivera Center, 1993.

Patterson, Orlando. *Slavery and Social Death: A Comparative Study*. Cambridge, MA: Harvard University Press, 1982.

Pease, Donald E. Introduction to C. L. R. James, *Mariners, Renegades, and Castaways: The Story of Herman Melville and the World We Live in*. Hanover, NH: University Press of New England, 2001.

Pérez, Loida Maritza. *Geographies of Home*. New York: Viking, 1999.

Pérez, Louis A. *Cuba in the American Imagination: Metaphor and the Imperial Ethos*. Chapel Hill: University of North Carolina Press, 2008.

Plascencia, Salvador. *The People of Paper*. Orlando: Harcourt, 2006.

Poblete, Juan, ed. Editor's introduction to *Critical Latin American and Latino Studies*. Minneapolis: University of Minnesota Press, 2003.

Polit Dueñas, Gabriela. *Cosas de Hombres: Escritores y caudillos en la literatura latinoamericana del siglo XX*. Rosario, Argentina: Beatriz Viterbo, 2008.

Porter, Carolyn. "What We Know That We Don't Know: Remapping American Literary Studies." *American Literary History* 6.3 (1994): 467–526.

Portes, Alejandro and Alex Stepick. *City on the Edge: The Transformation of Miami*. Berkeley: University of California Press, 1993.

Pratt, Mary Louise. *Imperial Eyes: Travel Writing and Transculturation*. New York: Routledge, 1992.

Quijano, Anibal, and Michael Ennis. "Coloniality of Power, Eurocentrism, and Latin America." *Nepantla: Views from South* 1.3 (2000): 533–580.

Quiroga, José. *Cuban Palimpsests*. Minneapolis: University of Minnesota Press, 2005.

Radio Ambulante. "Cuando La Habana era friki." January 24, 2017. http://radioambulante.org/audio/cuando-la-habana-era-friki-2.

Radiolab. "Los Frikis." March 24, 2015. http://www.radiolab.org/story/los-frikis/.

Rama, Ángel. *Los dictadores latinoamericanos*. Mexico City: Fondo de Cultura Económica, 1976.

Rama, Ángel. *Writing across Cultures: Narrative Transculturation in Latin America*. Trans. David Frye. Durham: Duke University Press, 2012.

Ramírez, Sergio. "La nueva novela latinoamericana." *La Insignia*, October 2008. http://www.lainsignia.org/2008/octubre/cul_002.htm.

Ramos, Juan Antonio. *Hacía el otoño del patriarca: La novela del dictador en hispanoamérica*. San Juan, Puerto Rico: Instituto de Cultura Puertorriqueña, 1983.

Randall, Margaret. *Gathering Rage: The Failure of Twentieth Century Revolutions to Develop a Feminist Agenda*. New York: Monthly Review Press, 1992.

Rebel Diaz. Website of Rebel Diaz. http://www.rebeldiaz.com/.

Rediker, Marcus. *Between the Devil and the Deep Blue Sea: Merchant Seamen, Pirates, and the Anglo-American Maritime World, 1700–1750*. New York: Cambridge University Press, 1987.

Rediker, Marcus. *The Slave Ship: A Human History*. New York: Viking, 2007.

Riofrio, John D. "Rio." *Continental Shifts: Migration, Representation, and the Struggle for Justice in Latin(o) America*. Austin: University of Texas Press, 2015.

Rivera, Tomás. *…y no se lo tragó la tierra / And the Earth Did Not Devour Him*. Trans. Evangelina Vigil-Piñón. Houston: Arte Público Press, 1992.

Roa Bastos, Augusto. *Yo el supremo*. Bogotá: Siglo Veintiuno Editores, 1988.

Roa Bastos, Augusto. *I the Supreme*. Trans. Helen Lane. New York: Dalkey Archive Press, 1986.

Robertis, Carolina de. *The Invisible Mountain*. New York: Vintage, 2010.

Robertis, Carolina de. *Perla*. New York: Vintage, 2012.

Robertis, Carolina de, ed. *Radical Hope: Letters of Love and Dissent in Dangerous Times*. New York: Vintage, 2017.

Rodríguez, Ana Patricia. *Dividing the Isthmus: Central American Transnational Histories, Literatures, and Cultures*. Austin: University of Texas Press, 2009.

Rodríguez, Ana Patricia. "Refugees of the South: Central Americans in the U.S. Latino Imaginary." *American Literature* 73.2 (2001): 387–412.

Rodríguez, Ileana. *Women, Guerrillas, and Love: Understanding War in Central America*. Minneapolis: University of Minnesota Press, 1996.

Rodríguez, Juana María. *Queer Latinidad: Identity Practices, Discursive Spaces*. New York: New York University Press, 2003.

Rodriguez, Ralph E. "Chicano Studies and the Need to Not Know." *American Literary History* 22.1 (2009): 180–190.

Rodriguez, Ralph E. "In Plain Sight: Reading the Racial Surfaces of Adrian Tomine's *Shortcomings*." In *Drawing New Color Lines: Transnational Asian American Graphic Narratives*, ed. Monica Chiu. Hong Kong: Hong Kong University Press, 2015.

Rodríguez, Richard T. *Next of Kin: The Family in Chicana/o Cultural Politics*. Durham: Duke University Press, 2009.

Román, Elda María. "'Post' Ethnic Form." In *American Literature in Transition: 2000–2010*, ed. Rachel Greenwald Smith. Cambridge: Cambridge University Press, forthcoming.

Román, Elda María. *Race and Upward Mobility: Seeking, Gatekeeping, and Other Class Strategies in Postwar America*. Stanford: Stanford University Press, 2017.

Roorda, Eric Paul. *The Dictator Next Door: The Good Neighbor Policy and the Trujillo Regime in the Dominican Republic, 1930–1945*. Durham: Duke University Press, 1998.

Rosario, Vanessa Pérez, ed. *Hispanic Caribbean Literature of Migration: Narratives of Displacement*. New York: Palgrave Macmillan, 2012.

Rothberg, Michael. *Multidirectional Memory: Remembering the Holocaust in the Age of Decolonization*. Stanford: Stanford University Press, 2009.

Rothenberg, Daniel, ed. *Memory of Silence: The Guatemalan Truth Commission Report*. New York: Palgrave Macmillan, 2012.

Saénz, Benjamin Alire. "Alligator Park." In *Flowers for the Broken*. Seattle: Broken Moon Press, 1992, 81–103.

Sae-Saue, Jayson Gonzales. *Southwest Asia: The Transpacific Geographies of Chicana/o Literature*. New Brunswick: Rutgers University Press, 2016.

Saldaña-Portillo, María Josefina. "From the Borderlands to the Transnational? Critiquing Empire in the Twenty-First Century." In *A Companion to Latina/o Studies*, ed. Juan Flores and Renato Rosaldo. Oxford: Blackwell, 2007.

Saldaña-Portillo, María Josefina. *The Revolutionary Imagination in the Americas and the Age of Development*. Durham: Duke University Press, 2003.

Saldívar, José David. "Conjectures on 'Americanity' and Junot Díaz's 'Fukú Americanus' in *The Brief Wondrous Life of Oscar Wao*." *Global South* 5.1 (Spring 2011): 120–136.

Saldívar, José David. *The Dialectics of Our America: Genealogy, Cultural Critique, and Literary History*. Durham: Duke University Press, 1991.

Saldívar, José David. *Trans-Americanity: Subaltern Modernities, Global Coloniality, and the Cultures of Greater Mexico*. Durham: Duke University Press Books, 2011.

Saldívar, Ramón. *Borderlands of Culture: Américo Paredes and the Transnational Imaginary*. Durham: Duke University Press, 2006.

Saldívar, Ramón. *Chicano Narrative: The Dialectics of Difference*. Madison: University of Wisconsin Press, 1990.

Saldívar, Ramón. "Historical Fantasy, Speculative Realism, and Postrace Aesthetics in Contemporary American Fiction." *American Literary History* 23.3 (2011): 574–599.

Sampson, Helen. *International Seafarers and Transnationalism in the Twenty-First Century*. Manchester, UK: Manchester University Press, 2013.

Sánchez, Rosaura, and Beatrice Pita. "Theses on the Latino Bloc: A Critical Perspective." *Aztlan: A Journal of Chicano Studies* 31.2 (2006): 25–53.

Sandoval, Adriana. *Los dictadores y la dictadura en la novela hispanoamericana (1851–1978)*. Mexico City: Universidad Nacional Autónoma de México, 1989.

Santa Ana, Otto. *Brown Tide Rising: Metaphors of Latinos in Contemporary American Public Discourse*. Austin: University of Texas Press, 2002.

Schmidt Camacho, Alicia R. *Migrant Imaginaries: Latino Cultural Politics in the U.S.-Mexico Borderlands*. New York: New York University Press, 2008.

Scott, James C. *Domination and the Arts of Resistance: Hidden Transcripts*. New Haven: Yale University Press, 1990.

Sellers-García, Sylvia. *When the Ground Turns in Its Sleep*. New York: Riverhead Books, 2008.

Seltzer, Mark. *Henry James and the Art of Power*. Ithaca, NY: Cornell University Press, 1984.

Shemak, April Ann. *Asylum Speakers: Caribbean Refugees and Testimonial Discourse*. New York: Fordham University Press, 2011.

Shoat, Ella. "Notes on the Post-colonial." In *Contemporary Postcolonial Theory: A Reader*. ed. Padmini Mongia. New York: Oxford University Press, 2003, 322–334.

Silko, Leslie Marmon. "The Border Patrol State." In *Yellow Woman and a Beauty of the Spirit*. New York: Simon and Schuster, 1997, 115–123.

Silverman, Max. *Palimpsestic Memory: The Holocaust and Colonialism in French and Francophone Fiction and Film.* New York: Berghahn Books, 2013.
Smith, Anna Deavere. *Twilight: Los Angeles, 1992.* New York: Anchor Books, 1994.
Socolovsky, Maya. *Troubling Nationhood in U.S. Latina Literature: Explorations of Place and Belonging.* New Brunswick: Rutgers University Press, 2013.
Sommer, Doris. *Proceed with Caution, When Engaged by Minority Writing in the Americas.* Cambridge, MA: Harvard University Press, 1999.
Song, Min Hyoung. *Strange Futures: Pessimism and the 1992 Los Angeles Riots.* Durham: Duke University Press, 2005.
Spitzer, Anais N. *Derrida, Myth, and the Impossibility of Philosophy.* New York City: Continuum, 2011.
Stonehill, Brian. *The Self-Conscious Novel: Artifice in Fiction from Joyce to Pynchon.* Philadelphia: University of Pennsylvania Press, 1988.
Taylor, Charles. *Modern Social Imaginaries.* Durham: Duke University Press, 2004.
Taylor, Diana. *The Archive and the Repertoire: Performing Cultural Memory in the Americas.* Durham: Duke University Press, 2003.
Taylor, Diana. *Disappearing Acts: Spectacles of Gender and Nationalism in Argentina's "Dirty War."* Durham: Duke University Press, 1997.
Thompson, Carl, ed. *Shipwreck in Art and Literature: Images and Interpretations from Antiquity to the Present Day.* New York: Routledge, Taylor and Francis Group, 2014.
Thomson, Rosemarie Garland. *Extraordinary Bodies: Figuring Physical Disability in American Culture and Literature.* New York: Columbia University Press, 1997.
Tierney-Tello, Mary Beth. *Allegories of Transgression and Transformation: Experimental Fiction by Women Writing under Dictatorship.* Albany: State University of New York Press, 1996.
Tobar, Héctor. "Reading Ferguson: Books on Race, Police, Protest and U.S. History." *Los Angeles Times*, August 18, 2014. http://www.latimes.com/books/jacketcopy/la-et-jc-reading-ferguson-books-on-race-police-protest-and-us-history-20140818-story.html.
Tobar, Héctor. *The Tattooed Soldier.* New York: Penguin Books, 1998.
Torres, María de los Angeles. *In the Land of Mirrors: Cuban Exile Politics in the United States.* Ann Arbor: University of Michigan Press, 1999.
Torres-Saillant, Silvio. "Divisible Blackness: Reflections on Heterogeneity and Racial Identity." In *The Afro-Latin@ Reader: History and Culture in the United States,* ed. Miriam Jiménez Román and Juan Flores. Durham: Duke University Press, 2010, 453–466.
Torres-Saillant, Silvio. *An Intellectual History of the Caribbean.* New York: Palgrave Macmillan, 2006.
Turits, Richard Lee. *Foundations of Despotism: Peasants, the Trujillo Regime, and Modernity in Dominican History.* Stanford: Stanford University Press, 2004.
Valenzuela, Luisa. *Cola de lagartija.* Mexico City: Rayuela International, 1992.
Valenzuela, Luisa. *The Lizard's Tail.* Trans. Gregory Rabassa. London: Serpent's Tail, 1987.
Valle, Victor M., and Rudolfo D. Torres. *Latino Metropolis.* Minneapolis: University of Minnesota Press, 2000.
Vargas Llosa, Mario. *La fiesta del chivo.* Madrid: Alfaguara, 2000.
Vázquez, David J. "Toxicity and the Politics of Narration: Imagining Social and Environmental Justice in Salvador Plascencia's *The People of Paper.*" In *Symbolism: An International Annual on Critical Aesthetics.* Forthcoming.

Vázquez, David J. *Triangulations: Narrative Strategies for Navigating Latino Identity.* Minneapolis: University of Minnesota Press, 2011.

Vázquez, Eric. "Héctor Tobar's *The Tattoed Soldier*: An Interrogative Mode of Justice" Manuscript in preparation.

Vigil, Ariana E. *Understanding Francisco Goldman.* Columbia: University of South Carolina Press, forthcoming.

Vigil, Ariana E. *War Echoes: Gender and Militarization in U.S. Latina/o Cultural Production.* New Brunswick: Rutgers University Press, 2014.

Viramontes, Helena María. "The Cariboo Café." In *The Moths and Other Stories.* Houston: Arte Público Press, 1995, 65–79.

Viramontes, Helena María. *Under the Feet of Jesus.* New York: Plume, 1996.

Vizenor, Gerald Robert, ed. *Survivance: Narratives of Native Presence.* Lincoln: University of Nebraska Press, 2008.

Weinreb, Amelia Rosenberg. *Cuba in the Shadow of Change: Daily Life in the Twilight of the Revolution.* Gainesville: University Press of Florida, 2009.

Weld, Kirsten. *Paper Cadavers: The Archives of Dictatorship in Guatemala.* Durham: Duke University Press, 2014.

Wenzel, Michael, Tyler G. Okimoto, Norman T. Feather, and Michael J. Platow. "Retributive and Restorative Justice." *Law and Human Behavior* 32.5 (2008): 375–389.

Williams, Raymond. *Marxism and Literature.* New York: Oxford University Press, 1977.

Williams, Raymond Leslie. *The Twentieth-Century Spanish American Novel.* Austin: University of Texas Press, 2003.

Whitfield, Esther Katheryn. *Cuban Currency: The Dollar and "Special Period" Fiction.* Minneapolis: University of Minnesota Press, 2008.

Wojczuk, Carla, and Julian Rowand, dirs. *These Walls Speak.* CalHumanities, 2015.

Woloch, Alex. *The One vs. The Many: Minor Characters and the Space of the Protagonist in the Novel.* Princeton: Princeton University Press, 2003.

Zuluaga, Conrado. *Novelas del dictador, dictadores de novela.* Bogotá: Valencia Editores, 1977.

{ INDEX }

Figures and notes are indicated by f and n following the page number.

Abrams, M. A., 151
Addis, Mary K., 197n14
Adichie, Chimamanda Ngozi, 60
African Americans. *See also* Black subjects
  in murals, 191
  injustice and, 129, 133–134, 147
  neo-slave narratives and, 200n32
  Rodney King uprisings (1992), 119, 121, 127–128, 131–135, 144–145, 219n18
  slave ships imagery and, 96–97, 102–103, 117
Afro-Latina/o, 46, 49–50, 196
Aldama, Frederick Luis, 200n33, 207n7
Agency, 91, 92, 114, 161, 174, 203n7
AIDS epidemic, 179
Alarcón, Daniel, 5, 18, 196n6, 206n22, 229n43
  At Night We Walk in Circles 224n17
  Lost City Radio, 215n27, 229n43
  Radio Ambulante, 229n43
Alarcón, Norma, 210n25
Alcaráz, Lalo, 232n18
Alicia, Juana, 230n11, 231n12
  "Resistance and Revolution," 191–192, 192*f*
  "Te oímos Guatemala/We Hear You Guatemala," 183–184, 191
  "Una ley inmoral, nadie tiene que cumplirla/No One Should Comply with an Immoral Law," 183–185, 183*f*, 191
Allende, Salvador, 26, 229n1
Alvarez, Julia, 5
  "Disappeared Does Not Take a Helping Verb in English," 215n27
  How the García Girls Lost Their Accents, 228n37
  In the Time of the Butterflies, 46, 195n1

Ambiguity, 48, 58–59, 110, 139
Anonymity, 40, 46, 51–53, 91, 131, 157, 184
Anti-institutionalism, 174
Anzaldúa, Gloria, *Borderlands/La Frontera*, 3, 8, 193, 210n25
Aparicio, Frances R., 13, 201n35
Araiza, Tirso, "Mission Makeover" (with Ippolito), 187–188, 188*f*
Argentina, political violence in, 60, 182, 202n45, 209n19, 216n31, 217n42
Arias, Arturo, 212n3
Armillas-Tisyera, Magalí, 197n14, 198n17, 200n29, 203n2
Artists' Call Against U.S. Intervention in Central America, 180
Asociación Madres de Plaza de Mayo (Mothers of the Plaza de Mayo), 182
Assassination trope, 42, 45, 61, 120–121, 130–131, 136, 138, 142, 152–153, 160, 183, 206n1
Assimilation, 12, 127, 140, 205n17, 211n36
Asturias, Miguel Ángel, 219n14
  El señor presidente/The President, 9, 34–35
Authoritarianism. *See also* Dictatorship
*Authori*tarianism, 11, 60–85
  author as dictator, 64–70
  narrative power and, 38
  narrative rights and narrative disclosure, 79–85
  narrative territory, 71–74
  resistance and dissent, 74–79
Autumnal decline theme, 78, 159
Avelar, Idelber, 200n30, 212n5

Bakhtin, Mikhail, 107, 211n34
Balaguer, Joaquin, 205n14
Balmy Alley murals, San Francisco.
    See also Murals
Bambara, Toni Cade, 177
Batchelor, David, 126, 219n13
Batista, Fulgencia, 225n21
Bay of Pigs invasion, 157–158, 224n15
Beckman, Erika, 94, 213n11
Belli, Gioconda, 177, 231n11
Bell-Villada, Gene, 198n21
Beltrán, Cristina, 24, 25, 201n37, 202n39
Benítez, Sandra
    Bitter Grounds, 206n2
    The Weight of All Things, 207n2
Benstock, Shari, 53
Bergman, Miranda, 231n12, 231n14
    "La Cultura Contiene la Semilla de la Resistencia que Retorña en la Flor de la Liberación/Culture Contains the Seed of Resistance which Blossoms into the Flower of Liberation" (with Thiele), 181–182, 181*f*
Bergner, Joel, "Un pasado que aún vive/A Past That Still Lives," 183–185, 183*f*
Bernard, Lourdes, "Anatomy of a Dictator," 232n18
Best, Stephen, 199n23
Blackmore, Josiah, 105–106, 216n32
Black subjects. *See also* African American; Afro-Latina/o
Black Power movement, 144, 191, 231n14
Bogotá 39 list, 196n6
Bolaño, Roberto, 9
Borderlands of authoritarianism, 60–85
    author as dictator, 64–70
    border militarization, 17, 22, 30, 63, 69–70, 82–83, 146, 186, 189, 209n19
    narrative rights and narrative disclosure, 79–85
    narrative territory, 71–74
    resistance and dissent, 74–79
    undocumented migration, 62, 63, 69–70, 79, 82–83, 98–103, 181, 185–187
Border militarization (U.S.-Mexico), 17, 22, 30, 63, 69–70, 82–83, 146, 186, 189, 209n19

Bourdieu, Pierre, 206n29
Brady, Mary Pat, 71, 199n24, 208n16
Brickhouse, Anna, 14
Brooks, Peter, 140, 220n25, 221n26
Brown, Michael, 146
Brown Berets, 26
Brown Power movement, 144

Cabral, Amílcar, 177, 230n6
Cacho, Lisa Marie, 99
Camacho, Alica Schmidt, 211n35
Caminero-Santangelo, Marta, 26, 110–111, 133, 201n37, 202n39, 220n23
Capitalism and neoliberalism, 6, 17, 21–22, 82, 87–89, 94, 102–103, 165, 189, 213n12, 214n20
Cardenál, Ernesto, 230n11
Carpentier, Alejo, 35
    El recurso del método/Reasons of State, 9, 18, 40
Carrillo, Guadalupe, 211n35
Castillo, Ana, *Sapagonia*, 206n2
Castro, Fidel, 26–28, 150, 203n46
CEH (Comisión para el Escalarecimiento Histórico, Guatemala), 218n5
Censorship, 10, 149
Cepeda, María Elena, 202n39
Chamoiseau, Patrick, *Texaco*, 206n25
Character interiority, 42, 67, 72, 80–81, 203n7
Character-space, 29, 39–41, 43, 49, 72, 78, 82, 135, 151, 167–168, 204n8, 221n31
Chatman, Seymour, 204n8
Chavez, Leo R., 212n38
Chávez-Silverman, Susana, 13
Chile
    artistic representations of political violence in, 177–179
    democratic transition in, 23, 145
    socialist movement in, 26
Choteo, 223n10, 224n18
Chromophobia, 126, 219n13
Chronotopes, 7, 46, 107
Cisneros, Sandra, *Caramelo*, 206n25
Citizenship. *See also* Class exploitation
    cultural, 133
    in Latina/o dictatorship novels, 10, 24

Index

power relations and, 17
representations of disability and, 82
Civil rights movement, 26, 228n40
Class. *See also* Capitalism and neoliberalism; Labor exploitation
consciousness of, 63
exploitation of, 7, 12, 79, 81, 94–95, 98
hierarchies of identity and, 10, 16–17, 50, 126
Coded narratives, 51–59
Cohen, Stanley, 95
Cold War ideologies, 99–100, 122, 129, 149, 201n35
Colonialism. *See also* Imperialism
Coloniality, 13–14, 37, 43, 59, 89, 115
Columbus, Christopher, 86
Comisión para el Escalarecimiento Histórico (CEH, Guatemala), 218n5
Comité de Madres y Familiares de El Salvador (COMADRES, Mothers and Family Members of El Salvador), 182
Commodification, 79, 81, 95, 98
Communism, 99, 123, 138, 149, 212n5
Consciousness
*authori*tarianism and, 61, 211n31
class, 63
decolonial, 8
of dictator, 10, 151, 170, 203n6
historical, 97
literary-political, 26, 221n31
trans-American, 55
Contact zone, 7, 71
Contamination trope, 137–138. *See also* Diseased trope
Contradiction, 30, 83–84, 93, 95, 163, 175
Contras, 93, 233n19
Coronado, Raúl, 196n7, 202n39
Cortés, Hernán, 96, 210n25
Counter-dictatorial imaginary
in murals, 179
decolonization and, 176
in Latina/o dictatorship novels, 5–8
narrative form and, 57–58
political memory and, 192–193
power relations and, 17, 22
social justice and, 190

Counterinsurgency tactics, 122, 127–128, 133, 182
Cruz, Angie, 195n3
Cuba.
Cold War ideologies and, 149
Cuban Missile Crisis, 172, 224n15
Cuban Revolution, 26–28, 150, 156, 197n15
exile politics, 149, 157, 226n24
in Latina/o dictatorship novels, 26–28, 197n15
Greater Cuba, 150–151, 160, 174–175
refugee program in U.S., 214n22
Culler, Jonathan, 65, 208n11
Cultural citizenship, 133
Cutler, John Alba, 16, 199n24, 211n36

Dalleo, Raphael, 25, 27
Danticat, Edwidge
Create Dangerously, 196n3
The Dew Breaker, 221n29
The Farming of Bones, 195n3, 219n11, 220n22
Daughters and heteropatriarchy, 168–176
Dávila, Arlene, 201n37
Davis, Mike, 128, 132, 134, 220
Dawson, Paul, 65
Day of the Dead altars, 192, 232n17
Death squads, 23, 88, 111, 144, 185, 217n2
Decolonial imagination, 32, 83, 176
Defiant daughters, 168–176
Delgadillo, Theresa, 201n356
Denning, Michael, 79, 99
Derby, Lauren, 56, 203n4, 204n10, 205n14
de Robertis, Carolina, 5
The Invisible Mountain, 3–4, 26, 215n27
Perla, 215n27
Radical Hope, 232n18
de Rosas, Juan Manuel, 11–12
Derrida, Jacques, 111
Díaz, Junot, 5, 18, 25, 28, 149, 196n6
"Apocalypse, What Disasters Reveal," 116
The Brief Wondrous Life of Oscar Wao, 11, 20, 30, 34–35, 38–59, 66, 78, 114, 139, 165–166, 220n22
on writing process, 215n28
Díaz, Porfirio, 209n24
Di Iorio, Lyn, 200n33

Dictatorship. *See also* Latina/o dictatorship novel; Latin American dictatorship novel; *specific individuals and countries*
  as archetypes, 12–13, 196n11, 198n19
  consciousness of dictator, 10, 40, 151
  dictatorial power, 5–8, 11, 14–17, 21–22, 25, 28–30, 38, 41, 43, 49–51, 55, 59, 146, 176
  egocentrism of dictator, 10, 155
  fall of, 61, 159–160
  as minor characters, 11, 17, 38–46, 204n9, 220n22
  solitude of, 10, 41, 152, 196n11, 210n28, 223n6
  as writers trope, 34–35, 61
Disappeared individuals (*los desaparecidos*), 3–4, 18, 32, 56–57, 60, 101–102, 131, 136, 143, 181–182, 191, 209n19, 215nn26–27, 216n31, 231n14
Diseased trope, 69, 122, 123, 137
Disorder, 121–129
Domestic abuse, 11, 155
Domestic dictatorship, 11, 170–171
Dominican Republic
  in *The Brief Wondrous Life of Oscar Wao*, 38–59
  Trujillo dictatorship in, 37, 38–39, 42, 50, 78, 191, 195n3, 204n12
Dorfman, Ariel, 3, 8, 118, 143, 145, 221n33, 232n18
  How to Read Donald Duck, 232n16
  La muerte y la doncella/Death and the Maiden, 118–119, 145
Dorfman, Rodrigo, 231–232n16
  Occupy the Imagination, Tales of Seduction and Resistance (film), 231–232n16
Dunn, Timothy J., 209n20

Eckstein, Susan, 226n28
Ellis Island, New York, 100–101, 173
El Mozote massacre, 217n2
El Salvador
  disappeared individuals in, 182
  U.S. intervention in, 143, 185
Eltit, Diamela, 9
Emanuel, Nicole, "Indigenous Beauty," 188–189, 189f
Evasive narration, 30, 54, 114, 166, 206n22

Fall of dictator trope, 61, 78, 167
Fancher, Brooke, "My Child Has Never Seen His Father," 184–185
Feitlowitz, Marguerite, 215n26
Feminist critique, 30, 155–156, 175
Ferguson, Missouri civil unrest (2015), 146–147
Fernandes, Sujatha, 163, 167, 226n28, 227n34
Filibustering, 21, 88, 94, 96, 213n12
Firmat, Gustavo Pérez, 9
Flags of convenience, 91, 213n9
Flores, Juan, 8, 135, 196n7, 200n34, 202n39
Focalization, 15, 38–40, 68, 110, 136–139, 149, 168, 203n6
Foil characters, 136, 150–152, 157, 174, 223n4
Footnotes, narrative usage of, 15, 20, 30, 38, 43–44, 51, 53–55, 114, 149, 160–161, 165–166, 206n26, 226n26
Forster, E. M., 42
Foucault, Michel, 68, 208n18
Franco, Jean, 13, 200n30, 212n5, 215n26, 220n21
Freedom Tower (Miami), 173–174
Friedman, Andrew, 94, 100, 134, 214n17
Fuentes, Carlos, 19
Fukú, 30, 36–37, 41, 43–44, 46, 51, 57, 59, 206n23, 214n18

Galeano, Eduardo, 86
Galíndez, Jesús de, 166
García, Cristina, 5, 25
  The Agüero Sisters, 225n22
  Dreaming in Cuban, 168, 171, 174
  King of Cuba, 11, 20, 26–28, 31–32, 54, 78, 136, 149–176, 203n1
García, Juan Carlos, 11, 44, 197n14, 198n17
García, María Cristina, 157, 214n22
García Márquez, Gabriel, 12, 222n2, 229n43
  El otoño del patriarca/Autumn of the Patriarch, 9, 19, 40, 86–87, 207n4
Gates, Henry Louis, Jr., 206n30
Gender. *See also* Feminist critique; Heteropatriarchy

Index

domestic abuse and, 11, 148, 155
identity politics and, 49, 199n24, 199n27, 201n38
in Latina/o dictatorship novels, 10, 24, 198n17
power relations and, 14, 16–17, 155
Genette, Gérard, 138
Genre criticism, 196n10
Gentrification, 179, 181, 185–188, 188f
Gerardi, Bishop Juan, 88, 218n5
Gill, Lesley, 121, 218n3, 218n7, 219n16
Gillman, Susan, 196n5
Gilroy, Paul, 89
Goldman, Francisco, 5, 28, 149, 215n28
  The Art of Political Murder, 88
  The Long Night of White Chickens, 88
  The Ordinary Seaman, 20–21, 31, 45, 70, 79, 87–117, 134, 174
Gómez-Barris, Macarena, 23, 177, 178, 197n12, 205n15, 229n1
González, Aníbal, 84
González, Christopher, 205n14
González, John Morán, 16
Gonzalez, Juan, 27, 88
González, Marcial, 199n24
González Echevarría, Roberto, 12, 197n14, 204n13
Gosse, Van, 224n19
Gordon, Avery, 102
Graeber, David, 214n19
Gruesz, Kirsten Silva, 24, 28–29, 96, 110, 196n7, 214n17
Guatemala
  National Police, 130
  U.S. intervention in, 121–122, 185
  violence against indigenous communities in, 23, 120, 183–184
Guerra, Lillian, 202n45, 224n14
Guevara, Ernesto "Che," 26, 142, 230n7
Guzmán, Jacobo Árbenz, 218n5

Haiti
  earthquake in, 116
  revolution in, 47
  Trujillo dictatorship and, 42, 195n3
Halperin, Laura, 200n33
Hames-García, Michael, 50, 196n5, 199n27

Hanif, Mohammed, *The Case of the Exploding Mangos*, 198n20
Hanna, Monica, 32, 196n7, 199n24, 206n28
Harvey, David, 212n5
Hernández, Ester, "Libertad," 228n40, 229n2
Heroism myths, 151–160, 223n8
Heteropatriarchy, 148–176
  in Balmy Alley murals, 189, 231n12
  defiant daughters and, 168–176
  as dictatorial mode of control, 22
  dictators and, 42–43, 50, 149, 152, 156, 159, 203n1
  domestic abuse and, 11, 149, 155
  domestic dictatorship and, 11, 154–156, 170, 228n37
  hypermasculine hero myths and, 20, 151–160
  power relations and, 17, 50
  resolver aesthetic and, 150, 160–168, 227n36
Hierarchies of identity, 10, 16–17, 50, 126. *See also* Class; Gender; Race and racism
Hirsch, Marianne, 22
hooks, bell, 148
Horn, Maja, 49, 204n12
Hutcheon, Linda, 80
Hypermasculinity, 20, 43, 125, 151–160, 204n12, 223n8. *See also* Heteropatriarchy

Identity
  hierarchies of, 16–17, 50, 126
  Latina/o, 24–29, 195n3, 201–202n38
  social, 199n27
Iglesias, Julio Calviño, 197n14
Immigration laws, 91, 99, 100, 101–102, 111, 114, 115, 186, 189, 214n22. *See also* Migrants
Imperialism
  in Balmy Alley murals, 179, 180, 185, 189
  capitalism and, 87, 89, 94
  counter-dictatorial imaginary and, 6–7
  cultural, 61
  failures of, 89, 98, 102, 133
  heteropatriarchy and, 153

Imperialism (*continued*)
  indigenous peoples impacted by, 98
  interventionism and, 6–7, 11, 13, 20, 27, 88, 89, 94, 96, 105, 112, 121, 144, 180, 192
  political, 27
  power relations and, 17, 22, 92
  ships and, 45, 86–87, 90, 96–97
  of United States, 13, 21–23, 27, 55, 98, 104–105, 125, 180, 185
Incarceration, 52, 187
Indigenous peoples
  assimilation of, 127, 140
  in Balmy Alley murals, 179–180, 183–185, 188–189, 189f
  imperialism's impact on, 98
  violence against, 88, 122, 183–184
Intersectionality, 17, 199n27
Ippolito, Lucia, "Mission Makeover" (with Araiza), 187–188, 188f
Irizarry, Ylce, 200n33, 225n22

Jackson, Kevin, 54
James, C. L. R., 90, 100–101, 105
Jameson, Fredric, 196n10, 199n23
Justice, 23, 118–147
  in Balmy Alley murals, 181, 231n13
  disorder and, 121–129
  individual retribution against collective impunity, 129–135
  narrative scales of, 59, 63, 135–147, 223n4
  restorative justice, 222n34
  retributive justice, 30, 119–120, 129–135, 146, 222n34
  social justice, 32, 119–120, 179, 181, 185, 190, 191, 206n30, 220n21, 228n40, 233n20

Kelk Cervantes, Susan, "Indigenous Eyes, War or Peace," 188–189, 189f
King, Martin Luther, Jr., 132
Kirkpatrick, Jean, 202n44
Kirkwood, Julieta, 148
Klein, Naomi, 212n5

Labor exploitation, 7, 79, 81, 94–95, 98
Lafourcade, Enrique, *La fiesta del rey acab/ King Ahab's Feast*, 9, 61, 213n7
Lagos, Roberto, 178

Lamas, Carmen E., 202n39
Latina/o dictatorship novel. *See also* Latin American dictatorship novel; *individual authors*
  authoritarianism in, 11, 38, 60–85
  as common literature of Americas, 4–5, 9–14
  counter-dictatorial imaginary in, 5–8, 17, 22, 26, 57–58, 176, 179, 190
  complicity and compromise in, 12, 38, 46, 74, 84, 198n17
  dictator as minor character in, 38–46
  dictator as writer and writer as dictator in, 34–35, 61, 64–70, 203n3, 207n3,
  heteropatriarchy and machismo in, 11, 17, 20, 22, 50, 148–176, 203n1
  justice in, 23, 32, 118–147, 222n34
  list of, 195n3
  modernity/coloniality world system in, 13–14, 37, 43, 59, 89, 115
  narrative form and power in, 16–17, 29–30, 34–59, 79–85, 178
  postdictatorship and postmemory hauntings in, 18–23
  power relationships in, 14–17, 22, 50, 71, 196n11
  resistance and political opposition in, 11–12, 15, 25–27, 37, 61, 64, 74–79, 83–84, 135, 166, 206n1
  stylistic and thematic features of, 5, 9–12, 20, 61
  terminology for, 11
Latina/o identity, 24–29. *See also* Afro-Latina/o; *specific national-origin groups*
  definition of, 201–202n38
  identity, 24–29, 195n3, 201–202n38
  narrative, 26
  panethnic, 24, 25, 28, 133, 193
  transnational, 24, 47, 193
Latin American dictatorship novel. *See also* Latina/o dictatorship novel; *individual authors*
  as common literature of Americas, 4–5, 9–14
  dictator as writer in, 39, 203n2

dictator as primary focalizer in, 10–11, 39–40
heteropatriarchy and machismo in, 11, 20, 153, 203n1
imperialism in, 86–87
list of, 9, 196n9
resistance and political opposition in, 11–1, 60–61, 84, 197n15, 198n17
stylistic and thematic features of, 9–14, 61–62, 196n11, 210n28, 218n6, 223n6
terminology for, 11, 197n14
typologies of, 9–10, 39, 198n18
Latorre, Guisela, 180, 230n5
Lazo, Rodrigo, 101, 196n7, 214n17
Levine, Caroline, 16–17, 199n25
Limón, Graciela, *In Search of Bernabé*, 207n2, 215n27
Lomas, Laura, 6, 196n5, 196n7, 223n10
López, Marissa K., 196n7, 201n35, 202n39, 204–205n13
López-Calvo, Ignacio, 197n14, 198n21, 201n35
Lugones, María, 13

Machado Sáez, Elena, 27, 200n33, 205n17
Machismo, 7, 169. *See also* Heteropatriarchy; Hypermasculinity
Madrigal, Oscar "the Oz," "Los Borrados," 207n2
Manifest Destiny, 94
Marchi, Regina, 232n17
Marcus, Sharon, 199n23
Marginalized hero, 46–51
Mármol, José, *Amalia*, 9
Martí, José, 6, 110, 117, 152, 191, 196n5, 223n8, 226n24
Martin, Gerald, 197n14
Martínez, Demetria, 5
Mother Tongue, 207n2, 215n27, 228n37
Martínez, Ernesto Javier, 199n24
Martínez, Oscar, 230n9
Marx, Karl, 48
Masculinity. *See also* Hypermasculinity
McClennen, Sophia, 222n33
McClintock, Anne, 21
McGurl, Mark, 207n9
Mendieta, Anna, *Facial Hair Transplant*, 158
Melville, Herman

"Benito Cereno," 222n2
Moby-Dick, 90, 100
Memory. *See also* Postmemory
justice and, 146
multidirectional, 189–190
palimpsestic, 185
political, 192–193
postdictatorship hauntings in, 18–23
symbolic, 23
Menchú, Rigoberta, 231n12
Middle Passage, 96–97
Mignolo, Walter, 13
Migrants. *See also* Undocumented subjects
exploitation of, 70, 79, 82–83, 88, 98–103, 211n37, 214n20, 214n23
farm labor, 77, 79
heteropatriarchy and, 176
immigration laws and, 91, 99
justice and, 133, 137, 146
migrant solidarity network and, 111
in murals, 181, 185–187, 230n9
migrant melancholia, 211n35
migrant rights movement, 83
refugees as, 99–100, 111–112, 133, 202n43
state repression of, 7, 84, 100–101, 209n19
U.S.–Mexico border and, 62, 63, 69–70
Milian, Claudia, 196nn6–7, 201–202n38, 212n3
Miliani, Domingo, 197n14, 198n18, 201n38
Militarization. *See also* Border militarization
Miller, D. A., 68
Minich, Julie Avril, 82, 123, 199n24, 220n24, 222n36
Mistral, Gabriela, 191
Monroe Doctrine, 94
Moraga, Cherríe, *This Bridge Called My Back*, 193, 210n25, 233n19
Moreiras, Alberto, 200n30
Moretti, Franco, 195n2
Morgan, Jamie, "Tribute to Archbishop Oscar Romero," 230n9
Mothers and Family Members of El Salvador (Comité de Madres y Familiares de El Salvador), 182
Mothers of the Plaza de Mayo (Asociación Madres de Plaza de Mayo), 182
Mourning, 46, 200n30

Moya, Paula M. L., 7, 17, 199nn23–25
Las Mujeres Muralistas, 229n2
Muñoz, José Esteban, 150, 175, 202n39, 223n10, 224n18, 2226n25
Murals, 32, 179–193
  "Enrique's Journey" (Rojas), 186–187, 186f
  "Indigenous Beauty" (Emanuel), 188–189, 189f
  "Indigenous Eyes, War or Peace" (Kelk Cervantes), 188–189, 189f
  "La Cultura Contiene la Semilla de la Resistencia que Retorña en la Flor de la Liberación/Culture Contains the Seed of Resistance which Blossoms into the Flower of Liberation" (Bergman & Thiele), 181–182, 181f
  "Mission Makeover" (Araiza & Ippolito), 187–188, 188f
  "Resistance and Revolution" (Alicia), 191–192, 192f
  "Una ley inmoral, nadie tiene que cumplirla/No One Should Comply with an Immoral Law" (Alicia), 183–185, 183f, 191
  "Un pasado que aún vive/A Past That Still Lives" (Bergner), 183–185, 183f

Naimou, Angela, 115, 213n9, 214n17, 215n25
Napoleon Bonaparte, 72–73, 209n24
Narrative form and power, 16–17, 29–30, 34–59, 178
  *author*itarianism and, 38, 79–85, 212n7
  coded narratives, 51–59, 114
  in counter-dictatorial imaginary, 5, 8
  dictator as minor character, 38–46
  evasive narratives, 54, 75, 114, 166, 206n22
  focalization, 15, 38, 40, 68, 110, 113, 136–141, 149, 203n6
  footnote and note usage, 15, 20, 30, 38, 43–44, 51, 53–55, 114, 149, 160–161, 165–166, 206n26, 226n26
  iterative narratives, 138
  justice and, 135–147
  marginalized hero, 46–51
  omniscient narration, 65, 67–69, 79, 81, 208n11

  underground storytelling, 51–59
Nava, Michael, *The City of Palaces*, 207n2
Nazario, Sonia, *Enrique's Journey*, 230n8
Neoliberalism, 17, 22, 88, 102, 189, 214n20. *See also* Capitalism and neoliberalism
Neo-slave narratives, 200n32
Nguyen, Viet Thanh, 146
Nicaragua
  revolution in, 87, 99, 156
  Somoza dictatorship in, 92–93, 96, 142, 213n10
  U.S. intervention in, 92–93
Notes, narrative usage of, 15, 20, 30, 38, 43–44, 51, 53–55, 114, 149, 160–161, 165–166, 206n26, 226n26

Obejas, Achy, 227n31
  Days of Awe, 172, 175
  "So We Came All the Way from Cuba So You Could Dress Like This?," 148–149, 168
Oboler, Suzanne, 201n37
Occupy Wall Street movement, 231–232n16
Olson, Barbara, 65, 208n11
Omniscient narration, 65, 67–70, 79, 81, 208n11
Ontiveros, Randy J., 211n32
Operation Condor, 4
Orbach, Michael, 212n6
Orchard, William, 199n24
Orozco, Daniel, "Somoza's Dream," 206n2, 221n28
Ortíz, Ricardo L., 195n3, 196n7, 201n36, 202n44, 223n3
Orwell, George, 34

Pacheco, Carlos, 11, 198n17, 198n19
Padilla, Yolanda, 196n7, 199n24
Pan-Latina/o fictions, 24–29
Paredes, Américo, 207n8
Parra, Violeta, 191
Parsley Massacre, 219n11
Patlán, Ray, 180
Patriarchy. *See also* Heteropatriarchy
Patterson, Orlando, 47, 99
Pease, Donald E., 214n24

Pérez, Loida Maritza, *Geographies of Home*, 228n37
Pérez, Louis A., 28
Pérez Firmat, Gustavo, 9
Peri Rossi, Cristina, 9
Phallic imagery, 153–154
Pinochet, Augusto, 145, 212n5, 229n1
Pita, Beatrice, 25
PLACA mural project, 180–193, 229n4
Plascencia, Salvador, 5, 28, 62, 149, 207n9
  The People of Paper, 11, 12, 30, 61–85, 95, 146, 203n3, 212n7
Poblete, Juan, 201n35, 201n37, 233n20
Polit Dueñas, Gabriela, 20, 35, 153, 197n14
Portes, Alejandro, 157, 224n15
Postcolonialism, 21
Postdictatorship, 18–23, 45, 48, 53, 58, 118, 166, 200n30
Postmemory, 18, 22, 23, 48, 51, 57, 58, 139, 166, 215nn27–28
Power. *See also* Narrative form and power
  authoritarian, 5–8, 17, 21, 23, 25, 29, 32, 68, 74, 82, 155–156, 178, 190, 193
  counter-dictatorial imaginary and, 17, 22
  dictatorial, 5–8, 11, 14–17, 21–22, 25, 28–30, 38, 41, 43, 49–51, 55, 59, 146, 176
  hierarchies of, 14, 16–17, 71
  monopolization of power trope, 196n11
  narrative form and, 14–17, 204n13
  white supremacy and, 17, 50
Pratt, Mary Louise, 71
Progressive politics, 27, 170, 224n15, 233n19
Propaganda, 157
Puig, Manuel, *El beso de la mujer araña*, 206n25

Quijano, Aníbal, 13
Quiroga, José, 151, 158

Race and racism. *See also* White supremacy
  environmental racism, 134, 138
  imperialism and, 22
  justice and, 120, 126, 134, 144
  power relations and, 16–17
  state repression and, 7, 12, 147
  violence associated with, 120, 134, 189
Radio Ambulante, 229n43

Rama, Ángel, 40, 196n10, 205n18
Ramírez, Sergio, 9, 18–20, 199n28
Ramos, Juan Antonio, 197n14, 223n6
Randall, Margaret, 148, 156
Reagan, Ronald, 93, 224n16
Realism, 71–72
Rebel Diaz (music group), 231n15
Recuperación de la Memoria Histórica (REMHI, Guatemala), 218n5
Rediker, Marcus, 86, 90, 98
Refugees, 85, 88, 99–100, 111–112, 117, 214n22. *See also* Migrants; Undocumented subjects
Resistance, 12, 15, 38, 52, 62, 64–68, 74–79, 83–84, 135, 166, 177, 181–184, 191
Resolver, 160–168
  aesthetic, 150, 165, 168, 227n36
  defined, 161–162
  reading practice, 150, 168
  Special Period, 161–162, 163, 227n29
Restorative justice, 222n34. *See also* Justice
Retributive justice, 30, 119–120, 129–135, 146, 222n34. *See also* Justice
Riofrio, John "Rio", 100n33, 196nn6–7, 201n35
Rios Montt, José Efraín, 220n19
Rivera, Tomás, *. . . y no se lo tragó la tierra / And the Earth Did Not Devour Him*, 77
Roa Bastos, Augusto, 34
  Yo el supremo/I, the Supreme, 9, 19, 40, 206n25, 207n3
Rodney King uprisings (1992), 119, 121, 127–128, 131–135, 144–145, 219n18
Rodríguez, Ana Patricia, 88, 120, 129, 180, 196n7, 201n35, 218n9, 229n2
Rodríguez, Ileana, 120, 224n13
Rodríguez, Juana María, 201n38, 202n39
Rodriguez, Ralph E., 16, 63, 199n23, 199n24
Rodríguez, Richard T., 156
Rodríguez, Silvio, 182, 230n7
Rojas, Josúe, "Enrique's Journey," 186–187, 186f
Román, Elda María, 80, 199n24, 211n37
Romero, Óscar, 177, 183, 183f, 184
Rothberg, Michael, 189–190
Rushdie, Salman, *Shame*, 34–35, 198n20

Sae-Saue, Jayson Gonzalez, 199n24, 233n19
Saldaña-Portillo, María Josefina, 27, 28, 154, 196n7, 201n35, 224n13
Saldívar, José David, 13–14, 32, 36, 196n5, 196n7,
Saldívar, Ramón, 7, 22, 59, 196n7, 199n24, 206n31, 207n8
Sampson, Helen, 212n6
Saénz, Benjamin Alire, "Alligator Park," 207n2
Sánchez, Rosaura, 25
Sanctuary Movement, 111, 230n10
Sandinista Revolution, 26, 99, 233n19
Santa Anna, Otto, 83
Sarmiento, Domingo Faustino, 196n8, 204n13
  Facundo, Civilización y barbaridad/Facundo, Civilization and Barbarism, 9, 218n6
School of the Americas, 121, 123, 217n2, 220n19
Schmidt Camacho, Alicia, 196n7, 211n35
Scott, James C., 52, 54, 217n47
Scraps trope, 108–117
Seltzer, Mark, 68
Sexuality, 10, 16, 24, 42, 47, 49. *See also* Feminism; Heteropatriarchy; Hypermasculinity
Sellers-García, Sylvia, *When the Ground Turns in its Sleep*, 195n3, 206n22
Shakur, Asata, 191
Shemak, April, 92, 111, 213n9, 214n21
Ships, 86–117
  captains of, 89–96
  micropolitics of, 89–91
  scraps, holes, and ruins on, 108–117, 217n46
  shipwreck narratives, 103–108, 215n30
  violence and death associated with, 96–103
Silence, 30, 38, 51, 55–58, 60–62, 77, 114, 206n22
Silko, Leslie Marmon, 209n19
Silverman, Max, 185
Slavery, 36, 47–48, 87–90, 96–99, 102–103, 117, 118. *See also* African Americans; Neo-slave narratives

Smith, Anna Deavere, *Twilight, Los Angeles, 1992*, 118, 145, 147
Social death, 47, 89, 92, 96–97, 99, 186
Solitude, 10, 41, 85, 152
Somoza, Anastasio, 92–93, 96, 142, 213n10
Sommer, Doris, 217n47
Song, Min Hyoung, 144
Sosa, Mercedes, 191, 231n14
Soviet Union, collapse of, 161–162, 226n28. *See also* Cold War ideologies
Special Period in Time of Peace (Cuba), 161–162, 163, 222n1, 226n28
Statue of Liberty, 109–110, 171–172, 228n40. *See also* Ellis Island
Stellar imagery, 154–155, 223n12
Stepick, Alex, 157, 224n15
Stranger Than Fiction (film), 210n30–31
Surveillance
  omniscient narration, 65, 67–70, 79, 81, 208n11
  repression via, 205n21, 213n7
  of U.S.–Mexico border, 12, 63, 69–70, 132, 146

Tattoos, 123–125
  jaguar imagery, 105, 123–125, 136, 218n9
  shipwreck imagery, 104
Taylor, Charles, 196n4
Taylor, Diana, 95, 196n7, 215n29, 218n10
Temporal ambiguity, 48, 139
These Walls Speak (film), 229n4
Thiang'o, Ngugi wa, *Wizard of the Crow*, 198n20
Thiele, O'Brien, 181, 231n14
  "La Cultura Contiene la Semilla de la Resistencia que Retorña en la Flor de la Liberación/Culture Contains the Seed of Resistance which Blossoms into the Flower of Liberation" (with Bergman), 181–182, 181f
Thompson, Carl, 216n35
Thomson, Rosemarie Garland, 50
Tierney-Tello, Mary Beth, 155–156
Tobar, Héctor, 5, 25, 28, 150, 217n1
  "Reading Ferguson, Books on Race, Police, Protest and U.S. History," 146–147

The Tattooed Soldier, 23, 31, 75, 105, 119–147, 223n4
Torres-Saillant, Silvio, 47, 205n14
Torture, 3–4, 18, 20, 52, 60, 90, 119, 122, 142, 182, 196n11, 209n19, 218n3, 218n5
Trans-American, 7, 9, 14, 36, 45, 46, 55, 111, 196n5, 196n7, 232n16
Transculturation, 8
Trans-Latina\o fictions, 24–29
Transnationalism
  *authori*tarianism and, 63, 77, 83
  heteropatriarchy and, 150, 173, 174, 176
  imperialism and, 4, 11
  justice and, 23, 119–122, 124, 134, 138, 139, 140, 144–145
  labor exploitation and, 83
  in Latina\o dictatorship novels, 10, 24, 26, 28
  migration narratives, 88
  narrative power and, 41, 45, 47, 49
  postmemory and, 23, 232n17
  power relations and, 17
  state repression and, 29, 32, 185, 220n20
  transnational imaginary, 7, 207n8
  U.S. interventionism and, 4, 27–29
Trujillo, Rafael, 37, 38–39, 42, 50, 78, 191, 195n3, 204n12
Trump, Donald, 232n18
Turits, Richard, 205n21
"Two 9/11s in a Lifetime, A Project and Exhibit on the Politics of Memory" (art exhibit), 177–179
Typography, 75–79

Underground storytelling, 51–59, 114, 166. *See also* Footnotes
Undocumented subjects. *also* Migrants
  in Balmy Alley murals, 181, 186–187, 230n9
  heteropatriarchy and, 176
  justice and, 133, 137, 146
  labor exploitation and, 70, 79, 82–83, 88, 98–103, 211n37, 214n20, 214n23
  race and white supremacy and, 49–50, 121, 134, 147, 196n5
  refugees as, 99
  representational exploitation of, 83
  resistance trope and, 12
  state repression of, 7, 84, 100–101, 209n19
  U.S.–Mexico border and, 62, 63, 69–70, 186–187
United States
  borderlands with Mexico, 18, 62, 63, 69–70, 186–187
  Cold War ideologies in, 99–100, 122, 129, 149, 201n35
  counter-dictatorial imaginary in, 5–8
  hierarchies of identity in, 10, 16–17, 50, 126
  imperialism of, 14, 21–23, 27, 98
  interventionism history in Latin American, 4, 13, 20–21, 27, 31, 55, 93–94, 121–122, 185
  marginalization in, 50, 126
  murals in, 32, 179–193
  neoliberalism in, 6, 17, 21–22, 82, 87–89, 94, 102–103, 165, 189, 213n12, 214n20
  Operation Condor, 4
  postmemory hauntings in, 18–19, 21–23
  power relations in, 5
  School of the Americas and, 121, 123, 217n2, 220n19
  systematic violence in, 8
  transnationalism and, 4, 27–29
  undocumented migrants in, 7, 62, 63, 69–70, 79, 82–83, 84, 98–103, 181, 185–187, 209n19
Uruguay, 4

Valenzuela, Luisa, 9
  Cola de lagartija/The Lizard's Tail, 60–61
Valle-Inclán, Ramón, *El tyrano banderas/The Tyrant Banderas*, 9
Vanderbilt, Cornelius, 213n12
Vargas Llosa, Mario, 9, 19, 203n6
  La fiesta del chivo/The Feast of the Goat, 40
Vázquez, David J., 26, 64, 200n33, 202n39, 211n33
Vázquez, Eric, 133–134, 221n32
Vigil, Ariana, 6, 100n33, 121, 196n7, 197n16, 201n36, 212n4, 216n37

Violence
- artistic representations of, 178–181, 183, 184–185, 187–189
- *authori*tarianism and, 83–84
- border militarization and, 17, 22, 30, 63, 69–70, 82–83, 146, 186, 189, 209n19
- counterinsurgency tactics and, 122, 214n23, 224n14
- domestic violence, 11, 149, 155
- heteropatriarchy and, 154–155, 165, 172, 176, 223n9
- imperialism and, 36, 130, 134, 205n15, 231n12
- against indigenous peoples, 88, 122, 183–184
- justice and, 25, 129, 135–136, 139, 143–148
- in Latina/o dictatorship novels, 4
- narrative power and, 41, 44–45, 47, 55
- postmemory hauntings of, 18–19, 22–23, 197n12
- retributive, 31–32, 120
- ships associated with, 96–103
- social, 102
- state-sponsored, 10, 30, 120–121, 128–130, 202n45, 215n27, 217n42, 219n16, 232n16
- structural, 90–91
- systemic violence, 8, 10, 23, 114, 128–129, 197n16, 209n19, 233n19
- tactical use of, 122
- transgenerational cycle of, 35, 139
- of Trujillo regime, 41, 44, 45
- writing linked to, 83–84, 210n29

Viramontes, Helena María,
 "The Cariboo Café," 207n2
 Under the Feet of Jesus, 77
Vizenor, Gerald, 217n47

Walker, William, 96, 213n12
Watts Riots (1965), 147
Weinreb, Amelia Rosenberg, 227n29, 227n31
Weld, Kirsten, 130
White supremacy, 6, 17, 22, 50, 147, 189, 196n5
Whitfield, Esther, 163
Williams, Raymond Leslie, 48, 69, 197n14
Woloch, Alex, 39–40, 42, 203n7, 204n8

Young Lords, 26

Zafa, 30, 37, 38, 41, 50, 57–59, 66, 166
Zapatistas, 191, 231n14
Zinn, Howard, 118
Zoot Suit Riots (1943), 147
Zuluaga, Conrado, 40, 197n14

www.ingramcontent.com/pod-product-compliance
Ingram Content Group UK Ltd.
Pitfield, Milton Keynes, MK11 3LW, UK
UKHW042006230426
12048UKWH00009B/579